Indians of North Carolina

Letter from the Secretary of the Interior

By O. M. McPherson

A DocSouth Books Edition
The University of North Carolina at Chapel Hill Library
Chapel Hill

A DocSouth Books Edition, 2018

ISBN 978-1-4696-4175-1 (pbk.: alk. paper)

Published by
The University of North Carolina at Chapel Hill Library
CB #3900 Davis Library
Chapel Hill, NC 27514-8890
http://library.unc.edu

Documenting the American South
http://docsouth.unc.edu
docsouth@unc.edu

Distributed by
The University of North Carolina Press
116 South Boundary Street
Chapel Hill, NC 27514-3808
1-800-848-6224
http://www.uncpress.org

This book was digitally printed.

About This Edition

This edition is made available under the imprint of DocSouth Books, a collaborative endeavor between the University of North Carolina at Chapel Hill Library and the University of North Carolina Press. Titles in DocSouth Books are drawn from the Library's Documenting the American South (DocSouth) digital publishing program, online at docsouth.unc.edu. These print and downloadable e-book editions have been prepared from the DocSouth electronic editions.

Both DocSouth and DocSouth Books present the transcribed content of historic books as they were originally published. Grammar, punctuation, spelling, and typographical errors are therefore preserved from the original editions. DocSouth Books are not intended to be facsimile editions, however. Details of typography and page layout in the original works have not been preserved in the transcription.

DocSouth Books editions incorporate two pagination schemas. First, standard page numbers reflecting the pagination of this edition appear at the top of each page for easy reference. Second, page numbers in brackets within the text (e.g., "[Page 9]") refer to the pagination of the original publication; online versions of the DocSouth works use this same original pagination. Page numbers shown in tables of contents and book indexes, when present, refer to the original works' printed page numbers and therefore correspond to the page numbers in brackets.

Summary

Indians of North Carolina: Letter from the Secretary of the Interior, Transmitting, in Response to a Senate Resolution of June 30, 1914, a Report on the Condition and Tribal Rights of the Indians of Robeson and Adjoining Counties of North Carolina, submitted in 1914 by Special Indian Agent Orlando M. McPherson, describes the history of a "body of mixed-blood people residing chiefly in Robeson County" (p. 7). This group, referred to variously as "Croatan Indians," "Cherokee Indians of Robeson County," "Hatteras Indians," and "Corees" (p. 7, p. 9, p. 15, p. 16), allegedly descended from the "Lost Colony" at Roanoke Island. This group of English settlers disappeared between 1588, when Governor John White left to seek reinforcements, and 1590, when he returned (Miller 193-200).

Special Agent McPherson's 25-page "Report" carefully examines historical evidence supporting and contradicting the claim that Robeson County's "Croatans" descended from indigenous peoples who intermixed with the lost English settlers, noting that "Croatan was . . . an island and Indian village just north of Cape Hatteras, N.C." (p. 8). He quotes and cites numerous histories of North Carolina's Native Americans, and in so doing provides an invaluable guide to documents dating back to the colonial era. Many of these original sources are attached to McPherson's report as "exhibits."

McPherson devotes special attention to early reports by "John Lederer, a learned German" explorer, whose notes are largely reprinted in "Hawks's History of North Carolina" (Exhibit D), John Lawson's "History of Carolina" (Exhibit E), the "Nineteenth Annual Report of the Bureau of Ethnology" (Exhibit G), and James Mooney's "Hand Book of Indians" (Exhibits H, J, and K). McPherson's appraisals of these sources are especially useful for the novice reader. He writes for example, that "Lawson's history is regarded as the standard authority for the period it covers; I find it extensively quoted from by all subsequent historians . . . [T]here are many facts and circumstances which confirm Lawson's record" (p. 15). In an editorial comment, McPherson takes issue with Hamilton McMillan and A.W. McLean's opinion that the Croatans are of Cherokee descent: "The history and traditions of the Cherokee Indians of North Carolina ... do not confirm the claim of the Robeson County Indians to Cherokee origin." McPherson explains that the "Cherokees were the mountaineers of the South. ... Indeed, interposed between the Cherokees and the coast were three or four powerful tribes with which they were in perpetual warfare" (p. 18).

McPherson concludes that while the Robeson County Indians were probably not Cherokees, they may very well have descended from the English settlers of the Lost Colony who intermixed with a friendly native tribe. As evidence, he cites numerous records describing the fair skin, gray eyes, English literacy, and "quaint old Anglo-Saxon" verbiage of the so-called Croatans (p. 16). He then provides a brief summary of the (successful) efforts to create separate schools for their children, and he reviews the legislation that first acknowledged the "Croatan Indians" before their legal designation changed to "Indians of Robeson County" (p. 29).

McPherson's federal report is essentially literature review in the guise of fact-finding. It relies heavily on Robeson county legislator Hamilton McMillan's musings on the relationship between Sir Walter Raleigh's Lost Colony and the Indians around Robeson County. Correspondence with McMillan and one of his histories are reprinted in Exhibits B and C or the McPherson's report. The report reaches many erroneous conclusions, in part because it was based in an anthropological framework of white supremacy, segregation-era politics, and assumptions about the value of racial "purity." In fact, later researchers would establish that the Lumbees, as Malinda Lowery writes, "are survivors from the dozens of tribes in that territory who established homes with the Native people, as well as free European and enslaved African settlers, who lived in what became their core homeland: the low-lying swamplands along the border of North and South Carolina." Excavations would later establish the presence of Native people in that homeland since at least 1000 A.D.

Ironically, McPherson's murky history connecting Lumbees to early colonial settlers was used to legitimize them and to deflect their categorization as African-Americans. "Like the Catawbas, Creeks, Choctaws, Seminoles, and other Indian groups in the East," observes Malinda Lowery, "Robeson County's Indians are a 'nation of nations,' for whom a formal name became necessary later on, primarily for negotiating with colonial, state, and federal authorities." The McPherson report documents one important phase of an Indian people's long path to self-determination and political recognition, a path that would designate them as Croatan, Cherokee Indians of Robeson

County, Siouan Indians of the Lumber River, and finally, Lumbee—the title of their own choosing and the one we use today.

Patrick E. Horn

| 63D CONGRESS 3d Session | SENATE | DOCUMENT No. 677 |

INDIANS OF NORTH CAROLINA

LETTER FROM
THE SECRETARY OF THE INTERIOR

TRANSMITTING,

IN RESPONSE TO A SENATE RESOLUTION OF JUNE 30, 1914, A REPORT ON THE CONDITION AND TRIBAL RIGHTS OF THE INDIANS OF ROBESON AND ADJOINING COUNTIES OF NORTH CAROLINA

JANUARY 5, 1915.—Referred to the Committee on Indian Affairs and ordered to be printed

JANUARY 13, 1915.—Accompanying illustrations ordered printed

WASHINGTON
1915

[Title Page Verso Image]

63D CONGRESS
3d Session
SENATE
DOCUMENT
No. 677
INDIANS OF NORTH CAROLINA
LETTER FROM
THE SECRETARY OF THE INTERIOR
TRANSMITTING,
IN RESPONSE TO A SENATE
RESOLUTION
OF JUNE 30, 1914, A REPORT ON THE
CONDITION
AND TRIBAL RIGHTS OF THE
INDIANS
OF ROBESON AND ADJOINING
COUNTIES
OF NORTH CAROLINA
JANUARY 5, 1915.—Referred to the
Committee on Indian Affairs and ordered
to be printed
JANUARY 13, 1915.—Accompanying
illustrations ordered printed

WASHINGTON
1915

CONTENTS.

Letter of transmittal.....5

Report on condition and tribal rights of Indians of Robeson and adjoining counties in North Carolina.....7

EXHIBIT A.....32
A1—Senate resolution No. 410.....32
A2—Office instructions, July 23, 1914.....32
A3—Eleventh Census, United States, 1890.....33
  EXHIBIT B.....36
B1—Petition of Croatan Indians.....36
B2—Office letter of Hon. J. W. Powell, January 7, 1889.....37
B3—Letter of J. W. Powell to Indian Office, January 11, 1889.....37
B4—Office letter to Hamilton McMillan, January 29, 1889.....38
B5—Letter of W. L. Moore to Indian Office, July 2, 1890.....38
B6—Office letter to Hamilton McMillan, July 14, 1890.....39
B7—Letter of Hamilton McMillan to Indian Office, July 17, 1890.....39
B8—Office letter to W. L. Moore, August 11, 1890.....40
  EXHIBIT C.—Sir Walter Raleigh's Lost Colony, by Hamilton McMillan.....41
  EXHIBIT CC.—The Lost Colony of Roanoke: Its Fate and Survival, by Stephen B. Weeks.....58
  EXHIBIT CCC.—Extract from History of North Carolina, by Samuel A'Court Ashe.....69
  EXHIBIT D.—Notes of Lederer's Travels in North Carolina, and Comments by Dr. Hawks.....88
  EXHIBIT E.—Lawson's History of Carolina.....99
  EXHIBIT F......120

Historical Sketch of the Indians of Robeson County, by A. W. McLean......120

Letter of A. W. McLean, dated September 7, 1914 128
Statement by Wash Lowrie, a Robeson County Indian 131
Office letter of September 14, 1914, to A. W. McLean 132
    EXHIBIT G.—History of the Cherokee Indians (from Nineteenth Annual Report of the Bureau of Ethnology) 133
    EXHIBIT H.—History of the Tuscaroras (from Handbook of American Indians) 180
    EXHIBIT I.—History of the Old Cheraws (from Greggs' History of the Old Cheraws) 196
    EXHIBIT J.—History of the Catawbas (from Handbook of American Indians) 215
    EXHIBIT K 218
History of the Cheraws (from Handbook of American Indians) 218
History of the Cherokees (from Handbook of American Indians) 220
    EXHIBIT L.—Legislation relative to Indians of Robeson County 223
    EXHIBIT M.—*Correspondence relative to the investigation of the condition, tribal rights, etc., of the Indians of Robeson County, N. C.* 233

[Page 4] *ILLUSTRATIONS.*

    Indians cooking fish. 76
    Map of the lost colony 83
    Ogilby's map of Carolina, 1671 89
    Lederer's map of Carolina, 1671 90
    Horne's map of Carolina, 1666 91
    Lawson's map of the Carolinas, 1709 100

Map of the Cherokee country (from the Nineteenth Annual Report of the Bureau of American Ethnology) 134

Map showing territory held by the Cherokees and their neighbors (from the Nineteenth Annual Report of the Bureau of American Ethnology) 136

Map of the sites of the Cheraws and Catawbas, from Greggs' History of the Old Cheraws 197

Map of Cheraws precinct and parts adjacent (from Greggs' History of the Old Cheraws) 198

LETTER OF TRANSMITTAL.

DEPARTMENT OF THE INTERIOR,

Washington, January 4, 1915.

The PRESIDENT OF THE SENATE.

SIR: Senate resolution 410, dated June 30, 1914, reads as follows:

That the Secretary of the Interior be, and he hereby is, directed to cause an investigation to be made of the condition and tribal rights of the Indians of Robeson and adjoining counties of North Carolina, recently declared by the Legislature of North Carolina to be Cherokees, and formerly known as Croatans, and report to Congress what tribal rights, if any, they have with any band or tribe; whether they are entitled to or have received any lands, or whether there are any moneys due them, their present condition, their educational facilities, and such other facts as would enable Congress to determine whether the Government would be warranted in making suitable provision for their support and education.

In conformity therewith, I have caused an investigation to be made by Special Indian Agent O. M. McPherson, and am transmitting herewith his report of September 19, 1914. This report is quite full, showing a careful investigation on the ground as well as extensive historical research.

It is believed that this report covers the matters mentioned in the resolution, and it is hoped that the information afforded thereby will "enable Congress to determine whether the Government will be warranted in making suitable provision for their support and education."

Respectfully,

FRANKLIN K. LANE.

[Page 7] REPORT ON CONDITION AND TRIBAL RIGHTS OF THE INDIANS OF ROBESON AND ADJOINING COUNTIES OF NORTH CAROLINA.

By Special Indian Agent O. M. MCPHERSON.

DEPARTMENT OF THE INTERIOR,

OFFICE OF INDIAN AFFAIRS,

Washington, September 19, 1914.

MY DEAR MR. SELLS: On June 30, 1914, the Senate passed a resolution (S. Res. 410) authorizing and directing the Secretary of the Interior to cause an investigation to be made of the condition and tribal rights of the Indians of Robeson and adjoining counties in North Carolina. Said resolution reads as follows:

Resolved, That the Secretary of the Interior be, and he hereby is, directed to cause an investigation to be made of the condition and tribal rights of the Indians of Robeson and adjoining counties of North Carolina, recently declared by the legislature of North Carolina to be Cherokees, and formerly known as Croatans, and report to Congress what tribal rights, if any, they have with any band or tribe; whether they are entitled to or have received any lands, or whether there are any moneys due them, their present condition, their educational facilities, and such other facts as would enable Congress to determine whether the Government would be warranted in making suitable provision for their support and education.

(See Exhibit A.)

On July 23, 1914, you instructed me to proceed to Robeson County, N. C., as early as convenient, and make the investigation called for by the resolution. In obedience to your instructions I immediately proceeded to Lumberton, in said State, and the results of my investigation will appear under appropriate headings in this report. (See Exhibit A1.)

HISTORICAL.

The Croatan Indians (designated "Cherokee Indians of Robeson County" by an act of the General Assembly of North Carolina ratified Mar. 11, 1913) comprise a body of mixed-blood people residing chiefly in Robeson County, N. C. A few of the same class of people reside in Bladen, Columbus, Cumberland, Scotland, and Hoke Counties, N. C., and in Sumter, Marlboro, and Dillon Counties, S. C. It is also said that a similar people, called "Redbones," reside in these counties in South Carolina, but I think it probable that they belong to the same class of people as those residing in Robeson County, N. C. In the Eleventh Census, of 1890, under the title "North Carolina [Page 8] Indians," they are described as "generally white, showing the Indian mostly in actions and habits." It is stated that—
They were enumerated by the regular census enumerator in part as whites; that they are clannish and hold with considerable pride to the tradition that they are the descendants of the Croatans of the Raleigh period of North Carolina and Virginia.

(See Exhibit A2.)

They are described in the Hand Book of American Indians, Bureau of American Ethnology, Bulletin No. 30, as a people evidently of mixed Indian and white blood, found in various sections in the eastern part of North Carolina, but chiefly in Robeson County. It is also stated that for many years they were classed with the free negroes, but steadfastly refused to accept such classification or to attend the negro schools or churches, claiming to be the descendants of the early native tribes and white settlers who had intermarried with them.

A bulletin of the Thirteenth Census (census of 1910), "Indians of North Carolina," shows their numbers to be as follows:

Bladen County	36
Columbus County	12
Cumberland County	48
Scotland County	74
Sampson County	213
Robeson County	5, 895
Total in North Carolina	6, 278

In a statement furnished the Committee on Indian Affairs, House of Representatives, February 14, 1913, in the hearing on Senate bill 3258, it is said: According to the census of 1910, the number of Indians in Robeson County was 5, 895. There are also about 1, 500 to 2, 000 in adjoining counties in North and South Carolina, making a settlement in all of about 8, 000 persons.

Apparently, the Indian Office had no knowledge of the existence of the Croatan Indians until the latter part of 1888. About that time 54 of these Indians, describing themselves as "a part of the Croatan Indians living in Robeson County," and claiming to be "a remnant of White's lost colony," petitioned Congress "for such aid as you may see fit to extend to us." This petition was referred to the Indian Office, and on January 7, 1889, a copy was sent to the Director of the Bureau of Ethnology, with the statement that there was no record in the Indian Office showing any such Indians or any such colony as that referred to, and requesting to be furnished with such information as said bureau had concerning these people. On January 11, 1889, the Director of the Ethnological Bureau replied:

I beg leave to say that Croatan was in 1585 and thereabouts the name of an island and Indian village just north of Cape Hatteras, N. C. White's colony of 120 men and women was landed on Roanoke Island just to the north in 1587, and in 1590 when White returned to revisit the colony he found no trace of it on Roanoke Island, save the name "Croatoan" carved upon a tree, which, according to a previous understanding, was interpreted to mean that the colonists had left Roanoke Island for Croatan. No actual trace of the missing colonists was ever found, but more than 100 years afterwards Lawson obtained traditional information from the Hatteras Indians which led him to believe that the colonists had been incorporated with the Indians. It It was thought that traces of white blood could be discovered among the Indians, some among them having gray eyes. It is probable that the greater number of the colonists were killed; but it was quite in keeping with Indian usages that a greater or less number, especially women and children, should have been made captive and subsequently incorporated into the tribe.

[Page 9](See Exhibit B2.)

On January 29, 1889, the Indian Office communicated with Mr. Hamilton McMillan, of Fayetteville, N. C., concerning these Indians, with the result that on July 17, 1890, Mr. McMillan sent the office a copy of his booklet relating to these people, entitled "Sir Walter Raleigh's Lost Colony." Further mention will be made of Mr. McMillan's views concerning the Robeson County Indians. On August 11, 1890, in reply to a letter of July 2 of that year, the Commissioner of Indian Affairs wrote Mr. W. L. Moore, of Osborne, N. C.:

It appears from his statement that this band is recognized by the State of North Carolina, has been admitted to citizenship, and the State has undertaken the work of their education.

While I regret exceedingly that the provisions made by the State of North Carolina seem to be entirely inadequate, I find it quite impracticable to render any assistance at this time. The Government is responsible for the education of something like 36, 000 Indian children and has provisions for less than half this number. So long as the immediate wards of the Government are so insufficiently provided for, I do not see how I can consistently render any assistance to the Croatans or any other civilized tribes.

(See Exhibit B7. See Exhibit C for the McMillan booklet.)

Much doubt and uncertainty has existed as to the source of the Indian blood of this people and as to whether their ancestors comprised a part of White's lost colony (sometimes spoken of as "Raleigh's lost colony"). Some of these Indians hold to a tradition that they are of Cherokee origin, and affect to believe that the action of the General Assembly of North Carolina in designating them as "Cherokee Indians of Robeson County" in some way confirms this tradition. I find that the question of the source of their Indian blood, and whether their ancestors were a part of Gov. White's lost colony are so inextricably bound together that it will be necessary to treat of both subjects under the same heading.

WHITE'S LOST COLONY.

The first explorer of the region originally known as Virginia, comprising the territory afterwards known as Virginia, North Carolina, and South Carolina (omitting for the present some explorations along the coast made by Lane), was John Lederer, a learned German, who resided in the Virginia colony during the administration of Sir William Berkeley. It appears that he made "three several marches" through the country referred to between March, 1669, and September, 1670. Copious extracts from Lederer's notes of travel are printed in Volume II of Hawks's History of North Carolina, together with lengthy explanatory notes. A map of Lederer's explorations accompanies Talbot's translation of the notes (which were written in Latin), by the aid of which Dr. Hawks endeavored to trace the explorer's wanderings in North Carolina. A facsimile of the map is printed in the history; also a facsimile of the map of Carolina drawn by Ogilby in 1671. Copies of these maps and the text relating to Lederer's notes as found in Dr. Hawks's History, Vol. II, accompany this report. (See Exhibit D.)

Dr. Hawks found himself unable to reconcile some of Lederer's narrative with later well-known geographical and historical facts. This was probably due to inaccuracies in courses and distances traveled by the explorer, to errors in names and locations, and to still [Page 10] greater inaccuracies in the orginal map. It is not my purpose to attempt to reconcile or explain these inaccuracies, but merely to call attention to some important facts which seem to have some relation to the early history of the so-called Croatan Indians.

There is a long-standing tradition among these Indians that their ancestors were white people, a part of Gov. White's lost colony, who amalgamated with the coast Indians and afterwards removed to the interior, where they now reside; and it is my purpose to inquire into the historical data which support or contradict this tradition. It is a matter of common knowledge that the Indians are a people of "traditions," being entirely destitute of written records. Indeed, I would regard the tradition of these people that their ancestors comprised a part of the "lost colony" as of little value were it not supported by what is regarded as authentic historical data. Mr. James Mooney, in the Hand Book of Indians, Bureau of American Ethnology, Bulletin No. 30, expresses doubt that these people originated from White's lost colony. He says:

The theory of descent from the lost colony may be regarded as baseless, but the name itself serves as a convenient label for a people who combine in themselves the blood of the wasted native tribes, the early colonists or forest rovers, the runaway slaves or other negroes, and probably also of stray seamen of the Latin races from coasting vessels in the West Indian or Brazilian trade.

Mr. Samuel A'Court Ashe, a most creditable historian, also seems to doubt the origin of the Croatan Indians from White's lost colony. He says in part:

Because names borne by some of the colonists have been found among a mixed race in Robeson County, now called Croatans, an inference has been drawn that there was some connection between them. It is highly improbable that English names would have been preserved among a tribe of savages beyond the second generation, there being no communication except with other savages. If English names had existed among the Hatteras Indians in Lawson's time, he probably would have mentioned it as additional evidence corroborating his suggestion deduced from some of them having gray eyes and from their valuing themselves on their affinity to the English. It is also to be observed that nowhere among the Indians were found houses or tilled lands or other evidences of improvement on the customs and manners of the aborigines. When this mixed race was first observed by the early settlers of the upper Cape Fear, about 1735, it is said that they spoke English, cultivated land, lived in substantial houses, and otherwise practiced the arts of civilized life, being in these respects different from any Indian tribe.

(See Exhibit CCC.)

Except for the doubt expressed by these writers, the universal opinion of those who have written concerning the early history of the Carolinas, as far as I have been able to ascertain, supports the tradition of the Indians.

Gov. White's notes of his voyage to Virginia (North Carolina) in search of the colony he planted on Roanoke Island in 1587 are printed at length in Hawks's History of North Carolina, extracts from which are reprinted in McMillan's pamphlet heretofore referred to. According to a secret understanding which White had with the colonists before he returned to England, if they departed from Roanoke Island before his return (and there had been talk that they might go 50 miles into the interior) they were to carve upon the trees or posts of the doors "the name of the place where they should be seated." When White and his men on August 16, 1590, landed on the north point of the island, where they had left the colony three years previously, and proceeded up the sandy bank, they saw upon a tree, in the very brow thereof, the fair roman letters [Page 11] "C. R. O.," which they "presently knew to signify the place where they should find the planters seated." It was also understood "that if they should happen to be distressed in any of those places" they should carve over the letters or name a cross; but White and his men found no such sign of distress. The narrative continues:

And having well considered of this we passed through the place where they were left in sundry houses, but we found the houses taken down and the place very strongly inclosed with a high palisade of great trees with curtains and flankers, very fortlike, and one of the chief trees or posts at the right side of the entrance had the bark taken off and 5 feet from the ground, in fair capital letters, was graven "CROATOAN," *without any cross or sign of distress.*

It should be noted that the word carved upon the tree was "Croatoan" and not "Croatan" as stated by some of the historians. White's narrative continues:

This done, we entered into the palisade, where we found many bars of iron, two pigs of lead, four iron fowlers, iron locker, shot, and such like heavy things thrown here and there, almost overgrown with grass and weeds. But although it grieved me much to see such spoil of my goods, yet on the other side I greatly joyed that I had safely found a certain token of their being at *Croatoan*, which is the place where Manteo was born, and the savages of the island our friends.

Manteo, it will be remembered, was one of two friendly Indians who had been carried to England by Sir Richard Grenville and returned to Virginia with Gov. White on the occasion of his first voyage, in 1587. On August 13 of that year, Manteo, by direction of Sir Walter Raleigh, was baptized, and in reward for his services to the English he was designated "Lord of Roanoke and Dasamonguepeuk."

Returning to Lederer's travels, it will be noted that on the map prepared in 1666—one of the earliest maps of the Carolina coast—*Croatoan* is represented as an island south of Cape Hatteras. This seems to accord with White's narrative, quoted above. On the map prepared by Ogilby, 1671, on the order of the lords proprietors, and on the map of "Carolina, described 1666" (facsimile by Schroeter), Croatan is marked as a part of the main land, directly west of Roanoke Island. Gov. White's narrative indicates that the colonists (or "planters," as he called them) originally removed to

Croatoan, an island south of Cape Hatteras, and not to Croatan, a part of the mainland. Mr. McMillan in his pamphlet (p. 11) says:

It is evident from the story of Gov. White, as given on a preceding page, that the colonists went southward along the coast to Croatoan Island, now a part of Carteret County, in North Carolina, and distant about 100 miles in a direct line from Albemarle Sound.

The Tuscarora Indians was a powerful and warlike tribe, occupying the central eastern part of North Carolina. They had frequent encounters with the Cherokees and Catawbas on the west and southwest, and with the Cheraws on the south, but stood as an impassable barrier to encroachments on their territory until the destructive war of 1711-1713. The exact location of the Tuscaroras can not be determined from Lederer's notes nor from Ogilby's or Lederer's map, further than that they occupied a very advantageous position in eastern North Carolina; but as indicative of the character of the people at this time (1670), especially the principal chief, Lederer says:

Not thinking fit to proceed farther, the 8th and 20th of June I faced about and looked homeward. To avoid Wisacky marsh I shaped my course northeast; and after [Page 12] three days' travel over hilly ways, where I met with no path or road, I fell into a barren, sandy desert, where I suffered miserably for want of water, the heat of summer having drunk all the springs dry and left no sign of any but the gravelly channels in which they run; so that if now and then I had not found a standing pool, which provident nature set round with shady oaks to defend it from the ardor of the sun, my Indian companion, horse, and self had certainly perished with thirst. In this distress we traveled till the 12th of July, and then found the head of a river, which afterwards proved Eruco, in which we received not only the comfort of a necessary and seasonable refreshment, but likewise the hopes of coming into a country again where we might find game for food at least, if not discover some new nation or people. Nor did our hopes fail us, for after we had crossed the river twice we were led by it, upon the 14th of July, to the town of Katearas, a place of great Indian trade and commerce and chief seat of the haughty emperor of the Taskiroras, called Kaskusara, vulgarly called Kaskous. His grim majesty, upon my first appearance, demanded my gun and shot, which I willingly parted with, to ransom myself out of his clutches; for he was the most proud, imperious barbarian that I met with in all my marches. The people here at this time seemed prepared for some extraordinary solemnity, for the men and the women of better sort had decked themselves very fine with pieces of bright copper in their hair and ears and about their arms and necks, which upon festival occasions they use as an extraordinary bravery; by which it would seem this country is not without rich mines of copper, but I durst not stay to inform myself in it, being jealous of some sudden mischief toward me from Kaskous, his nature being bloody and provoked upon any slight occasion.

Therefore, leaving Katearas, I traveled through the woods until the 16th, upon which I came to Kawitziokan, an Indian town upon a branch of Rorenoke River, which here I passed over, continuing my journey to Menchaerink; and on the 17th, departing from thence, I lay all night in the woods, and the next morning, betimes going by Natoway, I reached that evening Apamatuck, in Virginia, where I was not a little overjoyed to see Christian faces again.

(For the full text of Lederer's notes and Dr. Hawks's comments, see Exhibit D.)

John Lawson, surveyor general of North Carolina, was the next explorer who left a permanent record of his travels among the Indian tribes of the Carolinas. He commenced his journey at Charlestown, December 28, 1700, passed up the Santee and Wateree Rivers, and thence across the foothills to the headwaters of the tributaries of the Neuse and thence down these rivers to the coast. For many days he thought that he had crossed to the headwaters of the Cape Fear River, but after encountering Enoe-Will, an Indian who acted as his guide and interpreter during the latter part of his journey, discovered his mistake. He apparently passed through the country of the Santees, Waterus, Cheraws, and Catawbas, and on the return trip through the country of the Catawbas, Tuscaroras, and Corees. It is possible that he may have entered the country of the Cherokees on the Hiwassee River, though this is by no means certain. I was fortunate in obtaining an original copy of the Lawson history, printed in London in 1718, from which I have copied liberally by photostat process. As in the case of the Lederer notes, it is not my purpose to review the Lawson history in extenso, but merely to call attention to such parts as relate to the lost colony and to the Indians with whom it is supposed they amalgamated. The history is addressed to the "Lords-Proprietors of the Province of Carolina in America," and the author says in the preface:

Having spent most of my Time, during my eight Years Abode in Carolina, in travelling; I not only survey'd the Sea-Coast and those Parts which are already inhabited by the Christians, but likewise view'd a spatious Tract of land, lying betwixt the Inhabitants and the Ledges of Mountains, from whence our noblest Rivers have their Rise, running towards the Ocean, where they water as pleasant a country as any in Europe, the Discovery of which being never yet made publick, I have, in the following Sheets, given you a faithful Account thereof, wherein I have laid down everything [Page 13] with Impartiality, and Truth, which is indeed, the Duty of every Author, and preferable to a smooth Stile, accompany'd with Falsities and Hyperboles.

It seems evident that Lawson and his party were unable to converse with the Indians of the several tribes through which they passed, except in the sign language, until they encountered Enoe-Will, one of the headmen of the Coree tribe, a small tribe originally residing on the coast near the mouth of the Neuse River, and which was probably allied with the Hatteras, Pamlico, and other coast tribes. About the point of leaving the country of the Keyauwees, most of the party abandoned Lawson, with a view of proceeding to Virginia, leaving him and one companion to pursue their journey alone through North Carolina. On page 53 Lawson says:

This morning most of our Company having some Inclination to go straight away for Virginia, when they left this Place; I and one more took our leaves of them, resolving (with God's Leave) to see North Carolina, one of the Indians setting us in our way. The rest being indifferent which way they went, desired us, by all means, to leave a Letter for them, at the Achonechy-Town. The Indian that put us in our Path, had been a Prisoner amongst the Sinnagers; but had out-run them, although they had cut his Toes, and half his Feet away, which is a Practice common amongst them. They first raise the skin, then cut away half the Feet, and so wrap the Skin over the Stumps, and make a present Cure of the Wounds. This commonly disables them from making their Escape, they being not so good Travellers as before, and the Impression of their Half-Feet making it easy to trace them. However, this Fellow was got clear of them, but had little Heart to go far from home, and carry'd always a case of Pistols in his Girdle, besides a Cutlass, and a Fuzee.

Notwithstanding they were "put in their path" by the Indian referred to, Lawson and his companion apparently traveled a hundred miles or more without a guide. During this time they had nothing to subsist on but parched corn, and probably passed over the neutral territory between the Catawbas and the Tuscaroras. Near the "town" of Achonechy, probably 120 miles from the country of the Keyauwees, they encountered "30 horses coming on the road with four or five men on other jades, driving them." These proved to be a small company of Englishmen from Virginia, who were going into the Carolinas to trade with the Indians. The leading man was named Massey, and he advised Lawson by all means "to strike down the country for Roanoke, and not think of Virginia because of the Sinnegars." He also persuaded them to call upon Enoe-Will as they went to Adshusheer, "for that he would conduct them safe among the English," giving him the character of a very faithful Indian. About 3 o'clock they reached the town, and within two hours Enoe-Will came into the "King's" house, where they were staying. The next morning they set out with Enoe-Will "towards Adshusheer, leaving the Virginia path and striking more to the eastward for Roanoke." Lawson describes the journey to Adshusheer, where Enoe-Will resided "as a sad stony way" which made him quite lame. Here the Indians brought them two "cocks" (chickens), which to my mind is conclusive evidence that these Indians had previously come in contact with the whites, as Indians in their native state, as a rule, are destitute of domestic animals, except the horse and dog. Lawson says of Enoe-Will:

Our guide and landlord, Enoe-Will, was of the best and most agreeable temper that ever I met with in an Indian, being always ready to serve the English, not out of gain, but real affection.

The following day much rain fell and they stayed at the Indian town. The next morning they set out early and traveled about 10 miles, [Page 14] when they were stopped by the high water in the river. Lawson thought that they were on some tributary of the Cape Fear River, but on inquiry of Enoe-Will he learned that it was Enoe River and emptied into a place called "Enoe Bay," near his country, which he left when he was a boy; by which Lawson perceived that Will was one of the Corees and that the river they were waiting to cross was a branch of the Neuse River. This locates the Corees when Will was a boy—probably 50 or more years previously—on the coast near the mouth of the Neuse River, and for the first time the traveler learned that he was much farther north than he had supposed.

On page 58, the author says:

The next day, early, came two Tuskerora Indians to the other side of the river, but could not get over. They talked much to us, but we understood them not. In the afternoon, Will came with the mare and had some discourse with them. They told him the English, to whom he was going, were very wicked people; and that they threatened the Indians for hunting on their plantations.

This incident reveals the fact that the travelers were within or near the Tuscarora country, and that already friction existed between the English and the Tuscaroras. The author continues:

Will had a slave, a Sissipahan Indian by nation, who killed us several turkeys and other game, on which we feasted.

Showing the existence of Indian slavery among the Corees (or Schoccores, as Lawson sometimes called them) at this time.

A short distance after crossing the branch of the Neuse River referred to, they halted for the night. The traveler carried an illustrated Bible with him and as they lay in camp at this place Enoe-Will asked to see the book. Lawson describes what took place as follows:

My Guide Will desiring to see the Book that I had about me, I lent it him; and as he soon found the Picture of King David, he asked me several Questions concerning the Book, and Picture, which I resolved him, and invited him to become a Christian. He made me a very sharp Reply, assuring me, That he loved the English extraordinary well, and did believe their Ways to be very good for those that had already practiced them, and had been brought up therein, But as for himself, he was too much in Years to think of a Change, esteeming it not proper for Old People to admit of such an Alteration. However, he told me, If I would take his son Jack, who was then about 14 Years of Age, and teach him to talk in that Book, and make Paper speak, which they call our Way of Writing, he would wholly resign him to my Tuition; telling me, he was of Opinion, I was very well affected to the Indians.

This conversation between the traveler and his guide reveals several important things: First, that Enoe-Will must have been between 60 and 70 years old at this time, and that he was familiar with the fact that the English could "talk in a book" and "make paper speak." Couple this with the fact that the guide had an English name, "Will," which he probably assumed at the age of 20 or 21, and the information previously given by him that he lived on Enoe Bay when he was a boy, leads quite certainly to the conclusion that the Corees had come in contact with at least some portion of the lost colony. It must be remembered that when Will was a boy there were no English settlements on the east coast of North Carolina other than White's lost colony.

A few days after the conversation between the traveler and his guide, quoted above, Lawson reached the plantation of his friend, Mr. Richard Smith, on "Pamptigouch River," "where being well received by the inhabitants, and pleased with the goodness of the country, we all resolved to continue."

[Page 15]In the second part of his history, which the author designated "A description of North Carolina," he speaks of the early settlement of the country and of the lost colony as follows:

The first Discovery and Settlement of this Country was by the Procurement of Sir Walter Raleigh, in Conjunction with some publick-spirited Gentlemen of that Age, under the protection of Queen Elizabeth; for which Reason it was then named Virginia, being begun on that Part called Ronoak Island, where the Ruins of a Fort are to be seen at this day, as well as some old English Coins which have been lately found; and a Brass-Gun, a Powder-Horn, and one small Quarter deck-Gun, made of Iron Staves, and hooped with the same metal; which Method of making Guns might very probably be made use of in those Days, for the Convenience of Infant-Colonies.

A farther Confirmation of this we have from the Hatteras Indians, who either then lived on Ronoak-Island, or much frequented it. These tell us, that several of their ancestors were white People, and could talk in a Book, as we do; the Truth of which is confirmed by gray Eyes being found frequently amongst these Indians, and no others. They value themselves extremely for their Affinity to the English, and are ready to do them all friendly Offices. It is probable, that this Settlement miscarried for want of timely Supplies from England; or thro' the Treachery of the Natives, for we may reasonably suppose that the English were forced to cohabit with them, for Relief and Conversation; and that in process of Time, they conformed themselves to the Manners of their Indian Relations. And thus we see how apt Humane Nature is to degenerate.

I cannot forbear inserting here, a pleasant Story that passes for an uncontested Truth amongst the Inhabitants of this Place; which is, that the Ship which brought the first Colonies, does often appear amongst them, under Sail, in a gallant Posture, which they call Sir Walter Raleigh's Ship; And the truth of this has been affirmed to me, by Men of the best Credit in the Country.

A second Settlement of this Country was made about fifty Years ago, in that part we now call Albemarl County, and chiefly in Chuwon Precinct, by several substantial Planters, from Virginia, and other Plantations.

Lawson's history is regarded as the standard authority for the period it covers; I find it extensively quoted from by all subsequent historians; and if his statements concerning the amalgamation of the lost colony with the Hatteras Indians is not true, the "mystery" of what became of White's colony can never be solved. But there are many facts and circumstances which confirm Lawson's record.

When White returned to Roanoke Island in 1590, in accordance with the secret understanding between himself and the colonists, he found the word "Croatoan" graven upon a tree comprising one of the door posts of the palisade; and above it he found no cross or sign of distress. This, to my mind, indicated that the colonists were not captured in warfare by the Indians, but went with them voluntarily to find a better location than Roanoke Island. If they went with the Hatteras Indians voluntarily, amalgamation with them was inevitable.

I understand that when the act of the North Carolina Legislature designating them Croatans, was publicly read to the Indians, one aged Indian, a very intelligent man, remarked that he had always heard his ancestors say that they were Hatteras Indians. Manteo was friendly to the English, and would undoubtedly do everything in his power to protect them. On page 234 of his history Lawson describes the Hatteras Indians as consisting of one town residing on the Sand Banks, with 16 fighting men. The Hatteras Indians are described in the Hand Book of American Indians, Bureau of Ethnology (p. 537) as follows:

HATTERAS.—An Algonquian tribe living in 1701 on the sand banks about C. Hatteras, N. C., E. of Pamlico Sound, and frequenting Roanoke Id. Their single village, Sandbanks, had then only about 80 inhabitants. They showed traces of white blood and claimed that some of their ancestors were white. They may have been identical [Page 16] with the Croatan Indians (q. v.), with whom Raleigh's colonists at Roanoke Id. are supposed to have taken refuge.

The presence of gray eyes and fair skin among these people in Lawson's time can not be explained on any other hypothesis than that of amalgamation with the white race; and when Lawson wrote (1709) there was a tradition among the Hatteras Indians that their ancestors were white people "and could talk in a book"; and that "they valued themselves extremely for their affinity to the English and were ready to do them all friendly offices." I have already referred to the fact that Enoe-Will, a Coree Indian, who had been raised on the coast, and who was probably nearly 70 years of age when he acted as Lawson's guide, knew that the English could "talk in a book" and as he further expressed it, "could make paper talk," indicating that he was familiar with the customs of the English. The Corees are described in the "Hand Book," Bulletin No. 30 (p. 349), as follows:

COREE.—A tribe, possibly Algonquian, formerly occupying the peninsula S. of Neuse R., in Carteret and Craven Cos., N. C. They had been greatly reduced in a war with another tribe before 1696, and were described by Archdale as having been a bloody and barbarous people. Lawson refers to them as Coranine Indians, but in another place calls them Cannamox and gives them two villages in 1701—Coranine and Raruta—with about 125 souls. They engaged in the Tuscarora war of 1711, and in 1715 the remnants of the Coree and Machapunga were assigned a tract on Mattamuskeet Lake, Hyde Co., N. C., where they lived in one village probably until they became extinct.

There is an abiding tradition among these people at the present time that their ancestors were the lost colony, amalgamated with some tribe of Indians. This tradition is supported by their looks, their complexion, color of skin, hair and eyes, by their manners, customs and habits, and by the fact that while they are, in part, of undoubted Indian origin, they have no Indian names and no Indian language—not even a single word—and know nothing of Indian customs and habits. Speaking of the language of this people, Mr. McMillan says:

The language spoken is almost pure Anglo Saxon, a fact which we think affords corroborative evidence of their relation to the lost colony of White. Mon (Saxon) is used for man, father is pronounced "fayther," and a tradition is usually begun as follows:

"Mon, my fayther told me that his fayther told him," etc. "Mension," is used for measurement, "aks" for ask, "hit" for it, "hosen" for hose, "lovend" for loving, "housen" for houses. They seem to have but two sounds for the letter "a," one like short "o." Many of the words in common use among them have long been obsolete in English-speaking countries.

Col. Fred A. Olds, a newspaper correspondent of Raleigh, says of their language:

The language spoken by the Croatans is a very pure but quaint old Anglo-Saxon, and there are in daily use some 75 words which have come down from the great days of Raleigh and his mighty mistress, Queen Elizabeth. These old Saxon words arrest attention instantly. For man they say "mon," pronounce father "feyther," use "mension" for measurement, "ax" for ask, "hosen" for hose, "lovened" for loving, "wit" for knowledge, "housen" for houses; and many other words in daily use by them have for years been entirely obsolete in English-speaking countries.

Just when the colonists and the Indians with whom they amalgamated removed to the interior is not certainly known, but it is believed to have been as early as 1650. At the coming of the first white settlers to what is now known as Robeson County, there was found located on the banks of the Lumber River a large tribe of Indians, [Page 17] speaking the English language, tilling the soil, owning slaves, and practicing many of the arts of civilized life. McMillan says:

They occupied the country as far west as the Pee Dee, but their principal seat was on the Lumber, extending along that river for 20 miles. They held their lands in common and land titles only became known on the approach of white men. The first grant of land to any of this tribe, of which there is written evidence in existence, was made by King George II in 1732, to Henry Berry and James Lowrie, two leading men of the tribe, and was located on the Lowrie Swamp, east of Lumber River in present country of Robeson in North Carolina. A subsequent grant was made to James Lowrie in 1738. According to tradition there were deeds of land of older date, described as "White" deeds and "Smith" deeds, but no trace of their existence can be found at this date.

And what is of greater significance, a very large number of the names appearing among the lost colony are to be found among the Croatan Indians, a fact inexplicable upon any other hypothesis than that the lost colony amalgamated with the Indians.

These names, common to both, are printed in italics in the McMillan booklet. (Exhibit C.) The present investigation discloses that the Indian names, Indian language, and Indian customs and habits perished, while the English names, English language, and English customs and habits prevailed. Mr. McMillan adds:

The writer has been much interested in investigating the tradition prevalent among the Croatans and expresses his firm conviction that they are descended from the friendly tribe found on our east coast in 1587, and also descended from the lost colonists of Roanoke, who amalgamated with this tribe.

From the foregoing I have no hesitancy in expressing the belief that the Indians originally settled in Robeson and adjoining counties in North Carolina were an amalgamation of the Hatteras Indians with Gov. White's lost colony; the present Indians are their descendants with a further amalgamation with the early Scotch and Scotch-Irish settlers, such amalgamation continuing down to the present time, together with a small degree of amalgamation with other races.

I do not find that the Hatteras Indians or the so-called Croatan Indians ever had any treaty relations with the United States, or that they have any tribal rights with any tribe or band of Indians; neither do I find that they have received any lands or that there are any moneys due them.

CLAIM OF CHEROKEE ORIGIN.

Since writing the foregoing, the office has received and referred to me a communication, dated September 7, 1914, from Mr. A. W. McLean, of Lumberton, N. C., the local representative of these Indians, concerning their claim to Cherokee origin. Mr. McLean refers to a statement presented by him on February 14, 1913, to the House Committee on Indian Affairs, respecting the origin of these Indians, and asks that his communication be treated as supplemental to said statement. In the statement referred to Mr. McLean said in part:

We are of the opinion that they were originally a part of the great Cherokee Tribe of Indians, which inhabited the western and central portions of Carolina before the advance of the white man.

Indeed, Mr. McMillan, in his account before referred to, takes the position that they are of Cherokee descent, though we confess that we can not reconcile this contention with his main contention that they are descendants of Gov. White's or Sir Walter Raleigh's lost colony.

[Page 18]Long before historians began to study the origin of these people they claimed to be of Cherokee descent. In fact, they have always claimed that they were originally a part of the Cherokee Tribe and that they gave up their tribal relation after they had participated with the white man in the war against the Tuscaroras. These Indians had great roads or trails connecting their settlements with the principal seat of the Cherokee Tribe in the Allegheny Mountains. There is a well-authenticated tradition among them, handed down through several generations, that this small remnant after participating with the whites in the war against the Tuscaroras took up many of the habits and customs of the white man, and therefore refused to remove West with the great Cherokee Tribe. It is also certain that in this they were influenced by the admixture of Anglo-Saxon blood, which had taken place to some extent even in that remote period.

In the communication Mr. McLean says:

My opinion is, from a very exhaustive examination made before and after the hearing above mentioned, that these Indians are not only descendants of Sir Walter Raleigh's lost colony, as contended by Mr. Hamilton McMillan in his statement, a copy of which Mr. McPherson has in his possession, but that they are also mixed with the Cherokee Indians. In the first place, these Indians have contended from time immemorial that they were of Cherokee descent, and they further have had a tradition among them that their ancestors, or some of them, came from "Roanoke and Virginia." Roanoke and Virginia, of course, originally comprised all of eastern North Carolina, including Roanoke Island, the settlement of Sir Walter Raleigh's lost colony.

(For the full text of Mr. McLean's statement and communication see Exhibit F.)

The history and traditions of the Cherokee Indians of North Carolina, in my judgment, do not confirm the claim of the Robeson County Indians to Cherokee origin. The Cherokees were the mountaineers of the South, originally holding the entire Appalachian region from the headwaters of the Kanawha on the north to middle Georgia on the south. Their principal towns were upon the headwaters of the Savannah, Hiwassee, and Tuckasegee Rivers, and along the entire length of the Little Tennessee to its junction with the main stream. As far as I can learn, there is no tradition that they ever occupied the coast country in North Carolina or elsewhere. Indeed, interposed between the Cherokees and the coast were three or four powerful tribes with which they were in perpetual warfare. On the east and southeast the Tuscaroras and Catawbas were their inveterate enemies, with hardly even a momentary truce within historic times, and evidence is not wanting that the Sara or Cheraw were originally their deadly enemies. Had inclination led them toward the coast in the time of the earliest colonization they would probably have been driven back by other hostile tribes. In the Nineteenth Annual Report of the Bureau of Ethnology (p. 21), speaking of the early location of the Cherokees, it is stated:

From a careful sifting of the evidence, Haywood concludes that the authors of the most ancient remains in Tennessee had spread over that region from the south and southwest at a very early period, but that the latter occupants, the Cherokee, had entered it from the north and northeast in comparatively recent times, overrunning and exterminating the aborigines. He declares that the historical fact seems to be established that the Cherokee entered the country from Virginia, making temporary settlements upon New River and the upper Holston until, under the continued hostile pressure from the north, they were again forced to remove farther to the south, fixing themselves upon the Little Tennessee, in what afterwards became known as the middle towns. By a leading mixed blood of the tribe he was informed that they had made their first settlements within their modern home territory upon Nolichucky River, and that, having lived there for a long period, they could give no definite account of an earlier location. Echota, their capital and peace town, "claimed to be the eldest brother in the nation," and the claim was generally acknowledged. In confirmation of the statement as to an early occupancy of the upper Holston region, [Page 19] it may be noted that "Watauga Old Fields," now Elizabethton, were so called from the fact that when the first white settlement within the present State of Tennessee was begun there, so early as 1769, the bottom lands were found to contain graves and other numerous ancient remains of a former Indian town which tradition ascribed to the Cherokee, whose nearest settlements were then many miles to the southward.

In this historical statement there is no tradition that the Cherokees had ever occupied any portion of the coast country.

The strongest and most persistent tradition of the Robeson County Indians is that their ancestors were a part of the "lost colony"; and it seems most probable that the lost colony, if amalgamated with any Indian tribe (which seems historically certain), amalgamated with a *coast* tribe and not with a "mountain tribe" residing 300 miles to the westward, between whom and the coast settlements three or four hostile tribes were interposed. In this connection it should not be overlooked that at the time of the earliest attempts at colonization, and at the time of the great Tuscarora War, the Coree and Hatteras Indians, who resided on the coast, were firm allies of the Tuscaroras; in fact, they could not have maintained their position on the coast as against the tribes farther west and southwest except through a firm alliance with the stronger Tuscaroras.

The first definite history of the Cherokees begins with the year 1540, at which date they were firmly established where they have always afterwards been known to reside, namely, in the mountain section of the Carolinas and Georgia. The earliest Spanish adventurers failed to penetrate so far into the interior, and the earliest entry into their country was made by the intrepid De Soto, who advanced into the interior in May, 1540, by way of the Savannah River, in his fruitless quest for gold. There is no record of a second attempt to penetrate the Cherokee country for 26 years. In 1561 the Spaniards took formal possession of the Bay of Santa Elena, now St. Helena, near Port Royal, on the coast of South Carolina. The next year the French made an unsuccessful attempt at settlement at the same place, and in 1566 Menendez made the Spanish occupancy sure by establishing there a fort which he called San Felipe. In November of that year Capt. Juan Pardo was sent with a party from the fort to explore the interior and probably penetrated into the Cherokee country, but on account of the deep snow in the mountains he did not think it advisable to go farther, and so returned. The following summer Capt. Pardo left Fort Santa Elena with a small detachment of troops and penetrated the Cherokee country, but the trip was fruitless of important results, and he returned, having discovered nothing more valuable than some mica mines.

It was at about this time that the Catawbas, residing east of the Cherokees, were at the height of their power and influence, and for nearly a hundred years they were engaged in petty warfare with the northern Iroquoian tribes, particularly with the Cherokees. During this period the Catawbas stood as a barrier between the Cherokees and the coast.

Not until 1654 did the English come in contact with the Cherokees, called in the records of that period Rechahecrians, probably a corruption of Rickahockans, apparently the name by which they were then known to the Powhatan Tribe in Virginia. In this year the Virginia colony, which had recently concluded an exterminating war with the Powhatans, was alarmed at the news of the approach of a large body of Rechahecrian Indians who had invaded the country and [Page 20] established themselves at the falls of the James River. On page 30 of the Nineteenth Annual Report of the Bureau of Ethnology it is stated:

In 1670 the German traveler, John Lederer, went from the falls of James River to the Catawba country in South Carolina, following for most of the distance the path used by the Virginia traders, who already had regular dealings with the southern tribes, including probably the Cherokee. He speaks in several places of the Rickahockan, which seems to be a more correct form than Rechahecrian, and his narrative and the accompanying map put them in the mountains of North Carolina, back of the Catawba and the Sara and southward from the head of Roanoke River. They were apparently on hostile terms with the tribes to the eastward, and while the traveler was stopping at an Indian village on Dan River, about the present Clarksville, Va., a delegation of Rickahockan, which had come on tribal business, was barbarously murdered at a dance prepared on the night of their arrival by their treacherous hosts. On reaching the Catawba country he heard of white men to the southward, and incidentally mentions that the neighboring mountains were called tho Suala Mountains by the Spaniards. In the next year, 1671, a party from Virginia, under Thomas Batts, explored the northern branch of Roanoke River and crossed over the Blue Ridge to the headwaters of New River, where they found trace of occupancy, but no Indians. By this time all the tribes of this section, east of the mountains, were in possession of firearms.

This reveals the fact that the Cherokees in the earlier part of their known history were on hostile terms with the tribes to the eastward, which, as before stated, included the powerful and warlike tribe of the Tuscaroras. The Catawbas were in immediate contact with the Cherokees on the south and east, but the Tuscaroras also stood as an impassable barrier between them and the coast. To the south of the Tuscoraras were the Sara or Cheraws, who in the earliest historical periods were also hostile to the Cherokees.

On page 38 of the ethnological report above referred to it is stated: Throughout the eighteenth century the Cherokees were engaged in chronic warfare with their Indian neighbors. As these quarrels concerned the whites but little, however momentous they may have been to the principals, we have but few details. The war with the Tuscarora continued until the outbreak of the latter tribe against Carolina in 1711 gave opportunity to the Cherokee to cooperate in striking the blow which drove the Tuscarora from their ancient homes to seek refuge in the north. The Cherokee then turned their attention to the Shawano on the Cumberland, and with the aid of the Chickasaw finally expelled them from that region about the year 1715. Inroads upon the Catawba were probably kept up until the latter had become so far reduced by war and disease as to be mere dependent pensioners upon the whites. The former friendship with the Chickasaw was at last broken through the overbearing conduct of the Cherokee, and a war followed of which we find incidental notice in 1757, and which terminated in a decisive victory for the Chickasaw about 1768. The bitter war with the Iroquois of the far north continued, in spite of all the efforts of the colonial governments, until a formal treaty of peace was brought about by the efforts of Sir William Johnson (12) in the same year.

(For the full text of the history of the Cherokees as given in said report, see Exhibit G.)

Until after the exterminating war with the Tuscaroras in 1711-1713, it seems quite impossible that the Cherokees could have gotten to the coast of the Carolinas; but this was 124 years after the planting of the English colony on Roanoke Island by Gov. White.

As mentioned by Mr. McLean, it is quite probable that a small number of the Cherokees were allied with the whites, the Cheraw, and Catawba Indians against the Tuscaroras, for assertion to this effect is made by Williamson, Gregg and Mooney; but in a report of his Indian allies, made by Col. Barnwell himself, at Fort Narhantes (the stronghold of the Tuscaroras) on February 4, 1712, he does [Page 21] not mention the Cherokees. I quote from the Handbook of American Indians, page 845:

In a letter dated at Narhantes Fort, February 4, 1712, Col. Barnwell gives a list of the various tribes of southern Indians who composed his motley army. In his own spelling these were: The Amasses, Hog Logees, Apalatchees, Corsaboy, Watterees, Sagarees, Catawbas, Suterees, Waxams, Congarees, Sattees, Pedees, Weneaws, Cape Feare, Hoopengs, Wareperees, Saraws, and Saxapahaws. Fort Narhantes, according to Barnwell, was the largest and most warlike town of the Tuscarora.

When the Tuscaroras were first visited by Lawson they possessed the country lying between the coast of North Carolina and the foothills, having 16 towns and about 1, 200 warriors. (For their history, their alliance with the small coast tribes, their struggles with other tribes, the Tuscarora War, etc., see Exhibit H.)

After the close of the Tuscarora War it is possible that a few of the Cherokee Indians taking part therein remained in what is now Robeson County and amalgamated with the Indians then residing there; but it must be remembered that when the first Scotch settlers located in that section of country they found seated on the Lumber River and its tributaries a tribe of Indians *speaking English,* tilling the soil like white men, owning slaves, and practicing many of the arts of civilized life. This could not have been the Cherokees, for there is no tradition among them that they ever spoke the English language; but it does constitute one of the strongest links in the chain of evidence that this "Indian tribe" were the descendants of the "lost colony" which by force of necessity had become amalgamated with one of the coast tribes. While I say it is possible that some of the Cherokees who took part in the Tuscarora War may have remained in the east and amalgamated with the coast tribes, including the so-called Croatans in Robeson County, it is much more probable that they induced individual members of these tribes to migrate west with them, for it is a matter of history that the remnants of some of these small coast tribes did migrate west and became absorbed in the larger tribes, and in this way lost their identity. To my mind it is much more probable that some of the Croatans went west and became absorbed by the Cherokees than that a few Cherokees remained east and became absorbed by the Croatans. It is not unlikely that in this way the ancestors of the John Lowrie who signed the Cherokee treaty of 1806 may have been connected with the Croatans, but emigrated west after the Tuscarora War. But the circumstance of the similarity of names between the signer of the treaty of 1806 and one of the leading families of the Croatans would carry little weight as establishing identity between the two, for among the Cherokees in 1806 were a number of English and Scotch names, and a few of French origin; and the name Lowrie or Lowrey was then, as it is now, a very common English name, and might appear in several of the Indian tribes. The mere "tradition" that the two families were related, in the absence of record evidence to this effect, could have but little weight for, as explained in the earlier part of this report, the Indians are a people of traditions and in the absence of record evidence are content to accept tradition as fact.

The tradition obtained by Gregg from William H. Thomas that the Cherokees originally occupied the territory assigned to the Catawbas, and that there was a sanguinary battle between them, lasting from [Page 22] morning until night, resulting in frightful losses on both sides, as a result of which an agreement was entered into between them by the terms of which the Catawbas were to occupy the country formerly occupied by the Cherokees and the Cherokees were to remove farther west into the mountains, does not seem to be substantiated by the reports of the Ethnological Bureau. For the first chapter in Gregg's History of the Old Cheraws, in which he relates this tradition and gives the origin of the names of certain rivers in South Carolina, see Exhibit I. The map included in the narrative (p. 197) taken from map in Volume I, Transactions of American Ethnological Society, no doubt shows correctly the relative locations of the several tribes occupying the territory of the Carolinas when the earliest explorations were made by the whites. Reference is particularly made to this map for such locations.

The Catawbas were the most important of the Eastern Siouan tribes, and doubtless had a number of conflicts with the Cherokees, but the Cherokees were essentially mountaineers, and held dominion over the Appalachian

Chain from the headwaters of the Kanawha to central Georgia. The Cherokees were of Iroquoian stock while the Catawbas were of Siouan stock, and racial differences may have had something to do with their petty conflicts. The principal villages of the Catawbas were formerly on the west bank of the river, in what is now York County, S. C., opposite the mouth of Sugar Creek. I quote from the Hand Book of American Indians, pages 213 and 214:

Further investigations by Hale, Gatschet, Mooney, and Dorsey proved that several other tribes of the same region were also of Siouan stock, while the linguistic forms and traditional evidence all point to this E. region as the original home of the Siouan tribes. The alleged tradition which brings the Catawba from the N., as refugees from the French and their Indian allies about the year 1660 does not agree in any of its main points with the known facts of history, and if genuine at all, refers rather to some local incident than to a tribal movement. It is well known that the Catawba were in a chronic state of warfare with the northern tribes, whose raiding parties they sometimes followed, even across the Ohio.

The first notice of the Catawba seems to be that of Vandera in 1579, who calls them Issa in his narrative of Pardo's expedition. Nearly a century later, in 1670, they are mentioned as Ushery by Lederer, who claims to have visited them, but this is doubtful.

Lawson, who passed through their territory in 1701, speaks of them as a "powerful nation" and states that their villages were very thick. He calls the two divisions, which were living a short distance apart, by different names, one the Kadapau and the other the Esaw, unaware of the fact that the two were synonyms. From all accounts they were formerly the most populous and most important tribe in the Carolinas, excepting the Cherokee.

(For the full text of the history of the Catawbas as given in the Hand Book, see Exhibit J.)

Referring to the origin of certain names, as mentioned by Gregg, it is stated in the Nineteenth Annual Report of the Bureau of Ethnology that the word "Cherokee" has no meaning in the Cherokee language, and seems to be of foreign origin. As used among themselves the form is Tsa-lagi or Tsa-ragi. It first appears as Chalaque in the Portuguese narrative of De Soto's expedition, published originally in 1557. There is evidence that it is taken from the Choctaw word Choluk or Chiluk, signifying a pit or cave, derived from the Mobilian trade language, a corrupted Choctaw jargon formerly used as a medium of communication among all the tribes of the Gulf States. As given by Gatschet, the Catawba name for the Cherokees was Manteran,

meaning "coming out of the ground," which is nearly [Page 23] equivalent to the meaning contained in the Choctaw world. The report adds:
Adair's attempt to connect the name Cherokee with their word for fire, *atsila*, is an error, founded upon imperfect knowledge of the language.

(See Exhibit G, pp. 133 to 179.)

The word "Santee" (the name of an eastern Siouan tribe) is from the Sioux or Dakota word "insanyati," meaning Knife Lake.

The word "Wateree" (also the name of an eastern Siouan tribe) is probably from the Catawba word "wateran," meaning to float on the water.

Congaree is the name of a small eastern Siouan Tribe and the word is probably of Siouan origin; and Pedee is likewise the name of a small Siouan tribe and the word is thought to be of Siouan origin. While the word "Lumbee" is not found in the Hand Book (the Lumber River was anciently called the Lumbee) it is probably of the same origin. The "Lumbee" River is a branch of the Pedee and the similarity of the names would suggest the same origin. All these small Siouan tribes were originally parts of or confederated with the Cheraws, and about 1739, with the Cheraws, became incorporated with the Catawbas. For a complete history of all these small tribes, see Hand Book of American Indians.

The Cheraws are of Siouan stock, and originally ranged from southern Virginia to the Cape Fear River in South Carolina, their principal seat being near the town of Cheraw, S. C., which takes its name from them. In numbers they probably stood next to the Tuscaroras, but are much less prominent in history because of their almost complete destruction by the time the white settlements reached them. They were first visited by De Soto in 1540 and later by Lederer and Lawson. They were undoubtedly known to the Cherokees in very early times for they ranged over a part of the territory originally claimed by the Cherokees, but I find no authentic history that they were ever a part of the Cherokees or even allied with them. It is much more probable that they had numerous conflicts with the Cherokees in early times as they ranged over their territory and were continually harassed by the Iroquoian tribes. The Cherokees are of Iroquoian stock, while ethnologists claim that the Cheraws were of Siouan stock, and on account of this racial difference and difference in language, there is no reasonable probability that an alliance ever existed between them. The Cheraws were continually harassed by the Iroquoian tribes, and about 1710 were compelled to remove farther southeast and joined the Keyauwee, a small Siouan tribe. Being still subject to attacks by the Iroquois, between 1726 and

1739, they became incorporated with the Catawbas. The last historical notice of them was in 1768, when their remnant, reduced by war and disease, were still living with the Catawbas. The final absorption of the Cheraws by the Catawbas seems to refute the claim that the Cheraws were a branch of the Cherokee Tribe. It is not improbable, however, that there was some degree of amalgamation between the Indians residing on the Lumber River and the Cheraws, who were their nearest neighbors.

(For a full history of the Cheraws and Cherokees, as given in the Hand Book of American Indians, see Exhibit K.)

[Page 24] THEIR PRESENT CONDITION.

It is not altogether easy to describe the exact condition of these Indians. They are essentially a farming people, living almost exclusively in the country, and in many respects their condition is identical with that of their white neighbors among whom they live. A much less proportion of the heads of families, however, are landowners than among the whites, which means a much less degree of prosperity. It is conservatively estimated that not more than one-quarter of the heads of families are landowners, the holdings frequently amounting to only 4 or 5 acres; it follows that the great majority of them are renters. But in the communities where their land holdings are equal to that of the whites they give evidences of equal prosperity, and as I went through such settlements, from farm to farm, it was impossible for me to tell from outward appearance whether I was passing the farm of an Indian or that of a white man. One of these Indians is the owner of 500 acres of land; two or three others own about 300 acres each, and lesser amounts are owned by a considerable number. These men would be classed as prosperous farmers in any community. But it must be understood that most of the land in Robeson County is very level and a considerable proportion is included in swamps and lowlands. The tillable land of the county, however, would be classed as fertile bottom land, readily susceptible of raising large crops of cotton, tobacco, and corn.

Among the small landowners and renters a lesser degree of prosperity prevails, and among very many families there is much poverty and wretchedness. Many of the very old people who are unable to care for themselves are extremely needy and should be sent to the Home for the Aged and Infirm of Robeson County. It may be said of the entire body of Indians that they speak only the English language; that they are good farmers and cultivate their lands equally as well as the whites; that they are entirely self-supporting and self-reliant; that many of them live in substantial houses; and that all of them practice the arts and habits of civilized life. In these respects they are different from most of the Indian tribes.

The following statement of property owned by these Indians was furnished me by the State auditor:

Answering your letter of July 24, which you handed me this date, I give you the following information, taken from the records of this department:

	1912	1913
ROBESON COUNTY.		
Number of Indian polls.....	960	1,010
Value of property listed for taxation.	$493,900	$506,094
SCOTLAND COUNTY.		
Number Indian polls.....	38	44
Value of property listed for taxation.	$6,500	$5,689
HOKE COUNTY.		
Number of Indian polls.....	13	28
Value of property listed for taxation.	$3,574	$4,463

The records on file in this department from Cumberland, Bladen, and Columbus Counties do not show any Indian polls.

[Page 25] *EDUCATIONAL FACILITIES.*

Prior to 1835 the adult male Croatans exercised the right of franchise in North Carolina, and it seemed to be the current tradition that at least a few of the children attended the white schools, wherever schools for the whites had been established in Indian settlements; but for the most part they were compelled to attend "subscription" schools organized and conducted by themselves. By clause 3 of section 3 of the amendments to the constitution of 1835, the Croatans lost the right of franchise, and from that date until the adoption of the constitution of 1868 they were regarded and treated as "free persons of color"—which practically meant free negroes—and during this period they were not permitted to attend the schools for whites; there were practically no educational facilities open to the Indians at this time. There were doubtless some subscription schools, but they must have been of the poorest sort.

Between 1868 and 1885 efforts were made to compel the Indians to attend the negro schools, but they persistently refused to do this, preferring to grow up in ignorance rather than attend the colored schools. It would be more accurate to say that parents would not permit their children to attend the negro schools, preferring rather that they should grow up in total ignorance. The children raised to manhood and womanhood during this period are the most densely ignorant of any of these people.

Up to 1885 these people had been without name or designation, but through the efforts of Hon. Hamilton McMillan, by an act of the General Assembly of North Carolina of February 10, 1885, they were designated "Croatan Indians," and by the same act they were granted separate schools for their children, school committees of their own race and color, and were allowed to select teachers of their own choice, subject to the same rules and regulations applicable to all teachers under the general school laws. By section 2 of the act the county board of education was directed to see that the act was carried into effect, and to proceed to establish suitable school districts as shall be necessary for their convenience, and to do all necessary things to carry the act into effect. Under this act the number of free public schools has increased to such an extent as to fairly meet the needs of the Indians. I heard no complaint on account of their district schools. Their teachers are selected by their own school committees, and as a rule are of their own race. Practically all their teachers have attended their normal school.

Mr. J. R. Pool, the county superintendent of school for Robeson County, furnished me with the school statistics of the Indians for the school years 1912-13 and 1913-14. I glean the following facts from his statement:

Scholastic year 1912-13.

Census (6 to 21 years of age)....	2,643
Enrollment (6 to 21).....	1,662
Average daily attendance.....	970
Number of schools.....	27
Number of teachers (male 21, female 11).....	32
Number of districts.....	27
Value of school buildings.....	$7,900
Average length of term....days..	85.7
Average, special-tax districts.....days..	111.43

[Page 26][Scholastic year 1912-13.—Continued]

Expended for repairs.....	$500
Teachers' salaries.....	$5,475.25

Scholastic year 1913-14.

Census (6 to 21 years of age)....	2,948
Enrollment (6 to 21).....	1,854
Average daily attendance.....	1,164
Number of schools.....	27
Number of teachers.....	36
For repairs and new buildings.....	$1,160
Total value school buildings.....	$9,060
Average length of term (all schools).....days	102.66
Average in special tax exhibits.....days	104
Teachers' salaries.....	$6,410.25

(See Exhibit M.)

NORMAL SCHOOL.

The act of the General Assembly of North Carolina, ratified March 7, 1887, provided for a normal school for the Indians of Robeson County. Four Indian trustees were appointed and were given full power to select three additional trustees, to rent or acquire suitable buildings, to appoint teachers, and to do all necessary things to inaugurate a normal school. The sum of $500 was appropriated annually for two years for the support of the school. The school was at first located near Pates in a building formerly used for district school purposes, but after the destruction of this building by fire it was removed to the town of Pembroke, where a much larger building was erected, consisting of four rooms.

By the act of the general assembly of March 8, 1911, the board of trustees of the normal school was empowered to convey by deed the title to all the property of said school to the State board of education. Section 2 of the act authorized the State board of education to appoint seven members of the Indian race to constitute the board of trustees for the school. The appropriation for the school has been increased from time to time, the present appropriation being at the rate of $2,750 per annum. I have no statistics as to the enrollment and attendance at the school, but I understand that it has always been maintained to the exhaustion of the appropriation, and that it has contributed greatly to the educational advantages of these people in the preparation of teachers for their district schools.

LEGISLATION BY THE STATE OF NORTH CAROLINA.

Prior to the adoption of certain amendments to the constitution on the second Monday of November, 1835, the Croatan Indians voted and otherwise enjoyed all the rights and privileges of the elective franchise for State officials; but clause 3 of section 3 of the amendments adopted on said date provided that no free negro, free mulatto, or free person of mixed blood, descended from negro ancestors to the fourth generation, inclusive (though one ancestor of each generation may have been a white person) shall vote for members of the senate or house of commons. (See Exhibit L1.) Under this clause they were subsequently denied the right of franchise.

Section 7, chapter 68, of the acts of the general assembly of 1854, provides that all marriages since the 8th day of January, 1839, and all marriages in the future between a white person and a free negro, [Page 27] or free person of color, to the third generation, shall be void. It was held that the term "or free person of color" applied to the Croatans; but, notwithstanding this prohibition, I understand that occasional marriages between the Indians and white persons occurred. I was unable to ascertain whether or not any such marriages had been declared void. (See Exhibit L2.)

An amendment to the constitution of North Carolina in 1857 provides that every free white man of the age of 21 years, being a native or naturalized citizen of the United States, and who has been an inhabitant of the State for 12 months immediately preceding the day of any election, and shall have paid public taxes, shall be entitled to vote for a member of the senate for the district in which he resides. (See Exhibit L3.)

Section 1 of article 6 of the constitution of 1868 provides that every male person born in the United States, and every male person who has been naturalized, 21 years of age, and possessing the qualifications set out in said article, shall be entitled to vote at any election by the people in the State except as therein otherwise provided. After the adoption of the constitution of 1868 the right of franchise was restored to the Croatans.

The amendment of 1902 to section 4 of article 6 of the constitution of 1868 reads:

Every male person born in the United States, and every male person who has been naturalized, 21 years of age and possessing the qualifications set out in this article, shall be entitled to vote at any election by the people in the State except as herein otherwise provided.

SEC. 4. Every person presenting himself for registration shall be able to read and write any section of the constitution in the English language; and before he shall be entitled to vote he shall have paid, on or before the 1st day of May of the year in which he proposes to vote, his poll tax for the previous year as prescribed by article 5, section 1, of the constitution. But no male person who was on January 1, 1867, or at any time prior thereto, entitled to vote under the laws of any State in the United States wherein he then resided, and no lineal descendant of any such person, shall be denied the right to register and vote at any election in this State by reason of his failure to possess the educational qualifications herein prescribed: *Provided*, He shall have registered in accordance with the terms of this section prior to December 1, 1908. The general assembly shall provide for the registration of all persons entitled to vote without the educational qualifications herein prescribed, and shall, on or before November 1, 1908, provide for the making of a permanent record of such registration, and all persons so registered shall forever thereafter have the right to vote in all elections by the people in this State unless disqualified under section 2 of this article: *Provided*, Such person shall have paid his poll tax as above required.

(See Exhibit L4.)

This section is what is known as the "grandfather clause" of the constitution of North Carolina, which denies the right of franchise to those who are not able to read and write any section of the constitution in the English language; but this clause is held not to apply to the Indians of Robeson County for the reason that they, or their ancestors, prior to 1867, or at a time prior to said date, were entitled to vote under the laws of the State. The Indians, of course, must pay their poll tax and must comply with the registration provisions.

In the case of the State *v.* Manuel (20 N. C., 144) Justice Gaston held:
Upon the Revolution no other change took place in the laws of North Carolina than was consequent upon the transition from a colony dependent upon a European king to a free and sovereign State. Slaves remained slaves. British subjects in North Carolina became North Carolina freemen. Foreigners, until made members (citizens) of the State, continued aliens. Slaves manumitted here became freemen, and [Page 28] therefore if born within North Carolina are citizens of North Carolina; and all free persons born within the State are born citizens of the State.

(See Exhibit L5.)

Under this decision, which was subsequent to the constitution of 1835, which deprived free negroes and free mulattoes of the right to vote, "free persons of color" (the Croatan Indians) were not included, and it seems that they should not have been denied the right of suffrage.

Section 1 of chapter 51, laws of 1885, provides that the Indians of Robeson County and their descendants shall hereafter "be designated and known as the Croatan Indians." It should be noted that the act does not declare that they are Croatan Indians, but merely designates or names them Croatans, by which name they shall thereafter be known.

Section 2 of the act provides that said Indians and their descendants shall have separate schools for their children, school committees of their own race and color, and shall be allowed to select teachers of their own choice, subject to the same rules and regulations that are applicable under the general school law. The remaining sections of the act provide for putting the schools into operation under the general laws applicable to free schools within the State. (See Exhibit L5½.) Prior to this enactment the

Indians had no separate schools for the education of their children. Efforts had been made to compel them to attend the schools established for the negro population, but they steadfastly resisted such efforts and absolutely declined to attend the colored schools. The statistics respecting the number of schools, number of children of school age, attendance, etc., will be found under a separate heading.

Section 1, chapter 400 of the laws of 1887, provides that W. L. Moore, James Oxendine, James Dial, Preston Locklear, and others who may be associated with them shall constitute a body politic and corporate for educational purposes in the county of Robeson, under the name and style of the "Trustees of the Croatan Normal School"; that they shall have perpetual succession with the right to sue and be sued, etc. The other sections of the act provide for putting the said normal school into operation, and section 7 appropriates $500 annually for the period of two years for the support of the school. This appropriation has been increased from time to time, the present appropriation for the support of the school being $2,750. (See Exhibit L6.) The purpose of the normal school is to prepare persons as teachers for their public schools, and I understand that practically all the teachers in their district schools have attended the normal school.

Section 1, chapter 254 of the laws of 1887, amends section 1810 of the Code of North Carolina by adding thereto the words:
That all marriages between an Indian and a negro or between an Indian and a person of negro descent to the third generation, inclusive, shall be utterly void: *Provided,* That the act shall apply only to the Croatan Indians.

(See Exhibit L7.)

Section 1, chapter 458 of the laws of 1889, provides that the Croatan Indians of Richmond County and their descendants shall be entitled to the same school privileges and benefits as are the Croatan Indians of Robeson County. (See Exhibit L8.)

[Page 29]Section 1, chapter 60 of the laws of 1889, amends section 2 of the laws of 1885 by adding after the word "law," in the last line of said section, the words:
And there shall be excluded from such separate schools for the said Croatan Indians all children of the negro race to the fourth generation.

(See Exhibit L9.)

Section 1, chapter 536 of the laws of 1897, provides for the expenditure of an unexpended balance of $281.25, being the unexpended appropriation of 1895 for the support of the Croatan Normal School. (See Exhibit L10.)

Section 1, chapter 168 of the laws of 1911, authorizes the trustees of the Croatan Normal School to convey the property by deed to the State board of education, and authorizes said board to accept the same. Section 2 authorizes the State board of education to appoint seven members of the Indian race, formerly known as Croatans, to constitute a board of trustees for said school, and the remaining sections provide that such board of trustees and their successors shall manage and control the affairs of the Croatan Normal School. (See Exhibit L11.)

Section 1, chapter 215 of the laws of 1911, provides that chapter 51 of the public laws of North Carolina, session of 1885, be amended by striking out the words "Croatan Indians" wherever the same occur in said chapter and inserting in lieu thereof the words "Indians of Robeson County." Section 2 provides that in all laws enacted by the General Assembly of North Carolina relating to said Indians subsequent to the enactment of said chapter 51 of the laws of 1885 the words "Croatan Indians" shall be stricken out and the words "Indians of Robeson County" shall be inserted in lieu thereof. Section 3 provides that the said Indians residing in Robeson and adjoining counties, who have heretofore been known as Croatan Indians, together with their descendents, shall hereafter be known and designated as "Indians of Robeson County," and by that name shall be entitled to all the rights and privileges conferred by any of the laws of North Carolina upon the Indians heretofore known as Croatan Indians. Section 4 provides that the school situated near the town of Pembroke, in Robeson County, known as the Croatan Indian Normal School, shall hereafter be known and designated as "The Indian Normal School of Robeson County," and under that name shall be entitled to all the privileges and powers heretofore conferred by law upon said school.

Section 5 of the act takes up a new line of legislation and provides that the board of directors of the State hospital for the insane at Raleigh be authorized and directed to provide and set apart at said hospital, as soon after the passage of the act as practicable, suitable apartments and wards for the accommodation of any of said Indians of Robeson County who may be entitled under the laws relating to insane persons to be admitted to said hospital.

Section 6 authorizes and directs the sheriff, jailor, or other proper authorities of Robeson County to provide in the common jail of the county and in the Home for the Aged and Infirm of Robeson County separate cells, wards, or apartments for the said Indians in all cases where it shall be necessary under the laws of the State to commit any of said Indians to the jail or to the County Home for the Aged and Infirm. (See Exhibit L12.)

[Page 30]Section 1, chapter 123, of the laws of 1913, provides that chapter 215 of the public laws of North Carolina, session of 1911, be amended by striking out in the last line of section 1 of said act the words "Indians of Robeson County," and inserting in lieu thereof the words "Cherokee Indians of Robeson County"; that is to say, the designation of said Indians was changed from "Indians of Robeson County" to "Cherokee Indians of Robeson County." The other sections of the act make provision for the corresponding change in the designation of said Indians wherever the designation "Indians of Robeson County" occurs in the laws of the State. (See Exhibit L13.)

Section 1, chapter 199, of the laws of 1913, enacted March 12, 1913, provides for an appropriation of $500 in addition to the $2,500 already appropriated for the support of the normal school for said Indians, for the years 1913 and 1914. (See Exhibit L14.)

THEIR NEEDS.

As already indicated, a considerable number of these Indians, probably rather less than one-eighth, are prosperous farmers; another group, amounting approximately to one-eighth, are fairly well-to-do; about one-half of them would be classed as poor people, and about one-quarter of them as very poor, but entirely self-supporting. This classification relates to the families, considered as a unit. The families, as a rule, are very large, and the children under 18 years of age greatly outnumber the adults. Any financial assistance extended to the poorer classes, in the way of furnishing them with lands and with means to properly cultivate their lands, would be of great benefit to them and would undoubtedly be gratefully received.

In a personal canvas of a very large number of the heads of families I found that they differed widely as to what would be the best method of extending assistance to individual families, but there was entire unanimity of opinion as to the way in which the entire body of people could best be helped, namely, in providing them with some higher institution of learning where the more ambitious of their young people could obtain a better education than is now possible and better training for useful occupations in life.

Their district schools I am told will compare favorably with the district schools of the colored people and the whites residing in the same vicinities, and their normal school, if better equipped and better supported, would furnish them teachers for their district schools, but there are no higher institutions of learning in North Carolina, to which they have access, where they can send their youth who desire to obtain a more liberal education; the State institutions for the education of the white and colored youth are not open to the Indians of Robeson and adjoining counties. In consequence, their young people who desire to obtain a better education than that furnished through the medium of the normal school are unable at present to do so. It is true that these young people could attend the Carlisle Indian School, and other nonreservation Indian schools, but most of them are too poor to do so, and besides these nonreservation Indian schools do not furnish precisely the character of training they desire.

In addition to the common or district schools and the normal schools for both white and colored children, the State of North [Page 31] Carolina has provided the youth of both these races with institutions of learning imparting instruction in agriculture and the mechanic trades, and to some extent in domestic science; but there are no such schools of higher instruction open to these Indians. As I understand the matter, they are prohibited by law from attending these higher institutions of learning established for the education of white and colored youth. It is conjectured that the very limited number of these Indians, compared with the white and colored population, accounts for this discrimination.

I might say here that in my judgment, the children of these Indians, as a rule, are exceedingly bright, quick to learn from books, as well as from example, and are very eager to obtain further educational advantages than are now open to them. If the reverse were true, there would be little encouragement to furnish them with higher institutions of learning when they were incapable of taking advantage of their present educational facilities or indifferent about obtaining a higher education; but I believe the more ambitious of their youth to be eager to attend higher institutions of learning than those now provided.

While these Indians are essentially an agricultural people, I believe them to be as capable of learning the mechanical trades as the average white youth. The foregoing facts suggest the character of the educational institution that should be established for them, in case Congress sees fit to make the necessary appropriation, namely, the establishment of an agricultural and mechanical school, in which domestic science shall also be taught.

The preparation of this report has been somewhat delayed since my return from North Carolina because of the great amount of historical research called for by the investigation.

The correspondence in connection with the investigation is filed as Exhibit M.

Very respectfully submitted.

O. M. MCPHERSON,
Special Indian Agent

[Page 32] EXHIBIT A.

Exhibit A1.

SENATE RESOLUTION 410, SIXTY-THIRD CONGRESS, SECOND

SESSION.

Resolved, That the Secretary of the Interior be, and he hereby is, directed to cause an investigation to be made of the condition and tribal rights of the Indians of Robeson and adjoining counties of North Carolina, recently declared by the Legislature of North Carolina to be Cherokees, and formerly known as Croatans, and report to Congress what tribal rights, if any, they have with any band or tribe; whether they are entitled to or have received any lands, or whether there are any moneys due them, their present condition, their educational facilities, and such other facts as would enable Congress to determine whether the Government would be warranted in making suitable provision for their support and education.

Exhibit A2.

OFFICE INSTRUCTIONS JULY 23, 1914.

DEPARTMENT OF THE INTERIOR,

OFFICE OF INDIAN AFFAIRS,

Washington, *July 23, 1914.*

Mr. O. M. MCPHERSON, *Special Agent.*
MY DEAR MR. MCPHERSON: Upon the receipt of these instructions, or as soon thereafter as practicable, you will proceed to North Carolina for the purpose of investigating the affairs of the Croatan Indians of Robeson and adjoining counties of that State, as provided for by Senate resolution 410.

This resolution reads:

Resolved, That the Secretary of the Interior be, and he hereby is, directed to cause an investigation to be made of the condition and tribal rights of the Indians of Robeson and adjoining counties of North Carolina, recently declared by the Legislature of North Carolina to be Cherokees, and formerly kown as Croatans, and report to Congress what tribal rights, if any, they have with any band or tribe; whether they are entitled to or have received any lands, or whether there are any moneys due them, their present condition, their educational facilities, and such other facts as would enable Congress to determine whether the Government would be warranted in making suitable provision for their support and education.

Extreme care should be exercised by you in obtaining all pertinent facts relative to the condition and tribal rights of these Indians in order that this office may be prepared to submit to the next Congress, through the department, full information responsive to said resolution.

Very truly, yours,

CATO SELLS, *Commissioner.*

[Page 33] *Exhibit A3.*

ELEVENTH CENSUS UNITED STATES, 1890.

NORTH CAROLINA.

Indian population as of June 1, 1890.

Total.....	1, 516

Indians in prison, not otherwise enumerated.....	2
Indians, self-supporting and taxed (counted in the general census).....	1, 514

The civilized (self-supporting) Indians of North Carolina, counted in the general census, number 1, 514 (741 males and 773 females), and are distributed as follows:

Cherokee County, 47; Cumberland County, 28; Graham County, 151; Harnett County, 27; Jackson County, 314; Moore County, 15; Robeson County, 174; Swain County, 700; other counties (7 or less in each), 58.

The Indians of North Carolina are mostly descendants of the Cherokees, many of whom have so little Indian blood as in no way to attract the attention of a stranger. A considerable property interest attaches to membership in the Cherokee tribe, and it is claimed by some parties that there are more entitled to enumeration as Indians than were so designated by the census enumerators.

It is in no way surprising that enumerators should return so few Indians, as many of them are not distinguishable from whites except on special investigation as to their racial relations. On the other hand, the claims of some who wish to be enrolled as Cherokees would be disputed. There is a marked tendency among the eastern Cherokees to emigrate to the Indian Territory, and the number in North Carolina appears to be gradually diminishing from this cause.

By the laws of North Carolina the Indians vote and they are subject to a property tax, but they are not allowed within the third generation to marry whites.

The Indians of North Carolina were enumerated with the general population and were entered as 1, 514, of whom 174 are in Robeson County and are known as Croatans. Claims are made that both Croatans and Cherokees far exceed the numbers given by census enumerators for Indians in the counties in which these people live. The State of North Carolina recognizes a greater number as Croatans than are returned as Indians in Robeson County.

THE CROATANS.

A body of people residing chiefly in Robeson County, N. C., known as the Croatan Indians, are generally white, showing the Indian mostly in actions and habits. They were enumerated by the regular census enumerator in part as whites. They are clannish and hold with considerable pride to the traditions that they are the descendants of the Croatans of the Raleigh period of North Carolina and Virginia.

Mr. Hamilton McMillan, of Fayetteville, N. C., in 1888, published a pamphlet of 27 pages, the title page of which is as follows: "Sir Walter Raleigh's Lost Colony * * * with the traditions of an [Page 34] Indian tribe in North Carolina," Wilson, N. C. This pamphlet is to show that Raleigh's colony was carried off by the Indians, and that the Croatan Indians of North Carolina are their descendants. Mr. McMillan also, in answering an inquiry in reference to the Croatans, wrote the following to the Commissioner of Indan Affairs:

RED SPRINGS, N. C., *July 17, 1890.*

* * * The Croatan tribe lives principally in Robeson County, N. C., though there is quite a number of them settled in counties adjoining in North and South Carolina. In Sumter County, S. C., there is a branch of the tribe, and also in east Tennessee. In Macon County, N. C., there is another branch, settled there long ago. Those living in east Tennessee are called "Melungeans," a name also retained by them here, which is a corruption of "Melange," a name given them by early settlers (French), which means mixed. * * * In regard to their exodus from Roanoke Island their traditions are confirmed by maps recently discovered in Europe by Prof. Alexander Brown, member of the Royal Historical Society of England. These maps are dated in 1608 and 1610, and give the reports of the Croatans to Raleigh's ships which visited our coast in those years. * * * The particulars of the exodus preserved by tradition here are strangely and strongly corroborated by these maps. There can be little doubt of the fact that the Croatans in Robeson County and elsewhere are the descendants of the Croatans of Raleigh's day.

In 1885 I got the North Carolina Legislature to recognize them as Croatans and give them separate public schools. In 1887 I got $500 a year from the State for a normal school for them for 2 years. In 1889 the appropriation was extended three years longer.

Their normal school needs help; at least $500 more is needed. The appropriation for the public schools amounts to less than $1 a head per annum.

February 10, 1885, the general assembly of North Carolina provided by law for separate schools for the Croatan Indians of North Carolina. This act contained the following:

Whereas the Indians now living in Robeson County claim to be descendants of a friendly tribe who once resided in eastern North Carolina, on the Roanoke River, known as the Croatan Indians, therefore, the general assembly of North Carolina do enact:

SECTION 1. That the said Indians and their descendants shall hereafter be designated and known as the Croatan Indians.

The provisions for separate schools follow.

March 7, 1887, the general assembly of North Carolina established the Croatan normal school in Robeson County for the Croatan Indians, and February 2, 1889, the same body enacted that all children of the negro race to the fourth generation should be excluded from the Croatan separate Indian schools. The Croatan normal school is at Pates.

The census enumerators recognized 174 persons in Robeson County as Indians. The State school report for the year ending June 30, 1890, shows 649 boys and 593 girls between 6 and 21 years of age among the Croatans of Robeson County, of whom 188 boys and 422 girls attended school. The disbursements for the Croatan schools by the county treasurer were $765.75 to pay teachers and $284.87 for schoolhouses and sites.

J. W. Powell, under date of January 11, 1889, wrote of the Croatans:

Croatan was in 1585 and thereabouts the name of an island and Indian village just north of Cape Hatteras, N. C. White's colony of 120 men and women was landed on Roanoke Island, just to the north, in 1587, and in 1590, when White returned to revisit the colony, he found no trace of it on Roanoke Island, save the name "Croatoan" carved upon a tree, which, according to a previous understanding, was interpreted to mean that the colonists had left Roanoke Island for Croatan. No actual trace of the missing [Page 35] colonists was ever found, but more than 100 years afterward Lawson obtained traditional information from the Hatteras Indians which led him to believe that the colonists had been incorporated with the Indians. It was thought that traces of white blood could be discovered among the Indians, some among them having gray eyes. It is probable that the greater number of the colonists were killed; but it was quite in keeping with the Indian usages that a greater or less number, especially women and children, should have been made captive and subsequently incorporated into the tribe. The best authority to be consulted with regard to the above colony is Hawks' History of North Carolina, Fayetteville, N. C., 1859, volume I, pages 211, 225, 258.

The region inhabited by the Croatans is a low woodland, swampy region, locally known as pocoson land, abounding in whortleberries and blackberries, which bring some revenue to the people. The existence of a peculiar people, claiming Indian ancestry and nominally distinct from negroes and whites, has not prevented such admixture as to confuse every inquirer who has undertaken to solve their relations and the numbers of those rightfully claiming any defined racial distinctions, but it has made certain districts a refuge for men of all races who preferred the half wild life of the woods to regular labor, or who preferred the bullet to the slow forms of law to settle difficulties. In past years some of the most noted disturbances in the State seem due to a desperado whose racial connections are not clearly known, who married among the Croatans, and who was finally brought to justice only when the governor called out the militia. No such disturbance has occurred in recent years.

[Page 36] **EXHIBIT B.**

Exhibit B1.

PETITION OF CROATAN INDIANS.

STATE OF NORTH CAROLINA,

County of Robeson.

To the honorable the Congress of the United States:
The undersigned, your petitioners, a part of the Croatan Indians, living in the county and State aforesaid, their residence for a hundred years or more, respectfully petition your honorable body for such aid as you may see fit to extend to them, the amount to be appropriated to be used for the sole and exclusive purpose of assisting your petitioners and other Croatans in said county and State to educate their children and fit them for the duties of American citizenship.

Your petitioners would show that there are in said county, of legal school age, of the Croatan race, eleven hundred and sixty-five (1, 165 in December, 1887) children. That the Croatans in said county and State are industrious citizens, engaged for the most part in agricultural pursuits, and are unable to give to their children the benefits of proper educational training, and would, as aforesaid, most respectfully petition your honorable body to assist them.

Your petitioners are a remnant of White's lost colony and during the long years that have passed since the disappearance of said colony have been struggling unaided and alone to fit themselves and their children for the exalted privileges and duties of American freemen, and now for the first time ask your honorable body to come to their assistance.

And your petitioners as in duty bound, etc.

James Oxendine, Ashbury Oxendine, Zackriors Oxendine, J. J. Oxendine, Billey Locklear, Malakiah Locklear, Preston Locklear, John Ballard, Crolly Locklear, G. W. Locklear, Patrick Locklear, Luther Deas, Marcus Dial, Joseph Locklear, Alex Locklear, Frank Locklear, W. W. Locklear, J. E. Lovit, Beni Locklear, John Locklear, Joseph Locklear, jr., Soleomon Oxendine, A. J. Lowrie, John A. Locklear, Soleomon Locklear, Anguish A. Locklear, Silas Deas, Olline Oxendine, Isad Braboy, James Lowrie, John A. Lockler, Marcus Dial, Josep Lockler, Eliach Lockler, Frank Locklar, W. W. Lockler, J. E. Lovet, Buey Lockler, John Lockler, Jorge Brayboy, Pink Lockler, John E. Oxendine, William Sampson, Steven Carter, Evert Sampson, Wues Sampson, John Sampson, Rober Carter, Quin Gordan, Jordan Oxendine, James R. Sanderson, Peater Dyall, Willey Jacobs, Murdock Chavons.

[Page 37]Your petitioners above named respectfully ask that if your honorable body admits an educational aid that it be so appropriated for the trustees of the normal school in said county to use so much thereof as may be necessary to complete the normal-school building, and that the residue be applied for the purpose of training teachers among the Croatan race who may attend said school.

Exhibit B2.

OFFICE LETTER TO HON. J. W. POWELL, JANUARY 7, 1889.

DEPARTMENT OF THE INTERIOR,

OFFICE OF INDIAN AFFAIRS,

Washington, January 7, 1889.

DEAR SIR: I have the honor to inclose herewith copy of a communication signed with 54 names of persons who claim to be "Croatan Indians" and descendants of "White's lost colony," in Robeson County, N. C.

There is no record in this office of any such Indians or any such a colony, and I can find no reference to them in any history at my command.

Can you kindly furnish me with any information on the subject and much oblige,

Yours, respectfully,

JNO. H. OBERLY, *Commissioner.*

Exhibit B3.

LETTER OF J. W. POWELL TO INDIAN OFFICE, JANUARY 11, 1889.

SMITHSONIAN INSTITUTION,

BUREAU OF ETHNOLOGY,

Washington, D. C., January 11, 1889.

SIR: In reply to your letter of the 7th instant with inclosure requesting information in regard to the Croatan Indians, I beg leave to say that Croatan was in 1585 and thereabouts the name of an island and Indian village just north of Cape Hatteras, N. C. White's colony of 120 men and women was landed on Roanoke Island just to the north in 1587, and in 1590, when White returned to revisit the colony, he found no trace of it on Roanoke Island save the name "Croatoan," carved upon a tree, which, according to a previous understanding, was interpreted to mean that the colonists had left Roanoke Island for Croatan. No actual trace of the missing colonists was ever found, but more than 100 years afterwards Lawson obtained traditional information from the Hatteras Indians which led him to believe that the colonists had been incorporated with the Indians. It was thought that traces of white blood could be discovered among the Indians, some among them having gray eyes. It is probable [Page 38] that the greater number of the colonists were killed; but it was quite in keeping with Indian usages that a greater or less number, especially women and children, should have been made captive and subsequently incorporated into the tribe. The best authority to be consulted with regard to the above colony is Hawks' History of North Carolina, Fayetteville, N. C., 1859, Volume I, pages 211, 225, 228. The book may be obtained from the Congressional Library. Bancroft (History of U. S., Vol. I, p. 77, treated at great length in his early edition) and other authors mention the main facts, but their accounts rest upon Hawks'. It is understood that Mr. Hamilton McMillan, of Fayetteville, N. C., will soon publish a book attempting to show that Raleigh's colony was carried off by the Indians and that their descendants are now living in Robeson County, N. C.

I am, yours, with respect,

J. W. POWELL, *Director.*

Exhibit B4.

OFFICE LETTER TO HAMILTON MCMILLAN, JANUARY 29, 1889.

DEPARTMENT OF THE INTERIOR,

OFFICE OF INDIAN AFFAIRS,

Washington, January 29, 1889.

SIR: I have received a petition from parties in Robeson County, N. C., in which the claim is made that they are "Croatan" Indians, descendants of "White's lost colony," and asking Government aid for the education of their children, numbering about 1, 100.

I am informed that you are familiar with the history of these people, and if so, I will thank you for any information you will furnish me. Are they citizens of the United States, and are they entitled to the educational advantages furnished by the State of North Carolina?

Please answer at your earliest convenience and oblige,

Yours, respectfully,

JNO. H. OBERLY, *Commissioner.*

Exhibit B5.

LETTER OF W. L. MOORE TO INDIAN OFFICE JULY 2, 1890.

OSBORNE, N. C., July 2, 1890.

Mr. T. W. BELT, *Washington, D. C.*

DEAR SIR: Answering your letter of 7th ultimo will say that the people in whose behalf we wrote are not the Eastern Cherokees, but the Croatan Indians. Therefore they receive nothing appropriated for the Cherokees. The people for which I am officially interested have as a general thing grown up without so much as the rudiments of education, yet the youth who have had (to some degree) better opportunities for educating themselves show that the moral, intellectual, and social aptitudes in them are real. Can not something be [Page 39] obtained to assist them in a normal school for them? If so, please direct me how to proceed.

There are 1, 100 children between the ages of 6 and 21 years who need continual instruction.

Please reply at the earliest convenience.

Very respectfully,

W. L. MOORE.

Exhibit B6.

OFFICE LETTER TO HAMILTON MCMILLAN, JULY 14, 1890.

DEPARTMENT OF THE INTERIOR,

OFFICE OF INDIAN AFFAIRS,

Washington, July 14, 1890.

HAMILTON MCMILLAN, *Fayetteville, N. C.*

SIR: On the 29th of January, 1889, a report from the Bureau of Ethnology in regard to the Croatan Indians was mailed to you with the request that information be forwarded to this office in regard to these people. Inclosed find copy of the letter. No communication has been received from you in response to the office letter mentioned. The subject is again brought to the attention of the Indian Office by Mr. W. L. Moore, of Osborne, N. C., in a letter dated July 2, copy of which is also inclosed herewith.

I trust that you will promptly respond to this communication and return the document mailed to you January 29 with such information as you can give.

Very respectfully,

T. J. MORGAN, *Commissioner.*

Exhibit B7.

LETTER OF HAMILTON MCMILLAN TO INDIAN OFFICE, JULY 17, 1890.

RED SPRINGS, N. C., July 17, 1890.

MY DEAR SIR: Your letter of July 14 ultimo just to hand. The communication and report from the Bureau of Ethnology to which you refer were never received, and your letter just received conveys the first intimation of their having been sent. Had they been received I would have responded with pleasure.

I inclose to you to-day a copy of a pamphlet containing much of interest in this connection. The pamphlet was written very hastily nearly two years ago in order to give the North Carolina Legislature some information, as the Croatans were asking some legislation in their behalf.

The Croatan Tribe lives principally in Robeson County, N. C., though there are quite a number of them settled in counties adjoining in North and South Carolina. In Sumter County, S. C., there is a branch of the tribe and also in East Tennessee. In Lincoln County, N. C., there is another branch, settled there long ago. Those living in East Tennessee are called "Melungeans," a name also retained [Page 40] by them here, which is a corruption of *Melange,* a name given them by early settlers (French), which means *mixed*. The pamphlet sent you will outline their history as far as it can be discovered from their traditions. In regard to their *exodus from Roanoke Island* their traditions are confirmed by maps recently discovered in Europe by Prof. Alexander Brown, member of the Royal Historical Society of England. These maps are dated in 1608 and 1610, and give the reports of the Croatans to Raleigh's ships, which visited our coast in those years. These maps will be lithographed and published in a book, now being prepared by Prof. Brown. The particulars of the exodus preserved by tradition here are strangely and strongly corroborated by these maps. There can be little doubt of the fact that the Croatans in Robeson County and elsewhere are the descendants of the Croatans of Raleigh's day. In 1885 I got the North Carolina Legislature to recognize them as Croatans and give them separate public schools. In 1887 I got $500 a year from the State for a normal school for them for two years. In 1889 the appropriation was extended two years longer.

Their normal school needs help—at least $500 more is needed. The appropriation to the public schools amounts to less than a dollar a head per annum.

If you can aid them in the way desired we would be glad. They are citizens of the United States and entitled to the educational privileges enjoyed by other citizens, but those advanatges are not much.

Respectfully,

HAMILTON MCMILLAN.

Exhibit B8.

OFFICE LETTER TO W. L. MOORE, AUGUST 11, 1890.

DEPARTMENT OF THE INTERIOR,

OFFICE OF INDIAN AFFAIRS,

Washington, August 11, 1890.

W. L. MOORE, *Osborne, N. C.*
SIR: Referring to your letter of July 2 and office response thereto of the 16th, I have received a communication from Hamilton McMillan, of Red

Springs, N. C., setting forth the situation of the Croatan Indians very fully. It appears from his statement that this band is recognized by the State of North Carolina, has been admitted to citizenship, and the State has undertaken the work of their education.

While I regret exceedingly that the provisions made by the State of North Carolina seem to be entirely inadequate, I find it quite impracticable to render any assistance at this time. The Government is responsible for the education of something like 36, 000 Indian children and has provisions for less than half this number. So long as the immediate wards of the Government are so insufficiently provided for, I do not see how I can consistently render any assistance to the Croatans or any other civilized tribes.

I am obliged to you for calling my attention to the matter, and have been very much interested in the information furnished by Mr. McMillan regarding this very interesting tribe.

Very respectfully,

T. J. MORGAN, *Commissioner.*

[Page 41] EXHIBIT C.

SIR WALTER RALEIGH'S LOST COLONY.

[By Hamilton McMillan.]

AN HISTORICAL SKETCH OF THE ATTEMPTS OF SIR WALTER RALEIGH TO ESTABLISH A COLONY IN VIRGINIA, WITH THE TRADITIONS OF AN INDIAN TRIBE IN NORTH CAROLINA, INDICATING THE FATE OF THE COLONY OF ENGLISHMEN LEFT ON ROANOKE ISLAND IN 1587.

CHAPTER I.

In 1583, "Elizabeth, by the Grace of God, of England, France, and Ireland, Queen, defender of the faith," granted to Sir Walter Raleigh, his heirs and assigns forever, letters patent "to discover, search, find, and view such remote heathen and barbarous lands, countries, and territories, not actually possessed of any Christian Prince, nor inhabited by Christian people, as to him, his heirs and assigns, to every or any of them shall seem good, and the same to have, hold, and occupy and enjoy, to him, his heirs, and assigns forever."

It was provided further that a settlement should be made in the territory granted within six years next succeeding the date of the letters patent.

This grant was made during one of the most critical periods of British history. The Protestant Elizabeth had espoused the cause of the Netherlands and had given high offense to Spain by rejecting the proposed matrimonial alliance with Philip, the reigning monarch of that country. The

Armada, consisting of 140 ships of war and carrying fully 30, 000 men, threatened an early attack upon England. Powerful allies stood ready to assist King Philip. The length of time necessary to complete this powerful armament had afforded to Elizabeth opportunity to prepare for the impending danger. Sir Walter Raleigh then enjoyed high favor at court. The Queen early discovered his soldierly qualities and intellectual ability, and in addition to high rank which she bestowed upon him, readily granted him and his heirs extensive territory in North America. Raleigh was one of the most skillful generals of his times, and while actively engaged in the preparation for the threatened invasion of England, found opportunity to fit out an expedition to the coast of America to make discoveries and to locate a colony in compliance with the terms of his grant. The commanders of the expedition were Philip Amadas and Arthur Barlowe, who sailed with two barks from the coast of England on the 15th day of April, 1584, O. S., and reached the coast of America in July of the same year. They sailed along the coast for 120 miles before they found any entrance or river issuing into the sea. These navigators probably entered at Hatteras Inlet, on the coast of what is now North Carolina, and having anchored "within the [Page 42] haven's mouth on the left hand of the same," they went in boats "to view the land adjoining and to take possession of the same in right of the Queen's most excellent majesty as rightful Queen and Princess of the same." The land thus taken into possession was Roanoke Island, about 7 leagues distant from the anchorage.

After a stay of nearly two months, the expedition returned to England, carrying two of the natives, Manteo and Wanchese. The disposition of the natives toward the Englishmen was friendly, and though no reason is given for carrying the two Indians to England, it was probably understood that a second expedition would soon follow, and that they could return to their own country at an early day. There was good policy in impressing them, as prominent men of their own land, with the greatness of England. Manteo and Wanchese returned in another expedition to Roanoke, the former to become Lord of Roanoke, the latter to become the determined enemy of the English.

A second expedition, under Sir Richard Greenville, the cousin of Sir Walter Raleigh, sailed from England on the 9th of April, 1585. This expedition consisted of seven vessels, and arrived at Roanoke during the following July. In August following Sir Richard Greenville returned to England, after leaving a colony on Roanoke Island under Master Ralf Lane.

Lane explored the surrounding country, making many valuable discoveries, and finally, despairing of aid expected, embarked, with his entire colony, on the fleet of Sir Francis Drake, which stopped at Roanoke, and sailed for England.

The departure of Lane's colony left no Englishmen on the shores of North America.

CHAPTER II.

In less than one month from the departure of Lane Sir Richard Greenville arrived at Roanoke with supplies, and after a fruitless search for the colonists, he left 15 men on the island to hold possession of the country. After the departure of Greenville these men were seen no more by Englishmen.

Not discouraged by repeated failures, Sir Walter Raleigh fitted out another expedition under John White as governor, who, with others of the colonists, were incorporated as "The Governor and Assistants of the City of Raleigh in Virginia." The city of Raleigh was designed to be built on the shores of Chesapeake Bay.

Gov. White was instructed to call at Roanoke Island to ascertain the fate of the 15 men left there by Sir Richard Greenville. The commanders of the ships seemed to have been independent of the authority of Gov. White, and fully aware that a voyage to Chesapeake Bay would delay their expected cruise in the West Indies, refused to transport the colony to its destination, and thus compelled Gov. White to stop at Roanoke Island. The vessels departed soon after in search of Spanish prizes.

After reciting many incidents, Gov. White relates that "on the 13th of August, our savage Manteo, by the commandment of Sir Walter Raleigh, was christened in Roanoke and called Lord thereof, and of Dasamonguepeuk, in reward of his faithful service." "The 18th, Eleanor, daughter of Gov. White and wife to Ananias Dare, one of the colonists, was delivered of a daughter in Roanoke, and the [Page 43] same was christened there the Sunday following, and because this child was the first Christian born in Virginia, she was named Virginia."

Gov. White relates that a violent tempest arose on the 21st of August, which lasted for six days and threatened the destruction of one of the vessels then ready to sail for England. Gov. White was sent back to England by the planters, to act there as factor for the colony.

The Croatan Indians, who visited Roanoke Island, invited the colonists to reside with them, and the latter, prior to the departure of the governor, expressed to him their intention to accept the invitation and to remove 50 miles "up into the main." It was understood that if they went to Croatoan they were to carve the word *Croatoan* on the bark of a tree in some conspicuous place, that the governor might know where to find them on his return. It was further understood that if they left the island in distress they were to carve the Christian cross above the word Croatoan.

On the 27th of August, White sailed for England, and the colonists were seen no more by white men.

CHAPTER III.

On his arrival in England, Gov. White found all things in commotion. The long-threatened storm of war had burst upon England, and the services of Sir Walter Raleigh and others who were interested in the distant colony were enlisted in the national defense. It was a critical period of British history. Queen Elizabeth relied upon the skill of Raleigh, under whose guidance the Armada was defeated, and "liberty of person and liberty of conscience were once more free."

On the 22d of April, 1588, Gov. White, by aid of Sir Walter Raleigh, sailed from England with two barques to visit the colony at Roanoke. These vessels, disabled in fighting ships encountered during the voyage, were compelled to return to England. No further attempt to reach the colony was made till the 20th of March, 1590, when White again sailed for Virginia with three vessels. Nearly six months passed before the vessels reached Roanoke in the following August:

In his account of this voyage, as published by Hakluyt, Gov. White says that—

on the 15th of August, towards evening, we came to anchor at Hattorask in $36\frac{1}{3}°$, in five fathoms water three leagues from the shore. At our first coming to anchor on this shore we saw a great smoke rise in the Isle Roanoke, near the place where I left our colony in the year 1587, which smoke put us in good hope that some of the colony were there expecting our return out of England. The 16th and next morning our two boats went ashore, and Captain Cooke and Captain Spicer and their company with me, with intent to pass to the place at Roanoke where our countrymen were left. At our putting from the ship we commanded our master gunner to make ready two minions and a falcon, well loaded, and to shoot them off with reasonable space between every shot, to the end that their reports might be heard to the place where we hoped to find some of our people.

Omitting some unimportant details, we extract from White's narrative the following:

Our boats and all things filled again, we put off from Hattorask, being the number of nineteen persons in both boats; but before we could get to the place where our planters were left it was so exceeding dark that we overshot the place a quarter of a mile, when we espied towards the north end of the island (Roanoke) the light of a [Page 44] great fire through the woods, to which we presently rowed. When we came right over against it, we let fall our grapnel near the shore and sounded with a trumpet a call, and afterwards many familiar tunes and songs and called to them friendly; but we had no answer; we therefore landed at daybreak, and coming to the fire we found the grass and sundry rotten trees burning about the place. From hence we went through the woods to that part of the island directly over against Dasamonguepeuk, and from thence we returned by the waterside round about the north point of the island until we came to the place where I left our colony in the year 1587. In all this way we saw in the sand the print of the savage's feet of two or three sorts trodden in the night, and as we entered up the sandy bank, upon a tree in the very brow thereof, were curiously carved these fair Roman letters, C. R. O., which letters presently we knew to signify the place where I should find the planters seated, *according to a secret token agreed upon between them and me at my last departure from them,* which was that in any way they should not fail to write or carve, on the trees or posts of the doors, the name of the place where they should be seated; for at my coming away they were prepared to remove from Roanoke fifty miles into the main. Therefore at my departure from them in Aug., 1587, I willed them that if they should happen to be distressed in any of those places that they should carve over the letters or name a cross † in this form, but we found no such sign of distress. And having well considered of this we passed through the place where they were left in sundry houses, but we found the houses taken down and the place very strongly enclosed with a high palisade of great trees with curtains and flankers, very fortlike, and one of the chief trees or posts at the right side of the entrance had the bark taken off, and five feet from the ground, in fair capital letters, was graven "Croatoan," *without any cross or sign of distress.* This done, we entered into the palisado, where we found many bars of iron, two pigs of lead, four iron fowlers, iron locker, shot, and such like heavy things thrown here and there almost overgrown with grass and weeds. * * * But although it grieved me much to see such spoil of my goods, yet on the other side I greatly joyed that I had safely found a certain token of their being *at Croatoan*, which is the place where Manteo was born, *and the savages of the island our friends.*

Foul weather compelled Gov. White to return to the fleet, and on the following day with a favorable wind they prepared *to sail* to Croatan, but owing to the loss of all their anchors save one and the approaching foul weather it was determined to sail to St. John or some other island southward for fresh water, and after obtaining victuals and necessaries in the West Indies and spending the winter there to return in the spring to seek the colonists at Croatan. One of the vessels being in a leaky condition was compelled to sail for England. The other vessels after cruising for a while in search of Spanish prizes finally sailed for England and arrived at Plymouth on the 24th day of October, 1590.

From the story of Gov. White it is evident that Croatoan was sitated southward from Roanoke Island and upon the coast, for the voyagers attempted to sail to it upon the open sea. It is probable that the *island* mentioned was one of the long islands curtaining the coast and embraced within the present county of Carteret. It is so located on one of the oldest maps, bearing date of 1666. On a map published by order of the Lords Proprietors in 1671 the peninsula embracing the present county of Dare is called Croatan. Lawson's map of the year 1709 also locates Croatan in the same region. The sound immediately west of Roanoke Island still bears the name of Croatan. The name of the island belonging to the tribe was probably Croatoan, while the name of the tribe inhabiting it may have been Croatan. The name Croatan was given to the tribe by the English from the name of a locality within their territory. That part of their territory lying west of Roanoke Island was called Dasamonguepeuk by some of the natives. Manteo, by order of Sir Walter Raleigh, was made "Lord of Roanoke and Dasamonguepeuk," the first instance of a title of nobility being conferred on an American. [Page 45] There can be little doubt that the territory now embraced within the counties of Hyde, Tyrrell, and Dare was claimed and occupied by the friendly tribe of Manteo at one time, and was designated as Croatan, and at another time occupied by a different tribe of hostile Indians, who called it Dasamonquepeuk. Croatoan, the principal seat of Manteo and his tribe, lay to the southward. The name carved upon the tree according to a secret understanding between Gov. White and the planters prior to the departure of the former, was Croatoan, and was understood by him to mean an island southward from Roanoke, "for there," he relates, "Manteo was born and the savages *of the island* our friends."

For nearly 300 years after the departure of White no trace of the lost colony had been discovered, with the exception of the following related by Lawson, an early historian, who wrote in 1714: "The Hatteras Indians who lived on Roanoke Island, *or much frequented it,* tell us that several of their ancestors were white people and could talk in a book, as we do; the truth of which is confirmed by gray eyes being frequently found amongst these Indians, and no others. They value themselves extremely for their affinity to the English, and are ready to do them all friendly offices."

Purchas tells us that several subsequent voyages were made at the expense of Sir Walter Raleigh, to discover his lost countrymen, but without success. Commanders of ships in those days were more anxious to capture Spanish vessels than to find lost Englishmen, and it is doubtful if a single ship touched at Croatan or Roanoke to make inquiries after the departure of White in 1590.

CHAPTER IV.

Who were the Croatans? The term Croatan or Croatoan was applied by the English to the friendly tribe of Manteo whose chief abode was on an island on the coast southward from Roanoke. The name Croatan seems to indicate a locality in the territory claimed by Manteo and his tribe. Dr. Hawks speaks of this tribe as Hatteras Indians, and from an incident to be related hereafter this title seems to have been recognized by these Indians. From the first appearance of Amadas and Barlowe to the departure of Gov. White, in 1587 relations of the most friendly character are known to have existed between this tribe and the English colonists. Their chief, Manteo, in reward of his faithful services to the English, was, by command of Sir Walter Raleigh, baptized as a member of the Church of England and was made Lord of Roanoke and of Dasamonguepeuk. For reasons given in the succeeding pages we believe the term Roanoke, then applied to the island, was afterwards given to a large extent of territory contiguous to Pamlico Sound, in fact to all the territory claimed by Manteo. The tribes at that early day seemed to have had no settled boundaries to the territories claimed by them and occupied the land adjacent to their principal seats, alternately with other tribes, as hunting grounds.

The history of this tribe, as connected with the early attempts to colonize our eastern coast, is of peculiar interest and is worthy of extended notice.

[Page 46]Harriot, who accompanied Lane's expedition to Virginia, in describing the Indians on our coast, says:

They are a people clothed with loose mantles made of deerskins and aprons of the same around their middles, all else naked, of such a difference of stature as we of England, having no edge tools or weapons of iron or steel to offend us withal, neither know they how to make any. * * * The language of every government is different from any other, and the farther they are distant, the greater is the difference. * * * They believe that there are many gods, which they call Mantoac, but of different sorts and degrees, one only chief and great God which has been from all eternity. * * * They also believe the immortality of the soul, that after this life as soon as the soul is departed from the body according to the works it has done, it is either carried to heaven, the habitable of the gods, there to enjoy perpetual bliss and happiness, or else to a great pit or hole, which they think to be in the farther part of the world toward the sunset, there to burn continually, the place they call Popogusso.

In reading this account of the religion of the natives we conclude that at some period they had communication with more civilized races from the East who impressed upon them some idea of faith more exalted than that common among savages. Some may be ready to accept the absurdities of monkish fancy and readily believe them to be descendants of the "lost tribes" who had retained something of ancient Jewish faith. The difference in color, language, and other characteristics renders it difficult to accept such a theory. The knowledge of this western land is as old as the time of Plato and Solon, who mention an island in the West called Atlantis "and a great continent which lay beyond it." The Persians established a colony in the West Indies a thousand years ago, which, by "abstaining from all admixture with the black aborigines, differs but little from their progenitors in the parent country." The Welsh colonized the Carolina coast in the twelfth century. In 1660 Rev. Morgan Jones, in traveling in the Tuscarora country, was captured by the Doegs, a branch of that tribe who spoke Welsh. He describes them as settled upon Pontigo River near Cape Atross. This statement seems to confirm the Welsh chronicle which describes Madoc's colony. Long before the discovery of Columbus the Basques sent fishing vessels to the northern part of America. The Norse records describe voyages to the American coast, reciting facts and dates which are confirmed by Irish and Arabic chronicles, and also by the inscription on Womans Island on our northern coast bearing date of April 25, 1135. If we discredit the accounts of these early voyages we may discredit anything of ancient date recorded in history. The Sanscrit root syllable *ap* and the Latin root *ak*, both meaning water, are detected in the names of scores of rivers and bays on our Atlantic coast facing Europe, where vessels driven by the northeast trade winds, would probably reach our shores.

We cite these facts in support of the theory that colonies were in past times located on our coast and in course of time were neglected and forgotten by the parent countries and became absorbed by native tribes. If this theory is accepted it will account for traditions of wrecked vessels prevalent among the Indians described by Hariot, as well as for their religious notions so far above those commonly found among savages. Prescott, as quoted by Dr. Hawks, in speaking of the Indians found on the Atlantic coast of North America, says:

They had attained to the sublime conception of one Great Spirit, the creator of the universe, who, immaterial in his own nature, was not to be dishonored by an attempt at visible representation, and who, pervading all space, was not to be circumscribed within the walls of a temple.

[Page 47]What may have been the origin of the tribe, known to us through the English colonists as Croatan, can only be a matter of conjecture. They had traditions of vessels wrecked in past times, and they affirmed that iron implements found among them were obtained from such wrecks. Children with auburn hair and blue eyes were noticed among them, which impressed the belief that they had had communication with white people. From the appearance of Amidas and Barlowe in 1584 to the departure of Gov. White in 1587, their demeanor toward the whites was friendly. The treatment received by Manteo during his visit to England may have enhanced the good feeling toward the English. What became of them?

CHAPTER V.

After the departure of Gov. White from the coast of Virginia in 1590 five expeditions were fitted out at the expense of Sir Walter Raleigh for the relief of his distressed countrymen at Roanoke. These expeditions returned with no tidings of the planters and it became the settled conviction of those interested in the colony that it perished from starvation or savage cruelty.

After the settlement at Jamestown in 1607, Capt. John Smith sent a hardy woodsman to the Chowanoke Indians, who lived near the head of Albemarle Sound, under the pretense of sending presents to their king, but his object was to make inquiries concerning the Roanoke colony. Capt. Smith sent two other men to the Mangoaks, on the river Nottoway, but they returned as the other had done, without any information except that the white people were all dead. (Vide Williamson's His. of N. C., vol. 1, p. 73.)

It is evident from the story of Gov. White, as given on a preceding page, that the colonists went southward along the coast to Croatoan Island, now a part of Carteret County, in North Carolina, and distant about 100 miles in a direct line from Albemarle Sound. The Mangoacks were seated northwest from Albemarle and it is not surprising that the messengers returned without definite information. The statement of Lawson as to the tradition of the Hatteras Indians may throw some light on the fate of the English colonists, but it is a matter of surprise to us at this time that a *historian* would not pursue the investigation of that tradition far enough to ascertain who those ancestors were who could "talk in a book." Europeans had been upon the coast even before the arrival of Amidas and Barlowe in 1584. Persons were noticed among the natives *with auburn and chestnut colored hair,* and traditions existed concerning wrecked vessels. Iron implements were found among the Croatan Indians made of spikes and nails obtained from a wreck on their coast, which occurred about 20 years before the arrival of the English colony. A previous wreck in 1558 was mentioned; some of the crew were saved and were supposed to have been lost in their attempt to leave in the frail boats of the natives, Lawson wrote in 1714, 127 years after the colonists were last seen on Roanoke Island. Sixty-nine years after the settlement on that island and sixty years before the event related by Lawson, Roanoke was visited by an Englishman, Francis Yeardly, who, in a letter to John Farrar, Esq., [Page 48] dated May 8, 1654, relates a visit made to Roanoke Island by himself and others—

where or thereabouts they found the great commander of these parts with his Indians ahunting, who received them, civilly, and showed the ruins of Sir Walter Raleigh's fort, from which I received a sure token of their being there. After some days spent to and fro in the country, the young man, the interpreter, prevailed with the great man and his war captains to come in and make peace with the English, which they willingly condescended unto. (Vide Hawks, His. N. C., vol. 2, p. 17.)

So that at that early day the island was occupied by Indians who knew nothing of the lost Englishmen and who pointed out Raleigh's fort as an object of curiosity, without any tradition as to the fate of those who built it.

Rev. Mr. Blair, who was a missionary to the settlements on Pamlico Sound, after describing the difficulties of his situation, writes to his patron, Lord Weymouth, as follows:

I think it likewise reasonable to give you an account of a great nation of Indians, who live in that government, computed to be no less than 100, 000, many of which live among the English, and all, as far as I can understand, a very civilized people.

This letter was written in 1703. Mr. Blair speaks of a desert of 50 miles in extent to be crossed in reaching the place. At the time in which he writes the descendants of the missing colonists must have held only a tradition respecting the events attending the attempt at colonization on Roanoke Island. The number mentioned by Mr. Blair is evidently an exaggeration and the location of the tribe is indefinite. There is reason to believe that descendants of the colonists were living in a region of country southwest of Pamlico at the time in which he writes and that they emigrated westward toward the interior, where a large body of Croatan Indians and descendants of the lost colonists had previously located. It is probable that the civilized Indians mentioned were a portion of the Croatan tribe, as there was no other tribe to which the reference could apply. At that early day very little was known of the region to southwest of Pamlico Sound, and the missionary may have traveled 100 miles in reaching the place of his labor, which seemed to be at a great distance from other precincts visited by him.

At the time in which he writes (1703) there were no settlements of white men known to exist beyond the region around Pamlico Sound. Subsequent to that date white emigrants penetrated the wilderness, and in 1729 there was a settlement made on Hearts Creek, a tributary of the Cape Fear, and near the site of the present town of Fayetteville. Scotchmen arrived in what is now Richmond County in North Carolina as early as 1730. French Huguenots in large numbers emigrated to South Carolina after the revocation of the Edict of Nantes, and some of them had penetrated as far north as the present northern boundary of that State in the early part of the eighteenth century.

At the coming of white settlers there was found located on the waters of Lumber River a large tribe of Indians, *speaking English,* tilling the soil, owning slaves, and practicing many of the arts of civilized life. They occupied the country as far west as the Pee Dee, but their principal seat was on the Lumber, extending along that river for 20 miles. They held their lands in common, and land titles only became known on the approach of white men. The first grant of land to any of this tribe of which there is written evidence in [Page 49] existence was made by King George II in 1732 to *Henry Berry* and *James Lowrie,* two leading men of the tribe, and was located on the Lowrie Swamp, east of Lumber River in present county of Robeson, in North Carolina. A subsequent grant was made to James Lowrie in 1738. According to tradition, there were deeds of land of older date, described as "White" deeds and "Smith" deeds, but no trace of their existence can be found at this date.

Many of these people at a later period purchased their lands from persons who obtained large patents from the king.

Occasional bands of immigrants arrived on the Lumber River from ancient settlements toward the east, while others moved west toward the Pee Dee, Catawba and French Broad Rivers. These people were hospitable, and friendly relations were established between them and their white neighbors. Subsequent to the coming of white settlers a portion of the tribe went north toward the Great Lakes and some of their descendants can be found at this time in Canada, west of Lake Ontario. Another emigration occurred at a later date and the emigrants became incorporated with a tribe then located near Lake Michigan. Many families, described as white people, emigrated toward the Allegheny Mountains and there are many families in western North Carolina at this time, who are claimed by the tribe in Robeson County, as descendants of the lost English colonists, who had preserved their purity of blood to that degree that they could not be distinguished from white people. These Indians built great roads connecting the distant settlements with their principal seat on the Lumbee, as the Lumber River was then called. One of the great roads constructed by them can be traced from a point on Lumber River for 20 miles to an old settlement near the mouth of Hearts Creek, now Cross Creek. Another great highway still bearing the name of the "Lowrie Road" and used at this day as a public road, extends from the town of Fayetteville, through Cumberland and Robeson Counties, in a southwest direction toward an ancient Croatan settlement on the Pee Dee.

James Lowrie, previously mentioned as one of the grantees in the deed made by George the Second, and recognized as a chief man of his tribe, is described as an Indian who married Priscilla Berry, a sister of Henry Berry, the other grantee mentioned. James Lowrie was a descendant of James Lowrie, of Chesapeake, who married a Croatan woman *in Virginia* (as eastern North Carolina is still designated by the tribe) and became the progenitor of all the Lowries belonging to this tribe. According to the prevalent tradition respecting this family, the men were intellectual and ambitious, and, as a chronicler of the tribe described them, became "leaders among men." Many persons distinguished in the annals of North Carolina are claimed as descended from the original James Lowrie, of Chesapeake. "You will find the name of James Lowrie," remarked the chronicler, "wherever you find a Lowrie family."

Henry Berry, the grantee previously mentioned, was a lineal descendant of the English colonist, Henry Berry, who was left on Roanoke Island in 1587. (See list of names of lost colony.)

Many of this tribe served in the Continental Army during the Revolutionary War and enjoyed pensions within the memory of persons yet living. A considerable number served during the War [Page 50] of 1812, some of whom received pensions within the recollection of the writer. From the close of the Revolution to the year 1835 they exercised the elective franchise equally with white men, performed militia duties, encouraged schools and built churches, owned slaves, and lived in comfortable circumstances. By an ordinance of the North Carolina State convention of 1835, the elective franchise was denied to all "free persons of color." To effect a political purpose, it was contended that these citizens were "free persons of color," and afterwards they were debarred from voting till the year 1868, when a new constitution was adopted. After the adoption of the new State constitution, they were allowed the benefit of public schools, but having been classed for a long period as "free persons of color," they were compelled to patronize schools provided for the negro race. Owing to a bitter prejudice against negroes, but few availed themselves of the privilege, the greater part preferring that their children should grow up in ignorance, rather than that they should be forced to association with a race which they hold in utter contempt. Separate schools have since been provided for their race by the Legislature of North Carolina, which, by special act, recognized them as Croatan Indians.

CHAPTER VI.

During the late war between the States an incident occurred which caused the writer to investigate the traditions of this tribe. Three young men of the Lowrie family were drafted, according to military law, to work on the fortifications at Fort Fisher, in eastern North Carolina, and while on the road to the nearest depot in Robeson County they were killed, it is supposed, by a white man who had them in custody. An inquest was held, and at its conclusion, an old Indian named George Lowrie addressed the people assembled in substance as follows:

We have always been the friends of white men. We were a free people long before the white men came to our land. Our tribe was always free. They lived in Roanoke in Virginia. When the English came to Roanoke, our tribe treated them kindly. One of our tribe went to England in an English ship and saw that great country. When English people landed in Roanoke we were friendly, for our tribe was always friendly to white men. We took the English to live with us. There is the white man's blood in these veins as well as that of the Indian. In order to be great like the English, we took the white man's language and religion, for our people were told they would prosper if they would take white men's laws. In the wars between white men and Indians we always fought on the side of white men. We moved to this land and fought for liberty for white men, yet white men have treated us as negroes. Here are our young men shot down by a white man and we get no justice, and that in a land where our people were always free.

The incident above related occurred in the latter part of 1864, and owing to the troubled state of the country at that time and for several years afterwards, no investigation could be made till the year 1875, when the writer became a citizen and had opportunity of interviewing leading persons of the tribe.

After the year 1835 these Indians, who murmured greatly at the injustice done them in being classed as "mulattoes" or "free persons of color," became suspicious of white men, and at first we found difficulty in eliciting any facts relating to their past history. After years of patient investigation, gathering here and there, we present the following summary of traditions prevalent among them:

[Page 51]The tribe once lived in Roanoke in Virginia, as they persist in calling eastern North Carolina. The name Roanoke is applied to the country around Pamlico Sound, embracing Hyde, Tyrell, and Dare Counties on the north, with the series of islands as far south as Carteret County and embracing that county with Craven and Jones. Croatoan or Croatan was a locality far to the south, off the coast of Carteret, and was the principal seat of the tribe. Their leading man was made Lord of Roanoke. The name *Manteo* they do not recognize, but are familiar with *Mayno,* a name very common among them and representing a very quiet, law-abiding people.

At an early period after the English colony became incorporated with the tribe, they began to emigrate westward. The first settlement made was probably in what is now Sampson County on several small rivers, tributary to Black River. A portion located on the Cape Fear, near a place now bearing the name of "Indian Wells" and at Hearts Creek in Cumberland County, now Fayetteville. It is impossible to ascertain at what date the tribe located in Robeson, but it is probable that they have resided there for 200 years. According to their universal tradition they were located there long before the troubles with the Tuscaroras began in 1711. Some of the tribe fought under "Bonnul" as they term Col. Barnwell, and we have reliable evidence that they brought home a few Mattamuskeet Indians as prisoners and slaves. The descendants of these Mattamuskeets had their traditions also. The name Dare was not recognized by them in our first investigations but we afterwards discovered that they pronounce the name variously as *Darr, Durr,* and *Dorr.* This discovery was made when we related to an old chronicler of the tribe the story of Virginia Dare, the first white child born on American soil. This name Dorr or Durr has disappeared on the Lumber River since the war of 1812. The name Dorr appears on the muster roll of a company composed in part of Indians from Robeson County which served during that war, in the United States Army.

Several chroniclers, or old persons who keep the traditions of the tribe, have informed us that there are families bearing the name of Dorr or Durr, to be found in western North Carolina who are claimed by the tribe as descended from the English colonists of Roanoke. These chroniclers affirm that the Dares, Coopers, Harvies, and others retained their purity of blood and were generally the pioneers in emigration. Many names are corrupted, so that it is difficult to trace their history. The name *Goins* was originally O'Guin, as appears from ancient court records. The name Lumber, as applied to the river, was originally Lumbee or Lombee. The name Manteo is not familiar to them. While they have a tradition of their leader or chief who went to England, yet they have preserved no name for him. The nearest approach to the name Manteo, is Maino or Mainor. An old woman, whom we interviewed, spoke of their great man as *Wonoke*. This name may be a corruption of Roanoke, for we must remember Manteo was made Lord of Roanoke. Mattamuskeet Lake, according to a tradition preserved by these Indians, was a [Page 52]*burnt lake* or lake caused by water filling a hole burnt in the ground. We are indebted for this tradition to an aged gentleman of Robeson County who was familiar with the traditions of the tribe from about 1820 to 1824. He mentioned several persons who represented that they were descended from Mattamuskeet Indians who were taken prisoners, in the war between the Whites and Tuscaroras, by the tribe on the Lumber River. These Mattamuskeets could locate the dwelling places of their ancestors who lived in what is now Hyde County, in the vicinity of Mattamuskeet Lake. In our investigations we could find no tradition respecting these persons. The names given by our informant have all disappeared. Large numbers have emigrated since the beginning of the present century. Within half a century about 40 familes left the county of Robeson from about Plainview and went to the Northwest. "Traditions are fading fast," our informant remarked, "as far back as 1820 their traditions were more vivid than now and were familiar to old and young. Now, you will find their ancient traditions confined to comparatively a few old persons."

Pungo Lake is known among them as Mattapungo. They have no tradition as to any river named Roanoke. This name is invariably applied by them to the territory previously described as occupied by their tribe on the eastern coast. Hawks, as previously mentioned, speaks of the tribe in 1587 as Hatteras Indians. When the act of the North Carolina General Assembly was read to them, recognizing them as Croatans, an intelligent Indian remarked that he had always heard that they were called Hattoras Indians. The line of emigration extended westward from what is now Carteret County, and can be traced according to tradition as far west as the French Broad, in Buncombe County. Tradition respecting localities occupied by the tribe at the time of the absorption of the English colony is vague, but definite enough to establish the belief that their territory once embraced portions, at least, of the present counties of Carteret, Jones, and Craven. It is not at all probable that any of the English colonists left by Gov. White ever lived west of the county of Jones. The settlement on the Lumber River in Robeson County was made during the seventeenth century, possibly as early as 1650. The revocation of the Edict of Nantes occurred in 1685, and thousands of French Huguenots, driven to exile, found refuge in South

Carolina. As early as 1709, a colony of these exiles located in the eastern part of North Carolina. Some of these Huguenots penetrated the interior as far as the Lumber River in the early part of the last century, and found the country north and east of them thickly populated by Indians who had farms and roads and other evidences of civilized life, and had evidently resided there for a considerable time before the approach of white men.

Settlements were made toward the Pee Dee and at points beyond that river after their location on the Lumber.

The language spoken is almost pure Anglo Saxon, a fact which we think affords corroborative evidence of their relation to the lost colony of White. Mon (Saxon) is used for man, father is pronounced fayther, and a tradition is usually begun as follows: [Page 53] "Mon, my *fayther* told me that *his* fayther told him," etc. Mension is used for measurement, aks for ask, hit for it, hosen for hose, lovend for loving, housen for houses. They seem to have but two sounds for the letter a, one like short o. Many of the words in common use among them have long been obsolete in English-speaking countries.

They are a proud race, boasting alike of their English and Indian blood, hospitable to strangers, and ever ready to do friendly offices for white people.

They are peaceable in disposition, but when aroused by repeated injury they will fight desperately. The great mass shun notoriety and carefully avoid places where crowds of other races assemble. They generally live retired from public highways and seem to show Indian characteristics more strongly than in former times. There are sixteen churches owned by them in Robeson County, divided among Baptist and Methodist denominations. Their schoolhouses, built entirely by private means, are all framed buildings and provided far better than those of the colored race.

They are great road makers, like their ancestors. The best public roads in North Carolina are found among this tribe.

There has been no census taken separately from the other races, but the number in Robeson County is fully 2, 500, and, considering the settlements in other counties, the total is not less than 5, 000. The enrollment of Croatan children in Robeson County between the ages of six and twenty-one years, in accordance with an act of the general assembly passed in 1885, shows about eleven hundred entitled to the benefit of public instruction, provided separately for the race.

By an act of the general assembly passed in 1887 a normal school for teachers of the Croatan race was established, and the sum of $500 is annually appropriated for two years by the State for its support.

According to the law of North Carolina, all marriages between a white person and a negro or Indian, or between a white person and a person of negro or Indian descent to the third generation, inclusive, are null and void, but there was no inhibition of marriage between an Indian and a negro till the general assembly of 1887 amended the law by declaring all marriages between Croatan Indians and negroes or persons of negro descent to the third generation, inclusive, null and void.

CHAPTER VII.

In investigating the traditions prevalent among this singular people we found many family names identical with those of the lost colony of 1587. For the information of the reader we give a list of the names of all the men, women, and children of Raleigh's colony, which arrived in Virginia and remained to inhabit there. This list is found in first volume of Hawks' History of North Carolina and copied from Hakluyt, Volume III, page 280.

[Page 54]ANNO REGNI REGINÆ ELIZABETHÆ 29.

John White.
Roger *Baily.*
Ananias *Dare.*
Christopher *Cooper.*
Thomas *Stevens.*
John Sampson.
Dionys *Harvie.*
Roger Prat.
George *Howe.*
Simon Fernando.
Nicholas *Johnson.*
Thomas Warner.
Anthony *Cage.*
William *Willes.*
William *Brown.*
Thomas *Smith.*

Richard Kemme.
Thomas *Harris*.
Richard Taverner.
William Clement.
Robert *Little*.
Hugh *Tayler*.
William Berde.
Richard Wildye.
Lewes Wotton.
Michael Bishop.
Henry *Browne*.
Henry Rufotte.
Richard Tomkins.
Henry Dorrell.
John *Jones*.
John *Brooks*.
Cutbert *White*.
John Bright.
Clement *Taylor*.
William Sole.
John Cotsmuir.
Humphrey Newton.
Thomas *Colman*.
Thomas *Gramme*, or Graham, Graeme.
Mark *Bennet*.
John Gibbes.
John Stilman.
John Earnest.
Henry *Johnson*.
John Starte.
Richard Darige.
William *Lucas*.
Arnold Archard.
William Nichols.
Thomas Phevens.
John Borden.
Charles Florrie.

Henry Mylton.
Henry *Paine*.
Thomas *Harris*.
Thomas *Scot*.
Peter *Little*.
John Wyles.
Bryan Wyles.
Robert *Wilkinson*.
John Tydway.
Ambrose *Viccars*.
Edmund English.
Thomas Topan.
Henry Berry.
Richard *Berry*.
John Spendlove.
John Hemmington.
Thomas *Butler*.
Edward Powell.
John Burdon.
James Hynde.
Thomas Ellis.
John *Wright*.
William Dutton.
Maurice *Allen*.
William Waters.
Richard Arthur.
John *Chapman*.
James *Lasie*.
John *Cheven*.
Thomas Hewett.
George *Martin*.
Hugh *Pattenson*.
Martin Sutton.
John Farre.
John *Bridger*.
Griffin *Jones*.
Richard Shabedge.

WOMEN.

Eleanor *Dare*.
Margery *Harvie*.
Agnes *Wood*.
Winnifred *Powell*.
Joyce Archard.
Jane *Jones*.
Elizabeth Glane.
Jane *Pierce*.
Andry Tappan.
Alice *Charman*.
Emma Merimoth.
— Colman.
Margaret Lawrence.
Joan Warren.
Jane Mannering.
Rose *Payne*.
Elizabeth *Viccars*.

BOYS AND CHILDREN.

John Sampson.
Robert Ellis.
Ambrose *Viccas*.
Thomas Archard.
Thomas Humphrey.
Thomas Smart.
George Howe.
John Prat.
William Wythers.

CHILDREN BORN IN VIRGINIA.

Virginia Dare.
— *Harvie*.

[Page 55]Manteo and Towaye, or Wanchese, that were in England, returned to Virginia with the colony.

Gov. John White, at the solicitation of the colonists, returned to England. Simon Fernando, the Spanish pilot of the expedition, also returned. George Howe, one of the "Assistants" of Gov. White, was killed by the Indians on Roanoke Island soon after the arrival. Omitting the name of the perfidious Fernando, we have 120 persons in all, including men, women, and children, and about 90 family names, represented in the colony.

The names in the foregoing list in italics are those which are found at this time among the Indians residing in Robeson County and in other counties of North Carolina. The traditions of every family bearing the name of one of the lost colonists point to Roanoke as the country of their ancestors.

If we accept their traditions they held communication with the eastern coast long after their exodus, and it is not improbable that it was a party of this tribe which Lawson describes in 1714 as visiting their old hunting grounds and who described their ancestors as people who "could talk in a book."[1]

As to the intellectual character of this singular people but little can be written, as public schools were unknown prior to 1835 and such education as they obtained up to that date was limited to a knowledge of reading and writing and the fundamental rules of arithmetic. Hundreds have grown up to manhood and womanhood in perfect ignorance of books. By nature they are quick-witted, and, judging by the few examples of educated ones, they are equal to the whites in mental capacity. Ex-United States Senator Revels, of Mississippi, belongs to this tribe. He was born in Robeson County and emigrated to the northwest, where he was educated and subsequently resided in Mississippi.

The action of the North Carolina Legislature in establishing separate schools for this race and in recognizing them as the descendants of the friendly Croatans known to the early colonists is one great step toward their moral and intellectual elevation. They are almost universally landholders and occupy a territory in the county of Robeson of about 60, 000 acres, adapted to the growth of corn, cotton, and tobacco.

---

[1] Lawson's History was first published in 1709.

CHAPTER VIII.

It has long been a settled conviction that the lost colonists perished from starvation or savage cruelty.

This conviction has arisen from the fact that they were seen no more by white men.

The particulars given by Gov. White of the understanding which existed between him and the colonists prior to his departure for England in 1587, and his finding the word "Croatoan" on a tree, in a conspicuous place, on his return in 1590, seem to prove conclusively that the English had accepted the invitation of Manteo's tribe and had gone to Croatan Island. The fact that they were seen no more by white men does not prove that they perished. The same fact exists in regard to the Croatans and the same argument would prove their destruction also.

[Page 56] We must remember that the region embracing Croatan Island and the adjacent mainland was unexplored for a long period after the attempt at settlement on Roanoke Island. The history of those times shows that in 1609[1] the northeast corner of North Carolina was settled by a colony from Virginia.

In 1654, sixty-seven years after the English colonists were last seen on Roanoke, Virginia adventurers had explored as far south as the Pamlico and Neuse Rivers. In 1656[1] a settlement was made on Albemarle Sound. A colony from Massachusetts was located on the Cape Fear in 1660 and was soon abandoned. Sir John Yeamans' colony landed on the same river in 1664. In 1690 a French colony from Virginia settled on Pamlico Sound, and in 1698 emigrants from Albemarle also located in that region.

We have cited these facts to show how little was known from 1587 to 1690 of the region where tradition says the Croatans were settled.

In 1690, the date of the settlement of the French on Pamlico, all the English colonists must have been dead, and the sad story was held only in tradition, and it may be that the Croatans who were then remaining in that region, on the approach of the new colony, removed farther into the interior, where portions of that tribe had previously located.

---

1 Should read "about 1661."
1 Should read "about 1661."

As previously intimated, the traditions of the Indians now living in Robeson are sufficiently clear to prove that at an early period they located south of Pamlico Sound on the mainland. Tradition in regard to their ancient dwelling places on the tributaries of Black River in the present county of Sampson are more definite. The fact that French, English, Irish, and perhaps German names are found among them is accounted for by the tradition that marriages frequently occurred between them and the early immigrants. The name Chavis which is common among this people, is probably a corruption of the French name Cheves. Goins was O'Guin, as court records prove. Leary was O'Leary. Blauc or Blaux is French. Braboy is of recent origin and was originally "Brave Boy" and dates back to the war with the Tuscaroras in 1711 and was conferred on an Indian by the commander of the English for some meritorious act.

From the earliest settlement of the country along the Lumber River these Indians have been an English-speaking people. Their language has many peculiarities and reminds one of the English spoken in the days of Chaucer. The number of old English words in common use among them which have long been obsolete in English-speaking countries is corroborative of the truth of their tradition that they are the descendants of the lost Englishmen of Roanoke.

In traveling on foot they march in "Indian file" and exhibit a fondness for bright red colors. They unconsciously betray many other traits characteristics of Indians. The custom of raising patches of tobacco for their own use has been handed down from time immemorial.

In building they exhibit no little architectural skill. In road making they excel. Some of the best roads in North Carolina can be found within their territory. They are universally hospitable and polite to strangers. They are proud of their race and boast of their English ancestry. Like their ancestors, they are friendly to white men.

[Page 57]Their traditions are generally preserved by the old members of the tribe, but the tradition is universal among them from infancy to old age that their ancestors came from "Roanoke in Virginia." By Virginia they mean eastern North Carolina, and the term "Roanoke" means the territory occupied by the tribe in the vicinity of Pamlico Sound. In religious matters they are Baptists and Methodists. The latter belong to what is called the Indian Mission, which is of recent origin.

"They never forget a kindness, an injury, nor a debt," said an old citizen. * * * "They may not pay you when a debt is due, but they seldom forget an obligation and are sure to pay you after a time."

In common with all Indians they have a great respect for the Quakers and look upon them as the true friends of the Indian. In the olden time they had houses of entertainment for travelers.

The number of family names to be found among them identical with those of the colonists of Roanoke is further corroborative of their traditional descent.

The line of emigration from their original seat on the coast was westward and can be traced as far west as the French Broad, in Buncombe County. Though many families of this tribe emigrated from the Lumber River a long while ago, yet the locations of many of them have been located in western North Carolina with unerring certainty.

The writer has been much interested in investigating the traditions prevalent among the Croatans and expresses his firm conviction that they are descended from the friendly tribe found on our eastern coast in 1587 and also descended from the lost colonists of Roanoke who were amalgamated with this tribe.

Through many centuries of time there comes down to us the sad story of the lost legions of Varus. The mystery that so long hung over the fate of those legions was solved by Drusus, who found the bleaching bones of his countrymen in a German forest near the Baltic Sea.

The fate of the lost colonists of Roanoke, we submit, is revealed in the foregoing pages.

To the charitable who are interested in the moral elevation of humanity we heartily commend the Croatans.

[Page 58] EXHIBIT CC.

THE LOST COLONY OF ROANOKE: ITS FATE AND SURVIVAL.[1]

[By Stephen B. Weeks.]

The disappearance of the settlers of 1587 has been called the tragedy of American colonization. The greatest interest was manifested in their fate by all the early explorers. Numerous expeditions were sent in search of them. These brought back various rumors, but nothing certain could be learned. Their history became interwoven with legend and romance; but after a lapse of three hundred years they emerge again from the darkness and dust of oblivion.

It is now believed that the colonists of 1587 removed to Croatan soon after the return of Governor White to England; that they intermarried with the Croatan or Hatteras Indians; that their wanderings westward can be definitely traced; and that their descendants can be identified to-day.

It is to a discussion of the movements of the colonists after the departure of White, and to the identification of their descendants, that the remaining pages of this paper will be directed.

There can be no doubt that the colonists removed to Croatan. When White left them, "they were prepared to remove from Roanoak, fifty miles

---

[1] Reprinted from Papers American Historical Association, 1891, V, pp. 460-477. The late Dr. William T. Harris, when United States Commissioner of Education, took much interest in this theory of survival. He once expressed in the presence of this writer the belief that it was the greatest historical discovery of the nineteenth century.—S. B. W.

into the main." He agreed with them that they should carve in some conspicuous place the name of the section to which they went and if they went in distress a sign of the cross was to be carved above. The name Croatan was found, but there was no sign of distress. The colonists must have gone on the invitation of Manteo and his friends, and the fact that their chests and other heavy articles were buried indicates that it was their intention to revisit the island of Roanoke at some future time, and that it was then in the possession of hostile savages. These articles consisted largely of arms and other instruments of war. This indicates that they went into the land of friends and that that their new home was not far distant, otherwise they would have taken all their property with them rather than endure the fatigue of a second long journey to Roanoke for it. The question arises then, Where was Croatan? On the location of this place the future of the colony depended. Croatan, or more properly Croatoan, is an Indian word, and was applied by the Hatteras Indians to the place of their residence. Here Manteo was born, and here his relatives were living when he first met the English; the latter soon began to apply the name to the Indians themselves. The island of Roanoke was not at that time regularly inhabited, but was used as a hunting [Page 59] ground by the tribe to which Manteo belonged, and also by their enemies who lived on the main and were the subjects of Wingina.

The name Croatan first appears in the account of Grenville's voyage of 1585. It is there made an island; Lane says that it was an island; and White also bears witness to this, for he says, when describing his discovery of the deserted and dismantled fort: "I greatly joyed that I had found a certain token of their safe being at Croatoan, which is the place where Manteo was born and the savages of the island our friends." On White's map of the coast it is put down as an island. From these facts it is perfectly clear that the adventurers believed Croatan to be an island. The map of 1666 and the Nuremburg map make it a part of the banks lying between Cape Hatteras and Cape Lookout, perhaps what is now known as Core Banks, and consequently an island; but later maps have located Croatan on the mainland, just opposite Roanoke Island, in the present counties of Dare, Tyrrell, and Hyde. It is marked thus on Ogilby's map, published by the Lords Proprietors in 1671, on Morden's map of 1687, and on Lawson's map, published in 1709. A part of this region is still known as Croatan, while the sound between this section and Roanoke Island bears the name of Croatan. On the Nuremburg map and on the map of 1666 this peninsula is called Dasamonguepeuk. Now we know that in 1587 Manteo was baptized as Lord of Roanoke and Dasamonguepeuk. This title clearly indicates that the Hatteras tribe, to which Manteo belonged, laid claims to the peninsula. They doubtless made use of it for the cultivation of corn, as well as for hunting and fishing, while their principal seat was some eighty miles to the south on the island of Croatan. The English colonists have left us unimpeachable testimony that they removed from Roanoke Island to Croatan. The Croatan of the early explorers and maps was a long, narrow, storm-beaten sandbank, incapable in itself of supporting savage life, much less the lives of men and women living in the agricultural stage. It is not reasonable to suppose that the colonists would have gone from a fertile soil to a sterile one. It is probable, then, that in accordance with an understanding between each other, the Hatteras Indians having abandoned their residence on Croatan Island, and the English colonists having given up their settlements on Roanoke Island, both settled on the fertile peninsula of Dasamonguepeuk, which the Hatteras tribe had already claimed and partly occupied, but which they had not been able to defend against enemies. The name of their former place of residence followed the tribe, was applied to their new home, and thus got into the later maps. If this theory is accepted, it is easy to see how the Hatteras tribe may have come into communication with kindred tribes on the Chowan and Roanoke rivers, to which they seem to have gone at a later period. This is one end of the chain of evidence in this history of survivals.

The other end of the chain is to be found in a tribe of Indians now living in Robeson County and the adjacent sections of North Carolina, and recognized officially by the State in 1885 as Croatan Indians. These Indians are believed to be the lineal descendants of the colonists left by John White on Roanoke Island in 1587. The migrations of the Croatan tribe from former homes farther to the east can be traced by their tradition. It is pretty clear that the tribe removed to their present home from former settlements on Black River, in [Page 60] Sampson County. The time of their removal is uncertain; but all traditions point to a time anterior to the Tuscarora war in 1711, and it is probable that they were fixed in their present homes as early as 1650.[1] During the eighteenth century they occupied the country as far west as the Pee Dee, but their principal seats were on Lumber River, in

---

1 McMillan: Sir Walter Raleigh's Lost Colony, p. 20.

Robeson County, and extended along it for twenty miles. They held their lands in common, and titles became known only on the approach of white men. The first known grant made to any member of this tribe is located on the Lowrie Swamp east of Lumber River, and was made by George II in 1732 to Henry Berry and James Lowrie.[2] Another grant was made to James Lowrie in 1738. Traditions point to still older deeds that are not known to now exist. The tribe has never ceased to be migratory in its disposition. For many years after the main body had settled in Robeson, scattered detachments would join them from their old homes farther to the east, while parts would remove farther toward the west. They are now to be found all over western North Carolina, and many families there who have retained their purity of blood to such a degree that they can not be distinguished from white people are claimed by the tribe in Robeson. After the coming of the white people a part of the tribe removed to the region of the Great Lakes, and their descendants are still living in Canada, west of Lake Ontario. At a later period another company went to the Northwest and became incorporated with a tribe near Lake Michigan. Some time before the war a party drifted to Ohio; one of them, Lewis Sheridan Leary, was in John Brown's party when he invaded Harper's Ferry in 1859, and was killed there October 17, 1859, while guarding John Brown's "fort."[3] In 1890 a party removed to Kansas.

---

2 *Ibid.*, p. 14. The deeds for these grants are still extant and are in the possession of Hon. D. P. McEachin, of Robeson County, North Carolina.

3 The late Mr. John S. Leary wrote the author from Fayetteville, N. C., under date of July 22, 1891:"I do not know as to whether any considerable number of the 'Croatans' emigrated from the State at any time in a body. Quite a number who were connected with the Croatans in Robeson County left the State at different times. Senator Hiram R. Revels, his brothers, Willis B. & Absalom, and two sisters, some of the Oxendines, Learys, and Dials; I do not know the exact number. My father's mother was a Revels, born in Robeson County, was 2d cousin to Hiram. She married an Irishman named O'Leary. Father was born in Sampson County, on the Big Coharie, his parents having moved to that county. In 1806 they came to Fayetteville, where father lived until he died, in 1880. Father came from the 'Croatan stock.' My mother was born in France, and was brought to this country by her parents in 1812. Father & mother were married in 1825. In 1857 my father sent my brother, Lewis Sheridan Leary, to Oberlin, Ohio. While there he formed an acquaintance with John Brown and went with him to Harper's Ferry in October, 1859. He was killed on the 17th day of October, 1859. while guarding what is now known as 'John Brown's Fort.' I saw this fort for the first time in 1880. It is a small

The Croatans fought under Colonel Barnwell against the Tuscaroras in 1711, and the tribe of to-day speak with pride of the stand taken by their ancestors under "Bunnul" for the cause of the whites.[4] In this war they took some of the Mattamuskeet Indians prisoners and made them slaves. Many of the Croatans were in the Continental Army; in the War of 1812 a company was mustered into the Army of the United States, and members of the tribe received pensions for these services within the memory of the present generation; they also fought in the armies of the Confederate States. Politically they have had little chance for development. From 1783 to 1835 they had the [Page 61] right to vote, performed military duties, encouraged schools, and built churches; but by the constituent convention of 1835 the franchise was denied to all "free persons of color," and to effect a political purpose it was contended by both parties that the Croatans came under this catagory. The convention of 1868 removed this ban; but as they had long been classed as mulattoes they were obliged to patronize the negro schools. This they refused to do as a rule, preferring that their children should grow up in ignorance, for they hold the negro in utmost contempt,[1] and no greater insult can be given a Croatan than to call him "a nigger."

Finally, in 1885, through the efforts of Mr. Hamilton McMillan, who has lived near them and knows their history, justice long delayed was granted them by the General Assembly of North Carolina. They were officially recognized as Croatan Indians;[2] separate schools were provided for them and

---

brick house. I have a grand uncle, my father's mother's brother, living now in the Croatan settlement in Robeson County, 108 years old. As soon as I can make it convenient to see him I will have a talk with him and put on paper whatever information I can get from him and give you the benefit of it."

4 The traditions of the tribe that they fought in the Tuscarora war are verified by the Colonial Records of North Carolina. In vol. ii., p. 129, we find an entry: "Whereas, report has been made to this board that the Hateress Indyans have lately made their escape from the enemy Indyans," i. e., Tuscaroras. Again, on p. 171, we find: "Upon petition of the Hatterass Indyans praying some small relief from the country for their services," etc.

1 McMillan, Sir Walter Raleigh's Lost Colony, 14-16.

2 It has been suggested that the name "Croatan" was invented to strengthen the theory of their origin as here presented, but this is not the case. As we have seen, Croatan was the name of a locality and not of a tribe. The tribal name was Hattoras or Hatorask, or, as we now spell it, Hatteras. Lawson calls the Indians by this name. Dr. Hawks remarks on the error of the explorers in calling them Croatans: and when the

intermarriage with negroes was forbidden. Since this action on the part of the State they have become better citizens.[3]

They are almost universally landowners, occupying about sixty thousand acres in Robeson County. They are industrious and frugal, and anxious to improve their condition. No two families occupy the same house, but each has its own establishment.

They are found of all colors from black to white, and in some cases can not be distinguished from white people. They have the prominent cheek bones, the steel-gray eyes, the straight black hair of the Indian.[4] Those showing the Indian features most prominently have no beards; those in whom the white element predominates have beards. Their women are frequently beautiful; their movements are graceful, their dresses becoming, their figures superb.

In religious inclinations they are Methodists and Baptists, and own sixteen churches. The State has provided them a normal school for the training of teachers, and this action will go very far toward their mental and moral elevation. Their schoolhouses have been built entirely by private means; they are all frame buildings, and are furnished far better than those for the negro race. Their school enrollment in Robeson County is 422, according to the report of the eleventh census, and they employ eighteen teachers. Their entire school population, from six to twenty-one years, will probably amount to eleven hundred. Their whole population in this county is about twenty-five hundred, and their connections in other counties will perhaps swell this number to five thousand. They are quick-witted, and are capable of development. Mr. John S. Leary, a prominent politician of

---

act of the North Carolina Assembly recognizing them as Croatans was read to them, an intelligent Indian remarked that he had always heard that they were called "Hattoras" Indians.—McMillan, p. 20.

3 It is said by Mr. McMillan, that after the North Carolina act of 1887 went into effect the Croatans came near filling Lumberton jail with violators of law, the prosecutors in nearly all cases being Croatans.

4 A recent traveller among the Croatans writes of one of them: "Where in my life had I seen a handsomer man? The face was pure Greek in profile; the eyes *steel blue*, the figure of perfect mould, and the man as easily graceful in his attitude as any gentleman in a drawing-room. I sat in my buggy talking with this man for an hour, finding him far above ordinary intelligence and full of information." That night the traveller learned that the handsome Croatan was a brother of the famous Henry Berry Lowrie.

Raleigh, and professor of law in Shaw University, was a member of the tribe, and one of their number has reached the Senate of the United States, for Hon. Hiram R. Revels, who was born in [Page 62] Fayetteville, North Carolina, in 1822, and who was senator from Mississippi in 1870-71, is not a negro, but a Croatan Indian.[1]

This is the other end of the chain. To connect the two parts and show that the Croatan Indians of to-day are the descendants of the Hatteras Indians of 1587 and of the English colony left on Roanoke Island by John White in that year, we must examine, first, the evidence of historians and explorers on the subject; and, second, the traditions, character, and disposition, language, and family names of the Croatan Indians themselves.

We hear no more of the colonists left on Roanoke Island from the departure of White in 1591 until the settlement at Jamestown. We then have four sources of information in regard to them. The first of these is John Smith's "True Relation," first published in 1608. The second is a rude map of the coast of Virginia and North Carolina, which had probably been sent to England by Capt. Francis Nelson in June, 1608. It was intended to illustrate Smith's "True Relation," was not drawn from surveys, nor is it based on any accurate knowledge of the coast, nor had the maker seen the map of the

---

[1] At one time the Croatans were known as "Redbones," and there is a street in Fayetteville so called because some of them once lived on it. They are known by this name in Sumpter County, S. C., where they are quiet and peaceable, and have a church of their own. They are proud and high-spirited, and caste is very strong among them. There is in Hancock County, Tennessee, a tribe of people known by the local name of Malungeons or Melungeons. Some say they are a branch of the Croatan tribe, others that they are of Portuguese stock. They differ radically, however, in manners and customs from the accounts which we have received of the Croatans (*cf.* 2 articles in *The Arena* for 1891, by Miss Will Allen Dromgoole). Mr. McMillan favors the view that they are a part of the colony of Roanoke, and on this question Mr. John M. Bishop, a native of East Tennessee, now living in Washington, writes to the author: "My theory is that they are a part of the lost colony of Roanoke. Your utterances at the recent meeting in this city on the subject of the Lost Colony of Roanoke [meeting of Amer. Hist. Assn., Dec. 31, 1890] were so nearly in line with my ideas in this matter that I now write to call your attention to the subject.... You will mark the fact that the Malungeons are located on Newman's Ridge and Black Water Creek in Hancock County, Tenn., directly in the path of ancient westward emigration. Dan Boon tramped all over this immediate section.... The Malungeons, drifting with the tide of early emigration, stranded on the borderland of the wilderness and remained there."

coast made by John White. It was drawn presumably to illustrate a story told by the Indians, and based on the information derived from them. It was sent in September, 1608, by Zuñiga, the Spanish minister in London, to his master, Philip III, and is now first published in Mr. Alexander Brown's "Genesis of the United States." The third source is a pamphlet called "A True and Sincere Discourse of the Purpose and Ende of the *Plantation* begun in *Virginia,*" published in 1610. The fourth is Strachey's "History of Travaile into Virginia Britannia," published by the Hakluyt Society in 1849. Strachey came to Virginia as early as 1610, and became secretary of the council. His history is put by Mr. R. H. Major, his editor, between 1612 and 1616.

Captain Smith says in his "True Relation" that Opechancanough, one of the Indian kings, informed him "of certaine men cloathed at a place called Ocanahonan, cloathed like me." "The people cloathed at Ocamahowan, he also confirmed." Again: "We had agreed with the king of Paspahegh to conduct two of our men to a place called Panawicke, beyond Roonok, where he reported many men to be apparelled."[2]

The map illustrating this "Relation" shows three rivers which are probably intended to represent the Roanoke, the Tar, and the Neuse. On the south side of the Roanoke is a place called Ocanahowan. On the upper waters of the Neuse is Pakrakanick, and near it the legend "Here remayneth 4 men clothed that came from Roonock to Ochanahowan." The peninsula known to the explorers of 1585 as [Page 63] Dasamonguepeuk is called Pananiock, and the legend placed there says: "Here the king of Paspahege reported our men to be & wants to go." At a point on the James the map says: "Here Paspehege and 2 of our men landed to go to Panaweock." This expedition set out in January or February, 1608, and failed because the Indian king played the villain.

The managers of the Virginia Company in their "True and Sincere Declaration," referring to the Roanoke colony, say: "if with these [evils] we compare the advantages which we have gotten . . . in the *intelligence* of some of our nation planted by *Sir Walter Raleigh,* yet a live, within fifty mile of our fort, who can open the womb and bowels of this country; as is testified by two of our colony sent out to seek them, who (though denied

---

2 Smith's Works, Arber's edition, 1884, pp. 17-23. See map on p. 83.

by the savages speech with them) found *crosses* and *Letters* the *Characters* and assured Testimonies of *Christians* newly cut in the barks of trees."[1]

Strachey says: At Peccarecamek and Ochanahoen . . . the people have houses built with stone walls, and one story above another, so taught them by those English who escaped the slaughter at Roanoak, at what time this our colony, under the conduct of Captain Newport, landed within the Chesapeake Bay." Powhatan had been instigated to this massacre by his priests. Seven persons escaped, four men, two boys, and a young maid. These fled up the Chowan River and were preserved at Ritanoe by a chief named Eyanoco, and, in return for protection, began to teach the savages the arts of civilized life.[2]

We are to remember always that the reports of Indians are vague and indefinite. This is to be expected of an uneducated people, but while varying in detail the substance may be depended on as essentially true. The vagueness in these cases is further increased by the fact that the English knew little from actual exploration of the regions involved. We are safe then in identifying: (1) Smith's Panawicke with the Pananiock and the Pananeock of the map. This is the name given to the territory known to the earlier explorers as Dasamonguepeuk. (2) The Ochanahonan and Ocamahowan of Smith and the Ocanahowan of the map are identical with Strachey's Ochanahoen. (3) The Pakrakanick of the map is identical with Strachey's Peccarecamek.

Taking these sources of information together and identifying the localities as we have done, it seems reasonable to conclude: (1) That about 1607 the colonists left on Roanoke Island in 1587, now intermixed with the Croatan Indians, were on the peninsula of Dasamonguepeuk and that fresh traces of them were seen about this time by explorers sent out from Jamestown. (2) That they heard of the arrival of Captain Newport in Chesapeake Bay, and that some of them made an effort to reach the colony at Jamestown. It is not necessary to suppose that there was a general migration of the whole Croatan tribe toward the Chowan. We may conclude that most of the original colonists who were then alive and some of the half-breeds

---

[1] Brown, Genesis of the United States, i., 348.

[2] Strachey, pp. 50, 135. The expression used by Strachey with reference to the colony on page 152, where he says it will be related "in due place in this decade," indicates that he had some additional information in regard to their fate, but it was not given.

undertook the journey. They were met with hostility by the emissaries [Page 64] of Powhatan and some were slain.[1] (3) That others were protected and saved by a chief named Eyanoco, who was probably connected in some way with the Croatan tribe, for we must remember that when Lane was exploring these regions in 1586 he found Indians whose language Manteo could understand without an interpreter. (4) That according to the map they traveled from the region of the Chowan and Roanoke Rivers to the country known on it as Packrakanick and to Strachey as Peccarecamek. This was probably on the upper waters of the Neuse, in what may now be Wayne and Lenoir Counties. It is probable that they were rejoined by those who had not undertaken the expedition toward Virginia, and from this point they could have passed easily into Sampson and Robeson Counties in Conformity with their traditions, as related by Mr. McMillan.

Smith's "Relation," the map, and Strachey all tend to strengthen and explain the testimony of the next historical reference we have to the tribe. This is by John Lederer, a German, who made some explorations in eastern North Carolina, perhaps in the region south of the Roanoke River, in 1669-70. He mentions a powerful nation of bearded men two and one-half days' journey to the southwest, "which I suppose to be the Spaniards, because the Indians never have any" [beards].[2] Dr. Hawks thinks that these "bearded men" may have been the settlers on the Cape Fear, but we know that this colony was disbanded in 1667. We have no records of any Spanish settlements as far north as this; and according to Mr. McMillan (p. 20), the mongrel tribe now known as Croatan Indians were occupying their present homes as early as 1650. The statement of Lederer can only refer to the Croatan tribe.

The next account we have of them is in 1704, when Rev. John Blair, then traveling as a missionary through the Albemarle settlements, tells of a powerful tribe of Indians living to the south of what is now Albemarle Sound, "computed to be no less than 100, 000, many of which live amongst the

---

[1] Purchas says Powhatan confessed to Smith that he had been present at the slaughter of the English. But this account did not seem satisfactory to Smith, for he says in his condensation of White's narrative for his General History of Virginia: "And thus we left seeking our colony, that was never any of them found or seen to this day, 1622." This shows that Strachey's account was not known in 1609, when Smith had given up the search and returned to England.—Arber's edition, 1884, p. 331.

[2] Hawks, History of North Carolina, ii, 50.

English, and all, as I can understand, a very civilized people. This account is very vague and indefinite, and the numbers are largely overestimated; but it can refer to no other tribe than the Croatans. They were then living southwest of Pamlico Sound and they alone had had civilized influences to bear upon them.

The next reference to the tribe is more definite. John Lawson, the first historian of North Carolina, explored all the region southwest of Pamlico Sound. He was thoroughly acquainted with the Indians in those sections. In writing of the Roanoke settlements he says: A farther confirmation of this [the settlements of Raleigh] we have from the Hatteras (Croatan) Indians, who lived on Ronoack Island, or much frequented it. These tell us that several of their ancestors were white people and could talk in a book as we do; the truth of which is confirmed by gray eyes being frequently found amongst these Indians and no others. They value themselves extremely for their [Page 65] affinity to the English, and are ready to do them all friendly offices. It is probable that this settlement miscarried for want of timely supplies from England; or through the treachery of the natives, for we may reasonably suppose that the English were forced to cohabit with them for relief and conservation; and that in process of time they conformed themselves to the manners of their Indian relations; and thus we see how apt human nature is to degenerate."[1] Lawson wrote these words not later than 1709, as his book was first published in that year. It is impossible for the story told by him to be a tradition not founded on the truth, for he wrote within one hundred and twenty years of the original settlements at Roanoke, and he may have talked with men whose grandfathers had been among the original colonists.

The next witnesses in this chain of evidence are the early settlers in the Cape Fear section of North Carolina. Scotch settlements were made in Fayetteville as early as 1715.[2] In 1730 Scotchmen began to arrive in what is now Richmond County, and French Huguenots were at the same time pressing up from South Carolina. The universal tradition among the descendants of

---

3 Colonial Records of North Carolina, i, 603.

1 Lawson, History of North Carolina (ed. 1860), pp. 108, 109.

2 A house pulled down on Person Street, in Fayetteville, in 1889, fixes this date. This places the first settlements in this section at an earlier date than has been assigned them hitherto. (H. McMillan, in a letter to the writer.)

these settlers is that their ancestors found a large tribe of Indians located on Lumber River, in Robeson County, who were tilling the soil, owning slaves, and speaking English. The descendants of *this* tribe are known to be the Croatan Indians of to-day.

We see, then, that the historical arguments which tend to identify the Croatans of to-day as the descendants of the colonists of 1587 possess an historical continuity from 1591 to the present time. There is also a threefold internal argument based (1) on the traditions of the Croatan Indians of to-day; (2) from their character and disposition; (3) from their forms of language and family names.

I. *Traditions.*—The Croatan Indians believe themselves to be the descendants of the colonists of 1587, and boast of their mixed English and Indian blood. They always refer to eastern North Carolina as Virginia, and say their former home was in Roanoke, in Virginia, which means the present counties of Dare, Tyrrell, Hyde, Craven, Carteret, and Jones, and of this residence their traditions are sufficiently clear. They say that they held communication with the east long after their removal toward the west, and one of these parties may have met Lawson about 1709. They know that one of their leaders was made Lord of Roanoke and went to England, but his name has been lost, the nearest approach to it being in the forms Maino and Mainor. They have a word "mayno," which means a very quiet, law-abiding people; and this, by a kind of metonomy, may be a survival of Manteo. When an old chronicler was told the story of Virginia Dare he recognized it, but her name is preserved only as Darr, Durr, Dorr. They say that, according to their traditions, Mattamuskeet Lake, in Hyde County, is a burnt lake, and so it is; but they have no traditions in regard to Roanoke River. They say, also, that some of the earlier settlers intermarried with them, and this may explain the presence of such names among them as Chavis (Cheves), Goins (O'Guin), Leary (O'Leary).

[Page 66]II. *Character and disposition.*—These Indians are hospitable to strangers and are ever ready to do a favor for the white people. They show a fondness for gay colors, march in Indian file, live retired from highways, never forget a kindness, an injury, nor a debt. They are the best of friends and the most dangerous of enemies. They are reticent until their confidence is gained, and when aroused are perfect devils, exhibiting all the hatred, malice, cunning, and endurance of their Indian ancestors.[1] At the same time they are remarkably clean in their habits, a characteristic not found in the pure-blooded Indian. Physicians who practice among them say they never hesitate to sleep or eat in the house of a Croatan. They are also great road builders, something unknown to the savage. They have some of the best roads in the State, and by this means connect their more distant settlements with those on Lumber River. One of these, the Lowrie road, has been open for more than a hundred years, and is still in use. It extends southwest from Fayetteville, through Cumberland and Robeson counties, to a settlement on the Pee Dee. It was over this road that a special courier bore to General Jackson in 1815 the news of the treaty of Ghent.

---

[1] A fearful illustration of this spirit was shown in the career of Henry Berry Lowrie, "the great North Carolina bandit." In February, 1864, the Home Guard of Robeson County found Allen and William Lowrie, the father and brother of Henry Berry, guilty of receiving stolen goods, tried them by court-martial, and executed them under military law. The execution awakened the desire for revenge in the remaining brothers, and under the leadership of Henry Berry Lowrie they defied for ten years the authority of the county, the State, the Confederacy, and the United States. They killed the best men in the section, some for plunder, some for revenge, and some in self-defense. Henry Berry Lowrie was twenty-six at the time of his death, and in physique was a perfect Apollo. His countenance expressed the highest degree of firmness, courage, and decision of character. His forehead was high, broad, and massive; his eyes were a grayish hazel, his hair was straight and black, his chest was deep and broad; he was five feet ten inches high, weighed one hundred and fifty pounds, and was as elastic as rubber. He was always completely armed; in a belt he carried five long-range, six-barreled revolvers; a Henry rifle carrying sixteen cartridges was suspended at his back; a long knife and a double-barreled shotgun were found in his hands. His armament weighed not less than eighty pounds, but with it he could run, swim, bear weeks of exposure in the swamps, and travel by day and by night to an extent which would have killed a white man or negro. He slept on his arms, never seemed tired, and was never taken by surprise. During his long career of outlawry he was never untrue to a promise, never committed arson, nor insulted a white woman. A reward of ten thousand dollars was placed on his head; he was hunted by night and by day, but eluded all his pursuers, and perished on Feb. 20, 1872, from the accidental discharge of his gun. After the death of the chief the band lost much of the terror of its name, and two years later the last outlaw was slain. (*Cf.* The Lowrie History, as Acted in Part by Henry Berry Lowrie, the Great North Carolina Bandit, with Biographical Sketches of his Associates, by Mrs. Mary C. Norment, Wilmington, 1875. This book was written by Joseph B. McCallum; the chapter on the genealogy of the tribe is "notoriously unreliable"; it makes them all descendants of James Lowrie, who came to Robeson County from Virginia in 1769.)

III. *Language and Family Names.* The speech of the Croatans is very pure English; no classical terms are used. It differs from that of the whites and from that of the blacks among whom they live. They have preserved many forms in good use three hundred years ago, but which are now obsolete in the written language and are found only in colloquial and dialectical English. They drawl the penult or final syllable in every sentence. They begin their salutations with "mon-n-n," which means man. This seems to be frequently used much in the sense of the German *mann sagt,* or the French *on dit,* their traditions usually beginning: "Mon, my fayther told me that his fayther told him," etc. They retain the parasitic (glide) y, which was an extremely common development in Anglo-Saxon, in certain words through the palatal influence of the previous consonant, pronouncing cow as *cy*-ow, cart as *cy*-art, card as *cy*-ard, girl as *gy*-irl, kind as *ky*-ind. The voiceless form *wh*ing is retained instead of the voiced *w*ing. They have but two sounds for a, the short a being changed into o before nasals and representing Anglo-Saxon open o in mon. They use the northern lov*and* in place of the later hybrid loving. The Irish *fayther* is found for father. The dialectical [Page 67]*Jeans* is found in place of James. They regularly use *mon* for man; *mension* for measurement; *aks* for ask; *hit* for it; *hosen* for hose; *housen* for houses; *crone* is to push down and *wit* means knowledge.[1]

The strongest evidence of all is furnished us by the family names of the Croatan Indians of to-day. John White, in his account of the settlement of 1587, has left us "the names of all the men, women, and children which safely arrived in Virginia and remained to inhabit there." These settlers were one hundred and seventeen in number, and had ninety-five different surnames; out of these surnames forty-one, or more than forty-three per cent, including such names as Dare, Cooper, Stevens, Sampson, Harvie, Howe, Cage, Willes, Gramme, Viccars, Berry, Chapman, Lasie, and Chevin, which are now rarely met with in North Carolina, are reproduced by a tribe living hundreds of miles from Roanoke Island, and after a lapse of three hundred years.[2] The chroniclers of the tribe say that the Dares, the

---

1 The student of language will be interested in a paper on Early English Survivals on Hatteras Island, published by Prof. Collier Cobb, in which he points out the persistence of obsolete forms of speech still found among the "bankers" of the North Carolina coast and suggests that these people may themselves be connected with the Lost Colony.

2 Dr. Hawks reprints (History of North Carolina, i., 211, from Hakluyt) this list of names. Mr McMillan has compared it with the names of the Croatans, and, according to his authority,

Coopers, the Harvies, and others retained their purity of blood and were generally the pioneers in emigration. And still more remarkable evidence is furnished us by the fact that the traditions of every family bearing the name of one of the lost colonists point to Roanoke Island as the home of their ancestors.

TO SUMMARIZE: Smith and Strachey heard that the colonists of 1587 were still alive about 1607. They were then living on the peninsula of Dasamonguepeuk, whence they traveled toward the region of the Chowan and Roanoke Rivers. From this point they traveled toward the southwest and settled on the upper waters of the Neuse. John Lederer heard of them in this direction in 1670, and remarked on their beards, which were never worn by full-blooded Indians. Rev. John Blair heard of them in 1704. John Lawson met some of the Croatan Indians about 1709 and was told that their ancestors were white men. White settlers came into the middle section of North Carolina as early as 1715 and found the ancestors of the present tribe of Croatan Indians tilling the soil, holding slaves, and speaking English. The Croatans of to-day claim descent from the lost colony. Their habits, disposition, and mental characteristics show traces both of Indian and European ancestry. Their language is the English of three hundred years ago, and their names are in many cases the same as those borne by the original colonists. No other theory of their origin has been advanced, and it is confidently believed that the one here proposed is logically and historically the best, supported as it is both by external and internal evidence. If this theory is rejected, then the critic must explain in some other way the origin of a people which, after the lapse of three hundred years, show the characteristics, speak the language, and possess the family names of the second English colony planted in the western world.

[Page 68] *BIBLIOGRAPHY OF THE LOST COLONY.*

BAXTER, JAMES PHINNEY.—Raleigh's Lost Colony. New England Magazine, Jan., 1895, v, 565-587. ills.

BURNETT, SWAN M., M. D.—A note on the Melungeons. Amer. Anthropologist, Oct., 1889.

Also as separate, pp. 3.

---

those writer below in italics are now found among the Croatans. See p. 54.

COBB, COLLIER.—Early English Survivals on Hatteras Island. North Carolina Booklet, Oct., 1914, xiv, 91-99.

There are also various other earlier editions.

DROMGOOLE, Miss WILL ALLEN.—The Malungeons. Arena March, 1891. iii, 470-479. ill.

An unsympathetic article giving some account of their history, manners, and customs.

— The Malungeon tree and its four branches. Arena, May, 1891, iii, 745-751.

Historical and genealogical.

MCMILLAN, HAMILTON.—Sir Walter Raleigh's Lost Colony. An historical sketch of the attempts of Sir Walter Raleigh to establish a colony in Virginia with the traditions of an Indian tribe in North Carolina indicating the fate of the colony of Englishmen left on Roanoke Island in 1587. Wilson, N. C., 1888. D. pp. 29.

— Same. Revised edition. Raleigh [1907.]. O. pp. 46.

— The Croatans. North Carolina Booklet, Jan., 1911, x, 115-121.

MELTON, FRANCES JONES.—Croatans: the lost colony of America. Mid-Continent Magazine, July, 1895, vi, 195-202. ills.

NORMENT, Mrs. MARY C.—The Lowrie history. Wilmington, 1875. O. pp. 161.

Written by Joseph B. McCallum.

Reprinted in Charlotte (N. C.) Sunday Observer, March 19, 26, April 2, 9, 16, 23, 30, May 7, 14, 21, 28, June 4, 11, 1905.

— Another edition, Weldon, N. C., c. 1895. D. pp. 140.

— Another edition. Lumberton, N. C., 1909. pp. 192.

Contains article on the subject of the Croatans first published by Col. F. A. Olds about 1887.

PERRY, WM. STEVENS.—The first Christian born in Virginia. Iowa Churchman, Jan. and Feb., 1893.

TOWNSEND, GEORGE ALFRED (Gath). The Swamp Outlaws: or, the North Carolina bandits. New York [1872]. O. pp. [2]+]9]—84. ills.

A catch-penny reissue of letters sent to the New York Herald.

WEEKS, STEPHEN B.—Raleigh's Settlements on Roanoke Island. An historical survival. Magazine of American History, Feb., 1891, xxv, 127-139, 2 ills.

— The Lost Colony of Roanoke: Its fate and survival. Papers of the American Historical Association, 1891. v, 439-480.

— Same article reprinted as separate. New York, 1891. O. pp. 42.

— Same article summarized in Annual Report of American Historical Association, 1890, 97-98.

— Arguments of the article reprinted in Tom Watson's Jeffersonian Magazine, July, 1911, xiii, 192-201.

WILSON, E. Y.—Lost Colony of Roanoke. Canadian Magazine, April, 1895, iv, 500.

[Page 69] # EXHIBIT CCC

EXTRACT FROM HISTORY OF NORTH CAROLINA.

[By Samuel A'Court Ashe.]

CHAPTER I.

REFERENCES TO THE COLONY, 1591-1709.

Whereas as I wrote unto yow in my last that I was goun to Weymouth to speak with a pinnes of mine arrived from Virginia, I found this bearer, Captayne Gilbert, ther also, who went on the same voyage. But myne fell 40 leaugs to the west of it, and this bearer as much to the east; so as neither of them spake with the peopell. But I do sende both the barks away agayne, having saved the charg in sarsephraze woode; but this bearer bringing sume 2200 waight to Hampton, his adventurers have taken away their parts and brought it to London. I do therefore humblie pray yow to deal withe my Lord Admirale for a letter to make seasure of all that which is come to London, either by his Lordship's octoretye or by the Judge: because I have a patent that all shipps and goods are confiscate that shall trade their without my leve. And whereas Sassaphraze was worth 10s., 12s. and 20s. per pound before Gilbert returned, his cloying of the market, will overthrow all myne and his own also. He is contented to have all stayde: not only for this present; but being to go agayne, others will also go and destroy the trade, which otherwise would yield 8 or 10 for one, in certainty and a return in XX weeks. * * * Letter of Sir Walter Raleigh to Sir Robert Cecil. Aug. 21, 1602 Edwards' Life of Raleigh, II, 251.)

I beseich yow, favor our right: and yow shall see what a prety, honorabell and sauf trade wee will make.

Yours ever to serve yow,

W. RALEGH.

[William Strachey was secretary of the colony of Virginia, and his "Historie of Travaile into Virginia Britannia" was apparently written after the colony had been seated at Jamestown six years—in 1613.]

The men, women and children of the first plantation at Roanoke were by practize and commandment of Powhatan (he himself persuaded thereunto by his priests) miserably slaughtered, without any offense given him, either by the first planted (who twenty and od years had peaceably lyved intermyxed with those Savages and were out of his territory) or by those who nowe are come to inhabit some parte of his desarte lands. (1613. William Strachey's Travaile into Virginia, 85.)

[Page 70]Southward they [Newport's exploring party] went to some parts of Chowanook and the Mangoangs, to search there those left by Sir Walter Raleigh, which parts—to the towne of Chesepeak—hath formerly been discovered by Mr. Harriott and Sir Ralph Lane.

The high land is in all likelihoodes, a pleasant tract, and the mould fruitful, especially what may lye to the Southward, where at Peccarecamek and Ochanahoen by the relation of Machumps,[1] the people have houses built with stone walls, and one story above another, so taught them by the English who escaped the slaughter at Roanoke, at which time this our Colony, under the conduct of Captain Newport, landed within the Chesepeake Bay, where the people breed up tame turkeys about their houses, and take apes in the mountains, and where at Ritanoc the Weroance Eyanoco preserved seven of the English alive, four men, and two boys and one young mayde (who escaped and fled up the river of Choanook) to beat his copper, etc. (Strachey, 26.)

---

1 An Indian of Powhatan's tribe who had been to England.

[Powhatan] seems to command south and north from the Mangoangs and Chowanoaks, bordering upon Roanoke and the old Virginia, a town pallisadode standing at the north end of the bay. (Strachey, 48.)

He doth often send unto us to temporize with us, awaiting perhaps a fit opportunity (inflamed by his furious and bloody priests) to offer us a taste of the same cup which he made our poor countrymen drink of at Roanoke.

[In "The True and Sincere Declaration" made by the governor and councillors of the Jamestown settlement in December, 1609—they speak of having] intelligence of some of our nation planted by Sir Walter Raleigh, yet alive, within fifty miles of our fort, who can open the womb and bowels of this country; as is testified by two of our Colony sent out to seek them, who (though denied by the savages speech with them) found Crosses and Letters, the Characters and assured Testimonies of Christians, newly cut in the barks of trees. (Brown's Genesis, I, 349.)

[The discovery of these characters recently cut in the barks of trees at that time locates some of Raleigh's colony within fifty miles of Jamestown in 1608. The narrative continues:]

What he knew of the Dominions, he spared not to acquaint me with, as of certain men cloathed at a place called Ochanahonan, cloathed like me.

[And again:] We had agreed with the King of Paspehegh to conduct two of our men to a place called Panawicke, beyond Roanoke where he reported many men to be apparelled. We landed him at Warraskoyack, where playing the villain and deluding us for rewarde, returned within three or four days after, without going further.

[Smith sent from Warraskoyack, Master Scitlemore and two guides to seek for the Lost Colony of Sir Walter Raleigh. (Smith's True Relation.)

Alexander Brown has found and embodied in his work a rude drawing sent by Francis Nelson from Virginia in 1608 to illustrate Smith's "True Relation," and the same year sent to Spain from London. (Brown's Genesis, I, 184. February, 1608.)

[Page 71]On this map, on the Chowan, or on the Nottoway, falling into the Chowan River, Ochanahonan is placed: and on the Tar, or upper Pamlico River, "Pakrakanick" is located: and near it is a legend: "Here remayneth 4 men clothed that came from Roanoak to Ochanahonan." Between the Chowan and the Moratoc (Roanoke River) on this map is a legend: "Here the King of Paspehegh reported our men to be, and wants to go." And that region is marked "Pananiock."

On the map, the point Warraskoyack, from which Master Scitlemore and two guides started, and where Smith landed "the King of Paspehegh to conduct two of our men to a place called Panawicke, beyond Roanoke," is on a stream that probably is intended to represent Nansemond River. (December, 1608.)

This map was drawn on the relation of some Indian. The Indians of the James River had no connection with those farther south. Powhatan's jurisdiction did not extend over the Chowanists or the Mongoaks. The Indian who gave the information on which the drawing was based probably had but little familiarity with the localities, knowing about the rivers but nothing of the coast. He knew that the first river was the Chowan and its tributaries; that the next was the Moratoc, and that farther on there was a third—the Tar. He probably knew nothing of the sounds. He placed the chief town of the Chowan Indians on the northeast side of the Chowan River, and Ochanahonan on the other side. It seems to the author of this work that Ochanahonan is probably the town called by Lane Ohanoak. On DeBry's map this town is placed above the town of Chowanoak, but in Lane's narrative it is located below that town.

The Indian account places Pananiock, where White's colony settled, between the Moratoc and the Chowan rivers, but as the Indian was probably not acquainted with the waters of the sound, and only knew that the Moratoc discharged itself some distance below the Chowan, he inaccurately indicates that both emptied into the ocean. In that he was mistaken; but he probably was correct in locating the settlement north of the Moratoc River. It was between the mouth of the Moratoc and the Chowan that Lane observed the "goodly highlands," and that location being substantially "fifty miles in the interior" from Roanoke Island, it is there we would expect to find the place of permanent settlement. And it is there that the Indian relation places it.

After the massacre, "four men and two boys and one young mayde" escaped and fled up the river of Chowanoak, and were preserved by the Weroance at Ritanoe. This flight could have been readily made from a point north of the Moratoc River. It is also stated that four men came to Ochanahonan. If there were still other fugitives than those preserved at Ritanoe, their journey through the woods would also indicate that Pananiock was on the north of the Moratoc.]

LAWSON'S SUGGESTIONS.

The first discovery and settlement of this country was by the procurement of Sir Walter Raleigh, in conjunction with some public spirited gentlemen of that age, under the protection of Queen Elizabeth; for which reason it was then named Virginia, which begun on that part called Roanoke Island, where the ruins of a [Page 72] fort are to be seen at this day as well as some old English coins which have been lately found, and a brass gun, a powder horn and one small quarter-deck gun made of iron staves, which method of making guns might very probably be made use of in those days for the convenience of infant colonies. (Lawson's History of North Carolina, 108.)

A further confirmation of this we have from the Hatteras Indians who either then lived on Roanoke Island or much frequented it. These tell us that several of their ancestors were white people and could talk in a book as we do: the truth of which is confirmed by gray eyes being found frequently amongst these Indians and no others.

They value themselves extremely for their affinity to the English and are ready to do them all friendly offices. It is probable that this settlement miscarried for want of timely supplies from England, or through the treachery of the natives: for we may reasonably suppose that the English were forced to cohabit with them for relief and conversation: and that in process of time, they conformed themselves to the manners of their Indian relations; and thus we see how apt human nature is to degenerate.

THE HATTERAS INDIANS.

[The Hatteras Indians in 1585 were not under the same government as the savages on the mainland. They were a different tribe; and they were so few in numbers and so poor that when Lane was making a counterplot against Pemisapan and pretended that he was going to make a journey to Croatoan, he asked to be furnished with men to hunt for him while there, and with four days' provisions to last during his stay. No subsistence could be gotten from the Croatoans. A century later, in Lawson's time, that tribe had but sixteen fighting men, and even if all of these had a strain of English blood in them, their white ancestors might have been but a very small fraction of the English colonists. The tribe was still further reduced during the Indian War of 1711-15, when it adhered to the English. It lingered about its old home, suffering the fate of other small tribes, gradually becoming extinct. In 1763 some of the Hatteras and Mattamuskeet Indians were still living on the coast of Hyde, where a reservation had been set apart for them. Because names borne by some of the colonists have been found among a mixed race in Robeson County, now called Croatans, an inference has been drawn that there was some connection between them. (C. R., VI, 995.) It is highly improbable that English names would have been preserved among a tribe of savages beyond the second generation, there being no communication except with other savages. If English names had existed among the Hatteras Indians in Lawson's time, he probably would have mentioned it as additional evidence corroborating his suggestion deduced from some of them having gray eyes, and from their valuing themselves on their affinity to the English. It is also to be observed that nowhere among the Indians were found houses or tilled lands or other evidences of improvement on the customs and manners of the aborigines. When this mixed race was first observed by the early settlers of the upper Cape Fear, about 1735, it is said that they spoke English, [Page 73] cultivated land, lived in substantial houses, and otherwise practised the arts of civilized life, being in these respects different from any Indian tribe. In 1754 they were described as being on "Drowning Creek, on the head of Little Peedee, fifty families, a mixed crew, a lawless people, possessed the lands without patent or paying quit rents; shot a surveyor for coming to view vacant lands, being enclosed in great swamps." (C. R., V, 161.) From that time to the present these people have remained in their settlement on Drowning Creek. It is worthy of remark that in 1754 they were not considered Indians, for the military officers of Bladen County particularly reported that there were no Indians in that county. Whatever may have been their origin and the origin of their English names, neither their names nor their English manners and customs could have been perpetuated from the time of the Lost Colony without exciting some remark on the part of explorers, or historians. Apparently that community came into being at a later date. Yet it is to be observed that many persons believe them to be the descendants of the Lost Colony; and the Legislature has officially designated them as "Croatans," and has treated them as Indians.[1]]

---

[1] The subject of the connection of these Croatans with the colonists has been ably discussed by Mr. Hamilton McMillan and by Dr. Stephen B. Weeks, who maintain that view with much plausibility.

CHAPTER III.

LANE'S COLONY, 1585-86.

Lane's colony.—Arrival at Wokokon.—Secotan visited.—Aquascogoc burned by Grenville.—Disembarkation at Hattorask.—Settlement at Roanoke.—Fort Raleigh.—Explorations.—Manteo friendly.—Wanchese hostile.—The peril of famine.—Lane penetrates the Chowanoak; seizes Skyco; ascends the Moratoc.—Food exhausted.—The Indian conspiracy.—The hostiles gather at Dasamonquepeuc.—Lane strikes a blow and secures safety.—The arrival of Drake.—The departure of the colonists.—Arrival of Grenville's fleet.—Fifteen men left to hold possession.

THE FIRST COLONY.

Hastening to lay the foundations of a regal domain and with an eager anticipation of rich returns from his commercial dealings, Sir Walter now prepared a second expedition, which was to transport a hundred colonists for settlement in Virginia. Provisions were collected for a year's subsistence, by which time a new supply was to be furnished. The colonists were to be under the authority of Ralph Lane, as governor, who was chosen for this important post because he had already given the world assurance of his bravery, capacity, and resourcefulness. Among the enterprising men of that day he ranked high for energy, courage and versatile powers. Barlow, who, years before, had served with Raleigh in Flanders, was again to be with the party, and was to remain in Virginia as admiral; while Cavendish, afterward famous as a bold and skillful navigator, Thomas Hariot, highly distinguished as a mathematician and scientist, and John White, whose maps and admirable sketches, made in Virginia, are still extant, and who was deeply interested in the work of colonization, were likewise members of the company. At length, the preparations being completed, a fleet of seven vessels, all small, however, [Page 74] and capable of entering the inlets of the Virginia sounds, under the command of Sir Richard Grenville, a kinsman of Sir Walter Raleigh, and famous for his skill and bravery, set sail from Plymouth on April 9, 1585. After various adventures that caused delay, the fleet passed the Cape Fear on June 23d, and two days later came to anchor at Wokokon, now known as Ocracoke, southwest of Cape Hatteras. One of the vessels, under Captain Raymond, had, however, preceded the others, and having reached the vicinity twenty days earlier, had disembarked thirty-two men at Croatoan, a part of the sandbanks nearer the cape, that island also being called the "Admiral's Island," and Cape Hatteras itself was known as Cape Amadas.

EXPLORATION ON THE MAINLAND.

Some ten days were spent in examining the vicinity, and then, on July 11th, a considerable party embarked in four large boats, and taking provisions for eight days, passed over to the mainland, bordering on Pamlico Sound. They visited the Indian town of Pomeiok, and the great lake, Paquipe, and the town of Aquascogoc, and then Secotan, and explored the rivers of that region. During the expedition an Indian at Aquascogoc stole a silver cup from Sir Richard Grenville, and not restoring it, according to promise, Sir Richard went back from Secotan to that town for the purpose of regaining it; but the Indians had fled. So Sir Richard, to punish the theft, burned and spoiled their corn, which set those savages at enmity with the English.

Having gained some familiarity with those southern parts, the admiral weighed anchor, and turning the cape, reached Hattorask Inlet, having previously advised King Wingina at Roanoke Island of their coming. The colonists were accompanied by Manteo and Wanchese. The former had been strengthened in his friendship for the English, but the latter, whether because of apprehensions of their great power, which he had beheld in England, or because he belonged to that tribe on the Pamlico whose corn Sir Richard had destroyed, displayed an unfriendly disposition toward them. Arriving at Hattorask, the settlers disembarked on August 17th, and landed on Roanoke Island. Who now can enter fully into the feelings of those first adventurers, who in that summer time made their lodgment in the New World! The unknown country, the placid waters of the great sound, the delightful atmosphere and brilliant sunshine, and their difficult intercourse with the untutored savages who gathered around them—with their strange color, manners, and customs—and themselves so far removed from their distant homes—must have been constant subjects of reflection, mingling pleasure and apprehension, gratifying their spirit of adventure, and fostering hopes of personal reward, but ever startling them with the extreme novelty of their situation. A week after the landing Grenville took his departure, leaving the colonists established on Roanoke Island.

FORT RALEIGH ON ROANOKE ISLAND.

Lane at once began the erection of dwelling houses at a convenient point on the northern end of the island, and constructed a fort there, which he called Fort Raleigh; and from there excursions were made in every direction to get a better acquaintance with the country and [Page 75] its products. To the southward they went eighty miles to Secotan, that lay near the mouth of the Neuse; to the north they reached the Chesipeans, some fifteen miles inland from the head of Currituck Sound, and temporarily a small number of the English established themselves in that region. From these Indians, as well as from information derived from those on the Chowan, Lane learned that there was a larger and better harbor not far distant to the northward. On the west they penetrated to Chowanoak, a large Indian town on the Chowan River, and in that region they found an Indian sovereign, or Weroance, who ruled about eight hundred warriors, having subject to him eighteen towns. These towns, however, never consisted of more than thirty houses, and generally of only ten or twelve. The houses were made with small poles fastened at the top, the sides being covered with bark, and usually about twenty feet long, although some were forty and fifty feet, and were divided into separate rooms.

In these explorations the colonists ascended the various rivers emptying into the sound, and became familiar with the adjacent country. Hariot devoted himself to the study of the natural history of the region and wrote a valuable account of the animals, the vegetables, the plants, and the trees found there, and White made many sketches that are still preserved in the British Museum.

FAMINE THREATENS THE COLONISTS.

Among the savages, Ensinore, the old father of Wingina and Granganimeo, and Manteo were friendly with the white strangers; but the other chieftains were not favorable to them, although their bearing was not openly hostile. Granganimeo unfortunately died shortly after the arrival of the colonists, and upon that event Wingina, the king, according to some usage, took the name of Pemisapan, and as time passed he began to intrigue against the English, in which he was joined by Wanchese, Terraquine, Osacan, and other head men of the Indians. Relying on an additional supply of provisions by Easter, the colonists had been improvident, and by spring had exhausted their stock, and the planting time of vegetables and corn had hardly come when they found themselves without food. Their reliance now, temporarily at least, was on the corn of the Indians, and that was difficult to obtain. Their situation had become one of peril, especially as the Indians were reluctant to supply them. Pemisapan, understanding their difficulties, and at heart their enemy, now warily devised a plan for their destruction. He instilled into the Chowanists and into the Mangoaks, a strong and warlike tribe inhabiting the region on the Moratoc, or Roanoke River, that the English were their enemies; and then he informed Lane that the Mangoaks had much corn and that there were rich mines of gold and copper and other minerals in their country, and that they possessed stores of pearls and precious stones. This appealed strongly to Lane's cupidity, and he eventually determined to visit them, and applied to Pemisapan for guides, and three Indians besides Manteo were assigned to accompany him. So in March Lane set out on his expedition, taking the pinnace and two smaller boats, with some 50 or 60 men. He visited all the towns on the water's edge, and was especially pleased with some high land seen before reaching Chowanoak, subject to that king, where there was a goodly cornfield and a [Page 76] town called Ohanoak. Arriving at Chowanoak, he found a considerable assemblage there, the King Menatonon and his people being under apprehension that the English were enemies to them. Although Lane as a precautionary measure seized the person of the king and his young son, Skyco, he, nevertheless, was able to disarm their fears, and during a sojourn of two days with them obtained considerable information concerning the Mongoaks and their country, and also learned that by ascending the Chowan two days in a boat he would be within a four days' journey, by land, of a king's country that lay upon the sea. Obtaining some corn from Menatonon, and keeping Skyco as a hostage for further kindness, he sent the young Indian prince in the pinnace to the fort, and with the remaining boats and forty men pushed on up the Moratoc. His progress was slow, and he observed the difference between the strong current of that river and the sluggish waters of the great estuaries of the broad sound of Weapomeiok, as the country north of Albemarle Sound was then called.

EXPLORATION AND STARVATION.

The Mongoaks proved hostile, and when he had ascended the river two days, having progressed about thirty miles, they made an attack that was, however, easily repulsed. Then penetrating into the country, Lane found that the savages withdrew before him, removing all their corn and leaving nothing on which his men could subsist. His provisions being nearly out, he left it to the men to determine whether they should return or proceed; but they had two large mastiffs with them, and the men, declaring that the dogs prepared with sassafras would be good for two days' food, would not then abandon the expedition; and so they pushed on farther, but without any favorable result. At length, in danger of starvation, and their strength failing, they turned down stream, and in one day reached an island at the mouth of the river.

Their provisions now were entirely exhausted; but here, because of a heavy wind raising great billows in the sound, they were constrained to remain the whole of the next day. It was Easter eve; and Lane says they truly kept the fast. But Easter morn brought them new hope, and the storm ceasing, they entered the sound, and by four o'clock reached the Indian town of Chepanum (apparently on Durant's Neck, between Little and Perquimans rivers), which they found deserted; but fortunately there were fish in the weirs that furnished timely food; "for some of our company of the light-horsemen were far spent," those sailors who managed the canoes or light boats since called gigs being facetiously designated as "light-horsemen."

The next morning, refreshed and strengthened, they resumed their journey and returned to Roanoke in safety.

THE INDIANS BECOME HOSTILE.

In their absence, Pemisapan had stirred up the neighboring Indians to enmity against the remaining colonists, and hoping that his devices for the destruction of Lane's party had succeeded, he sought to strengthen the resolution of his followers by declaring that [Page 76a]
[Page 77] Lane and his party had either died of starvation or had been cut off by the Mongoaks. Ensinore, who had urged more friendly counsels, had unfortunately died toward the end of March, and there was now no influence to counteract Pemisapan's hostility; and urged by him, the

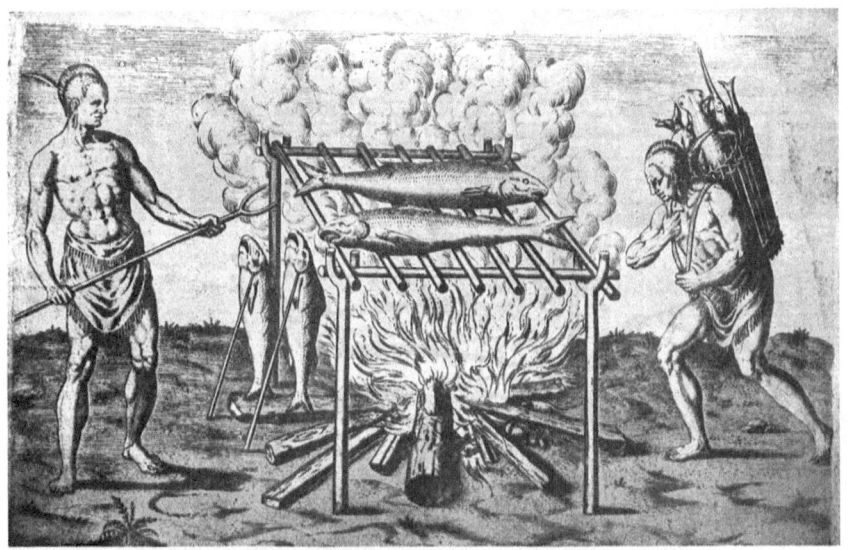

INDIANS COOKING FISH.

(From the John White drawings in Ashe's History of North Carolina.)

Indians would no longer render any assistance in the way of obtaining either fish or other food, and the situation of the colony was becoming extremely critical. The protracted absence of Lane's party added to their despondency, while it gave color to the report of their destruction. Such was the deplorable condition on the island when Lane's reappearance, contrary to the prophecies of his enemies, together with the accounts given by the Indians who had accompanied him of the ease with which he had overcome those Mongoaks who had fought him, caused a reaction in favor of the whites, and the Indians once more began to set weirs for them and aided them in planting corn, the planting season having now arrived. Still, until relief should come from England, or the crops just planted should mature, the colonists had to rely on such supplies as they could gather for themselves. In this extremity resort was had to the oyster beds found in the sound; and the better to subsist, the men were divided into small companies, and located at different points. Captain Stafford and twenty others were sent to Croatoan, where, while getting oysters, they could watch for the approach of the expected vessels bearing relief; at Hattorask a dozen more were stationed for the same purpose, while every week companies of fifteen or twenty were sent to the mainland to hunt for food. Thus they managed to exist through the month of May, waiting and watching in vain for the promised supplies from home.

In the meantime, Pemisapan, while preserving a friendly guise, began to plot anew against them, and instigated the hostile Indians to take the whites at a disadvantage, falling upon them while scattered and cutting them off in detail. To carry out this scheme he proposed to hold a great assembly of Indians, to last a month, by way of solemnizing the death of his father, Ensinore. This meeting was to be held on the mainland, at Desamonguepeuk, opposite Roanoke Island; and besides seven hundred neighboring warriors, it was to be attended by an equal number of the Mangoaks and Chesipeans, who were to come and lie secretly in the woods until the signal fires should give them the order to rise. As a part of the same plan, it was arranged that Terraquine, one of Pemisapan's chieftains, with twenty men, should set fire to the thatched roof of Lane's house, and when he should come out, they were to murder him. Another leader and squad were to deal with Hariot the same way; and, similarly, all of the principal men of the colony were to be surprised and overcome. Toward the end of May the neighboring Indians began to assemble on Roanoke Island, the night of June 10th being the time appointed for the others to meet and carry into effect the murderous plot.

Skyco, being the son of a king, on reaching the island had been taken by Pemisapan to reside with his own family, and as the young prince was held a prisoner and was deemed hostile to the English, the plot became known to him; but Lane had treated him with kindness and consideration, and the young boy in gratitude revealed to him all the details of the conspiracy. Confronted with such an emergency, Lane's strength of character and resolution promptly displayed [Page 78] itself. Had he been a weaker man, not so resourceful, the colonists would probably have fallen victims to Indian strategy.

LANE'S STRATEGY.

Pemisapan had gone over to the mainland, ostensibly to see about his growing corn crops, but really to attend to collecting the hostile Indians. Lane, realizing that safety could only be secured by the death of this wily foe and of his coadjutors, resolved on an immediate stroke. He sent him word to return to the island, for having heard of the arrival of his fleet at Croatoan, he himself proposed to go there; and he wished Pemisapan to detail some of his men to fish and hunt for him at Croatoan, and he also wanted to purchase four days' supply of corn to take with him. Pemisapan, however, did not fall into the trap; but while promising to come, postponed doing so from day to day, waiting for the assembling of the hostile Indians. At length, on the last of May, all of Pemisapan's own people having begun to congregate on the island, Lane determined to wait no longer. So that night he ordered "the master of the light-horsemen," as he termed his chief boatman, with a few others to gather up at sunset all the canoes in the island, so as to prevent any information being conveyed to the mainland. As the "light-horsemen" were performing this duty, they saw a canoe departing from the island, and in seizing it two of the savages were killed. This aroused the Indians who were present, and they at once took themselves to their bows and the Englishmen to their muskets. Some few of the savages were killed in the encounter and the others fled down the island. At dawn the next morning, with the "light-horsemen" and a canoe carrying twenty-five others, with the "colonel of the Chesipeans," and "the sergeant major," Lane hastened to the mainland, and sent word to Pemisapan that he was coming to visit him, as he was about to depart for Croatoan, and wished to complain of the conduct of Osacan, who the night before had tried to convey away the prisoner Skyco, whom he had there handcuffed. The Indian king, ignorant of what had happened on the island, and not suspecting any hostile purpose, received Lane and his attendants, who, coming up, found him surrounded by seven or eight of his principal Weroances, together with many other warriors.

As soon as they met, Lane gave the agreed signal, "Christ, our Victory," and immediately the colonel of the Chesipeans, the sergeant major, and their company opened fire, and Pemisapan and his chief men were slain and the others dispersed. A blow so sudden and terrible paralyzed the Indians; the plot was abandoned and the danger averted.

DRAKE ARRIVES AND THE COLONISTS RETURN TO ENGLAND.

A week later, on June 8th, the colony was thrown into an ecstasy of excitement by the hasty arrival of a messenger from Stafford, who reported seeing off Croatoan a fleet consisting of more than twenty vessels; but war had the year before broken out between Spain and England, and it was not at first known whether the ships belonged to friends or foes. The next day, however, Stafford himself came, having walked twenty miles by land, bringing a letter, proffering [Page 79] food and assistance, from Sir Francis Drake, then at Hattorask, who had just returned from sacking Santo Domingo, Cartagena and St. Augustine. With a joyful heart, Lane hastened to the fleet "riding at his bad harbor"; and Drake proposed to leave him a sufficient supply of provisions and a small vessel that could pass the inlet and lie within the sound. But before the necessary arrangements were completed a terrific storm came up that lasted three days, and the vessel which was to have been left was blown to sea and did not return; and much damage was done to the other ships of the fleet, and many pinnaces and smaller boats were entirely lost. After the storm had abated, Drake offered to leave another vessel, but he then had none that could enter the harbor; so the ship, if left, would have had to remain on the perilous coast. As an alternative proposition Drake offered to take the colonists aboard and transport them to England. After consideration, it was deemed best to accept this last offer, and the different companies into which the colony had been broken being again collected, they embarked on June 19th and safely reached Portsmouth on July 27th. Thus, after a nine months' residence, ended the first attempt to plant a colony on Roanoke Island.

In the meantime, a bark bearing advice that a new fleet was coming had been despatched from England, and somewhat later Sir Richard Grenville sailed with three vessels freighted with supplies and bringing other colonists. The first bark arrived immediately after the departure of Lane, and finding the settlement abandoned, returned to England; but when Sir Richard came, a fortnight later, he remained three weeks searching for the settlers and making explorations; and then putting fifteen men in the fort, with an ample supply of provisions, he sailed away on a cruise against the Spaniards.

CHAPTER IV.

WHITE'S COLONY, 1587-91.

Raleigh's embarrassments.—Conveys an interest in Virginia to Thomas Smith, John White, and associates.—The Citie of Raleigh in Virginia.—White's colony departs.—Howe murdered.—White despoils the fields of the hostiles.—Baptism of Manteo.—Birth and christening of Virginia Dare.—White returns to England.—The Armada.—White's first attempt to return to Virginia.—Raleigh makes further conveyance of his interest.—White sails in February, 1591.—Finds colony removed.—Mace's voyage.—Elizabeth dies.—Raleigh arrested for treason.—The settlement at Jamestown.—Fate of the Lost Colony.

RALEIGH'S EMBARRASSMENTS.

The unexpected return of Lane's colonists greatly disappointed Raleigh. His efforts at exploration and colonization had involved great expenditures. He had already disbursed forty thousand pounds in the enterprise, a sum approximating in this age half a million dollars, and that at a period when there was no great accumulation of wealth in England. He had now been at court some years and was a member of Parliament; and his fine powers and accomplishments, his versatility of genius and varied learning, commended him to the high favor of the queen, who gave substantial evidence of her inclination to push his fortunes. In 1584 she had bestowed on him a grant of [Page 80] twelve thousand acres of forfeited land in Munster, Ireland, which he attempted to colonize with English tenants and where he employed a large force in cutting timber for market, which, however, did not turn out a profitable enterprise. Also, beginning in the same year, he received annually for five years profitable grants allowing him to export quantities of broadcloth from England—a sort of monopoly; and he likewise obtained a lucrative monopoly in the grant of the "farm of wines," vesting in him the power of selling licenses for the vending of wine and, in some measure, of regulating the price of that commodity throughout the kingdom. Some months after Lane's return, on the attainder of Anthony Babbington, the queen was also pleased to bestow on Raleigh all of the estates that had come to the Crown by the attainder, which gave him rich manors and broad acres in five counties of England. In July, 1585, when the war broke out with Spain, he was created Lord Warden of the Stannaries (Cornwall and Devon) and Vice-Admiral of Cornwall and Devon; and two years later he was appointed captain of the Queen's Guard, the office of a courtier, to succeed Hatton, who was to become Lord Chancellor. But neither his outlays in Ireland nor his expenditures for Virginia had yielded him any return, while his living at court, where he indulged in magnificent display, involved large expenses.

THE CITIE OF RALEIGH IN VIRGINIA.

Such were his circumstances when Lane's colony returned to England in the fall of 1586. But unwilling to abandon the enterprise and still hoping for profit from establishing a trade in Virginia, he now determined to associate merchants with him who would share the profits and the expenses. At that time some of the wealthy merchants of London were looking with eager eyes for new avenues of trade and commerce. Chief among these was Thomas Smith, whose subsequent enterprises led to his receiving knighthood at the hands of his appreciative sovereign; and of their number was Richard Hakluyt, to whom posterity is indebted for the collection and publication of many narratives of exploration and discovery in that interesting period. To Smith and eighteen other merchants who risked their money in the enterprise Raleigh granted free trade forever with his colony in Virginia, and to thirteen others he assigned the right of governing the colony. Of these John White, who had been in all the previous expeditions to Virginia, was constituted the governor, and the other twelve, who also were to accompany the colony, were nominated his assistants; among them Ananias Dare and Dionysius Harvie, who carried their wives with them, and the former of whom was White's son-in-law. These thirteen Raleigh, by patent, under the powers contained in his own charter, on January 7, 1587, erected into a corporation under the name of "The Governor and Assistants of the Citie of Raleigh in Virginia"; and the nineteen merchants were made members, "free of the corporation."

A PERMANENT SETTLEMENT ATTEMPTED.

These preliminaries being arranged, a new colony was collected, consisting of one hundred and twenty-one persons, of whom seventeen were women, twelve apparently being wives accompanying their [Page 81] husbands, and nine being children. On April 26, 1587, three vessels bearing the colonists left Portsmouth for Plymouth; and on May 8th finally took their departure from that port for Hattorask, where, after many adventures, two of them arrived on July 22d, and a few days later the other. Raleigh had given written directions that after taking in the fifteen men left by Grenville the vessels were to proceed to Chesapeake Bay, where a new settlement was to be made, and such was the purpose of Governor White. But when White with a part of his men had left the ship to visit Roanoke Island for the purpose of taking off the fifteen men, Ferdinando, the admiral, influenced the sailors to say that they could not be received back into the ship, thus constraining all the colonists to disembark. At sunset White's boat reached the island, but the only trace he could find of the men left by Grenville was the bones of one that lay unburied where he had been slain. The fort had been razed down, but the cottages were still standing, some of the outer planks, however, being torn off. Forced to remain there, White set the men at once to work to repair the buildings and to construct others. The colonists had hardly gotten established in their new homes, when George Howe, one of the assistants, having strayed off two miles from the fort catching crabs on the shore opposite the mainland, was set upon by some savages, receiving sixteen wounds from arrows, and was slain. This was an evidence of hostility that White at once sought to allay. He sent Stafford with twenty men, accompanied by Manteo, who along with another Indian, Towaye, had gone to England and had now returned to Croatoan, where Manteo's mother and kindred were; and from these friendly Indians it was learned that some savages from the mainland had taken the men left by Grenville unawares, had killed some of them, set fire to the house where they had taken refuge, and driven them from the island; they taking their boat and going to an island near Hattorask, after which they had never been seen. They also said that it was a remnant of Wingina's men dwelling at Dasamonquepeuc who had slain Howe. To establish more amicable relations with these hostile Indians, the Croatoans were requested to go over to their towns and proffer them the friendship of the English, who promised to forgive and forget all past offences; and it was agreed that this embassy was to return with the answer within seven days. At the end of the time, no answers being received, White deemed it best to strike a blow to show that the colonists were to be dreaded. At night, accompanied by Stafford and twenty-four men and Manteo, he crossed over to Dasamonquepeuc and secreted his force near the Indian town; and early in the morning he opened fire on some Indians discovered there. Unfortunately, these were not the hostiles, who, fearing punishment for the murder of Howe, had fled, leaving their corn standing in the fields; but they were some of the Croatoans who had gone there to gather the corn. White, disappointed in his revenge, despoiled the fields and returned home. The colony being now settled, on August 13th a ceremony was performed at Roanoke that gave expression to the gratitude of Raleigh and the colony for the faithful and friendly services of Manteo.

By command of Sir Walter, the rite of baptism was administered to Manteo, and there was conferred on him the order of Knighthood; [Page 82] and he was created Lord of Roanoke and Dasamonguepeuk. And five days later another interesting event occurred, the birth of the first English child born in America. On August 18, 1587, Eleanor Dare, wife of Ananias Dare and a daughter of the governor, gave birth to a daughter, who the next Sunday was christened Virginia, because she was the first Christian born in the new country. A few days later, also, was born to Dionysius Harvie and his wife, Margery, a child, whose name, however, has not been preserved.

THE COLONISTS TO REMOVE INTO THE INTERIOR.

It was now discovered that certain other particular supplies were needed, as this was intended to be a permanent settlement; and there was consultation as to who should return with the fleet to obtain them. It was finally determined that White himself would answer the purpose best, and he agreed to go with the vessels back to England. But before his departure it was resolved that the colony should remove to some point about fifty miles in the interior; and it was agreed that they would, on departing from the island, leave some sign indicating their location; and if in distress, a cross would be the sign. It is probable that this point, fifty miles in the interior, where the colony was to locate, was the highland near Ohanoak, where there were goodly cornfields and pleasant surroundings.

At length, the fleet being ready to sail, on August 27th, after a month's sojourn with the colony, White embarked and departed for England. On the return voyage he met with many perilous adventures, but finally, about the middle of October, made land at Smerwick, on the west coast of Ireland, and in November reached Hampton. With him came to England still another Indian, who, accepting Christianity, was baptized at Bideford Church; but a year later died, and was interred there. When the colonists receded from White's view, as he left the shores of Virginia, they passed from the domain of history, and all we know is that misfortune and distress overtook them; and that they miserably perished, their sad fate being one of those deplorable sacrifices that have always attended the accomplishment of great human purposes.

CONDITIONS IN ENGLAND ON WHITE'S ARRIVAL.

On White's arrival, in November, 1587, seeking aid for the colony, doubtless the merchants and others who had ventured their means with Raleigh in this last attempt at colonization and trade in Virginia, were willing to respond; but there were rumors of the preparation in Spain of a great Armada to invade England, and an order had been issued forbidding the departure of any vessel from any English port. In that period of excitement and alarm, the necessities of the distant colonists were of less moment than the pressing matters at home. Still Raleigh, exerting his personal influence, obtained a license for two small vessels to sail, and on April 25, 1588, White departed with them from Bideford for Virginia. The captains, however, were more intent on a gainful voyage than on the relief of the colonists, and betook themselves to the hazardous business of making prizes. At length one of them, meeting with two ships of war, was after a bloody fight overcome and rifled, despoiled and disabled, and [Page 83]
 she returned to England within a month; and three weeks later, the other, equally badly served, came home without having completed the voyage. Soon afterward, the great Armada appeared, and Raleigh was among those who made havoc of the Spanish galleons in the "morris dance of death," that, beginning in the straits, lasted around the north of Scotland and on the coast of Ireland. Immediately on his return he was challenged to mortal combat by the queen's favorite, the handsome boy, Essex, and for a time retired to Ireland in seclusion. But soon all his powers and resources were employed in distressing Spanish commerce and in taking rich prizes, while England was again and again threatened with Spanish invasion. In the following March, 1589, because, perhaps, both of his [Page 84] public employments and of the greater facilities of the merchants to care for the colonists, he transferred his rights in Virginia by an assignment or lease to Thomas Smith, White and others, and relinquished his interest in the colony. What particular efforts these merchants made to relieve the planters are not recorded; but White afterward mentioned "having at sundry times been chargeable and troublesome to Sir Walter for the supplies and relief of the planters in Virginia." Because of the inhibition of the sailing of merchant ships from England, no opportunity presented for White to return to Virginia until early in 1591. He then ascertained that John Watts of London, merchant, was about to send three vessels to the West Indies; but when they were ready to depart, a general stay was again commanded of all

ships throughout England. Taking advantage of this circumstance, White applied to Sir Walter to obtain a special license for these vessels to sail, on condition that they would transport a convenient number of passengers with their furniture and necessaries to Virginia. The license was obtained by Raleigh, but the condition was not observed; and the only passenger they would take was White himself, and no provisions for the relief of the colonists.

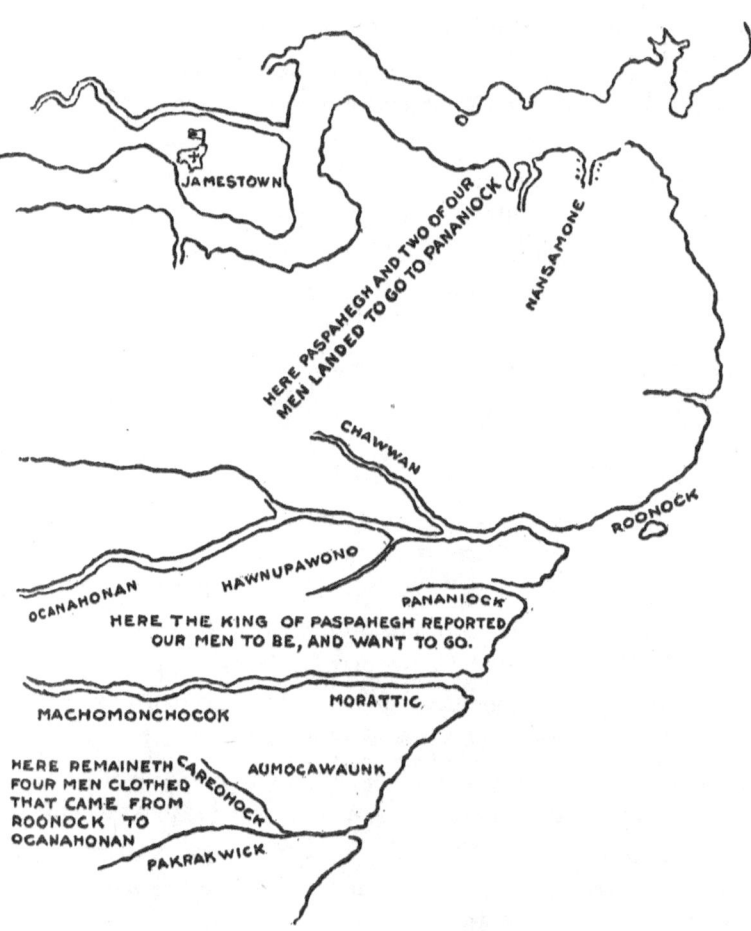

Map of the lost colony. From Ashe's History of North Carolina.

WHITE SAILS FOR ROANOKE.

Leaving Plymouth on March 20, 1591, they sailed for the West Indies and sought to make prizes, and had some desperate encounters. Eventually, on August 3d, they reached Wokokon, but were driven off by a storm. On Monday, the 9th, however, the weather being fair, they returned and anchored and went on shore, obtaining a supply of fresh water and catching great stores of fish. On the morning of the 12th they departed, and toward night dropped anchor at the north end of Croatoan. The next morning they sounded the inlet there, and then, on August 15th, came to anchor at Hattorask, seeing a great smoke on Roanoke Island. The next morning, after directing signal guns to be fired, to warn the colonists of their presence, they entered the inlet; but observing a great smoke toward the southwest, they landed and proceeded to it, only to meet with disappointment. Returning to their vessels, the morning following they set off again; but on passing the bar one of the boats was upset, and seven of the crew, including the captain, the mate and the surgeon, were drowned, and the remaining men protested against proceeding further. Distressing, indeed, was the situation of White and unpropitious the outlook of a journey begun with such a calamity. But at length the men reluctantly yielded and the boats proceeded to the island, arriving after night, anchoring off the shore and sounding a trumpet call and familiar tunes to evoke a response. But all in vain. No answer came, although in the distance a firelight was seen. At break of day they landed and hastened to the fire, finding no sign of the English. Then pressing across the island, they skirted along its western shore until they came to the north point near where the settlement had been. There on the shore they found a tree on which had been cut the Roman letters C. R. O. With despondent hearts they proceeded to the place of settlement, and saw that the houses had been taken down and the place strongly enclosed with a high palisade of great trees, very like a fort; and on a tree was cut the word "Croatoan," but without the cross or sign of distress. The boats [Page 85] were gone; the pieces of light ordnance had been taken away, only some of the heavier pieces remaining, and the fort was all grown up with grass and weeds, as if long since deserted. A trench in which White had buried his boxes had been opened and his maps and property scattered, and his armor lay on the ground, almost eaten through with rust. It was a scene of desolation. There was still a hope, yet it must have been but faint, that the colonists could be found at Croatoan. White had just sailed along that island and had anchored at its northern end and had beheld no sign of the presence of any English there. Returning to the inlet, it was, however, determined to go again to that island. But after they had weighed anchor, the design was relinquished; and one vessel returned to England and the other steered for the West Indies. From that time onward the English who settled in Virginia were known as Raleigh's Lost Colony. They were not forgotten, but were never discovered.

RALEIGH'S EFFORTS TO RELIEVE THE COLONY.

Greater enterprises now absorbed Raleigh, who had become one of the most heroic of that splendid company of heroes who brought lustre to the Elizabethan Age; but still, between 1587 and 1602, it is said that he sent out no less than five expeditions to seek his unfortunate company in Virginia. In 1602 he bought a ship, hired a crew, placed it under the command of Samuel Mace, who had twice before sailed for Virginia, and in March sent it forth to search for the colonists. Mace struck Virginia forty leagues southwest of Hatteras, and spent a month trading with the Indians as he scoured along the coast; but without going to Croatoan or Hattorask, he returned to Weymouth in August. Raleigh hastened there to meet him, and found in the same harbor another vessel likewise just arrived from Virginia, but which had missed Roanoke also, by forty leagues to the northward. He, however, proposed to send them both away again, having saved the cost in the sassafras they brought, which he claimed because of his ownership of the land under his patent, no one having the right, he asserted, to trade in Virginia except by his license. The next year Richard Hakluyt, one of the grantees in the charter of the City of Raleigh, formally applied to Sir Walter for permission to sail to northern Virginia; but in the spring of that year, 1603, Elizabeth died, and before the summer had passed Raleigh was arrested for treason.

JAMESTOWN SETTLED—THE ROANOKE COLONY DISAPPEARS.

In the meantime the spirit of enterprise which had been stimulated by Raleigh's efforts at colonization had grown, and Thomas Smith and a few other London merchants, in 1599, had laid the foundations of the East India Company, whose great success led, in 1606, to the formation of another corporation, called the Virginia Company, with two divisions, at the head of one division being Thomas Smith, now knighted, and other London merchants and gentlemen who had been associated with Raleigh in his enterprise; and on December 19, 1606, Christopher Newport set sail with one hundred and forty-three immigrants and, on May 13th, settled Jamestown. The next year Newport [Page 86] was directed to make an expedition to find Raleigh's Lost Colony.

THE FATE OF WHITE'S COLONISTS.

The colonists, warned by previous mishaps, certainly brought with them sufficient supplies to last until a crop would mature in the fall of 1588, and they did not neglect to begin their planting operations.

On his return White found no sign of any planting on Roanoke Island; nor was there evidence of any conflict with the savages—no graves, no butchery. The dwellings had been taken down and removed, and the light ordnance had been carried away. The growth of weeds indicated that two seasons had passed since the removal, and apparently the spot had not been revisited by the colonists in many months.

On his departure for England, the avowed intention was for the colonists to settle fifty miles in the interior; and when he coasted along Croatoan leisurely he observed no sign of their presence on the shore. Instead of establishing themselves on that barren sandbank, exposed to the attacks of the Spaniards, with no inviting streams, nor fertile fields, nor shady forests, they looked westward for a secure and agreeable location for their permanent settlement. Fifty miles would have brought them to the "goodly highlands, on the left hand between Muscamunge and Chowanoak," where the Indians already had fertile cornfields; and there, according to Indian statements of different sources, they appear to have seated themselves on what are now the pleasant bluffs of Bertie County.

Several vessels were at different times despatched to search for them; but none of these entered the great sounds. At length, after Jamestown was settled, Newport in 1608 was specially directed to make an exploration to discover them. An expedition by water did not proceed far and was without result. A searching party by land penetrated to the territory of the Chowanists and Mangoaks, but did not find the colonists.

Smith in his "True Relation" (1608) repeats information derived from the king of the Paspehegh Indians, who resided above Jamestown, to the effect that there were men apparelled like himself at Ochanahonan, which seems to have been on the Nottoway; and that there were many at Panawicke, a region apparently between the Chowan and Roanoke rivers. Five years later, William Strachey, the secretary of the Jamestown colony, gave some account of the missing colonists derived from Machumps, a friendly Indian of considerable intelligence, who had been to England and who came freely and often to Jamestown. At Peccarecamek and Ochanahonan, the Indians had houses built with stone walls, one story above another, having been taught by the English who escaped the slaughter at the time of the landing at Jamestown. And at Ritanoe there were preserved seven of the colonists, four men, two boys and a young maid, who having escaped, fled up the Chowan.

For more than twenty years the colonists were reported to have lived peaceably with the Indians and to have intermixed with them in their locality, beyond the territory of Powhatan; and then on the arrival of the colonists at Jamestown, Powhatan, persuaded by his bloody priests, procured their slaughter, he being present on the [Page 87] occasion. Some escaped; but none ever had communication with the Jamestown settlers.

Peccarecamek was apparently on the upper Pamlico, or Tar River; and perhaps a trace of English blood might be found in the aggressiveness and fierceness of the Indians of that region a century later.

TRACES OF THE COLONISTS.

If others were preserved on the sandbanks, as they might well have been, escaping in their pinnace through the waters of the sound, a trace of them possibly came down to posterity through their intermixture with the Hatteras Indians. That small tribe had always been friendly with the whites; and as late as 1709, grey eyes were found among them and they cherished a friendship with the English because of their affinity, according to their own traditions. Yet there were other opportunities for an admixture of the races. Thirty-two men of Captain Raymond's company were among them twenty days before the arrival of Lane's colony, and the following summer Captain Stafford and twenty men were with them until Drake came in June, and doubtless others were stationed there the next year to keep watch for the expected return of White, until all hope had expired. Other than these possible traces no memorial has ever been discovered of the existence of the Lost Colony, whose mournful fate, involved in mystery, has ever been a fruitful theme of song and story.

[Page 88] EXHIBIT D.

NOTES OF LEDERER'S TRAVELS IN NORTH CAROLINA AND COMMENTS BY DR. HAWKS.

[Reprinted from Hawks' History of North Carolina, Vol. 2.]

No. VII.

EXTRACTS FROM THE DISCOVERIES OF JOHN LEDERER.

In three several Marches from Virginia to the west of Carolina, and other parts of the Continent; begun in March, 1669, and ended in September, 1670. Collected and translated out of Latin from his discourse and writings, by Sir William Talbot, Baronet. Printed in London, in 1672. [Reprinted from a copy in the author's library.]

[John Lederer was a learned German, who lived in Virginia during the administration of Sir William Berkeley. Little was then known of the mountainous part of that State, or of what was beyond. Berkeley commissioned Lederer to make explorations, and accordingly he went upon three several expeditions. The first was from the head of York River due west to the Appalachian Mountains; the second was from the falls of James River, west and southwest, and brought him into North Carolina, through several of the counties of which he travelled; the third was from the falls of the Rappahannock, westward, to the mountains.

Certain Englishmen were appointed by Berkeley to accompany him; these, however, forsook him and turned back. Lederer proceeded, notwithstanding, alone; and on his return to Virginia (which, by the way, was never expected), met with insult and reproaches, instead of the cordial welcome to which he was entitled. For this he was indebted to his English companions who had forsaken him; and so active were they in creating a prejudice against him, that he was not safe among the people of Virginia, who had been told that the public taxes of that year had all been expended in his wanderings.

Under these circumstances he went into Maryland, and there succeeded finally in obtaining a hearing from the governor, Sir William Talbot, and in submitting his papers to him. The governor, though at first much prejudiced against the man by the stories he had heard, yet found him, as he says, "a modest, ingenious person, and a pretty scholar;" and Lederer vindicated himself "with so convincing reason and circumstance," as Talbot says, that he quite removed all unfavorable impressions, and the governor himself took the trouble to translate from the Latin and publish Lederer's account of his journeyings.

A map of his explorations accompanies Talbot's translation, and by the aid of that we have endeavored to trace, as well as we could, the German's wanderings within the present boundaries of North Carolina.]

[Page 89]The twentieth of May, 1670, one Major Harris and myself, with twenty Christian horse and five Indians, marched from the falls of James River, in Virginia, towards the Monakins; and on the two-and-twentieth were welcomed by them with volleys of shot. Near this village we observed a pyramid of stones piled up together, which, their priests told us, was the number of an Indian colony drawn out by lot from a neighbor country over-peopled, and led hither by one Monack, from whom they take the name of Monakin. Here inquiring the way to the mountains, an ancient man described, with a staff, two paths on the ground, one pointing to the *Mahocks*, and the other to the *Nahyssans*.

[Page 90][The Mahocks, from Lederer's map, would appear to have been living near the dividing line of Nelson and Albemarle counties, at the junction of the Rockfish with the James River. The locality of the Nahyssans appears, from Robert Morden's map of Carolina (1687), and also from Ogilby's, to have been west of the Mahocks, between them and the first range of the mountains.]

Ogilby's map of Carolina. From Hawks' History of North Carolina.

But my English companions, slighting the Indian's direction, shaped their course by the compass due west; and therefore it fell out with us, as it does with those land-crabs that, crawling backwards in a direct line, avoid not the trees that stand in their way, but climbing over their very tops come down again on the other side, and so, after a day's labor, gain not above two feet of ground. Thus we, obstinately pursuing a due west course, rode over steep and craggy cliffs [Page 91] which beat our horses quite off the hoof. In these mountains we wandered from the 25th of May till the 3d of June, finding very little sustenance for man or horse, for these places are destitute both of grain and herbage.

The third of June we came to the south branch of James River, which Major Harris, observing to run northwardly, vainly imagined to be an arm of the Lake of Canada, and was so transported with this fancy that he would have raised a pillar to the discovery, if the fear of the Mahock Indian and want of food had permitted him to stay. Here I moved to cross the river and march on; but the rest of the company were so weary of the enterprise, that, crying out, one and all, [Page 92] they would have offered violence to me, had I not been provided with a private commission from the Governor of Virginia to proceed, though the rest of the company should abandon me—the sight of which laid their fury.

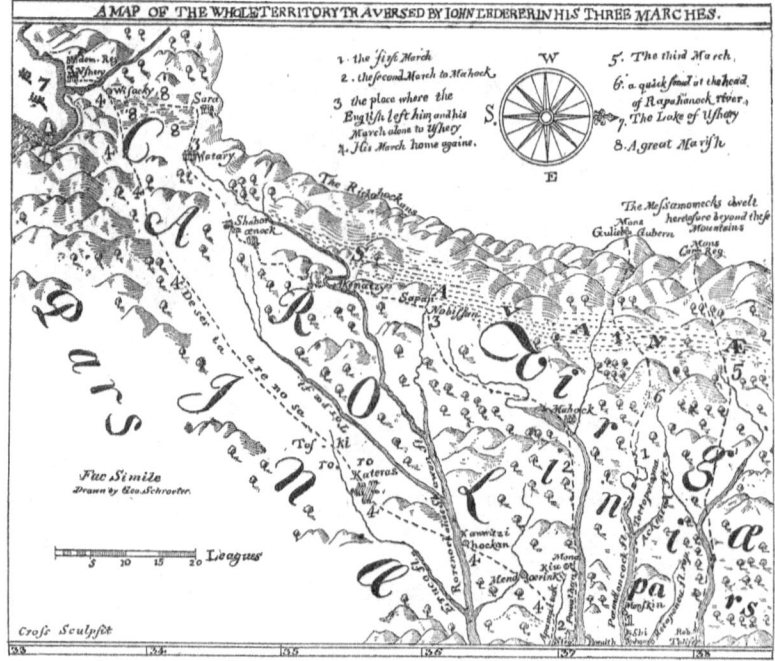

Lederer's map of Carolina, 1671. From Hawk's History of North Carolina.

The lesser hills, or *Akontshuck,* are here impassable, being both steep and craggy. The rocks seemed to me, at a distance, to resemble eggs set up on end.

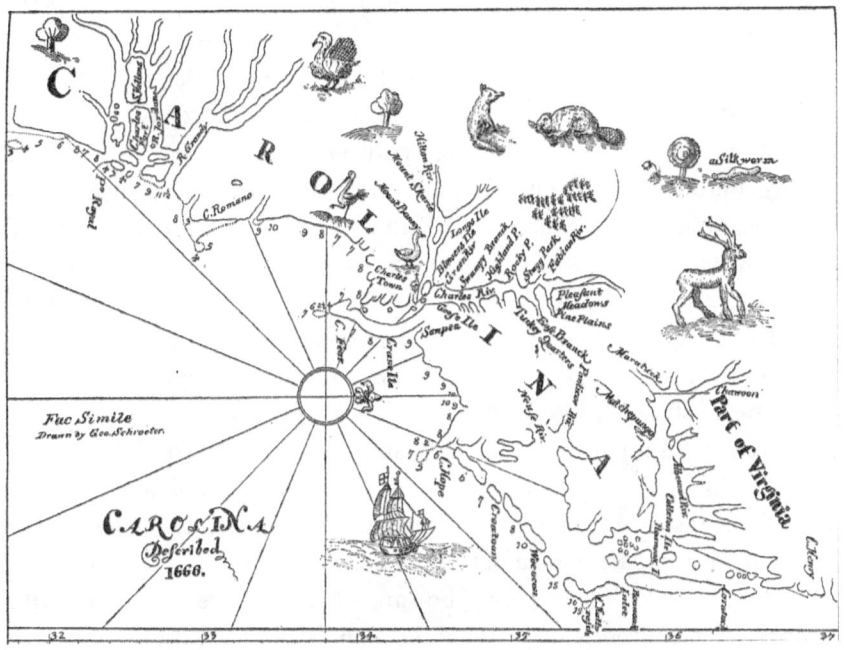

Horne's map of Carolina. From Hawks' History of North Carolina.

James River is here as broad as it is about a hundred miles lower, at Monakin; the passage over it is very dangerous by reason of the rapid torrents made by rocks and shelves forcing the water into narrow channels. From an observation which we made of straws and rotten chunks[1] hanging in the boughs of trees on the bank, and two-and-twenty feet above water, we argued that the melted snow falling from the mountains swelled the river to that height, the flood carrying down that rubbish which, upon the abatement of the inundation, remained in the trees.

---

1 This word is very generally used at the South, and means sometimes the end of small logs, partly burned, and then extinguished; and at others, as in this case, broken fragments of moderate size from decayed trees.

The air in these parts was so moist that all our biscuits became mouldy and unfit to be eaten, so that some nicer stomachs, who, at our setting out, laughed at my provision of Indian-meal parched, would gladly now have shared with me; but I being determined to go upon further discoveries, refused to part with any of that which was to be my most necessary sustenance.

The fifth of June, my company and I parted, good friends, they back again, and I, with one Susquehanna Indian, named Jackzetavon, only, in pursuit of my first enterprise, changing my course from west to southwest and by south to avoid the mountains. Major Harris, in parting, gave me a gun, believing me a lost man, and given up as a prey to Indians or savage beasts, which made him the bolder to report strange things in his own praise and my disparagement, presuming I would never appear to disprove him. This, I suppose, and no other, was the cause that he did with so much industry procure me discredit and odium; but I have lost nothing by it but what I never studied to gain, which is popular applause.

From the fifth, which was Sunday, until the ninth of June, I travelled through difficult ways, without seeing any town or Indian, and then I arrived at Sapon, a town of the Nahyssans, about a hundred miles distant from Mahock, situate upon a branch of *Shawan,* alias *Rorenock* River.

[By *Shawan,* Lederer means Chowan, which he here confounds with Roanoke. On Morden's map (1687), and on Ogilby's (1671), the Chowan is called *Rokahak,* while the Moratoc or Roanoke is called *Noratoke.* The Staunton and the Dan form the latter river, and it was probably on some of the tributaries of the first-named stream he struck, perhaps on the Staunton itself, just before its junction with the Dan. He had changed his course, as he tells us, to S. W. by S., to avoid the mountains, and the only streams to which this course would bring him are the Staunton and its northern tributaries.]

And though I had just cause to fear these Indians, because they had been in continual hostility with the Christians for ten years before, yet presuming that the truck which I carried with me would procure [Page 93] my welcome, I adventured to put myself into their power, having heard that they never offer any injury to a few persons, from whom they apprehend no danger; nevertheless they examined me strictly, whence I came, whither I went, and what my business was. But after I had bestowed some trifles of glass and metal amongst them, they were satisfied with reasonable answers, and I received with all imaginable demonstrations of kindness, as offering of sacrifice, a compliment showed only to such as they design particularly to honor; but they went further, and consulted their gods, whether they should not admit me into their nation and councils, and oblige me to stay among them by a marriage with the king's or some of their great men's daughters. But I, though with much ado, waived their courtesy, and got my passport, having given my word to return to them within six months.

Sapon is within the limits of the province of Carolina, and as you may perceive by the figure, has all the attributes requisite to a pleasant and advantageous seat; for, though it stands high and upon a dry land, it enjoys the benefit of a stately river and a rich soil, capable of producing many commodities, which may hereafter render the trade of it considerable.

[We must here remember that the dividing line between the present States of Virginia and Carolina was not then established as it is now recognized. From Lederer's map, it appears that all that part of Virginia lying south of James River, and extending as far westward as the Blue Ridge, was considered by him as part of Carolina, and is so designated on his map. Sapon, however, would appear from his map to have been in North Carolina, or just beyond the present boundary, in Virginia. Morden places it just south of the dividing line, in Carolina, on the upper waters of what we call the Roanoke. It was the chief town of the Nahyssans.]

Not far distant from hence, as I understood from the Nahyssan Indians, is their king's residence, called *Pintahœ*, upon the same river, and happy in the same advantages both for pleasure and profit, which my curiosity would have led me to see, were I not bound, both by oath and commission, to a direct pursuance of my intended purpose of discovering a passage to the further side of the mountains. This nation is governed by an absolute monarch; the people of a high stature, warlike, and rich. I saw great store of pearl unbored in their little temples or oratories, which they had won, amongst other spoils, from the Indians of Florida, and hold in as great esteem as we do.

From hence, by the Indians' instructions, I directed my course to *Akenatzy*, an island bearing south and by west, and about fifty miles distant, upon a branch of the same river, from Sapon.

[This island *Akenatzy* is possibly what is found on Lawson's map of 1709, under the name of *Aconeche*, in the Roanoke River.]

The country here, though high, is level, and for the most part a rich soil, as I judged by the growth of the trees; yet where it is inhabited by Indians it lies open in spacious plains, and is blessed with a very healthful air, as appears by the age and vigor of the people; and though I travelled in the month of June, the heat of the weather hindered me not from riding at all hours without any great annoyance from the sun. By easy journeys I landed at *Akenatzy* upon the twelfth of June. The current of the river is here so strong that my [Page 94] horse had much difficulty to resist it, and I expected every step to be carried away with the stream.

This island, though small, maintains many inhabitants, who are fixed here in great security, being naturally fortified with fastnesses of mountains, and water on every side. Upon the north shore they yearly reap great corps of corn, of which they always have a twelve-month's provision aforehand, against an invasion from their powerful neighbors. Their government is under two kings, one presiding in arms, the other in hunting and husbandry. They hold all things, except their wives, in common; and their custom in eating is, that every man, in his turn, feasts all the rest, and he that makes the entertainment is seated betwixt the two kings, when, having highly commended his own cheer, they carve and distribute it among the guests.

At my arrival here I met four stranger Indians, whose bodies were painted in various colors with figures of animals whose likeness I had never seen; and by some discourse and signs which passed between us, I gathered that they were the only survivors of fifty who set out together in company from some great island, as I conjecture, to the northwest; for I understood that they crossed a great water, in which most of their party perished by tempest, the rest dying in the marshes and mountains by famine and hard weather, after a two months' travel by land and water in quest of this island of *Akenatzy*.

The most reasonable conjecture that I can frame out of this relation is, that these Indians might come from the island of *New Albion* or *California*, from whence we may imagine some great arm of the Indian Ocean or bay stretches into the continent towards the *Apalatæan* Mountains in the nature of a midland sea, in which many of these Indians might have perished. To confirm my opinion in this point, I have heard several Indians testify that the nation of *Rickohockans*, who dwell not far to the westward of the *Apalatæan* Mountains, are seated upon a land, as they term it, of great waves—by which, I suppose, they mean the sea-shore.

[However reasonable this conjecture may have appeared at the time to Lederer, with such geographical knowledge as was then possessed, we think, if we mistake not the locality in which the German then was, a much more reasonable supposition can be formed by us at this day. He was on an island in the Roanoke River, and, as we think, in that part of the river that flows between Halifax and Northampton counties. The four Indians had probably come from the northeast or east, and the great water they crossed was nothing more than the Sound, for their whole journey had occupied a space of time much too short for a travel from any great body of water to the west or northwest. If, however, they came from the northwest, it must have been from the borders of the great lakes, which, we think, was the land of the *Rickohockans,* whom he mentions in the next paragraph as *distinct* from these four Indians. He entertained, it will be observed, an opinion very common at that day, that the Gulf of Mexico extended northwardly into the continent much further than it does, and he had a very imperfect conception of the entire breadth of the continent.]

The next day after my arrival at *Akenatzy,* a *Rickohockan* ambassador, attended by five Indians whose faces were colored with *auripigmentum* (in which mineral these parts do much abound), was [Page 95] received, and that night invited to a ball, of their fashion; but in the height of their mirth and dancing, by a smoke contrived for that purpose, the room was suddenly darkened, and, for what cause I know not, the Rickohockan and his retinue barbarously murdered. This struck me with such an affrightment, that the very next day, without taking my leave of them, I slunk away with my Indian companion. Though the desire of informing myself further concerning some minerals, as *auripigmentum,*&c., which I there took especial notice of, would have persuaded me to stay longer among them, had not the bloody example of their treachery to the Rickohockans frightened me away.

The fourteenth of June, pursuing a south southwest course, sometimes by a beaten path and sometimes over hills and rocks, I was forced to take up my quarters in the woods; for though the *Oenock* Indians, whom I then sought, were not, in a direct line, above thirty odd miles distant from *Akenatzy,* yet the ways were such, and obliged me to go so far about, that I reached not *Oenock* until the sixteenth.

[We are not without knowledge of the locality of the *Ohanoaks.* They were in the present county of Bertie, on its eastern side (see vol. i., p. 113). It would, therefore, seem that Lederer travelled down from Northampton, on the eastern side of the Roanoke into Bertie, towards the Chowan.]

The country here, by the industry of these Indians, is very open, and clear of wood. Their town is built round a field, where, in their sports, they exercise with so much labor and violence and in so great numbers, that

I have seen the ground wet with the sweat that dropped from their bodies. Their chief recreation is slinging of stones.

Fourteen miles west-southwest of the *Oenocks* dwell the *Shackory* Indians, upon a rich soil, and yet abounding in antimony, of which they showed me considerable quantities. Finding them agree with the *Oenocks* in customs and manners, I made no stay there, but passing through their town I travelled till the nineteenth of June, and then, after a two days' troublesome journey through thickets and marsh-grounds, I arrived at *Watary*, above forty miles distant, and bearing west-southwest to *Shakor*.

I departed from *Watary* the one-and-twentieth of June, and keeping a west course for near thirty miles I came to *Sara*. Here I found the ways more level and easy. I did likewise, to my no small admiration, find hard cakes of white salt among them; but whether they were made of sea-water or taken out of salt-pits I know not, but am apt to believe the latter, because the sea is so remote from them.

From *Sara* I kept a south-southwest course until the five-and-twentieth of June, and then I reached *Wisacky*. This three days' march was more troublesome to me than all my travels besides, for the direct way which I took from *Sara* to *Wisacky* is over a continued marsh overgrown with reeds, from whose roots spring knotty stumps, as hard and sharp as flint. I was forced to lead my horse most part of the way, and wonder that he was not either plunged in the bogs or lamed by those rugged knots.

This nation is subject to a neighbor king residing upon the bank of a great lake called *Ushery*, environed of all sides with mountains and *Wisacky* marsh.

The six-and-twentieth of June, having crossed a fresh river which runs into the lake of Ushery, I came to the town, which was more [Page 96] populous than any I had seen before in my march. The king dwells some three miles from it, and therefore I had no opportunity of seeing him the two nights which I stayed there. This prince, though his dominions are large and populous, is in continual fear of the *Oustack* Indians, seated on the opposite side of the lake, a people so addicted to arms that even their women come into the field and shoot arrows over their husbands' shoulders, who shield them with leathern targets.

The water of *Ushery* Lake seemed to my taste a little brackish, which I rather impute to some mineral waters which flow into it, than to any saltness it can take from the sea, which we may reasonably suppose is a great way from it. Many pleasant rivulets fall into it, and it is stored with great plenty of excellent fish. I judged it to be about ten leagues broad, for were not the other shore very high it could not be discerned from *Ushery*. How far this lake tends west-wardly, or where it ends, I could neither learn nor guess.

[It is difficult to determine what lake it is that Lederer calls *Ushery*; it was, however, in the midst of extensive swampy lands, or, as he terms them, marsh. We have such lands in Bertie, Martin, Beaufort, Washington, Tyrrel, and Hyde counties, and particularly in the three last named, where such lands, reclaimed, form some of our richest plantations. Was he somewhere in this region of swamp lands? The only lakes, however, of much importance are Lake Phelps and Matamuskeet Lake. If he were on the eastern side of the Roanoke, he could not have reached these without crossing the river, and yet his itinerary mentions no such crossing. Neither are we aided by the name he gives to the Indians on the opposite side of the lake: we know of no tribe called *Oustack* Indians. The nearest approach to it is *Newsiok,* on the waters of Neuse, and not on any lake. If, when he left the island *Akenatzy* in the Roanoke, he crossed to the *western* bank of the river, he might have found swampy lands in Martin, Beaufort, and Washington counties, supposing him to have been wandering towards *Hyde;* but how then would he have passed through the region of the *Ohanoaks,* which was certainly in Bertie? Beside, Matamuskeet, if that be the lake referred to, was not called *Ushery* by the natives. Its Indian name was *Paquipe*. If we suppose Lake Phelps to be meant, how shall we reconcile such a conjecture with the size he gives? Lake Phelps, we think, is not thirty miles broad. We believe him to have been somewhere in the region of marshy lands we have named; but as to Lake *Ushery,* we freely confess we cannot fix its locality. Col. Byrd says that the Indians living *on the Santee River* were called the Usheries.]

Here I made a day's stay to inform myself further in these countries; and understood both from the *Usheries* and some *Sara* Indians that came to trade with them, that two days' journey and a half from hence to the southwest, a powerful nation of bearded men were seated, which I suppose to be the Spaniards, because the Indians never have any, it being a universal custom among them to prevent their growth by plucking the young hair out by the roots.

[Lederer made his journey in 1669-70, and may be correct in supposing the bearded men to be Spaniards; but at that date there was a settlement of Englishmen that would answer the description here given. The settlers on the Cape Fear from Barbadoes commenced their colony in 1664, and these may have been the bearded men referred [Page 97] to. He is in error, however, as to the distance of the bearded men from the Indians. It was more than a journey of two days and a half.]

Not thinking fit to proceed further, the eight-and-twentieth of June I faced about and looked homewards. To avoid *Wisacky* marsh I shaped my course northeast; and after three days' travel over hilly ways, where I met with no path or road, I fell into a barren, sandy desert, where I suffered miserably for want of water,—the heat of summer having drunk all the springs dry, and left no sign of any, but the gravelly channels in which they run: so that if now and then I had not found a standing pool, which provident nature set round with shady oaks, to defend it from the ardor of the sun, my Indian companion, horse, and self had certainly perished with thirst. In this distress we travelled till the twelfth of July, and then found the head of a river, which afterwards proved *Eruco;* in which we received, not only the comfort of a necessary and seasonable refreshment, but likewise the hopes of coming into a country again, where we might find game for food at least, if not discover some new nation or people. Nor did our hopes fail us; for after we had crossed the river twice, we were led by it, upon the fourteenth of July, to the town of *Katearas,* a place of great Indian trade and commerce, and chief seat of the haughty emperor of the *Taskiroras,* called *Kaskusara,* vulgarly called *Kaskous.* His grim majesty, upon my first appearance, demanded my gun and shot, which I willingly parted with, to ransom myself out of his clutches; for he was the most proud, imperious barbarian that I met with in all my marches. The people here at this time seemed prepared for some extraordinary solemnity; for the men and the women of better sort had decked themselves very fine with pieces of bright copper in their hair and ears and about their arms and necks, which upon festival occasions they use as an extraordinary bravery: by which it would seem this country is not without rich mines of copper. But I durst not stay to inform myself in it, being jealous of some sudden mischief towards me from *Kaskous,* his nature being bloody, and provoked upon any slight occasion.

Therefore, leaving *Katearas,* I travelled through the woods until the sixteenth, upon which I came to *Kawitziokan,* an Indian town upon a branch of *Rorenoke* River, which here I passed over, continuing my journey to *Menchœrink;* and on the seventeenth departing from thence, I lay all night in the woods, and the next morning betimes going by *Natoway,* I reached that evening *Apamatuck,* in Virginia, where I was not a little overjoyed to see Christian faces again.

[From Lederer's account, the conjecture that seems most probable is, that taking a course southwest and by south from the falls of James River, he came upon the Roanoke in North Carolina, and crossed it at the island which he calls *Akenatzy,* if he crossed it at all. This island is between Halifax and Northampton, I apprehend. His wandering then took him into some of those counties where our swamp lands are most abundant, and he certainly was in Bertie, from which, pursuing a northeast course, he returned to Virginia, and crossing the Nottoway, proceeded to the Appomatox, which he followed to its junction with the James. The distances he gives, added together, after his entrance into North Carolina, would make his wanderings in our State some two hundred miles; and as he was among [Page 98] the *Ohanoaks* and *Tuscaroras,* he was certainly in Bertie. He, however, was not the first European who had seen that land. Eighty-five years before, the hardy adventurers under Lane had placed their feet upon it, though their inland explorations were much less extensive than those of Lederer. It is proper, however, to add, that from the localities he names, as they appear on Ogilby's map (1671), which we subjoin to this account, his wanderings would appear to have been much more extensive than we have made them. *Watery, Sara, Wisacki,* and *Ushery* would all appear to have been in South Carolina, the last directly west of Charleston. If he made this journey, then, entering the State somewhere in Warren county, he must have crossed it in a southwestern line, and passing through Robeson county into South Carolina, must have traversed that State also in its entire width. We cannot believe this. The time occupied would not have been sufficient for it. Lederer's itinerary presents difficulties which we confess we cannot satisfactorily solve.

On the map of Lederer, as well as on that of Ogilby, both of which we subjoin, the reader will perceive a river named *Torpœo.* This is erroneously made to empty into the Roanoke. A comparison of its position with other localities shows it to have been what is commonly, though improperly, called the *Tar* River. Its name is not Tar, though Col. Byrd called it by that name more than one hundred years ago. Others have supposed its original Indian name to be *Taw* or *Tau,* which Williamson, with his customary dogmatism, ignorantly states meant "Health." It never had such a meaning in any dialect of the Algonquin or Iroquois that we have met with—and these were the two mother languages of the Indians of the eastern side of

North Carolina—nor was there any such Indian word, as far as we can discover; though such a *syllable,* formed from an Indian word, is found in the composition of Indian words, according to the known polythinseticism of our Indian tongues. But the river was, notwithstanding, called *Taw,* for we find (as I am informed by a friend[1]) that name applied in a patent of 1729. Wheeler, Simms, Emmons, and Cook, all modern authorities, repudiating "Tar," call it "*Tau.*" Mr. Clark thinks that, from analogy, it should be written Taw, and cites the names H*aw,* Ca*taw*ba, Chicka*saw,* Cho*ctaw,* where the syllable terminates with *w.* But the fact is, that in the orthography of Indian names and words, it is important to know to what country the individual belonged who first wrote them down for the eye of civilized man; otherwise the pronunciation may be mistaken. For ourselves, while we are quite sure the river's true name never was Tar, we doubt whether Taw is the original word. Words of one syllable are exceedingly rare in the Indian languages, and especially in the names of *places.* They are almost invariably compounds. Its Indian name was *Torpœo,* and we think it should be so called now. Taw is but a corruption of the first syllable *Tor.* We have tried in vain to discover the meaning of the compound Tor-pæo.]

[Page 99] EXHIBIT E.

LAWSON'S HISTORY OF CAROLINA.

The history of Carolina; containing the exact description and natural history of that country; together with the present state thereof. And a journal of a thousand miles, travel'd thro' several nations of Indians, giving a particular account of their customs, manners, &c. By John Lawson, Gent. Surveyor-General of North Carolina. London: Printed for T. Warner, at the Black-Boy in Pater-Noster Row, 1718. Price bound five shillings.

MY LORDS, As Debts of Gratitude ought most punctually to be paid, so, where the Debtor is uncapable of Payment, Acknowledgments ought, at least, to be made. I cannot, in the least, pretend to retaliate *Your Lordships* Favours to me, but must farther intrude on that Goodness of which I have already had so good Experience, by laying these Sheets at *Your Lordships* Feet, where they beg Protection, as having nothing to recommend them, but Truth; a Gift which every Author may be Master of, if he will.

I here present *Your Lordships* with a Description of your own Country, for the most part, in her Natural Dress, and therefore less vitiated with Fraud and Luxury. A Country, whose Inhabitants may enjoy a Life of the greatest Ease and Satisfaction, and pass away their Hours in solid Contentment.

Those Charms of *Liberty* and *Right,* the Darlings of an *English* Nature, which *Your Lordships* grant and maintain, make you appear Noble Patrons in the Eyes of all Men, and we a happy People in a Foreign Country; which nothing less than Ingratitude and Baseness can make us disown.

As Heaven has been liberal in its Gifts, so are *Your Lordships* favourable Promoters of whatever may make us an easy People; which, I hope, *Your Lordships* will continue to us and our Posterity; and that we and they may always acknowledge such Favours, by banishing from among us every Principle which renders Men factious and unjust, which is the hearty Prayer of,

MY LORDS, *Your Lordships most obliged, most humble, and most devoted Servant,*

JOHN LAWSON.

PREFACE.

'TIS *a great Misfortune, that most of our Travellers, who go to this vast Continent in* America, *are Persons of the meaner Sort, and generally of a very slender Education; who being hir'd by the Merchants, to trade amongst the* Indians, *in which Voyages they often spend several Years, are yet, at their Return, uncapable of giving any reasonable Account of*[Page 100]*what they met withal in those remote Parts; tho' the Country abounds with Curiosities worthy a nice Observation. In this Point, I think, the* French *outstrip us.*

First, *By their Numerous Clergy, their Missionaries being obedient to their Superiors in the highest Degree, and that Obedience being one great Article of their Vow, and strictly observ'd amongst all their Orders.*

Secondly, *They always send abroad some of their Gentlemen in Company of the Missionaries, who, upon their Arrival, are order'd out into the Wilderness, to make Discoveries, and to acquaint themselves with the Savages of* America; *and are oblig'd to keep a strict Journal of all the Passages they meet withal, in order to present the same not only to their Governors and Fathers, but likewise to their Friends and Relations in* France; *which is industriously spread about that Kingdom, to their Advantage. For their Monarch being a very good Judge of Mens Deserts, does not often let Money or Interest make men of Parts give Place to others of less Worth. This breeds an Honourable Emulation amongst them, to outdo one another, even in Fatigues, and Dangers whereby they gain a good Correspondence with the* Indians, *and acquaint themselves with their Speech and Customs; and so make considerable Discoveries in a short time. Witness, their Journals from* Canada, *to the*

Missisipi, *and its several Branches, where they have effected great Matters, in a few Years.*

Having spent most of my time, during my eight Years Abode in Carolina, *in travelling; I not only survey'd the Sea-Coast and those Parts which are already inhabited by the Christians, but likewise view'd a spatious Tract of Land, lying betwixt the Inhabitants and the Ledges of Mountains, from whence our noblest Rivers have their Rise, running towards the Ocean, where they water as pleasant a Country as any in* Europe; *the Discovery of which being never yet made publick, I have, in the following Sheets, given you a faithful Account thereof, wherein I have laid down every thing with Impartiality, and Truth, which is indeed, the Duty of every* Author, *and preferable to a smooth stile, accompany'd with Falsities and Hyperboles.*

Great Part of this pleasant and healthful Country is inhabited by none but Savages, who covet a Christian Neighborhood, for the Advantage of Trade, and enjoy all the Comforts of Life, free from Care and Want.

But not to amuse my Readers any longer with the Encomium of Carolina, *I refer 'em to my* Journal, *and other more particular Description of that Country and its Inhabitants, which they will find after the* Natural History *thereof, in which I have been very exact, and for Method's sake, rang'd each Species under its distinct and proper Head.*

Friday.—The next day, we were preparing for our Voyage, and baked some Bread to take along with us. Our Landlord was King of the *Kadapau Indians,* and always kept two or three trading Girls in his Cabin. Offering one of these to some of our Company, who refused his Kindness, his Majesty flew into a violent Passion, to be thus slighted, telling the *Englishmen,* they were good for nothing. Our old Gamester, particularly, hung his Ears at the Proposal, having too lately been a Loser by that sort of Merchandize. It was observable, that we did not see one Partridge from the *Waterrees* to this place, tho' my Spaniel-Bitch, which I had with me in this Voyage, had put up a great many before.

[Page 101]*Saturday.*—On *Saturday* Morning, we all set out for *Sapona,* killing, in these Creeks, several Ducks of a strange Kind, having a red Circle about their Eyes, like some Pigeons that I have seen, a Top-knot reaching from the Crown of their Heads, almost to the middle of their Backs, and abundance of Feathers of pretty Shades and Colours. They prov'd excellent Meat. Likewise, here is good store of Woodcocks, not so big as those in *England,* the Feathers of the Breast being of a Carnation-Colour, exceeding ours for Delicacy of Food. The Marble here is of different Colours, some or other of the Rocks representing most Mixtures, but chiefly the white having black and blue Veins in it, and some that are red. This day, we met with seven heaps of Stones, being the Monuments of seven *Indians,* that were slain in that place by the *S'nnagers,* or *Troquois.* Our *Indian* Guide added a Stone to each heap. We took up our Lodgings near a Brook-side, where the *Virginia* Man's Horses got away; and went back to the *Kadapau's.*

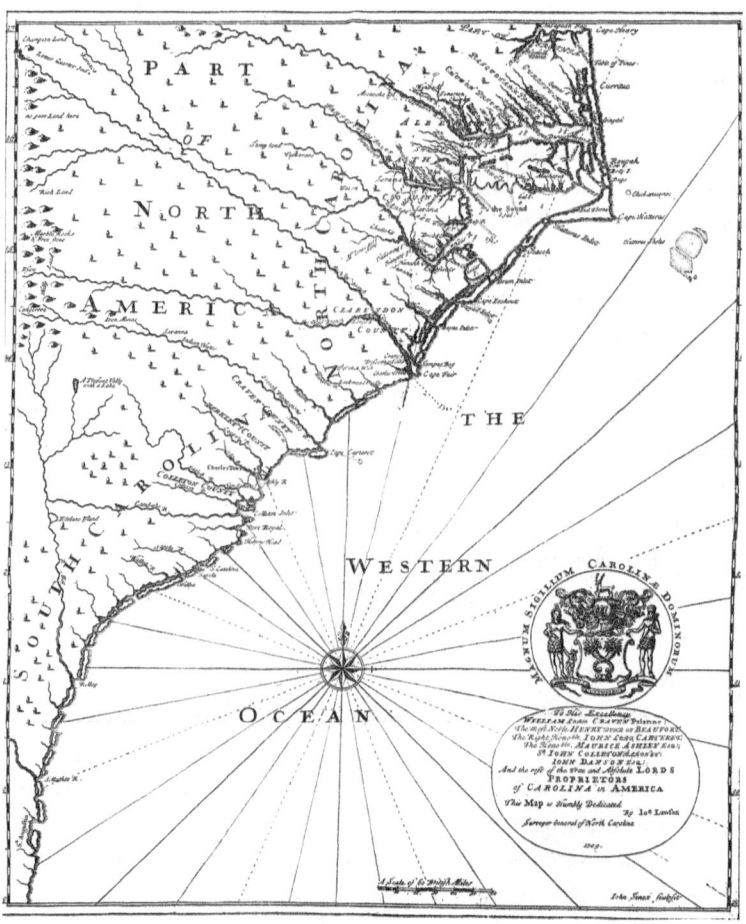

LAWSON'S MAP OF THE CAROLINAS.

Sunday.—This day, one of our Company, with a *Sapona Indian,* who attended *Stewart,* went back for the Horses. In the mean time, we went to shoot Pigeons, which were so numerous in these Parts, that you might see many

Millions in a Flock; they sometimes split off the Limbs of stout Oaks, and other Trees, upon which they roost o' Nights. You may find several *Indian* Towns, of not above 17 Houses, that have more than 100 Gallons of Pigeons Oil, or Fat; they using it with Pulse, or Bread, as we do Butter, and making the Ground as white as a sheet with their Dung. The *Indians* take a Light, and go among them in the Night, and bring away some thousands, killing them with long Poles, as they roost in the Trees. At this time of the Year, the Flocks, as they pass by, in great measure, obstruct the Light of the day.

Monday.—On *Monday*, we went about 25 Miles, travelling through a pleasant dry Country, and took up our Lodgings by a Hillside, that was one entire Rock, out of which gush'd out pleasant Fountains of well-tasted Water.

Tuesday.—The next day, still passing along such Land as we had done for many days before, which was, Hills and Vallies, about 10 a Clock we reach'd the Top of one of these Mountains, which yielded us a fine Prospect of a very level Country, holding so, on all sides, farther than we could discern. When we came to travel through it, we found it very stiff and rich, being a sort of Marl. This Valley afforded as large Timber as any I ever met withal, especially of Chesnut Oaks, which render it an excellent Country for raising great Herds of Swine. Indeed, were it cultivated, we might have good hopes of as pleasant and fertile a Valley, as any our *English* in *America* can afford. At Night, we lay by a swift Current, where we saw plenty of Turkies, but perch'd upon such lofty Oaks, that our Guns would not kill them, tho' we shot very often, and our Guns were very good. Some of our Company shot several times, at one Turkey, before he would fly away, the Pieces being loaded with large Gooseshot.

Wednesday.—Next Morning, we got our Breakfast; roasted Acorns being one of the Dishes. The *Indians* beat them into Meal, and thicken their Venison-Broth with them; and oftentimes make a palatable Soop. They are used instead of Bread, boiling them till the Oil swims on the top of the Water, which they preserve for use, [Page 102] eating the Acorns with Flesh-meat. We travell'd, this day, about 25 Miles, over pleasant *Savanna* Ground, high, and dry, having very few Trees upon it, and those standing at a great distance. The Land was very good, and free from Grubs or Underwood. A Man near *Sapona* may more easily clear 10 Acres of Ground, than in some places he can one; there being much loose Stone upon the Land, lying very convenient for making of dry Walls, or any other sort of durable Fence. This Country abounds likewise with curious bold Creeks, (navigable for small Craft) disgorging themselves into the main Rivers, that vent themselves into the Ocean. These Creeks are well stor'd with sundry sorts of Fish, and Fowl, and are very convenient for the Transportation of what Commodities this Place may produce. This Night, we had a great deal of Rain, with Thunder and Lightning.

Thursday.—Next Morning it proving delicate Weather, three of us separated ourselves from the Horses, and the rest of the Company, and went directly for *Sapona* Town. That day, we pass'd through a delicious Country, (none that I ever saw exceeds it.) We saw fine bladed Grass, six Foot high, along the Banks of these pleasant Rivulets: We pass'd by the Sepulchres of several slain *Indians.* Coming, that day, about 30 Miles, we reach'd the fertile and pleasant Banks of *Sapona* River, whereon stands the *Indian* Town and Fort. Nor could all *Europe* afford a pleasanter Stream, were it inhabited by *Christians,* and cultivated by ingenious Hands. These *Indians* live in a clear Field, about a Mile square, which they would have sold me; because I talked sometimes of coming into those Parts to live. This most pleasant River may be something broader than the *Thames* at *Kingston,* keeping a continual pleasant warbling Noise, with its reverberating on the bright Marble Rocks. It is beautified with a numerous Train of Swans, and other sorts of Water-Fowl, not common, though extraordinary pleasing to the Eye. The forward Spring welcom'd us with her innumerable Train of small Choristers, which nhabit those fair Banks; the Hills redoubling, and adding Sweetness to their melodious Tunes by their shrill Echoes. One side of the River is hemm'd in with mountainy Ground, the other side proving as rich a Soil to the Eye of a knowing Person with us, as any this Western World can afford. We took up our Quarters at the King's Cabin, who was a good Friend to the *English,* and had lost one of his Eyes in their Vindication. Being upon his march towards the *Appallache* Mountains, amongst a Nation of *Indians* in their Way, there happen'd a Difference, while they were measuring of Gunpowder; and the Powder, by accident, taking fire, blew out one of this King's Eyes, and did a great deal more mischief, upon the spot: Yet this *Sapona* King stood firmly to the *English* Man's Interest, with whom he was in Company, still siding with him against the *Indians.* They were intended for the *South Sea,* but were too much fatigued by the vast Ridge of Mountains, tho' they hit the right Passage; it being no less than five days Journey through a Ledge of Rocky Hills, and sandy Desarts. And which is yet worse, there is no Water, nor scarce a Bird to be seen, during your Passage over these barren Crags and Valleys. The *Sapona* River proves to be the *West* Branch of *Cape-Fair,* or *Clarendon* River, whose Inlet, with other Advantages, makes it appear as noble a River to plant a Colony in, as any I have met withal.

[Page 103] The *Saponas* had (about 10 days before we came thither) taken Five Prisoners of the *Sinnagers* or *Jennitos,* a Sort of People that range several thousands of Miles, making all Prey they lay their Hands on. These are fear'd by all the savage Nations I ever was among, the Westward *Indians* dreading their Approach. They are all forted in, and keep continual Spies and Out-Guards for their better Security. Those Captives they did intend to burn, few Prisoners of War escaping that Punishment. The Fire of Pitch-Pine being got ready, and a Feast appointed, which is solemnly kept at the time of their acting this Tragedy, the Sufferer has his Body stuck thick with Light-Wood-Splinters, which are lighted like so many Candles, the tortur'd Person dancing round a great Fire, till his Strength fails, and disables him from making them any farther Pastime. Most commonly, these Wretches behave themselves (in the Midst of their Tortures) with a great deal of Bravery and Resolution, esteeming it Satisfaction enough, to be assur'd, that the same Fate will befal some of their Tormentors, whensoever they fall into the Hands of their Nation. More of this you will have in the other Sheets.

The *Toteros,* a neighbouring Nation, came down from the Westward Mountains, to the *Saponas,* desiring them to give them those Prisoners into their Hands, to the Intent they might send them back into their own Nation, being bound in Gratitude to be serviceable to the *Sinnagers,* since not long ago, those Northern-*Indians* had taken some of the *Toteros* Prisoners, and done them no Harm, but treated them civilly whilst among them, sending them, with Safety, back to their own People, and affirming, that it would be the best Method to preserve Peace on all Sides. At that, time these *Toteros, Saponas,* and the *Keyauwees,* 3 small Nations, were going to live together, by which they thought they should strengthen themselves, and become formidable to their Enemies. The Reasons offer'd by the *Toteros* being heard, the *Sapona* King, with the Consent of his Counsellors, deliver'd the *Sinnagers* up to the *Toteros,* to conduct them home.

Friday Morning, the old King having shew'd us 2 of his Horses, that were as fat, as if they had belong'd to the *Dutch* Troopers, left us, and went to look after his Bever-Traps, there being abundance of those amphibious Animals in this River, and the Creeks adjoining. Taken with the Pleasantness of the Place, we walk'd along the River-side, where we found a very delightful island, made by the River, and a Branch; there being several such Plots of Ground environ'd with this Silver Stream, which are fit Pastures for Sheep, and free from any offensive Vermin. Nor can any thing be desired by a contented Mind, as to a pleasant Situation, but what may here be found; Every Step presenting some new Object, which still adds Invitation to the Traveller in these Parts. Our *Indian* King and his Wife entertain'd us very respectfully.

Saturday. Jan. 31.—On *Saturday,* the *Indians* brought in some Swans, and Geese, which we had our Share of. One of their Doctors took me to his Cabin, and shew'd me a great Quantity of medicinal Drugs, the Produce of those Parts; Relating their Qualities as to the Emunctories they work'd by, and what great Maladies he had heal'd by them. This Evening, came to us the Horses, with the Remainder of our Company, their *Indian* Guide (who was a Youth of this Nation) [Page 104] having kill'd in their Way, a very fat Doe, Part of which they brought to us.

Sunday.—This day, the King sent out all his able Hunters, to kill Game for a great Feast, that was to be kept at their Departure, from the Town, which they offer'd to sell me for a small matter. That Piece of Ground, with a little Trouble, would make an *Englishman* a most curious Settlement, containing above a Mile square of rich Land. This Evening, came down some *Toteros,* tall, likely Men, having great Plenty of Buffelos, Elks, and Bears, with other sort of Deer amongst them, which strong Food makes large, robust Bodies. Enquiring of them, if they never got any of the *Bezoar* Stone, and giving them a Description how it was found, the *Indians* told me, they had great plenty of it; and ask'd me, What use I could make of it? I answer'd them, That the white Men us'd it in Physick, and that I would buy some of them, if they would get it against I came that way again. Thereupon, one of them pull'd out a Leather-Pouch, wherein was some of it in Powder; he was a notable Hunter, and affirm'd to me, That that Powder, blown into the Eyes, strengthen'd the Sight and Brain exceedingly, that being the most common Use they made of it. I bought, for 2 or 3 Flints, a large Peach-Loaf, made up with a pleasant sort of Seed; and this did us a singular Kindness, in our Journey. Near the Town, within their clear'd Land, are several *Bagnios,* or Sweating-Houses, made of Stone, in Shape like a large Oven. These they make much Use of; especially, for any Pains in the Joints, got by Cold, or Travelling. At Night, as we lay in our Beds, there arose the most violent N. W. Wind I ever knew. The first Puff blew down all the *Palisadoes* that fortify'd the Town; and I thought it would have blown us all into the River, together with the Houses. Our one-ey'd King, who pretends much to the Art of Conjuration, ran out in the most violent Hurry, and in the Middle of the Town, fell to his Necromantick Practice; tho' I thought he would have been blown away or kill'd, before the *Devil* and he could have exchang'd half a dozen Words; but in two Minutes, the Wind was ceas'd, and it became as great a Calm, as I ever knew in my Life. As I much admir'd at that sudden Alteration, the old Man told me, the *Devil* was very angry, and had done thus, because they had not put the *Sinnagers* to Death.

On *Monday* Morning, our whole Company, with the Horses, set out from the *Sapona-Indian* Town, after having seen some of the Locust, which is gotten thereabouts, the same Sort that bears Honey. Going over several Creeks, very convenient for Water-Mills, about 8 Miles from the Town, we pass'd over a very pretty River, call'd Rocky River, a fit Name, having a Ridge of high Mountains running from its Banks, to the Eastward; and disgorging itself into *Sapona*-River; so that there is a most pleasant and convenient Neck of Land, betwixt both Rivers, lying upon a Point, where many thousand Acres may be fenced in, without much Cost or Labour. You can scarce go a Mile, without meeting with one of these small swift Currents, here being no Swamps to be found, but pleasant, dry Roads all over the Country. The Way that we went this day, was as full of Stones, as any which *Craven*, in the West of *Yorkshire*, could afford, and having nothing but *Moggisons* on my Feet, I was so lam'd by this stony Way, that I thought I must have taken up some Stay in those Parts. We went, this day, not above 15 or 20 [Page 105] Miles. After we had supp'd, and all lay down to sleep, there came a Wolf close to the Fire-side, where we lay. My Spaniel soon discover'd him, at which, one of our Company fir'd a Gun at the Beast; but, I believe, there was a Mistake in the loading of it, for it did him no Harm. The Wolf stay'd till he had almost loaded again, but the Bitch making a great Noise, at last left us and went aside. We had no sooner laid down, but he approach'd us again, yet was more shy, so that we could not get a Shot at him.

Tuesday.—Next day, we had 15 Miles farther to the *Keyauwees*. The Land is more mountainous, but extremely pleasant, and an excellent Place for the breeding Sheep, Goats, and Horses; or Mules, if the *English* were once brought to the Experience of the Usefulness of those Creatures. The Valleys are here very rich. At Noon, we pass'd over such another stony River, as that eight Miles from *Sapona*. This is call'd *Heighwaree,* and affords as good blue Stone for Mill-Stones, as that from *Cologn,* good Rags, some Hones, and large Pebbles, in great abundance, besides Free-Stone of several Sorts, all very useful. I knew one of these Hones made use of by an Acquaintance of mine, and it prov'd rather better than any from *Old Spain,* or elsewhere. The Veins of Marble are very large and curious on this River, and the Banks thereof.

Five Miles from this River, to the N. W. stands the *Keyauwees* Town. They are fortify'd in, with wooden Puncheons, like *Sapona,* being a People much of the same Number. Nature hath so fortify'd this Town, with Mountains, that were it a Seat of War, it might easily be made impregnable; having large Corn-Fields joining to their Cabins, and a *Savanna* near the Town, at the Foot of these Mountains, that is capable of keeping some hundred Heads of Cattle. And all this environ'd round with very high Mountains, so that no hard Wind ever troubles these Inhabitants. Those high Clifts have no Grass growing on them, and very few Trees, which are very short, and stand at a great Distance one from another. The Earth is of a red Colour, and seems to me to be wholly design'd by Nature for the Production of Minerals, being of too hot a Quality, to suffer any Verdure upon its Surface. These *Indians* make use of Lead-Ore, to paint their Faces withal, which they get in the neighbouring Mountains. As for the refining of Metals, the *Indians* are wholly ignorant of it, being content with the *Realgar.* But if it be my Chance, once more to visit these Hilly Parts, I shall make a longer Stay amongst them: For were a good Vein of Lead found out, and work'd by an ingenious Hand, it might be of no small Advantage to the Undertaker, there being great Convenience for smelting, either by Bellows or Reverberation; and the Working of these Mines might discover some that are much richer.

At the Top of one of these Mountains, is a Cave that 100 Men may sit very conveniently to dine in; whether natural, or artificial, I could not learn. There is a fine Bole between this Place, and the *Saps.* These Valleys thus hemm'd in with Mountains, would (doubtless) prove a good place for propagating some sort of Fruits, that our Easterly Winds commonly blast. The Vine could not mis of thriving well here; but we of the Northern Climate are neither Artists, nor curious, in propagating that pleasant and profitable Vegetable. Near the Town, is such another Current, as *Heighwaree.* We being six in Company, divided ourselves into Two Parties; and it was my [Page 106] Lot to be at the House of *Keyavwees Jack,* who is King of that People. He is a *Congree-Indian,* and ran away when he was a Boy. He got this Government by Marriage with the Queen; the Female Issue carrying the Heritage, for fear of Impostors; the Savages well knowing, how much Frailty possesses the *Indian* Women, betwixt the Garters and the Girdle.

Wednesday.—The next day, having some occasion to write, the *Indian* King, who saw me, believ'd that he could write as well as I. Whereupon, I wrote a Word, and gave it him to copy, which he did with more Exactness, than any *European* could have done, that was illiterate. It was so well, that he who could read mine, might have done the same by his. Afterwards, he took great Delight in making Fish-hooks of his own Invention, which would have been a good Piece for an Antiquary to have puzzled his Brains withal, in tracing out the Characters of all the Oriental Tongues. He sent for several *Indians* to his Cabin, to look at his Handy-work, and both he and they thought, I could read his Writing as well as I could my own. I had a Manual in my Pocket, that had King *David's* Picture in it, in one of his private Retirements. The *Indian* ask'd me, Who that Figure represented? I told him, It was the Picture of a good King, that liv'd according to the Rules of Morality, doing to all as he would be done by, ordering all his Life to the Service of the Creator of all things; and being now above us all, in Heaven, with God Almighty, who had rewarded him with all the delightful Pleasures imaginable in the other World, for his Obedience to him in this; I concluded, with telling them, that we received nothing here below, as Food, Raiment, *&c.* but what came from that Omnipotent Being. They listned to my Discourse with a profound Silence, assuring me, that they believ'd what I said to be true. No Man living will ever be able to make these *Heathens* sensible of the Happiness of a future State, except he now and then mentions some lively carnal Representation, which may quicken their Apprehensions, and make them thirst after such a gainful Exchange; for, were the best Lecture that ever was preach'd by Man, given to an ignorant sort of People, in a more learned Style, than their mean Capacities are able to understand, the Intent would prove ineffectual, and the Hearers would be left in a greater Labyrinth than their Teacher found them in. But dispense the Precepts of our Faith according to the Pupil's Capacity, and there is nothing in our Religion, but what an indifferent Reason is, in some measure, able to comprehend; tho' a *New-England* Minister blames the *French* Jesuits for this way of Proceeding, as being quite contrary to a true Christian Practice, and affirms it to be no ready, or true Method, to establish a lively Representation of our Christian Belief amongst these Infidels.

All the *Indians* hereabouts carefully preserve the Bones of the Flesh they eat, and burn them, as being of Opinion, that if they omitted that Custom, the Game would leave their Country, and they should not be able to maintain themselves by their Hunting. Most of these *Indians* wear Mustachoes, or Whiskers, which is rare; by reason the *Indians* are a People that commonly pull the Hair of their Faces, and other Parts, up by the Roots, and suffer none to grow. Here is plenty of Chesnuts, which are rarely found in *Carolina,* and never near the Sea, or Salt-Water; tho' they are frequently in such Places in *Virginia.*

[Page 107] At the other House, where our Fellow Travellers lay, they had provided a Dish, in great Fashion amongst the *Indians,* which was Two young Fawns, taken out of the Doe's Bellies, and boil'd in the same slimy Bags Nature had plac'd them in, and one of the Country-Hares, stew'd with the Guts in her Belly, and her Skin with the Hair on. This new-fashion'd Cookery wrought Abstinence in our Fellow-Travellers, which I somewhat wonder'd at, because one of them made nothing of eating *Allegators,* as heartily as if it had been Pork and Turneps. The *Indians* dress most things after the Wood-cock Fashion, never taking the Guts out. At the House we lay at, there was very good Entertainment of Venison, Turkies, and Bears; and which is customary amongst the *Indians,* the Queen had a Daughter by a former Husband, who was the beautifullest *Indian* I ever saw, and had an Air of Majesty with her, quite contrary to the general Carriage of the *Indians.* She was very kind to the *English,* during our Abode, as well as her Father and Mother.

Thursday.—This Morning, most of our Company having some Inclination to go straight away for *Virginia,* when they left this Place; I and one more took our leaves of them, resolving (with God's Leave) to see *North-Carolina,* one of the *Indians* setting us in our way. The rest being indifferent which way they went, desired us, by all means, to leave a Letter for them, at the *Achonechy-*Town. The *Indian* that put us in our Path, had been a Prisoner amongst the *Sinnagers;* but had out-run them, although they had cut his Toes, and half his Feet away, which is a Practice common amongst them. They first raise the Skin, then cut away half the Feet, and so wrap the Skin over the Stumps, and make a present Cure of the Wounds. This commonly disables them from making their Escape, they being not so good Travellers as before, and the Impression of their Half-Feet making it easy to trace them. However, this Fellow was got clear of them, but had little Heart to go far from home, and carry'd always a Case of Pistols in his Girdle, besides a Cutlass, and a Fuzee. Leaving the rest of our Company at the *Indian-*Town, we travell'd, that day, about 20 Miles, in very cold, frosty Weather; and pass'd over two pretty Rivers, something bigger than *Heighwaree*, but not quite so stony. We took these two Rivers to make one of the Northward Branches of *Cape-Fair* River, but afterwards found our Mistake.

Friday.—The next day, we travell'd over very good Land, but full of Free-Stone, and Marble, which pinch'd our Feet severely. We took up our Quarters in a sort of *Savanna*-Ground, that had very few Trees in it. The Land was good, and had several Quarries of Stone, but not loose, as the others us'd to be.

Saturday.—Next Morning, we got out Breakfasts of Parch'd Corn, having nothing but that to subsist on for above 100 Miles. All the Pine-Trees were vanish'd, for we had seen none for two days. We pass'd through a delicate rich Soil this day; no great Hills, but pretty Risings, and Levels, which made a beautiful Country. We likewise pass'd over three Rivers this day; the first about the bigness of *Rocky* River, the other not much differing in Size. Then we made not the least Question, but we had pass'd over the North-West Branch of *Cape-Fair*, travelling that day above 30 Miles. We were much taken with the Fertility and Pleasantness of the Neck of Land between these two Branches, and no less pleas'd, that we had pass'd the River, which us'd to frighten Passengers from fording it. At last, determining [Page 108] to rest on the other side of a Hill, which we saw before us; when we were on the Top thereof, there appear'd to us such another delicious, rapid Stream, as that of *Sapona*, having large Stones, about the bigness of an ordinary House lying up and down the River. As the Wind blew very cold at N.W. and we were very weary, and hungry, the Swiftness of the Current gave us some cause to fear; but, at last, we concluded to venture over that Night. Accordingly, we stripp'd, and with great Difficulty, (by God's Assistance) got safe to the North-side of the famous *Hau*-River, by some called *Rearkin;* the *Indians* differing in the Names of Places, according to their several Nations. It is call'd *Hau*-River, from the *Sissipahau Indians,* who dwell upon this Stream, which is one of the main Branches of *Cape-Fair*, there being rich Land enough to contain some Thousands of Families; for which Reason, I hope, in a short time, it will be planted. This River is much such another as *Sapona;* both seeming to run a vast way up the Country. Here is plenty of good Timber, and especially, of a Scaly-bark'd Oak; And as there is Stone enough in both Rivers, and the Land is extraordinary Rich, no Man that will be content within the Bounds of Reason, can have any grounds to dislike it. And they that are otherwise, are the best Neighbours, when farthest off.

Sunday.—As soon as it was day, we set out for the *Achonechy*-Town, it being, by Estimation, 20 Miles off, which, I believe, is pretty exact. We were got about half way, (meeting great Gangs of Turkies) when we saw, at a Distance, 30 loaded Horses, coming on the Road, with four or five Men, on other Jades, driving them. We charg'd our Piece, and went up to them: Enquiring, whence they came from? They told us, from *Virginia*. The leading Man's Name was *Massey*, who was born about *Leeds* in *Yorkshire*. He ask'd, from whence we came? We told him. Then he ask'd again, Whether we wanted any thing that he had? telling us, we should be welcome to it. We accepted Two Wheaten Biskets, and a little Ammunition. He advised us, by all means, to strike down the Country for *Ronoack*, and not think of *Virginia*, because of the *Sinnagers*, of whom they were afraid, tho' so well arm'd, and numerous. They persuaded us also, to call upon one *Enoe Will*, as we went to *Adshusheer*, for that he would conduct us safe among the *English*, giving him the Character of a very faithful *Indian*, which we afterwards found true by Experience. The *Virginia*-Men asking our Opinion of the Country we were then in? we told them, it was a very pleasant one. They were all of the same Opinion, and affirm'd, That they had never seen 20 Miles of such extraordinary rich Land, lying all together, like that betwixt *Hau*-River and the *Achonechy* Town. Having taken our Leaves of each other, we set forward; and the Country, thro' which we pass'd, was so delightful, that it gave us a great deal of Satisfaction. About Three a Clock, we reach'd the Town, and the *Indians* presently brought us good fat Bear, and Venison, which was very acceptable at that time. Their Cabins were hung with a good sort of Tapestry, as fat Bear, and barbakued or dried Venison; no *Indians* having greater Plenty of Provisions than these. The Savages do, indeed, still possess the Flower of *Carolina*, the *English* enjoying only the Fag-end of that fine Country. We had not been in the Town 2 Hours, when *Enoe-Will* came into the King's Cabin; which was our Quarters. We ask'd him, if he would conduct us to [Page 109] the *English*, and what he would have for his Pains; he answer'd, he would go along with us, and for what he was to have, he left that to our Discretion.

Monday.—The next Morning, we set out, with *Enoe- Will*, towards *Adshusheer*, leaving the *Virginia* Path, and striking more to the Eastward, for *Ronoack*. Several *Indians* were in our Company belonging to *Will's* Nation, who are the *Shoccories*, mixt with the *Enoe-Indians*, and those of the Nation of *Adshusheer*. *Enoe-Will* is their chief Man, and rules as far as the Banks of *Reatkin*. It was a sad stony Way to *Adshusheer*. We went over a small River by *Achonechy*, and in this 14 Miles, through several other Streams, which empty themselves into the Branches of *Cape-Fair*. The stony Way made me quite lame; so that I was an Hour or two behind the rest; but honest *Will* would not leave me, but bid me welcome when we came to his House, feasting us with hot Bread, and Bears-Oil; which is wholsome Food for Travellers. There runs a pretty Rivulet by this Town. Near the Plantation, I saw a prodigious overgrown Pine-Tree, having not seen any of that Sort of Timber for above 125 Miles: They brought us 2 Cocks, and pulled their larger Feathers off, never plucking the lesser, but singeing them off. I took one of these Fowls in my Hand, to make it cleaner than the *Indian* had, pulling out his Guts and Liver, which I laid in a Bason; notwithstanding which, he kept such a Struggling for a considerable time, that I had much ado to hold him in my Hands. The *Indians* laugh'd at me, and told me, that *Enoe- Will* had taken a Cock of an *Indian* that was not at home, and the Fowl was designed for another Use. I conjectur'd, that he was design'd for an Offering to their God, who, they say, hurts them, (which is the Devil.) In this Struggling, he bled afresh, and there issued out of his Body more Blood than commonly such Creatures afford. Notwithstanding all this, we cook'd him, and eat him; and if he was design'd for him, cheated the Devil. The *Indians* keep many Cocks, but seldom above one Hen, using very often such wicked Sacrifices, as I mistrusted this Fowl was designed for.

Our Guide and Landlord *Enoe-Will* was of the best and most agreeable Temper that ever I met with in an *Indian*, being always ready to serve the *English*, not out of Gain, but real Affection; which makes him apprehensive of being poison'd by some wicked *Indians*, and was therefore very earnest with me, to promise him to revenge his Death, if it should so happen. He brought some of his chief Men into his Cabin, and 2 of them having a Drum, and a Rattle, sung by us, as we lay in Bed, and struck up their Musick to serenade and welcome us to their Town. And tho' at last, we fell asleep, yet they continu'd their Consort till Morning. These *Indians* are fortify'd in, as the former, and are much addicted to a Sport they call *Chenco*, which is carry'd on with a Staff and a Bowl made of Stone, which they trundle upon a smooth Place, like a Bowling-Green, made for that Purpose, as I have mention'd before.

Tuesday.—Next Morning, we set out, with our Guide, and several other *Indians,* who intended to go to the *English,* and buy Rum. We design'd for 'a

Nation about 40 Miles from *Adshusheer*, call'd the Lower Quarter: The first Night, we lay in a rich *Perkoson*, or low Ground, that was hard-by a Creek, and good dry Land.

[Page 110] *Wednesday.*—The next day, we went over several Tracts of rich Land, but mix'd with Pines and other indifferent Soil. In our way, there stood a great Stone about the Size of a large Oven, and hollow; this the *Indians* took great Notice of, putting some Tobacco into the Concavity, and spitting after it. I ask'd them the Reason of their so doing, but they made me no Answer. In the Evening, we pass'd over a pleasant Rivulet, with a fine gravelly Bottom, having come over such another that Morning. On the other side of this River, we found the *Indian* Town, which was a Parcel of nasty smoaky Holes, much like the *Waterrees;* their Town having a great Swamp running directly through the Middle thereof. The Land here begins to abate of its Height, and has some few Swamps. Most of these *Indians* have but one Eye; but what Mischance or Quarrel has bereav'd them of the other I could not learn. They were not so free to us, as most of the other *Indians* had been; Victuals being somewhat scarce among them. However, we got enough to satisfy our Appetites. I saw, among these Men, very long Arrows, headed with Pieces of Glass, which they had broken from Bottles. They had shap'd them neatly, like the Head of a Dart; but which way they did it, I can't tell. We had not been at this Town above an Hour, when two of our Company, that had bought a Mare of *John Stewart*, came up to us, having receiv'd a Letter by one of *Will's Indians*, who was very cautious, and asked a great many Questions, to certifie him of the Person, e'er he would deliver the Letter. They had left the Trader, and one that came from *South-Carolina* with us, to go to *Virginia;* these Two being resolved to go to *Carolina* with us.

Thursday.—This Day fell much Rain, so we staid at the *Indian* Town.

Friday.—This Morning, we set out early, being four *English*-Men, besides several *Indians*. We went 10 Miles, and were then stopp'd by the Freshes of *Enoe*-River, which had rais'd it so high, that we could not pass over, till it was fallen. I enquir'd of my Guide, Where this River disgorg'd it self? He said, It was *Enoe*-River, and run into a Place call'd *Enoe*-Bay, near his Country, which he left when he was a Boy; by which I perceiv'd, he was one of the *Cores* by Birth: This being a Branch of *Neus*-River.

Saturday.—This Day, our Fellow-Traveller's Mare ran away from him; wherefore, *Will* went back as far as the lower Quarter, and brought her back.

Sunday.—The next Day, early, came two *Tuskeruro Indians* to the other side of the River, but could not get over. They talk'd much to us, but we understood them not. In the Afternoon, *Will* came with the Mare, and had some Discourse with them; they told him, The *English*, to whom he was going, were very wicked People; and, That they threatned the *Indians* for Hunting near their Plantations. These Two Fellows were going among the *Schoccores* and *Achonechy Indians*, to sell their Wooden Bowls and Ladles for Raw-Skins, which they make great Advantage of, hating that any of these Westward *Indians* should have any Commerce with the *English*, which would prove a Hinderance to their Gains. Their Stories deterr'd an Old *Indian* and his Son, from going any farther; but *Will* told us, Nothing they had said should frighten him, he believing them to be a couple of Hog-stealers; and that the *English* only sought Restitution of their Losses, by them; and that this was the [Page 111] only ground for their Report. *Will* had a Slave, a *Sissipahau-Indian* by Nation, who killed us several Turkies, and other Game, on which we feasted.

Monday.—This River is near as large as *Reatkin*; the South-side having curious Tracts of good Land, the Banks high, and Stone-Quarries. The *Tuskeruros* being come to us, we ventur'd over the River, which we found to be a strong Current, and the Water about Breast-high. However, we all got safe to the North-Shore, which is but poor, white, sandy Land, and bears no Timber, but small shrubby Oaks. We went about 10 Miles, and sat down at the Falls of a large Creek, where lay mighty Rocks, the Water making a strange Noise, as if a great many Water-Mills were going at once. I take this to be the Falls of *Neus*-Creek, called by the *Indians, Wee quo Whom*. We lay here all Night. My Guide *Will* desiring to see the Book that I had about me, I lent it him; and as he soon found the Picture of King *David*, he asked me several Questions concerning the Book, and Picture, which I resolv'd him, and invited him to become a Christian. He made me a very sharp Reply, assuring me, That he lov'd the *English* extraordinary well, and did believe their Ways to be very good for those that had already practis'd them, and had been brought up therein; But as for himself, he was too much in Years to think of a Change, esteeming it not proper for Old People to admit of such an alteration. However, he told me, If I would take his Son *Jack*, who was then about 14 Years of Age, and teach him to talk in that Book, and make Paper speak, which they call our Way of Writing, he would wholly resign him to my Tuition; telling me, he was of Opinion, I was very well affected to the *Indians*.

Tuesday.—The next Morning, we set out early, and I perceiv'd that these *Indians* were in some fear of Enemies; for they had an Old Man with them, who was very cunning and circumspect, wheresoever he saw any Marks of Footing, or of any Fire that had been made; going out of his Way, very often, to look for these Marks. We went, this day, above 30 Miles, over a very level Country, and most Pine Land, yet intermix'd with some Quantities of Marble; a good Range for Cattel, though very indifferent for Swine. We had now lost our rapid Streams, and were come to slow, dead Waters, of a brown Colour, proceeding from the *Swamps,* much like the Sluices in *Holland,* where the Track-*Scoots* go along. In the Afternoon, we met two *Tuskeruros,* who told us, That there was a Company of Hunters not far of, and if we walk'd stoutly, we might reach them that Night. But *Will* and He that own'd the Mare, being gone before, and the Old *Indian* tired, we rested, that Night, in the Woods, making a good light Fire, Wood being very plentiful in these parts.

Wednesday.—Next Day, about 10 a Clock, we struck out of the Way, by the Advice of our Old *Indian.* We had not gone past two Miles, e'er we met with about 500 *Tuskeruros* in one Hunting-Quarter. They had made themselves Streets of Houses, built with Pine-Bark, not with round Tops, as they commonly use, but Ridge-Fashion, after the manner of most other *Indians.* We got nothing amongst them but Corn, Flesh being not plentiful, by reason of the great Number of their People. For tho' they are expert Hunters, yet they are too populous for one Range; which makes Venison very scarce to what it is amongst other *Indians,* that are fewer; no Savages [Page 112] living so well for Plenty, as those near the Sea. I saw, amongst these, a Humpback'd *Indian,* which was the only crooked one I ever met withal. About two a Clock, we reach'd one of their Towns, in which there was no body left, but an Old Woman or two; the rest being gone to their Hunting Quarters. We could find no Provision at that Place. We had a *Tuskeruro* that came in company with us, from the lower Quarter, who took us to his Cabin, and gave us what it afforded, which was Corn-meat.

Thursday.—This Day, we pass'd through several Swamps, and going not above a dozen Miles, came to a Cabin, the Master whereof us'd to trade amongst the *English.* He told us, If we would stay Two Nights, he would conduct us safe to them, himself designing, at that time, to go and fetch some Rum; so we resolved to tarry for his Company. During our Stay, there happen'd to be a Young Woman troubled with Fits. The Doctor who was sent for to assist her, laid her on her Belly, and made a small Incision with

Rattle-Snake-Teeth; then laying his Mouth to the Place, he suck'd out near a Quart of black conglutinated Blood, and *Serum*. Our Landlord gave us the Tail of a Bever, which was a choice Food.

Friday.—There happen'd also to be a Burial of one of their Dead, which Ceremony is much the same with that of the *Santees,* who make a great Feast at the Interment of their Corps. The small Runs of Water hereabout, afford great Plenty of Craw-Fish, full as large as those in *England,* and nothing inferior in Goodness.

Saturday Morning, our Patron, with *Enoe Will,* and his Servant, set out with us, for the *English*. In the Afternoon, we ferried over a River, (in a *Canoe*) called by the *Indians, Chattookau,* which is the N. W. Branch of *Neus*-River. We lay in the *Swamp,* where some *Indians* invited us to go to their Quarters, which some of our Company accepted, but got nothing extraordinary, except a dozen Miles March out of their Way: The Country here is very thick of *Indian* Towns and Plantations.

Sunday.—We were forced to march, this day, for Want of Provisions. About 10 a Clock, we met an *Indian* that had got a parcel of Shad-Fish ready barbaku'd. We bought 24 of them, for a dress'd Doe-Skin, and so went on, through many *Swamps,* finding, this day, the long ragged Moss on the Trees, which we had not seen for above 600 Miles. In the Afternoon, we came upon the Banks of *Pampticough,* about 20 Miles above the *English* Plantations by Water, though not so far by Land. The *Indian* found a *Canoe,* which he had hidden, in which we all got over, and went about six Miles farther. We lay, that Night, under two or three Pieces of Bark, at the Foot of a large Oak. There fell abundance of Snow and Rain in the Night, with much Thunder and Lightning.

Monday.—Next Day, it clear'd up, and it being about 12 Miles to the *English,* about half-way we passed over a deep Creek, and came safe to Mr. *Richard Smith's,* of *Pampticough-River,* in *North-Carolina;* where being well receiv'd by the Inhabitants, and pleas'd with the Goodness of the Country, we all resolv'd to continue.

[Page 113] *A DESCRIPTION OF NORTH-CAROLINA.*

CAROLINA HOW BOUNDED.

THE Province of *Carolina* is separated from *Virginia* by a due West-Line, which begins at *Currituck*-Inlet, in 36 Degrees, 30 Minutes, of Northern-Latitude, and extends indefinitely to the Westward, and thence to the Southward, as far as 29 Degrees; which is a vast Tract of Sea-Coast. But having already treated, as far as is necessary, concerning South-*Carolina*, I shall confine myself, in the ensuing Sheets, to give my Reader a Description of that Part of the Country only, which lies betwixt *Currituck* and *Cape-Fair*, and is almost 34 Deg. North. And this is commonly call'd *North Carolina*.

This Part of *Carolina* is faced with a Chain of Sand-Banks, which defends it from the Violence and Insults of the *Atlantick* Ocean; by which Barrier, a vast Sound is hemm'd in, which fronts the Mouths of the Navigable and Pleasant Rivers of this Fertile Country, and into which they disgorge themselves.

INLETS.

Thro' the same are Inlets of several Depths of Water. Some of their Channels admit only of Sloops, Brigantines, small Barks, and Ketches; and such are *Currituck, Ronoak,* and up the Sound above *Hatteras:* Whilst others can receive Ships of Burden, as *Ocacock, Topsail*-Inlet, and *Cape-Fair;* as appears by my Chart.

FIRST COLONY OF CAROLINA.

The first Discovery and Settlement of this Country was by the Procurement of Sir *Walter Raleigh,* in Conjunction with some publick-spirited Gentlemen of that Age, under the Protection of Queen *Elizabeth;* for which Reason it was then named *Virginia,* being begun on that Part called *Ronoak*-Island, where the Ruins of a Fort are to be seen at this day, as well as some old *English* Coins which have been lately found; and a Brass-Gun, a Powder-Horn, and one small Quarter deck-Gun, made of Iron Staves, and hoop'd with the same Metal; which Method of making Guns might very probably be made use of in those Days, for the Convenience of Infant-Colonies.

HATTERAS INDIANS.

A farther Confirmation of this we have from the *Hatteras Indians,* who either then lived on *Ronoak*-Island, or much frequented it. These tell us, that several of their Ancestors were white People, and could talk in a Book, as we do; the Truth of which is confirm'd by gray Eyes being found frequently amongst these *Indians,* and no others. They value themselves extremely for their Affinity to the *English,* and are ready to do them all friendly Offices. It is probable, that this Settlement miscarry'd for want of timely Supplies from *England;* or thro' the Treachery of the Natives, for we may reasonably suppose that the *English* were forced to cohabit with them, for Relief and Conversation; and that in process of Time, [Page 114] they conform'd themselves to the Manners of their *Indian* Relations. And thus we see, how apt Humane Nature is to degenerate.

SIR WALTER RALEIGH'S SHIP.

I cannot forbear inserting here, a pleasant Story that passes for an uncontested Truth amongst the Inhabitants of this Place; which is, that the Ship which brought the first Colonies, does often appear amongst them, under Sail, in a gallant Posture, which they call Sir *Walter Raleigh's* Ship; And the truth of this has been affirm'd to me, by Men of the best Credit in the Country.

SECOND SETTLEMENT OF NORTH CAROLINA—PLEASANTNESS OF

CAROLINA.

A second Settlement of this Country was made about fifty Years ago, in that part we now call *Albemarl*-County, and chiefly in *Chuwon* Precinct, by several substantial Planters, from *Virginia,* and other Plantations; Who finding mild Winters, and a fertile Soil, beyond Expectation, producing every thing that was planted, to a prodigious Increase; their Cattle, Horses, Sheep, and Swine, breeding very fast, and passing the Winter, without any Assistance from the Planter; so that every thing seem'd to come by Nature, the Husbandman living almost void of Care, and free from those Fatigues which are absolutely requisite in Winter-Countries, for providing Fodder and other Necessaries; these Encouragements induc'd them to stand their Ground, altho' but a handful of People, seated at great Distances one from another, and amidst a vast number of *Indians* of different Nations, who were then in *Carolina*. Nevertheless, I say, the Fame of this new-discover'd Summer-Country spread thro' the neighbouring Colonies, and, in a few Years, drew a considerable Number of Families thereto, who all found Land enough to settle themselves in, (had they been many Thousands more) and that which was very good and commodiously seated, both for Profit and Pleasure. And indeed, most of the Plantations in *Carolina* naturally enjoy a noble Prospect of large and spacious Rivers, pleasant Savanna's, and fine Meadows, with their green Liveries, interwoven with beautiful Flowers, of most glorious Colours, which the several Seasons afford; hedg'd in with pleasant Groves of the ever-famous Tulip-tree, the stately Laurel, and Bays, equalizing the Oak in Bigness and Growth; Myrtles, Jessamines, Wood-bines, Honeysuckles, and several other fragrant Vines and Ever-greens, whose aspiring Branches shadow and interweave themselves with the loftiest Timbers, yielding a pleasant Prospect, Shade and Smell, proper Habitations for the Sweet-singing Birds, that melodiously entertain such as travel thro' the Woods of *Carolina*.

The Planters possessing all these Blessings, and the Produce of great Quantities of Wheat and *Indian* Corn, in which this Country is very fruitful, as likewise in Beef, Pork, Tallow, Hides, Deer-Skins, and Furs; for these Commodities the *New-England*-Men and *Bermudians* visited *Carolina* in their Barks and Sloops, and carry'd out what they made, bringing them, in Exchange, Rum, Sugar, Salt, Molosses, and some wearing Apparel, tho' the last at very extravagant Prices.

As the Land is very fruitful, so are the Planters kind and hospitable to all that come to visit them; there being very few Housekeepers, [Page 115] but what live very nobly, and give away more Provisions to Coasters and Guests who come to see them than they expend amongst their own families.

AN ACCOUNT OF THE INDIANS OF NORTH-CAROLINA.

THE *Indians*, which were the Inhabitants of *America*, when the *Spaniards* and other *Europeans* discover'd the several Parts of that Country, are the People which we reckon the Natives thereof; as indeed they were, when we first found out those Parts, and appear'd therein. Yet this has not wrought in me a full Satisfaction, to allow these People to have been the Ancient

Dwellers of the New-World, or Tract of Land we call *America*. The Reasons that I have to think otherwise, are too many to set down here; but I shall give the Reader a few, before I proceed; and some others he will find scatter'd in my Writings elsewhere.

WOOD UNDER GROUND—SHELLS SOME FATHOMS IN THE EARTH, THE

SEA PROBABLY HAS THROWN UP IN PART OF THIS COUNTRY—MEXICO

BUILDINGS.

In *Carolina* (the Part I now treat of) are the fairest Marks of a Deluge, (that at some time has probably made strange Alterations, as to the Station that Country was then in) that ever I saw, or, I think, read of, in any History. Amongst the other Subterraneous Matters, that have been discover'd, we found, in digging of a Well that was twenty six foot deep, at the Bottom thereof, many large Pieces of the Tulip-Tree, and several other sorts of Wood, some of which were cut and notch'd, and some squared, as the Joices of a House are, which appear'd (in the Judgment of all that saw them) to be wrought with Iron Instruments; it seeming impossible for any thing made of Stone, or what they were found to make use of, to cut Wood in that manner. It cannot be argu'd, that the Wood so cut, might float from some other Continent; because Hiccory and the Tulip-Tree are spontaneous in *America,* and in no other Places, that I could ever learn. It is to be acknowledg'd, that the *Spaniards* give us Relations of magnificent Buildings, which were raised by the *Indians* of *Mexico* and other Parts, which they discover'd, and conquer'd; amongst whom no Iron Instruments were found: But 'tis a great Misfortune, that no Person in that Expedition was so curious, as to take an exact Draught of the Fabricks of those People, which would have been a Discovery of great Value, and very acceptable to the Ingenious; for, as to the Politeness of Stones, it may be effected by Collision, and Grinding, which is of a contrary Nature, on several Accounts, and disproves not my Arguments, in the least.

EARTHEN POTS UNDER GROUND.

The next is, the Earthen Pots that are often found under Ground, and at the Foot of the Banks where the Water has wash'd them away. They are for the most part broken in pieces; but we find them of a different sort, in Comparison of those the *Indians* use at this day, [Page 116] who have had no other, ever since the *English* discover'd *America*. The Bowels of the Earth cannot have alter'd them, since they are thicker, of another Shape, and Composition, and nearly approach to the Urns of the Ancient *Romans*.

INDIAN PEACHES—THE STONE—WATERMELON AND GOURDS THE

INDIANS HAVE ALWAYS HAD.

Again, the Peaches, which are the only tame Fruit, or what is Foreign, that these People enjoy, which is an Eastern Product, and will keep and retain its vegetative and growing Faculty, the longest of any thing of that Nature, that I know of. The Stone, as I elsewhere have remark'd, is thicker than any other sort of the Peaches in *Europe,* or of the *European* sort, now growing in *America,* and is observed to grow if planted, after it has been for several years laid by; and it seems very probable, that these People might come from some Eastern Country; for when you ask them whence their Fore-Fathers came, that first inhabited the Country, they will point to the Westward and say, *Where the Sun sleeps, our Forefathers came thence,* which, at this distance, may be reckon'd amongst the Eastern Parts of the World. And to this day, they are a shifting, wandring People; for I know some *Indian* Nations, that have chang'd their Settlements, many hundred Miles; sometimes no less than a thousand, as is prov'd by the *Savanna Indians,* who formerly lived on the Banks of the *Messiasippi,* and remov'd thence to the Head of one of the Rivers of South-*Carolina;* since which, (for some dislike) most of them are remov'd to live in the Quarters of the *Iroquois* or *Sinnagars,* which are on the Heads of the Rivers that disgorge themselves into the Bay of *Chesapeak.* I once met with a young *Indian* Woman, that had been brought from beyond the Mountains, and was sold a Slave into *Virginia.* She spoke the same language, as the *Coranine Indians,* that dwell near Cape-*Look-out,* allowing for some few words, which were different, yet no otherwise, than that they might understand one another very well.

INDIAN WELL SHAP'D PEOPLE.

The *Indians* of North-*Carolina* are a well-shap'd clean-made People, of different Statures, as the *Europeans* are, yet chiefly inclin'd to be tall. They are a very streight People, and never bend forwards, or stoop in the Shoulders, unless much overpower'd by old Age. Their Limbs are exceeding well-shap'd. As for their Legs and Feet, they are generally the handsomest in the World. Their Bodies are a little flat, which is occasion'd, by being laced hard down to a Board, in their Infancy. This is all the Cradle they have, which I shall describe at large elsewhere. Their Eyes are black, or of a dark Hazle; the White is marbled with red Streaks, which is ever common to these People, unless when sprung from a white Father or Mother. Their Colour is of a tawny, which would not be so dark, did they not dawb themselves with Bears Oil, and a Colour like burnt Cork. This is begun in their Infancy, and continued for a long time, which fills the Pores, and enables them better to endure the Extremity of the Weather. They are never bald on their Heads, although never so old, which, I believe, proceeds from their Heads being always uncover'd, [Page 117] and the greasing their Hair (so often as they do) with Bears Fat, which is a great Nourisher of the Hair, and causes it to grow very fast. Amongst the Bears Oil (when they intend to be fine) they mix a certain Red Powder, that comes from a Scarlet Root which they get in the hilly Country, near the Foot of the great Ridge of Mountains, and it is no where else to be found. They have this Scarlet Root in great Esteem, and sell it for a very great Price, one to another. The Reason of its Value, is because they not only go a long way for it, but are in great Danger of the *Sinnagars* or *Iroquois,* who are mortal Enemies to all our *Indians,* and very often take them Captives, or kill them, before they return from this Voyage. The *Tuskeruros* and other *Indians* have often brought this Seed with them from the Mountains; but it would never grow in our Land. With this and Bears Grease they anoint their Heads and Temples, which is esteem'd as ornamental, as sweet Powder to our Hair. Besides this Root has the Virtue of killing Lice, and suffers none to abide or breed in their Heads. For want of this Root, they sometimes use *Pecoon*-Root, which is of a Crimson Colour, but it is apt to die the Hair of an ugly Hue.

NO DWARF—INDIAN TOBACCO.

Their Eyes are commonly full and manly, and their Gate sedate and majestick. They never walk backward and forward as we do, nor contemplate on the Affairs of Loss and Gain; the things which daily perplex us. They are dexterous and steady both as to their Hands and Feet, to Admiration. They will walk over deep Brooks, and Creeks, on the smallest Poles, and that without any Fear or Concern. Nay, an *Indian* will walk on the Ridge of a Barn or House and look down the Gable-end, and spit upon the Ground, as unconcern'd, as if he was walking on *Terra firma.* In Running, Leaping, or any such other Exercise, their Legs seldom miscarry, and give them a Fall; and as for letting any thing fall out of their Hands, I never yet knew one Example. They are no Inventors of any Arts or Trades worthy mention; the Reason of which I take to be, that they are not possess'd with that Care and Thoughtfulness, how to provide for the Necessaries of Life, as the *Europeans* are; yet they will learn any thing very soon. I have known an *Indian* stock Guns better than most of our *Joiners,* although he never saw one stock'd before; and besides, his Working-Tool was only a sorry Knife. I have also known several of them that were Slaves to the *English,* learn Handicraft-Trades very well and speedily. I never saw a Dwarf amongst them, nor but one that was Hump-back'd. Their Teeth are yellow with Smoaking Tobacco, which both Men and Women are much addicted to. They tell us, that they had Tobacco amongst them, before the *Europeans* made any Discovery of that Continent. It differs in the leaf from the sweet-scented, and *Oroonoko,* which are the Plants we raise and cultivate in *America.* Theirs differs likewise much in the Smell, when green, from our Tobacco, before cured. They do not use the same way to cure it as we do; and therefore, the Difference must be very considerable in Taste; for all Men (that know Tobacco) must allow, that it is the Ordering thereof which gives a Hogoo to that Weed, rather than any Natural Relish it possesses, [Page 118] when green. Although they are great Smokers, yet they never are seen to take it in Snuff, or chew it.

They have no Hairs on their Faces (except some few) and those but little, nor is there often found any Hair under their Arm-Pits. They are continually plucking it away from their Faces, by the Roots. As for their Privities, since they wore Tail-Clouts, to cover their Nakedness, several of the Men have a deal of Hair thereon. It is to be observ'd, that the Head of the *Penis* is cover'd (throughout all the Nations of the *Indians* I ever saw) both in Old and Young. Although we reckon these a very smooth People, and free from Hair; yet I once saw a middle-aged Man, that was hairy all down his Back; the Hairs being above an Inch long.

FEW CRIPPLES—INDIANS GOOD EYES.

As there are found very few, or scarce any, Deformed, or Cripples, amongst them, so neither did I ever see but one blind Man; and then they would give me no Account how his Blindness came. They had a Use for him, which was, to lead him with a Girl, Woman, or Boy, by a String; so they put what Burdens they pleased upon his Back, and made him very serviceable upon all such Occasions. No People have better Eyes, or see better in the Night or Day, than the *Indians*. Some alledge, that the Smoke of the Pitch-Pine, which they chiefly burn, does both preserve and strengthen the Eyes; as, perhaps, it may do, because that Smoak never offends the Eyes, though you hold your Face over a great Fire thereof. This is occasion'd by the volatile Part of the Turpentine, which rises with the Smoke, and is of a friendly balsamick Nature; for the Ashes of the Pine-Tree afford no fix'd Salt in them.

NOT PAIR THEIR NAILS.

They let their Nails grow very long, which, they reckon, is the Use Nails are design'd for, and laugh at the *Europeans* for pairing theirs, which they say disarms them of that which nature designed them for.

And since I hinted at a Regulation of the Savages, and to propose a way to convert them to Christianity, I will first particularize the several Nations of *Indians* that are our Neighbours, and then proceed to what I promis'd.

Tuskeruro Indians are fifteen Towns, *viz. Haruta, Waqui, Contahnah, Anna Ooka, Conaub-Kare Harooka, Una Nauban, Kentanuska, Chunaneets, Kenta, Eno, Naur-begh-ne, Oonoffoora, Tofneoc, Nonawharitse, Nursoorooka*; Fighting Men 1200. *Waccon.* Towns 2, *Tupwauremau, Tooptatmeer,* Fighting Men 120. *Machapunga,* Town 1, *Maramiskeet,* Fighting Men 30. *Bear* River, Town 1, *Raudauquaquank,* Fighting Men 50. *Maberring Indians,* Town 1, *Maberring* River, Fighting Men 50. *Chuwon Indians,* Town 1, *Bennets* Creek, Fighting Men 15. *Paspatank Indians,* Town 1, *Paspatank* River, Fighting Men 10. *Poteskeit,* Town 1, *North* River, Fighting Men 30. *Nottaway Indians,* Town 1, *Winoack* Creek, Fighting

Men 30. *Hatteras* Town 1, Sand Banks, Fighting Men 16. *Connamox Indians*, Towns 2, *Coranine, Raruta*, Fighting Men 25. *Neus Indians*, Towns [Page 119] 2, *Chattooka, Rouconk*, Fighting Men 15. *Pampticough Indians*, Town 1, *Island*, Fighting Men 15. *Taupim Indians*, 6 People. These five Nations of the *Totero's, Sapona's, Keiauwee's, Aconechos*, and *Schoccories*, are lately come amongst us, and may contain, in all, about 750 Men, Women and Children. Total 4780

Now, there appears to be one thousand Six hundred and twelve Fighting Men, of our Neighbouring *Indians;* and probably, there are three Fifths of Women and Children, not including Old Men, which amounts to four thousand and thirty Savages, besides the five Nations lately come. Now, as I before hinted, we will see what grounds there are to make these People serviceable to us, and better themselves thereby.

On a fair Scheme, we must first allow these Savages what really belongs to them, that is, what good Qualities, and natural Endowments, they possess, whereby they being in their proper Colours, the Event may be better guess'd at, and fathom'd.

First, they are as apt to learn any Handicraft, as any People that the World affords; I will except none; as is seen by their Canoes and Stauking Heads, which they make of themselves; but to my purpose, the *Indian* Slaves in South *Carolina,* and elsewhere, make my Argument good.

Secondly, we have no disciplin'd Men in *Europe*, but what have, at one time or other, been branded with Mutining, and Murmuring against their Chiefs. These savages are never found guilty of that great Crime in a Soldier; I challenge all Mankind to tell me of one Instance of it; besides, they never prove Traitors to their Native Country, but rather chuse Death than partake and side with the Enemy.

They naturally possess the Righteous Man's Gift; they are Patient under all Afflictions, and have a great many other Natural Vertues, which I have slightly touch'd throughout the Account of these Savages.

They are really better to us than we are to them; they always give us Victuals at their Quarters, and take care we are arm'd against Hunger and Thirst: We do not so by them (generally speaking) but let them walk by our Doors Hungry, and do not often relieve them. We look upon them with Scorn and Disdain, and think them little better than Beasts in Humane Shape, though if well examined, we shall find that, for all our Religion and Education, we possess more Moral Deformities, and Evils than these Savages do, or are acquainted withal.

[Page 120] EXHIBIT F.

HISTORICAL SKETCH OF THE INDIANS OF ROBESON COUNTY.

[By A. W. McLean.]

It is our purpose to state some facts relating to the Indians now residing in Robeson and adjoining counties in North Carolina. These peculiar and interesting people have been the subject of much historical research during the last half century.

The first white settlers who located in the section now comprised in Robeson County were French Huguenots, who immigrated in large numbers from France to South Carolina after the revocation of the Edict of Nantes, and some of them had penetrated as far north as the boundary line of North Carolina, only a few miles from the present location of the Indians in Robeson County, in the early part of the eighteenth century. Scotch immigrants settled in the upper section of what is now Robeson County as early as 1730. When these white settlers first arrived they found located on the waters of the Lumbee, as Lumber River was then called, a tribe of Indians speaking broken English, tilling the soil in a rude manner, and practicing in rather imperfect ways some of the arts practiced by the civilized people of Europe. There is abundant evidence that the land lying on the Lumbee River and upon the large creeks and swamps which are tributary to it was a great Indian camping ground. While there were many small tribes of Indians inhabiting this section of eastern North Carolina, the tribe formerly known as "Croatans," now known as "Indians of Robeson County," occupied the territory as far southwest as the Peedee River, in South Carolina, but the principal seat was on the Lumber River, a tributary of the Peedee, and the settlement extended along this river for at least 20 miles, the center of this settlement being about the site of the present town of Pembroke. At first they held their lands in common by right of possession, and this continued until the coming of the white man, when ownership in severalty gradually took the place of ownership in common; however, up to this day most of the people own their lands by right of possession, which has ripened into perfect title.

Hon. Hamilton McMillan, an experienced historian of marked ability, published in 1888 and again in 1907 an account of these people under the title of "Sir Walter Raleigh's Lost Colony." Mr. McMillan's opinion is that the Indians now residing in Robeson and adjoining counties are descended from Sir Walter Raleigh's lost colony, left by Gov. White on Roanoke Island in 1587, and there are many plausible arguments advanced by Mr. McMillan for his theory. Another school of local historians contend that these Indians are descended from some other settlement of English-speaking people along the coast of North Carolina, probably near Lockwoods Folly, in Brunswick County, N. C. It is generally admitted by the adherents of both of these theories that these people are of undoubted [Page 121] Indian origin and that they have at some time in the past become mixed to a more or less extent with persons of English blood. The purpose of this sketch is not to decide between these conflicting contentions, for this is immaterial to the purpose of this inquiry.

"TO WHAT TRIBE OF INDIANS DO THEY BELONG?"

We are of the opinion that they were originally a part of the great Cherokee Tribe of Indians which inhabited the western and central portions of Carolina before the advance of the white man.

Indeed, Mr. McMillan, in his account before referred to, takes the position that they are of Cherokee descent, though we confess that we can not reconcile this contention with his main contention that they are descendants of Gov. White's or Sir Walter Raleigh's lost colony.

Long before historians began to study the origin of these people they claimed to be of Cherokee descent. In fact, they have always claimed that they were originally a part of the Cherokee Tribe and that they gave up their tribal relation after they had participated with the white man in the war against the Tuscaroras. These Indians had great roads or trails connecting their settlements with the principal seat of the Cherokee Tribe in the Allegheny Mountains. There is a well-authenticated tradition among them, handed down through several generations, that this small remnant, after participating with the whites in the war against the Tuscaroras, took up many of the habits and customs of the white man, and therefore refused to remove west with the great Cherokee Tribe. It is also certain that in this they were influenced by the admixture of Anglo-Saxon blood, which had taken place to some extent even in that remote period.

On a map (being map No. 1) of the transactions of the American Ethnological Society the Yemassees are assigned to the region bordering on the Savannah River; the Cherokees to the mountain region; the Cheraws from the Yemassees along the coastal region to the Pamlicos on Pamlico Sound; the Tuscaroras along the Roanoke River, and just south of them, on the Nuese, the Woocons; and the Catawbas in central North and South Carolina.

It appears from Gregg's History of The Old Cheraws that originally the Cherokees occupied the territory assigned on the map to the Catawbas. According to their tradition, the Catawbas, about the time of the settlement of North America by the whites, occupied a region far to the northward, from whence they removed to the South. Being a numerous and warlike race, they vanquished the tribes with whom they came in conflict on the way, until they met the Cherokees on the banks of the river now called the Catawba. Here a sanguinary battle ensued, the loss on both sides being heavy, though neither party gained a victory. Terms of peace were agreed on, the Cherokees moving to the west and the Catawbas taking their country. This tradition is said to be confirmed by ethnological research. The Cheraws embraced all the small tribes of the Santee, Congaree, Wateree, Waccamaw, and Pedee. The Cheraws appear to have been a branch of the Cherokees. In the language of the Cherokees "chera" means fire. From the terminals of names Gregg connects the two tribes. He says: "If, about the period of their distinctive existence [Page 122] as a tribe, being possibly an offshoot from the Cherokees, at the era of some internal struggle and partial dismemberment of that once powerful and widely extended nation," etc. And, otherwise, he suggests that the Cheraws once belonged to the Cherokees.

In the early days of the settlement he says that there were 28 small tribes in South Carolina, and, in 1700, William Gale, of Albermarle, mentioned that he "was just setting out on a four months' voyage to the Cape Fear, where he had sent a shallop's load of goods to trade with the Indians."

Apparently he intended to pass up that river and go as far west as the mountains to trade with the Indians. He said that there were 13 different tribes with which he was well acquainted and had free commerce.

There were many small tribes of Indians from the Neuse to the Savannah, those on the Cape Fear being Congarees, who were really "Cheraws," and the Cheraws, as Gregg indicates, were doubtless an offshoot of the original Cherokees who remained in their several localities at the time of the settlement by the Catawbas and the removal of the great bulk of the Cherokees to the mountains.

These circumstances are corroborative of the opinion of Giles Leitch that the Indians of Robeson County possessed the characteristics of the Cherokees.

The first permanent settlement on the Cape Fear, at old Brunswick, was about 1725. At that time there were many small Indian tribes throughout that region. Some ten years later settlers had penetrated well into the interior and found on the upper Cape Fear a community who had some European characteristics, evidently having mingled to some extent with some of the European races. Such is the first known reference to this settlement. Later, in 1752, there is a reference to them as occupying the territory which they now hold in what is now Robeson County, and it was then reported that they shot at a surveyor who went among them to survey land against their claims.

At that time the remnants of small Indian tribes still existed throughout that region.

The last battle with the Indians in making the original settlements near the seacoast was, according to tradition, at the Sugar Loaf, a few miles north of the site of Fort Fisher, in 1725, when the whites took possession of the lower part of the Cape Fear River. The royal governor eight years later estimated the Indians who were considered a part of the population for their friendly associations as numbering 800. On the outskirts of the settlements there were various small tribes of Indians inhabiting the wilderness in lower North Carolina and in South Carolina. In 1740 a Mr. Vaughn appropriated a large tract of land in Duplin County, together with a hundred slaves, to the purpose of Christianizing five Indian tribes in that vicinity. As the country became settled these remnants disappeared, and doubtless many of the Indians of that region went to live with that nucleus in the territory now confined in Robeson County. This seems to be the most probable account of the origin of this peculiar people, many of whom throughout all the generations appear to have been full-blood Indians, having, as Leitch says, the characteristics of the Cherokees, with whom, in the previous century, they were closely allied. By their traditions some Indians from that region accompanied Col. Barnwell to the Albemarle in January, 1712, and it appears that Barnwell passed close by their settlements.

[Page 123]It was among the Cherokees that many men were enlisted to fight the Tuscaroras in 1713, when North Carolina called upon South Carolina for assistance. This call was responded to by hundreds of white men, Cherokees and other Indians under Col. Barnwell. Along the great Lowrie road Col. Barnwell passed with his army to fight the Tuscaroras. The army took the upper road at Fayetteville and crossed the Cape Fear at Averasboro. Ramsay, in his history of South Carolina, says, in volume 1, page 156: "Gov. Craven lost no time in forwarding a force to their assistance. The assembly voted £4, 000 for the service of the war. A body of militia, consisting of 600 men under the command of Col. Barnwell, marched against the savages; 218 Cherokees under the command of Capts. Harford and Turston, 79 Creeks under Capt. Hastings, 41 Catawbas under Capt. Cantey, 28 Yemassees under Capt. Pierce, joined the Carolinians in this expedition." This army passed through Robeson County, and there are traditions among the Indians of Robeson County regarding the army of "Bonnul," as they pronounced the name of Barnwell. One of these traditions is that several of the Cherokees, on their return from the Tuscarora war, located in Robeson County, bringing their prisoners with them as slaves. These prisoners intermarried among the Cherokees and became free, as was the custom among Indian tribes.

The Cherokees, from whom the Indians of Robeson County claim descent, were to some extent an agricultural people. The clay pottery found in this section is ornamented by having a full ear of corn rolled over the surface while the material of the pottery was in a plastic state. In the beginning of the War of Independence the colonial troops captured thousands of bushels of corn among the Cherokees in the mountains of western North Carolina.

The universal tradition among the Indians found in Robeson County, N. C., and counties adjoining is that they are the descendants of English people and the Cherokees.

Their Indian ancestors, the Cherokees, according to their tradition, had their principal abiding place in the mountains to the west, and had trails or roads lead ng to various points on the coast. On the principal one of these roads, known as the Lowrie road, they had settlements on the Neuse River, on the waters of Black River, on the Cape Fear, Lumbee, and as far as the Santee in South Carolina. Their principal settlement was in the territory along the Lumbee and covering a large part of the present county of Robeson, and extending through what is now Cumberland County as far as Averasboro on the Cape Fear. They had other trails leading from the mountains eastward, and three of them united with the Lowrie road or trail where there was a crossing of the Cape Fear where the present town of Fayetteville is situated.

John Brooks (ancestor of Aaron Brooks, now living near Pates, in Robeson County) was a soldier in the American Army at the Battle of Eutaw Springs. Soon after returning from the Revolutionary War he died, leaving his widow, Betsy Brooks. Her name appears in the United States census of 1790 as the head of a family.

Jacob Locklear also served in the American Army at the Battle of Eutaw Springs, and at other places. This Jacob Locklear had a brother, William Locklear, who was known as "Lazy Will." This "Lazy Will Locklear" spoke the Cherokee language and often held [Page 124] conversations in Cherokee with Randall Locklear, Elizabeth Lowery, and others. The tradition handed down by the descendants of Lazy Will Locklear is that he and certain others of the Indians remained and settled on Long Swamp and Lumber River, in Robeson County, when the other Indians left for the West. It is also a tradition in this family that Lazy Will Locklear and others of the Indians fought under Gen. Barnwell. It is also stated that there was a battle between some of the Indians and others near the present town of Red Springs, and there is an Indian mound there which is pointed out to this day. Recent investigations disclose the skeletons of a number of Indians who were buried there. The remains were found to be buried in the usual manner of Indian burying grounds.

Daniel Locklear, now living near Buie, in Robeson County, is a great-great-grandson of the Jacob Locklear above mentioned.

The original Lowery Road, now known by that name which passes through Robeson County and referred to in the Hamilton McMillan History of the Indians, was said to have been used by the Indians in traveling from Eastern North Carolina, then known as Roanoke in Virginia, to the Cheraw and other Indian settlements in South Carolina. It was first an Indian trail and was afterwards a post road.

Jordon Chavis, son of Julia Chavis and grandson of Ishmael Chavis, is now 75 years of age. He states that his father and grandfather always told him that their people were Cherokee Indians.

Preston Locklear, age 75 years, states that he and his ancestors were always known as Indians and that his parents taught him that his people lived here in Robeson County long before the white people came here.

Isaac Brayboy, age 74, states that his parents and grandparents told him that their people were Cherokee Indians; that the name was originally "Braveboy." This name is recorded in the census of 1790.

James Brayboy, now 82 years of age, states that his father and grandfather always told him that his people were Indians by the name of Braveboy. That they were living on Lumber River and Long Swamp, in Robeson County, when the white people first came to this country; that they were friendly with the white people and that they helped the white people to drive out the unfriendly Indians.

It will be noted that in the census of 1790 the name now known as "Locklear" is spelled "Lockaleer." It is said among the Indians to-day that this name in Indian language was originally "Locklaha."

As further confirming the Cherokee origin of these people, they have a tradition that the brother of James Lowery, and one of those who fought in the Revolution, was John Lowery, who was the head man among the Cherokees, and that he was one of those who made a treaty on behalf of the Cherokees with the Federal Government. Of this they had a tradition, none of them being able to read or write. On examination, it has been found that John Lowery did sign the treaty on behalf of the Cherokees made in 1806. (See second volume, Treaties, p. 91, Congressional Library.)

This John Lowery was the great-granduncle of Sinclair Lowery, now living in Robeson County, at the age of 78 years.

From the "War Map," in Winsor's History of America, giving the routes taken by Barnwell and taken by the two Moores, it appears that Barnwell, who had 50 whites and some 400 Indians, passed along [Page 125] the Santee to the Congaree, then up the Wateree to the vicinity of the Catawba, embodying detachments of all these tribes in his force; that turning east he crossed the Peedee, and then continued east a considerable distance and took a northeast course, crossing the Cape Fear about where Fayetteville is; then ascending that river to about the vicinity of Averasboro he took a northeast course to Torhunte, on the Cotechne. He reached the Neuse, about Fort Barnwell, in January 1712.

After a great battle, in which his Indians made many prisoners, they returned to South Carolina; and later he, being wounded, likewise returned.

The war breaking out again, South Carolina sent another force under Col. James Moore, 33 whites and 1, 000 Indians. Col. Moore pursued the same route to the Pedee, but then turned to the northeast and crossed the Cape Fear at the junction of the Haw and Deep, and then went on to Torhunte. He arrived December 1, 1712. His brother, Maj. Maurice Moore, quickly followed him with another large force of Indians. His route lay still farther west by Trading Ford (near Salisbury), and after crossing the Deep he came east by Occoneechee, where Hillsboro is, and eastward to Torhunte. All these routes were Indian trails. It is to be noted that Barnwell alone passed through what is now Robeson County, and as until recently there never was any publication made of his route, it may be affirmed that the tradition stated is remarkable and noteworthy.

Although many other Indians from South Carolina accompanied Col. James Moore to the Albemarle the following winter, and a few weeks later still others accompanied Col. Maurice Moore, these expeditions did not pass through the Robeson region, and the local traditions are connected only with Barnwell. It is safe to say that these people could have known nothing of these matters except from actual tradition.

In 1756 a similar force of Indians from South Carolina accompanied Col. Hugh Waddell in his expedition to the north for the relief of the more northern colonies in the French and Indian War. While there is no particular record of the fact, yet as small numbers of Indians from almost every settlement composed this force, doubtless some belonged to these tribes that finally made up the population in Robeson County.

Gregg says that most of these smaller tribes eventually united with the Catawbas, and about 1743 the language of the Catawbas is said to have consisted of twenty different dialects.

The remaining Indians, in the course of settlement, passed from view, although "brief allusions are found in our early period to the several tribes in the acts of the assembly passed for the regulation and support of the Indian trade."

As the Indian element in the present population of Robeson County is certainly derived from the former Indians of that region, these people are entitled to share in any feeling of appreciation we may have of the general conduct of all these friendly tribes during the period of settlement and in colonial times.

During the Revolution some of these Indians served in the Continental ranks, as well as in the more local organizations raised by the State of North Carolina.

[Page 126]The territory embraced in Robeson County was much divided in sentiment, and toward the close of the Revolution it was the scene of a murderous civil warefare of unparalleled atrocity.

The tradition of these people that some of their leaders fought on the side of the Colonies seems to be corroborated by certain circumstances. Giles Leitch says that during the Revolution some of these families acquired a considerable number of slaves. Had they acquired them from North Carolinians, these slaves would have been recovered on the return of peace. Such slaves as the British captured, they sent either to Florida or Nova Scotia. It is therefore probable that these slaves held by these Robeson County Indians were acquired from South Carolina. Marion raised his celebrated band largely in that part of North Carolina, and as an inducement for serving with him he offered as pay to his North Carolina troopers slaves taken from the South Carolina Loyalists. So many of these slaves were thus taken and held by his North Carolina troopers that after the war the question of their return became a matter of State legislation.

After the war, feeling against the local Tories ran so high that they were discriminated against and severe tests of loyalty were applied. There seems to have been no feeling against these Indians, for although not white they were allowed to vote as "freemen," without any change being made in the law to include them, although only whites had earlier been allowed to vote. They voted until 1835, when the Constitution was changed by the insertion of the word "white."[1]

Had they been of the Tory element probably they would not have been allowed the right of suffrage, because the feeling against the Tories was very bitter, especially in that region where they lived.

During the War of 1812 they were enrolled in the militia; and among others, Charles Oxendine, Thomas Locklier, John Drinkwater, Hugh Locklear, William Bullard, Elias Bullard, Richard Bullard, and Stephen Cumboe were in the companies of militia detached from the Robeson regiments for service in that war. (See Muster Rolls Troops of 1812, State Library at Raleigh.)

---

1 All freemen voted before 1835.—S.B.W.

Up to 1835 these Indians were entitled to vote, and some of them owned slaves. A number of them appear as heads of families in the United States census of 1790.

After 1835 these people could not vote, nor were they prior to the Civil War admitted to the public schools when they were established.

In 1867 they were allowed to vote under the reconstruction acts, and under the constitution adopted in 1868, and were entitled to attend the negro schools, but not the schools for the whites. But they refused absolutely to attend the negro schools, and thus were debarred from school privileges.

Attention was drawn to their peculiar social status, and as they were of undoubted Indian extraction Hon. Hamilton McMillan, who inquired into their history, reached the conclusion that they were descended from the Indians on Croatan Sound and derived their white blood from the lost colony of 1587. This idea was based on their partly civilized condition when first observed by the early settlers of that region about 1730. Under that impression, the legislature in 1885 provided separate common schools for them under the name of the "Croatan Indians."

[Page 127]The word "Croatan" is not a generic or tribal name, but was purely local, and this appellation was given to these Indians in the act of the legislature in 1885 at the instance of the Hon. Hamilton McMillan. The name having been suggested by the word "Croatan" which was found on a tree after the disappearance of Gov. John White's lost colony. In 1911 the legislature changed the name to "Indians of Robeson County."

But whatever the origin of the Indians of this community was, it is certain that from the first settlement they have been separated from the other inhabitants of that region, and are of Indian descent, with Indian characteristics, with complexion, features, and hair of the Indian race, and are now borne on the census rolls as Indians.

NEED OF BETTER SCHOOL FACILITIES.

While they have the ordinary common schools and a small normal school, as they can not attend the high institutions provided on the one hand for the whites and on the other hand for the negroes, their educational facilities are limited.

It is very desirable, therefore, that additional educational facilities should be afforded them, especially in the way of higher academic and industrial education.

It appears that they have capacity for agriculture and the mechanic arts, and readily become skilled in them when trained. A mechanical and industrial school would be of great benefit to them.

In like manner the training of the girls in the domestic arts and economics would be of great benefit.

These people never had a reservation set apart for them, as the Catawbas had not far to the west of them.

The bill under consideration, which has passed the Senate, provides for an appropriation of $50, 000 to erect buildings for a school for these Indians at or near Pembroke, in Robeson County.

According to the census of 1910, the number of these Indians in Robeson County was 5, 895. There are also about 1, 500 to 2, 000 in adjoining counties in North and South Carolina, making a settlement in all of about 8, 000 persons. In 1909 there were enrolled in the ordinary common free schools provided by the State 1, 594 of these Indian children. The average length of the term of their school districts was 82 days. The only school facilities enjoyed by them other than the ordinary common school above mentioned is a normal school for the training of teachers, provided for by the State at an annual cost of $2, 250. Under the laws of North Carolina, which provide for the absolute separation of the races, they are not entitled to attend the university for men, the State normal and industrial college for women, or the agricultural and mechanical college for either the white or negro races. They are therefore entirely without the facilities for industrial or higher academic education. There has always been a feeling among these people and their white neighbors that the Federal Government should make some provision for them, for the reason that the Government does expend large sums of money every year in providing schools for other nonreservation Indians in all sections of the country. The present Indian appropriation bill provides for [Page 128] more than a million dollars for this purpose, some provisions in that bill being as follows:

For support and education of three hundred and seventy-five Indian pupils at the Indian school at Genoa, Nebraska, and for pay of superintendent, $62, 300; for general repairs and improvements, $4, 500; in all, $66, 800.

For support and education of one hundred and eighty Indian pupils at the Indian school at Cherokee, North Carolina, and for pay of superintendent, $30, 000; for general repairs and improvements, $6, 000; in all, $36, 000.

For support and education of one hundred Indian pupils at the Indian school, Bismarck, North Dakota, and for pay of superintendent, $18, 200; for general repairs and improvements, $2, 000; in all, $20, 200.

For support and education of Indian pupils at the Indian school at Carlisle, Pennsylvania, and for pay of superintendent, $132, 000; for general repairs and improvements, $20, 000; in all, $152, 000.

For support and education of one hundred and seventy-five Indian pupils at the Indian school at Pierre, South Dakota, and for pay of superintendent, $32, 000; for general repairs and improvements, $10, 000; in all, $42, 000.

For the support and education of two hundred and ten Indian pupils at the Indian school at Hayward, Wisconsin, and for pay of superintendent, $36, 670; for general repairs and improvements, $2, 500; in all, $39, 170.

It appears from a letter from the Department of the Interior, Bureau of Indian Affairs, that there are 22 nonreservation Indian schools in various parts of the United States now supported by the Government, none of these being situated in the Southern States.

It appears that these schools are not connected with reservations or agencies, but are maintained especially for Indians of any tribe coming usually from that part of the country in which the school is situated, and pupils are admitted whose parents are entirely free from governmental control or guardianship, and who in some cases hold their lands without restriction, the only condition of admittance being that they would otherwise be deprived of an opportunity to obtain an education, academic or industrial. It is submitted that the condition of the Indians in question fully meets these requirements, because they are debarred by the laws of the State of North Carolina from attending the colleges and schools of higher education, both academic and industrial.

LETTER OF A. W. McLEAN, SEPTEMBER 7, 1914.

LUMBERTON, N. C., September 7, 1914.

DEAR SIR: I promised Mr. O. M. McPherson, special Indian agent, who recently spent some time in Lumberton investigating the Cherokee Indians of Robeson County, that I would probably send him some further information in connection with these Indians which he might be able to use in making his report.

I have made a very careful study of the history of these Indians for a number of years. In a hearing before the Committee on Indian Affairs of the House of Representatives on Friday, February 14, 1913, I submitted an historical sketch of these Indians, a copy of which I furnished to Mr. McPherson. Supplementing that sketch, I desire to submit the following as bearing upon their contention that they are of Cherokee origin:

My opinion is, from a very exhaustive examination made before and after the hearing above mentioned, that these Indians are not [Page 129] only descendants of Sir Walter Raleigh's lost colony, as contended by Mr. Hamilton McMillan in his statement, a copy of which Mr. McPherson has in his possession, but that they are also mixed with the Cherokee Indians. In the first place, these Indians have contended from time immemorial that they were of Cherokee descent, and they further have had a tradition among them that their ancestors, or some of them, came from "Roanoke and Virginia." Roanoke and Virginia, of course, originally comprised all of eastern North Carolina, including Roanoke Island, the settlement of Sir Walter Raleigh's lost colony.

In the great war with the Tuscaroras in eastern North Carolina Barnwell's army was made up largely of Indians, and especially Cherokee Indians. The only serious contention made against the claim that they are Cherokees is that the Cherokees live farther west. In view of their tradition that upon their return from eastern North Carolina with Barnwell's army some of them stopped and settled in Robeson County, there seems to be nothing in this contention. This tradition is borne out by the fact that the great road traveled by Barnwell in his expedition to eastern North Carolina was along the Lowrie Road, which passes immediately through the present settlement of these Indians. (See Williamson's History of North Carolina, Vol. I, pp. 194, etc. See also History of the Old Cheraws, by Gregg, pp. 1 to 31. See especially map between pp. 2 and 3, which shows that the Cheraws were located in all that section between the Cape Fear River and the Catawba River. See also on page 7 reference to Lederer's journey, in which it is stated that he made his journey entering the State of North Carolina somewhere in Robeson County, crossing in a southwestern line, and passing through

Robeson County into South Carolina. His road was along the Great Lowrie Road, which was originally an Indian trail, and which passes directly through the heart of the Indian settlement in Robeson County. See also Hawks's History of North Carolina.)

As will be noted from the historical sketch given by me at the committee hearing hereinbefore mentioned, John Lowrie signed a treaty on the part of the Cherokee Indians with the United States Government in 1806. This John Lowrie was the ancestor of some of the Lowrie Indians now living in Robeson County. His brother, James Lowrie, was one of the most prominent Indians in the county in the year 1810.

Several of these Indians served in the Revolutionary War. John Brooks was granted a pension by the United States Government for services in the Revolutionary War. (See warrant No. 80030, issued to John Brooks for 160 acres of bounty land for his services in the Revolutionary War. See also Revolutionary War pension file No. 6732, pension order.) In Volume XXII of the North Carolina State Records, pages 56 and 57, it appears that the following Indians of Robeson County received a pension from the Government for service in the Revolutionary War: John Brooks, James Brooks, Berry Hunt, Thomas Jacobs, Michael Revells, Richard Bell, Samuel Bell, Primas Jacobs, Thomas Cummings, and John Hammond, these pensions having been granted under the Federal acts of 1818 and 1832.

In 1871, while Congress was investigating the operations of the Ku-Klux, the Hon. Giles Leach, then a prominent lawyer residing [Page 130] at Lumberton, Robeson County, was summoned to appear before a congressional committee in Washington to testify in regard to the condition of affairs in Robeson County. He was naturally very unfriendly to the Indians, because he admitted in his testimony that he was employed by the State of North Carolina to prosecute some of them. Notwithstanding his prejudice, when asked the question as to what race the Lowries and the other Indians belonged to, he said:

Well, sir, I desire to tell you the truth as near as I can. I think they are a mixture of Spanish and Indian. They have straight black hair and many of the characteristics of the Cherokee Indians in our State.

When asked the question as to what blood there was in the Lowrie family, he said:

I think the father was an Indian. I think the family had about all the characteristics of the Cherokee Indians of our State. The mother was named

Cumboe, and I think it very likely that there may have been some white blood in the Cumboe family. The Lowrie family is Indian.

I regard this testimony of the Hon. Giles Leach as very important as bearing upon the fact that these Indians are of Cherokee descent, because, as stated, he was strongly prejudiced against them and evidently gave no testimony favorable to them except where he felt obliged to do so.

It is inconceivable that these Indians should have had a tradition in their families which can be traced for more than a hundred years to the effect that they were of Cherokee origin unless there was something in the statement. It will be noted in the pamphlet published by the Hon. Hamilton McMillan that they always claimed to him that they were of Cherokee origin. The investigation I have made of them for the last 20 or 25 years has elicited the universal tradition and history that their Indian blood was Cherokee. It is entirely possible, of course, that there may have been a mixture of some other Indian blood. In fact, it is generally believed that the Cheraws and a number of other native Indian tribes who originally lived on the border line of North and South Carolina were mixed more or less with the Cherokee Indians.

The fact that such reliable historians as Capt. S. A. Ashe, the author of a history of North Carolina, Hon. Hamilton McMillan, a man now over 80 years of age, who has lived in this section all his life and who has made a special study of these Indians, and the Hon. Giles Leach, who was one of the most noted local historians who ever lived in this section—the very fact, I say, that they have all stated that it is their positive opinion from their investigations that these people have Cherokee blood in them is, when coupled with their own universal tradition to that effect, conclusive proof that they have Cherokee blood in their veins. Indeed, it would be practically impossible to prove the family or tribal relation of any people by stronger or more convincing proof.

I inclose statement of Wash Lowrie, a very old Indian, which is practically the same as the others with whom I have talked for the last 25 years.

Yours, truly,

A. W. MCLEAN.

[Page 131] *STATEMENT OF WASH LOWRIE TO A. W. MCLEAN.*

On July 14, 1914, I interviewed Wash Lowrie at his home on the Lowrie Road, about 2 miles north of Pembroke. He stated that he lacked a few months of being 80 years of age. That his father was Daniel Lowrie, who died about 1864, age 73 years, and Daniel Lowrie was a natural son of James Lowrie. This James Lowrie was one of the original Indians in this section and was very well off at the time of his death in 1810. (See his will, recorded in book of wills No. 1, p. 121, office clerk superior court, Robeson County.) The mother of Daniel Lowrie was Sarah Locklear. Other descendants of James Lowrie now living in this section are the following: Luther Dees and John Dees, sons of Silas Lowrie, who was a son of Thomas Lowrie, and Thomas Lowrie was a son of James Lowrie. Sinclair Lowrie and James Lowrie and Pert Ransom are all children of Allen Lowrie, who was a son of the original James Lowrie. This James Lowrie first lived in the upper part of Robeson County, now Hoke County. He afterwards moved to Harpers Ferry, on Lumber River, and maintained first a ferry and afterwards a toll bridge at that point. He laid out and constructed the Lowrie Road. Wash Lowrie says that this James Lowrie was a nephew of Col. John Lowrie, who was one time chief of the Cherokees and who signed a treaty on behalf of the Cherokees to the United States Government. He further states that he knew old John Brooks well, having seen him a number of times before he died. This John Brooks was a soldier in the Revolutionary War. (See application for pension in the records of the War Department at Washington.) Wash Lowrie says that old John Brooks died at the age of about 110 years. His application for pension states that he was about 90 or 96 years old when the pension was granted. Says that he was told by Aaron Revels, then 100 years old, and Daniel Lowrie, his father, then 73 years old, and Joe Chavis, age 90, that these Indians in Robeson County came from Roanoke, in Virginia. That after remaining in Robeson County for some time they went to the mountains with the other Cherokees, but a number returned on account of leaving relatives in Robeson County, where they had mixed with the other tribes and probably with several of the whites.

The United States census of 1790 shows only a few Indian families in Robeson County at the time of taking that census.

Wash Lowrie states further that he has often heard of Hugh Locklear, who served in the War of 1812, and that Nelson Locklear, now living in Robeson County, is a great grandson of this Hugh Locklear, and that

Hector Locklear's wife is a great granddaughter. That he has often heard of Stephen Cumbo, who was a soldier in the War of 1812. That Abbie Cumbo, who married Allen Lowrie, was a daughter of this Stephen Cumbo.

This Wash Lowrie is now in very bad health, having suffered a stroke of paralysis, but his mind and memory seem to be good. He has many of the characteristics of the Indians. An enlarged photograph can be obtained, as he has one hanging in his bedroom.

[Page 132] *OFFICE LETTER OF SEPTEMBER 14, 1914, TO A. W. MCLEAN.*

SEPTEMBER 14, 1914.

DEAR SIR: The office has received your letter of September 7, 1914, submitting certain matter relating to the Indians of Robeson County, N. C., and the same has been referred to Special Agent McPherson for consideration in connection with his investigation of the affairs of said Indians, in obedience to Senate resolution 410 and the instructions of this office.

Very respectfully,

E. B. MERITT,
Assistant Commissioner.

[Page 133] EXHIBIT G.

HISTORY OF THE CHEROKEE INDIANS.

[From Nineteenth Annual Report of the Bureau of Ethnology.]

THE TRADITIONARY PERIOD.

The Cherokee were the mountaineers of the South, holding the entire Allegheny region from the interlocking head-streams of the Kanawha and the Tennessee southward almost to the site of Atlanta, and from the Blue Ridge on the east to the Cumberland Range on the west, a territory comprising an area of about 40, 000 square miles, now included in the States of Virginia, Tennessee, North Carolina, South Carolina, Georgia, and Alabama. Their principal towns were upon the headwaters of the Savannah, Hiwassee, and Tuckasegee, and along the whole length of the Little Tennessee to its junction with the main stream. Itsâtĭ, or Echota, on the south bank of the Little Tennessee, a few miles above the mouth of Tellico River, in Tennessee, was commonly considered the capital of the nation. As the advancing whites pressed upon them from the east and northeast the more exposed towns were destroyed or abandoned and new settlements were formed lower down the Tennessee and on the upper branches of the Chattahoochee and the Coosa.

As is always the case with tribal geography, there were no fixed boundaries, and on every side the Cherokee frontiers were contested by rival claimants. In Virginia, there is reason to believe, the tribe was held in check in early days by the Powhatan and the Monacan. On the east and southeast the Tuscarora and Catawba were their inveterate enemies, with hardly even a momentary truce within the historic period; and evidence goes to show that the Sara or Cheraw were fully as hostile. On the south there was hereditary war with the Creeks, who claimed nearly the whole of upper Georgia as theirs by original possession, but who were being gradually pressed down toward the Gulf until, through the mediation of the United States, a treaty was finally made fixing the boundary between the two tribes along a line running about due west from the mouth of Broad River on the Savannah. Toward the west, the Chickasaw on the lower Tennessee and the Shawano on the Cumberland repeatedly turned back the tide of Cherokee invasion from the rich central valleys, while the powerful Iroquois in the far north set up an almost unchallenged claim of paramount lordship from the Ottawa River of Canada southward at least to the Kentucky River.

On the other hand, by their defeat of the Creeks and expulsion of the Shawano, the Cherokee made good the claim which they asserted to all the lands from upper Georgia to the Ohio River, including the rich hunting grounds of Kentucky. Holding as they did the great mountain barrier between the English settlements on the coast and the French or Spanish garrisons along the Mississippi and the Ohio, their geographic position, no less than their superior number, would [Page 134] have given them the balance of power in the South but for a looseness of tribal organization in striking contrast to the compactness of the Iroquois league, by which for more than a century the French power was held in check in the north. The English, indeed, found it convenient to recognize certain chiefs as supreme in the tribe, but the only real attempt to weld the whole Cherokee Nation into a political unit was that made by the French agent, Priber, about 1736, which failed from its premature discovery by the English. We frequently find their kingdom divided against itself, their very number preventing unity of action, while still giving them an importance above that of neighboring tribes.

The proper name by which the Cherokee call themselves is Yûñ'wiyä', or Ani'-Yûñ'wiyä' in the third person, signifying "real people," or "principal people," a word closely related to Oñwe-hoñwe, the name by which the cognate Iroquois know themselves. The word properly denotes "Indians," as distinguished from people of other races, but in usage it is restricted to mean members of the Cherokee Tribe, those of other tribes being designated as Creek, Catawba, etc., as the case may be. On ceremonial occasions they frequently speak of themselves as Ani'-Kitu' hwagĭ, or "people of Kĭtu'hwa," an ancient settlement on Tuckasegee River and apparently the original nucleus of the tribe. Among the western Cherokee this name has been adopted by a secret society recruited from the full-blood element and pledged to resist the advances of the white man's civilization. Under the various forms of Cuttawa, Gattochwa, Kittuwa, etc., as spelled by different authors, it was also used by several northern Algonquian tribes as a synonym for Cherokee.

Cherokee, the name by which they are commonly known, has no meaning in their own language, and seems to be of foreign origin. As used among themselves the form is Tsa'lăgĭ' or Tsa'răgĭ'. It first appears as Chalaque in the Portuguese narrative of De Soto's expedition, published originally in 1557, while we find Cheraqui in a French document of 1699, and Cherokee as an English form as early, at least, as 1708. The name has thus an authentic history of 360 years. There is evidence that it is derived from the Choctaw word *choluk* or *chiluk,* signifying a pit or cave, and comes to us through the so-called Mobilian trade language, a corrupted Choctaw jargon formerly used as the medium of communication among all the tribes of the Gulf States, as far north as the mouth of the Ohio. Within this area many of the tribes were commonly known under Choctaw names, even though of widely differing linguistic stocks, and if such a name existed for the Cherokee it must undoubtedly have been communicated to the first Spanish explorers by De Soto's interpreters. This theory is borne out by their Iroquois (Mohawk) name, Oyata'ge'ronoñ', as given by Hewitt, signifying "inhabitants of the cave country." the Allegheny region being peculiarly a cave country, in which "rock shelters," containing numerous traces of Indian occupancy, are of frequent occurrence. Their Catawba name also, Mañterañ, as given by Gatschet, signifying "coming out of the ground," seems to contain the same reference. Adair's attempt to connect the name Cherokee with their word for fire, *atsila,* is an error founded upon imperfect knowledge of the language.

Among other synonyms for the tribe are Rickahockan, or Rechahecrian, the ancient Powhatan name, and Tallige', or Tallige'wi, the [Page 134a] [Page 135] ancient name used in the Walam Olum chronicle of the Lenape'. Concerning both the application and the etymology of this last name there has been much dispute, but there seems no reasonable doubt as to the identity of the people.

Linguistically the Cherokee belong to the Iroquoian stock, the relationship having been suspected by Barton over a century ago, and by

Gallatin and Hale at a later period, and definitely established by Hewitt in 1887.¹ While there can now be no question of the connection, the marked lexical and grammatical differences indicate that the separation must have occurred at a very early period. As is usually the case with a large tribe occupying an extensive territory, the language is spoken in several dialects, the principal of which may, for want of other names, be conveniently designated as the Eastern, Middle, and Western. Adair's classification into "Ayrate" (*e'ladĭ*), or low, and "Ottare" (*â'talĭ*), or mountainous, must be rejected as imperfect.

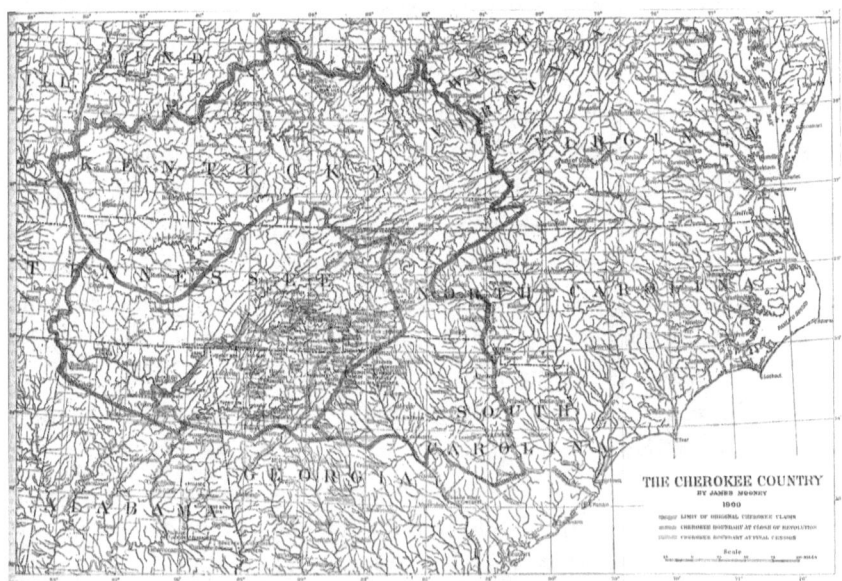

MAP OF THE CHEROKEE COUNTRY.

(From Nineteenth Annual Report of the Bureau of American Ethnology.)

---

1 Barton, Benj. S., New Views on the Origin of the Tribes and Nations of America, p. xlv, passim; Phila., 1797; Gallatin, Albert, Synopsis of Indian Tribes, Trans. American Antiquarian Society, II, p. 91; Cambridge, 1836; Hewitt, J. N. B., The Cherokee an Iroquoian Language, Washington, 1887, (MS. in the archives of the Bureau of American Ethnology).

The Eastern dialect, formerly often called the Lower Cherokee dialect, was originally spoken in all the towns upon the waters of the Keowee and Tugaloo, head streams of Savannah River, in South Carolina and the adjacent portion of Georgia. Its chief peculiarity is a rolling *r*, which takes the place of the *l* of the other dialects. In this dialect the tribal name is Tsa'răgĭ', which the English settlers of Carolina corrupted to Cherokee, while the Spaniards, advancing from the south, became better familiar with the other form, which they wrote as Chalaque. Owing to their exposed frontier position, adjoining the white settlements of Carolina, the Cherokee of this division were the first to feel the shock of war in the campaigns of 1760 and 1776, with the result that before the close of the Revolution they had been completely extirpated from their original territory and scattered as refugees among the more western towns of the tribe. The consequence was that they lost their distinctive dialect, which is now practically extinct. In 1888 it was spoken by but one man on the reservation in North Carolina.

The Middle dialect, which might properly be designated the Kituhwa dialect, was originally spoken in the towns on the Tuckasegee and the headwaters of the Little Tennessee, in the very heart of the Cherokee country, and is still spoken by the great majority of those now living on the Qualla Reservation. In some of its phonetic forms it agrees with the Eastern dialect, but resembles the Western in having the *l* sound.

The Western dialect was spoken in most of the towns of east Tennessee and upper Georgia and upon Hiwassee and Cheowa Rivers in North Carolina. It is the softest and most musical of all the dialects of this musical language, having a frequent liquid *l* and eliding many of the harsher consonants found in the other forms. It is also the literary dialect, and is spoken by most of those now constituting the Cherokee Nation in the West.

Scattered among the other Cherokee are individuals whose pronunciation and occasional peculiar terms for familiar objects give indication of a fourth and perhaps a fifth dialect, which can not now be localized. It is possible that these differences may come from foreign [Page 136] admixture, as of Natchez, Taskigi, or Shawano blood. There is some reason for believing that the people living on Nantahala River differed dialectically from their neighbors on either side.

The Iroquoian stock, to which the Cherokee belong, had its chief home in the North, its tribes occupying a compact territory which comprised portions of Ontario, New York, Ohio, and Pennsylvania, and extended down the Susquehanna and Chesapeake Bay almost to the latitude of

Washington. Another body, including the Tuscarora, Nottoway, and perhaps also the Meherrin, occupied territory in northeastern North Carolina and the adjacent portion of Virginia. The Cherokee themselves constituted the third and southernmost body. It is evident that tribes of common stock must at one time have occupied contiguous territories, and such we find to be the case in this instance. The Tuscarora and Meherrin, and presumably also the Nottoway, are known to have come from the north, while traditional and historical evidence concur in assigning to the Cherokee as their early home the region about the headwaters of the Ohio, immediately to the southward of their kinsmen, but bitter enemies, the Iroquois. The theory which brings the Cherokees from northern Iowa and the Iroquois from Manitoba is unworthy of serious consideration.

The most ancient tradition concerning the Cherokee appears to be the Delaware tradition of the expulsion of the Talligewi from the North as first noted by the missionary Heckewelder in 1819, and published more fully by Brinton in the Walam Olum in 1885. According to the first account, the Delawares, advancing from the west, found their further progress opposed by a powerful people called Alligewi or Talligewi, occupying the country upon a river which Heckewelder thinks identical with the Mississippi, but which the sequel shows was more probably the Upper Ohio. They were said to have regularly built earthen fortifications, in which they defended themselves so well that at last the Delawares were obliged to seek the assistance of the "Mengwe," or Iroquois, with the result that after a warfare extending over many years the Alligewi finally received a crushing defeat, the survivors fleeing down the river and abandoning the country to the invaders, who thereupon parceled it out amongst themselves, the "Mengwe" choosing the portion about the Great Lakes while the Delawares took possession of that to the south and east. The missionary adds that the Allegheny (and Ohio) River was still called by the Delawares the Alligewi Sipu, or river of the Alligewi. This would seem to indicate it as the true river of the tradition. He speaks also of remarkable earthworks seen by him in 1789 in the neighborhood of Lake Erie, which were said by the Indians to have been built by the extirpated tribe as defensive fortifications in the course of this war. Near two of these, in the vicinity of Sandusky, he was shown mounds under which it was said some hundreds of the slain Talligewi were buried.[1] As is usual in such traditions, the Alligewi were said to have been of giant stature, far exceeding their conquerors in size.

In the Walam Olum, which is, it is asserted, a metrical translation of an ancient hieroglyphic bark record discovered in 1820, the main tradition is given in practically the same way, with an appendix which follows the fortunes of the defeated tribe up to the beginning of the historic period, thus completing the chain of evidence.

MAP SHOWING TERRITORY HELD BY THE CHEROKEES.

(From Nineteenth Annual Report of the Bureau of American Ethnology.)

---

1 Heckewelder, John, Indian Nations of Pennsylvania, pp. 47-49, ed. 1876.

[Page 137]In the Walam Olum also we find the Delawares advancing from the west or northwest until they come to "Fish River"—the same which Heckewelder makes the Mississippi. On the other side, we are told, "The Talligewi possessed the East." The Delaware chief "desired the eastern land," and some of his people go on, but are killed by the Talligewi. The Delawares decide upon war and call in the help of their northern friends, the "Talamatan," i. e., the Wyandot and other allied Iroquoian Tribes. A war ensues which continues through the terms of four successive chiefs, when victory declares for the invaders, and "all the Talega go south." The country is then divided, the Talamatan taking the northern portion, while the Delawares "stay south of the lakes." The chronicle proceeds to tell how, after eleven more chiefs have ruled, the Nanticoke and Shawano separate from the parent tribe and remove to the south. Six other chiefs follow in succession until we come to the seventh, who "went to the Talega Mountains." By this time the Delawares have reached the ocean. Other chiefs succeed, after whom "the Easterners and the Wolves"—probably the Mahican or Wappinger and the Munsee—move off to the northeast. At last, after six more chiefs, "the whites came on the eastern sea," by which is probably meant the landing of the Dutch on Manhattan in 1609. We may consider this a tally date, approximating the beginning of the seventeenth century. Two more chiefs rule, and of the second we are told that "He fought at the south; he fought in the land of the Talega and Koweta," and again the fourth chief after the coming of the whites "went to the Talega." We have thus a traditional record of a war of conquest carried on against the Talligewi by four successive chiefs, and a succession of about twenty-five chiefs between the final expulsion of that tribe and the appearance of the whites, in which interval the Nanticoke, Shawano, Mahican, and Munsee branched off from the parent tribe of the Delawares. Without venturing to entangle ourselves in the devious maze of Indian chronology, it is sufficient to note that all this implies a very long period of time—so long, in fact, that during it several new tribes, each of which in time developed a distinct dialect, branch off from the main Lenapé stem. It is distinctly stated that all the Talega went south after their final defeat; and from later references we find that they took refuge in the mountain country in the neighborhood of the Koweta (the Creeks), and that Delaware war parties were still making raids upon both these tribes long after the first appearance of the whites.

Although at first glance it might be thought that the name Talligewi is but a corruption of Tsalagi, a closer study leads to the opinion that is a true Delaware word, in all probability connected with *waloh* or *walok*, signifying a cave or hole (Zeisberger), whence we find in the Walam Olum the word *oligonunk* rendered as "at the place of caves." It would thus be an exact Delaware rendering of the same name, "people of the cave country," by which, as we have seen, the Cherokee were commonly known among the tribes. Whatever may be the origin of the name itself, there can be no reasonable doubt as to its application. "Name, location, and legends combine to identify the Cherokees or Tsalaki with the Tallike; and this is as much evidence as we can expect to produce in such researches."[1]

[Page 138]The Wyandot confirm the Delaware story and fix the identification of the expelled tribe. According to their tradition, as narrated in 1802, the ancient fortifications in the Ohio Valley had been erected in the course of a long war between themselves and the Cherokee, which resulted finally in the defeat of the latter.[1]

The traditions of the Cherokee, so far as they have been preserved, supplement and corroborate those of the northern tribes, thus bringing the story down to their final settlement upon the headwaters of the Tennessee in the rich valleys of the southern Alleghenies. Owing to the Cherokee predilection for new gods, contrasting strongly with the conservatism of the Iroquois, their ritual forms and national epics had fallen into decay even before the Revolution, as we learn from Adair. Some vestiges of their migration legend still existed in Haywoods's time, but it is now completely forgotten both in the East and in the West.

According to Haywood, who wrote in 1823 on information obtained directly from leading members of the tribe long before the Removal, the Cherokee formerly had a long migration legend, which was already lost, but which, within the memory of the mother of one informant—say about 1750—was still recited by chosen orators on the occasion of the annual green-corn dance. This migration legend appears to have resembled that of the Delawares and the Creeks in beginning with genesis and the period of animal monsters, and thence following the shifting fortune of the chosen band to the historic period. The tradition recited that they had originated in a land toward the rising sun, where they had been placed by the command of "the four councils sent from above." In this pristine home were

---

1 Brinton, D. G., Walam Olum, p. 231; Phila., 1885.
1 Schoolcraft, H. R., Notes on the Iroquois, p. 162: Albany, 1847.

great snakes and water monsters, for which reason it was supposed to have been near the sea-coast, although the assumption is not a necessary corollary, as these are a feature of the mythology of all the eastern tribes. After this genesis period there began a slow migration, during which "towns of people in many nights' encampment removed;" but no details are given. From Heckewelder it appears that the expression, "a night's encampment," which occurs also in the Delaware migration legend, is an Indian figure of speech for a halt of one year at a place.[2]

In another place Haywood says, although apparently confusing the chronologic order of events: "One tradition which they have amongst them says they came from the west and exterminated the former inhabitants; and then says they came from the upper parts of the Ohio, where they erected the mounds on Grave creek, and that they removed thither from the country where Monticello (near Charlottesville, Virginia) is situated."[3] The first reference is to the celebrated mounds on the Ohio near Moundsville, below Wheeling, West Virginia; the other is doubtless to a noted burial mound described by Jefferson in 1781 as then existing near his home, on the low grounds of Rivanna river opposite the site of an ancient Indian town. He himself had opened it and found it to contain perhaps a thousand disjointed skeletons of both adults and children, the bones piled in successive layers, those near the top being least decayed. They showed no signs of violence, but were evidently the accumulation of long years from the neighboring Indian town. The distinguished [Page 139] writer adds: "But on whatever occasion they may have been made, they are of considerable notoriety among the Indians: for a party passing, about thirty years ago (i. e., about 1750), through the part of the country where this barrow is, went through the woods directly to it without any instructions or inquiry, and having staid about it some time, with expression which were construed to be those of sorrow, they returned to the high road, which they had left about half a dozen miles to pay this visit, and pursued their journey."[1] Although the tribe is not named, the Indians were probably Cherokee, as no other southern Indians were then accustomed to range in

---

2 Heckewelder, Indian Nations, p. 47, ed. 1876.

3 Haywood, John, Natural and Aboriginal History of Tennessee, pp. 225-226; Nashville, 1823.

1 Jefferson, Thomas, Notes on Virginia, pp. 136-137; ed. Boston, 1802.

that section. As serving to corroborate this opinion we have the statement of a prominent Cherokee chief, given to Schoolcraft in 1846, that according to their tradition his people had formerly lived at the Peaks of Otter, in Virginia, a noted landmark of the Blue Ridge, near the point where Staunton river breaks through the mountains.[2]

From a careful sifting of the evidence Haywood concludes that the authors of the most ancient remains in Tennessee had spread over that region from the south and southwest at a very early period, but that the later occupants, the Cherokee, had entered it from the north and northeast in comparatively recent times, overrunning and exterminating the aborigines. He declares that the historical fact seems to be established that the Cherokee entered the country from Virginia, making temporary settlements upon New River and the upper Holston, until, under the continued hostile pressure from the north, they were again forced to remove farther to the south, fixing themselves upon the Little Tennessee, in what afterward became known as the middle towns. By a leading mixed blood of the tribe he was informed that they had made their first settlements within their modern home territory upon Nolichucky River, and that, having lived there for a long period, they could give no definite account of an earlier location. Echota, their capital and peace town, "claimed to be the eldest brother in the nation," and the claim was generally acknowledged.[3] In confirmation of the statement as to an early occupancy of the upper Holston region, it may be noted that "Watauga Old Fields," now Elizabethtown, were so called from the fact that when the first white settlement within the present State of Tennessee was begun there, so early as 1769, the bottom lands were found to contain graves and other numerous ancient remains of a former Indian town which tradition ascribed to the Cherokee, whose nearest settlements were then many miles to the southward.

While the Cherokee claimed to have built the mounds on the upper Ohio, they yet, according to Haywood, expressly disclaimed the authorship of the very numerous mounds and petroglyphs in their later home territory, asserting that these ancient works had exhibited the same appearance when they themselves had first occupied the region.[4] This accords with

---

2 Schoolcraft, Notes on the Iroquois, p. 163, 1847.
3 Haywood, Natural and Aboriginal History of Tennessee, pp. 233, 236, 269, 1823.
4 Haywood, Nat. and Aborig. Hist. Tennessee, pp. 226, 234, 1823.

Bartram's statement that the Cherokee, although sometimes utilizing the mounds as sites for their own town houses, were as ignorant as the whites of their origin or purpose, having only a general tradition that their forefathers had found them in much the same condition on first coming into the country.[5]

[Page 140]Although, as has been noted, Haywood expresses the opinion that the invading Cherokee had overrun and exterminated the earlier inhabitants, he says in another place, on half-breed authority, that the newcomers found no Indians upon the waters of the Tennessee, with the exception of some Creeks living upon that river, near the mouth of the Hiwassee, the main body of that tribe being established upon and claiming all the streams to the southward.[1] There is considerable evidence that the Creeks preceded the Cherokee, and within the last century they still claimed the Tennessee, or at least the Tennessee watershed, for their northern boundary.

There is a dim but persistent tradition of a strange white race preceding the Cherokee, some of the stories even going so far as to locate their former settlements and to identify them as the authors of the ancient works found in the country. The earliest reference appears to be that of Barton in 1797, on the statement of a gentleman whom he quotes as a valuable authority upon the southern tribes. "The Cheerake tell us, that when they first arrived in the country which they inhabit, they found it possessed by certain 'moon-eyed people,' who could not see in the daytime. These wretches they expelled." He seems to consider them an albino race.[2] Haywood, twenty-six years later, says that the invading Cherokee found "white people" near the head of the Little Tennessee, with forts extending thence down the Tennessee as far as Chickamauga Creek. He gives the location of three of these forts. The Cherokee made war against them and drove them to the mouth of Big Chickamauga Creek, where they entered into a treaty and agreed to remove if permitted to depart in peace. Permission being granted, they abandoned the country. Elsewhere he speaks of this extirpated white race as having extended into Kentucky and probably also into western Tennessee, according to the concurrent traditions of different tribes. He describes

---

5 Bartram, Wm., Travels, p. 365; reprint, London, 1792.
1 Haywood, op. cit., pp. 234-237.
2 Barton, New Views, p. xliv, 1797.

their houses, on what authority is not stated, as having been small circular structures of upright logs, covered with earth which had been dug out from the inside.³

Harry Smith, a half-breed born about 1815, father of the late chief of the East Cherokee, informed the author that when a boy he had been told by an old woman a tradition of a race of very small people, perfectly white, who once came and lived for some time on the site of the ancient mound on the northern side of Hiwassee, at the mouth of Peachtree Creek, a few miles above the present Murphy, North Carolina. They afterward removed to the West. Colonel Thomas, the white chief of the East Cherokee, born about the beginning of the century, had also heard a tradition of another race of people, who lived on Hiwassee, opposite the present Murphy, and warned the Cherokee that they must not attempt to cross over to the south side of the river or the great leech in the water would swallow them.⁴ They finally went west, "long before the whites came." The two stories are plainly the same, although told independently and many miles apart.

[Page 141] *THE PERIOD OF SPANISH EXPLORATION—1540-?*

The definite history of the Cherokee begins with the year 1540, at which date we find them already established, where they were always afterward known, in the mountains of Carolina and Georgia. The earliest Spanish adventurers failed to penetrate so far into the interior, and the first entry into their country was made by De Soto, advancing up the Savannah on his fruitless quest for gold, in May of that year.

While at Cofitachiqui, an important Indian town on the lower Savannah governed by a "queen," the Spaniards had found hatchets and other objects of copper, some of which was of finer color and appeared to be mixed with gold, although they had no means of testing it.¹ On inquiry they were told that the metal had come from an interior mountain province called Chisca, but the country was represented as thinly peopled and the way as impassable for horses. Some time before, while advancing through eastern Georgia, they had heard also of a rich and plentiful province called Coca,

---

3 Haywood, Nat. and Aborig. Hist. Tennessee, pp. 166, 234-235, 287-289, 1823.
4 See story, "The Great Leech of Tlanusi'yĭ," p. 328.
1 Garcilaso de la Voga, La Florida del Inca, pp. 129, 133-134; Madrid, 1723.

toward the northwest, and by the people of Cofitachiqui they were now told that Chiaha, the nearest town of Coca province, was twelve days inland. As both men and animals were already nearly exhausted from hunger and hard travel, and the Indians either could not or would not furnish sufficient provision for their needs, De Soto determined not to attempt the passage of the mountains then, but to push on at once to Coca, there to rest and recuperate before undertaking further exploration. In the meantime he hoped also to obtain more definite information concerning the mines. As the chief purpose of the expedition was the discovery of the mines, many of the officers regarded this change of plan as a mistake, and favored staying where they were until the new crop should be ripened, then go directly into the mountains, but as the general was "a stern man and of few words," none ventured to oppose his resolution.[2] The province of Coca was the territory of the Creek Indians, called Ani'-Kusa by the Cherokee, from Kusa, or Coosa, their ancient capital, while Chiaha was identical with Chehaw, one of the principal Creek towns on Chattahoochee River. Cofitachiqui may have been the capital of the Uchee Indians.

The outrageous conduct of the Spaniards had so angered the Indian queen that she now refused to furnish guides and carriers, whereupon De Soto made her a prisoner, with the design of compelling her to act as guide herself, and at the same time to use her as a hostage to command the obedience of her subjects. Instead, however, of conducting the Spaniards by the direct trail toward the west, she led them far out of their course until she finally managed to make her escape, leaving them to find their way out of the mountains as best they could.

Departing from Cofitachiqui, they turned first toward the north, passing through several towns subject to the queen, to whom, although a prisoner, the Indians everywhere showed great respect and obedience, furnishing whatever assistance the Spaniards compelled her to demand for their own purposes. In a few days they came to "a province called Chalaque," the territory of the Cherokee Indians, probably upon the waters of Keowee River, the eastern head stream of the Savannah. It is described as the poorest country for corn that [Page 142] they had yet seen, the inhabitants subsisting on wild roots and herbs and on game which they killed with bows and

---

2 Gentleman of Elvas, Publications of the Hakluyt Society, IX, pp. 52, 58, 64; London, 1851.

arrows. They were naked, lean, and unwarlike. The country abounded in wild turkeys ("gallinas"), which the people gave very freely to the strangers, one town presenting them with seven hundred. A chief also gave De Soto two deerskins as a great present.[1] Garcilaso, writing on the authority of an old soldier nearly fifty years afterward, says that the "Chalaques" deserted their towns on the approach of the white men and fled to the mountains, leaving behind only old men and women and some who were nearly blind.[2] Although it was too early for the new crop, the poverty of the people may have been more apparent than real, due to their unwillingness to give any part of their stored-up provision to the unwelcome strangers. As the Spaniards were greatly in need of corn for themselves and their horses, they made no stay, but hurried on. In a few days they arrived at Guaquili, which is mentioned only by Ranjel, who does not specify whether it was a town or a province—i. e., a tribal territory. It was probably a small town. Here they were welcomed in a friendly manner, the Indians giving them a little corn and many wild turkeys, together with some dogs of a peculiar small species, which were bred for eating purposes and did not bark.[3] They were also supplied with men to help carry the beggage. The name Guaquili has a Cherokee sound and may be connected with *wa'gulï*, "whippoorwill," *uwâ' gi'ï*, "foam," or *gi'lï*, "dog."

Traveling still toward the north, they arrived a day or two later in the province of Xuala, in which we recognize the territory of the Suwali, Sara, or Cheraw Indians, in the piedmont region about the head of Broad River in North Carolina. Garcilaso, who did not see it, represents it as a rich country, while the Elvas narrative and Biedma agree that it was a rough, broken country, thinly inhabited and poor in provision. According to Garcilaso, it was under the rule of the queen of Cofitachiqui, although a distinct province in itself.[4] The principal town was beside a small rapid stream, close under a mountain. The chief received them in friendly fashion, giving them corn, dogs of the small breed already mentioned, carrying baskets,

---

1 Gentleman of Elvas, Publications of the Hakluyt Society, IX, p. 60, London, 1851.
2 Garcilaso, La Florida del Inca, p. 136, ed. 1723.
3 Ranjel, in Oviedo, Historia General y Natural de las Indias, I, p. 562; Madrid, 1851.
4 Garcilaso, La Florida del Inca, p. 137, 1723.

and burden bearers. The country roundabout showed greater indications of gold mines than any they had yet seen.³

Here De Soto turned to the west, crossing a very high mountain range, which appears to have been the Blue Ridge, and descending on the other side to a stream flowing in the opposite direction, which was probably one of the upper tributaries of the French Broad.⁵ Although it was late in May, they found it very cold in the mountains.⁶ After several days of such travel they arrived, about the end of the month, at the town of Guasili, or Guaxule. The chief and principal men came out some distance to welcome them, dressed in fine robes of skins, with feather head dresses, after the fashion of the country. Before reaching this point the queen had managed to make her escape, together with three slaves of the Spaniards, and the last that was heard of her was that she was on her way back to her own [Page 143] country with one of the runaways as her husband. What grieved De Soto most in the matter was that she took with her a small box of pearls, which he had intended to take from her before releasing her, but had left with her for the present in order "not to discontent her altogether."¹

Guaxule is described as a very large town surrounded by a number of small mountain streams which united to form the large river down which the Spaniards proceeded after leaving the place.² Here, as elsewhere, the Indians received the white men with kindness and hospitality—so much so that the name of Guaxule became to the army a synonym for good fortune.³ Among other things they gave the Spaniards 300 dogs for food, although, according to the Elvas narrative, the Indians themselves did not eat them.⁴ The principal officers of the expedition were lodged in the "chief's house," by which we are to understand the townhouse, which was upon a high hill with a roadway to the top.⁵ From a close study of the nar-

---

3 Ranjel, in Oviedo, Historia General y Natural de las Indias, I, p. 562; Madrid, 1851.
5 See note 8, De Soto's route.
6 Ranjel, op. cit., I, p. 562.
1 Elvas, Hakluyt Society, IX, p. 61, 1851.
2 Garcilaso, op. cit., p. 139.
3 Ranjel, in Oviedo, Historia, I, p. 563, 1851.
4 Elvas, Biedma, and Ranjel, all make special references to the dogs given them at this place; they seem to have been of the same small breed ("perrillos") which Ranjel says the Indians used for food.
5 Garcilaso, La Florida del Inca, p. 139, 1723.

rative it appears that this "hill" was no other than the great Nacoochee mound, in White county, Georgia, a few miles northwest of the present Clarkesville.[6] It was within the Cherokee territory, and the town was probably a settlement of that tribe. From here De Soto sent runners ahead to notify the chief of Chiaha of his approach, in order that sufficient corn might be ready on his arrival.

Leaving Guaxule, they proceeded down the river, which we identify with the Chattahoochee, and in two days arrived at Canasoga, or Canasagua, a frontier town of the Cherokee. As they neared the town they were met by the Indians, bearing baskets of "mulberries,"[7] more probably the delicious service berry of the southern mountains, which ripens in the early summer, while the mulberry matures later.

From here they continued down the river, which grew constantly larger, through an uninhabited country which formed the disputed territory between the Cherokee and the Creeks. About five days after leaving Canasagua they were met by messengers, who escorted them to Chiaha, the first town of the province of Coça. De Soto had crossed the State of Georgia, leaving the Cherokee country behind him, and was now among the Lower Creeks, in the neighborhood of the present Columbus, Georgia. With his subsequent wanderings after crossing the Chattahoochee into Alabama and beyond we need not concern ourselves.

While resting at Chiaha De Soto met with a chief who confirmed what the Spaniards had heard before concerning mines in the province of Chisca, saying that there was there "a melting of copper" and of another metal of about the same color, but softer, and therefore not so much used.[8] The province was northward from Chiaha, somewhere in upper Georgia or the adjacent part of Alabama or Tennessee, through all of which mountain region native copper is found. The other mineral, which the Spaniards understood to be gold, may have been iron pyrites, although there is some evidence that the Indians occasionally found and shaped gold nuggets.

[Page 144] Accordingly two soldiers were sent on foot with Indian guides to find Chisca and learn the truth of the stories. They rejoined the army some time after the march had been resumed, and reported according to

---

6 See note 8, De Soto's route.
7 See Elvas, Hakluyt Society, IX, p. 61, 1851; and Ranjel, op. cit., p. 563.
8 Elvas, op. cit., p. 64.

the Elvas chronicler, that their guides had taken them through a country so poor in corn, so rough, and over so high mountains that it would be impossible for the army to follow; wherefore, as the way grew long and lingering, they had turned back after reaching a little poor town where they saw nothing that was of any profit. They brought back with them a dressed buffalo skin which the Indians there had given them, the first ever obtained by white men, and described in the quaint old chronicle as "an ox hide as thin as a calf's skin, and the hair like a soft wool between the coarse and fine wool of sheep."[1]

Garcilaso's glowing narrative gives a somewhat different impression. According to this author the scouts returned full of enthusiasm for the fertility of the country, and reported that the mines were of a fine species of copper, and had indications also of gold and silver, while their progress from one town to another had been a continual series of feastings and Indian hospitalities.[2] However that may have been, De Soto made no further effort to reach the Cherokee mines, but continued his course westward through the Creek country, having spent altogether a month in the mountain region.

There is no record of any second attempt to penetrate the Cherokee country for twenty-six years. In 1561 the Spaniards took formal possession of the Bay of Santa Elena, now Saint Helena, near Port Royal, on the coast of South Carolina. The next year the French made an unsuccessful attempt at settlement at the same place, and in 1566 Menendez made the Spanish occupancy sure by establishing there a fort which he called San Felipe.[3] In November of that year Captain Juan Pardo was sent with a party from the fort to explore the interior. Accompanied by the chief of "Juada" (which from Vandera's narrative we find should be "Joara," i. e., the Sara Indians already mentioned in the De Soto chronicle), he proceeded as far as the territory of that tribe, where he built a fort, but on account of the snow in the mountains did not think it advisable to go farther, and returned, leaving a sergeant with thirty soldiers to garrison the post. Soon after his return he received a letter from the sergeant stating that the chief of Chisca—the

---

1 Elvas, Hakluyt Society, IX, p. 66, 1851.

2 Garcilaso, La Florida del Inca, p. 141, ed. 1723.

3 Shea, J. G., in Winsor, Justin, Narrative and Critical History of America, II, pp. 260, 278: Boston, 1886.

rich mining country of which De Soto had heard—was very hostile to the Spaniards, and that in a recent battle the latter had killed a thousand of his Indians and burned fifty houses with almost no damage to themselves. Either the sergeant or his chronicler must have been an unconscionable liar, as it was asserted that all this was done with only fifteen men. Immediately afterward, according to the same story, the sergeant marched with twenty men about a day's distance in the mountains against another hostile chief, whom he found in a strongly palisaded town, which, after a hard fight, he and his men stormed and burned, killing fifteen hundred Indians without losing a single man themselves. Under instructions from his superior officer, the sergeant with his small party then proceeded to explore what lay beyond, and, taking a road which they were told led to the territory of a great chief, after four [Page 145] days of hard marching they came to his town, called Chiaha (Chicha, by mistake in the manuscript translation), the same where De Soto had rested. It is described at this time as palisaded and strongly fortified, with a deep river on each side, and defended by over three thousand fighting men, there being no women or children among them. It is possible that in view of their former experience with the Spaniards, the Indians had sent their families away from the town, while at the same time they may have summoned warriors from the neighboring Creek towns in order to be prepared for any emergency However, as before, they received the white men with the greatest kindness, and the Spaniards continued for twelve days through the territories of the same tribe until they arrived at the principal town (Kusa?), where, by the invitation of the chief, they built a small fort and awaited the coming of Pardo, who was expected to follow with a larger force from Santa Elena, as he did in the summer of 1567, being met on his arrival with every show of hospitality from the Creek chiefs. This second fort was said to be one hundred and forty leagues distant from that in the Sara country, which latter was called one hundred and twenty leagues from Santa Elena.[1]

In the summer of 1567, according to previous agreement, Captain Pardo left the fort at Santa Elena with a small detachment of troops, and after a week's travel, sleeping each night at a different Indian town, arrived at "Canos, which the Indians call Canosi, and by another name, Cofetaçque" (the Cofitachiqui of the De Soto chronicle), which is described as situated

---

[1] Narrative of Pardo's expedition by Martinez, about 1568, Brooks manuscripts.

in a favorable location for a large city, fifty leagues from Santa Elena, to which the easiest road was by a river (the Savannah) which flowed by the town, or by another which they had passed ten leagues farther back. Proceeding, they passed Jagaya, Gueza, and Arauchi, and arrived at Otariyatiqui, or Otari, in which we have perhaps the Cherokee *â'tărĭ* or *â'ătaĭ*, "mountain." It may have been a frontier Cherokee settlement, and, according to the old chronicler, its chief and language ruled much good country. From here a trail went northward to Guatari, Sauxpa, and Usi, i. e., the Wateree, Waxhaw (or Sissipahaw?), and Ushery or Catawba.

Leaving Otariyatiqui, they went on to Quinahaqui, and then, turning to the left, to Issa, where they found mines of crystal (mica?). They came next to Aguaquiri (the Guaquili of the De Soto chronicle), and then to Joara, "near to the mountain, where Juan Pardo arrived with his sergeant on his first trip." This, as has been noted, was the Xuala of the De Soto chronicle, the territory of the Sara Indians, in the foothills of the Blue Ridge, southeast from the present Asheville, North Carolina. Vandera makes it one hundred leagues from Santa Elena, while Martinez, already quoted, makes the distance one hundred and twenty leagues The difference is not important, as both statements were only estimates. From there they followed "along the mountains" to Tocax (Toxaway?), Cauchi (Nacoochee?), and Tanasqui—apparently Cherokee towns, although the forms can not be identified—and after resting three days at the last-named place went on "to Solameco, otherwise called Chiaha," where the sergeant met them. The combined forces afterward went on, through Cossa (Kusa), Tasquiqui (Taskigi), and other Creek towns, as far as Tascaluza, [Page 146] in the Alabama country, and returned thence to Santa Elena, having apparently met with a friendly reception everywhere along the route. From Cofitachiqui to Tascaluza they went over about the same road traversed by De Soto in 1540.[1]

We come now to a great gap of nearly a century. Shea has a notice of a Spanish mission founded among the Cherokee in 1643 and still flourishing when visited by an English traveler ten years later,[2] but as his information is derived entirely from the fraudulent work of Davies, and as no such mission is mentioned by Barcia in any of these years, we may regard the story

---

1 Vandera narrative, 1569, in French, B. F., Hist. Colls. of La. new series, pp. 289-292; New York, 1875.
2 Shea, J. G., Catholic Missions, p. 72; New York, 1855.

as spurious. The first mission work in the tribe appears to have been that of Priber, almost a hundred years later. Long before the end of the sixteenth century, however, the existence of mines of gold and other metals in the Cherokee country was a matter of common knowledge among the Spaniards at St. Augustine and Santa Elena, and more than one expedition had been fitted out to explore the interior.[3] Numerous traces of ancient mining operations, with remains of old shafts and fortifications, evidently of European origin, show that these discoveries were followed up, although the policy of Spain concealed the fact from the outside world. How much permanent impression this early Spanish intercourse made on the Cherokee it is impossible to estimate, but it must have been considerable.

THE COLONIAL AND REVOLUTIONARY PERIOD—1654-1784.

It was not until 1654 that the English first came into contact with the Cherokee, called in the records of the period Rechahecrians, a corruption of Rickahockan, apparently the name by which they were known to the Powhatan tribes. In that year the Virginia colony, which had only recently concluded a long and exterminating war with the Powhatan, was thrown into alarm by the news that a great body of six or seven hundred Rechahecrian Indians—by which is probably meant that number of warriors—from the mountains had invaded the lower country and established themselves at the falls of James River, where now is the city of Richmond. The assembly at once passed resolutions "that these new come Indians be in no sort suffered to seat themselves there, or any place near us, it having cost so much blood to expel and extirpate those perfidious and treacherous Indians which were there formerly." It was therefore ordered that a force of at least 100 white men be at once sent against them, to be joined by the warriors of all the neighboring subject tribes, according to treaty obligation. The Pamunkey chief, with a hundred of his men, responded to the summons, and the combined force marched against the invaders. The result was a bloody battle, with disastrous outcome to the Virginians, the Pamunkey chief with most of his men being killed, while the whites were forced to make such terms of peace with the Rechahecrians that the assembly cashiered the commander of the expedition and compelled him to pay the

---

3 See Brooks manuscripts in the archives of the Bureau of American Ethnology.

whole cost of the treaty from his own estate.⁴ Owing to the imperfection of the Virginia records we have no means of knowing the causes of the sudden invasion or how long the invaders retained their position at the falls. In all probability it [Page 147] was only the last of a long series of otherwise unrecorded irruptions by the mountaineers on the more peaceful dwellers in the lowlands. From a remark in Lederer it is probable that the Cherokee were assisted also by some of the piedmont tribes hostile to the Powhatan. The Peaks of Otter, near which the Cherokee claim to have once lived, as has been already noted, are only about one hundred miles in a straight line from Richmond, while the burial mound and town site near Charlottesville, mentioned by Jefferson, are but half that distance.

In 1655 a Virginia expedition sent out from the falls of James River (Richmond) crossed over the mountains to the large streams flowing into the Mississippi. No details are given and the route is uncertain, but whether or not they met Indians, they must have passed through Cherokee territory.¹

In 1670 the German traveler, John Lederer, went from the falls of James River to the Catawba country, in South Carolina, following for most of the distance the path used by the Virginia traders, who already had regular dealings with the southern tribes, including probably the Cherokee. He speaks in several places of the Rickahockan, which seems to be a more correct form than Rechahecrian, and his narrative and the accompanying map put them in the mountains of North Carolina, back of the Catawba and the Sara and southward from the head of Roanoke River. They were apparently on hostile terms with the tribes to the eastward, and while the traveler was stopping at an Indian village on Dan River, about the present Clarksville, Virginia, a delegation of Rickahockan, which had come on tribal business, was barbarously murdered at a dance prepared on the night of their arrival by their treacherous hosts. On reaching the Catawba country he heard of white men to the southward, and incidentally mentions that the neighboring mountains were called the Suala Mountains by the Spaniards.² In the next year, 1671, a party from Virginia under Thomas Batts explored the

---

4 Burk, John, History of Virginia, II, pp. 104-107; Petersburg, 1805.

1 Ramsey, J. G. M., Annals of Tennessee, p. 37; Charleston, 1853 (quoting Martin, North Carolina, I, p. 115, 1853).

2 Lederer, John, Discoveries, pp. 15, 26, 27, 29, 33, and map; reprint, Charleston, 1891; Mooney, Siouan Tribes of the East (bulletin of Bureau of Ethnology), pp. 53-54, 1894.

northern branch of Roanoke River and crossed over the Blue Ridge to the headwaters of New River, where they found traces of occupancy, but no Indians. By this time all the tribes of this section, east of the mountains, were in possession of firearms.[3]

The first permanent English settlement in South Carolina was established in 1670. In 1690 James Moore, secretary of the colony, made an exploring expedition into the mountains and reached a point at which, according to his Indian guides, he was within twenty miles of where the Spaniards were engaged in mining and smelting with bellows and furnaces; but on account of some misunderstanding he returned without visiting the place, although he procured specimens of ores, which he sent to England for assay.[4] It may have been in the neighborhood of the present Lincolnton, North Carolina, where a dam of cut stone and other remains of former civilized occupancy have recently been discovered. In this year, also, Cornelius Dougherty, an Irishman from Virginia, established himself as the first trader among the Cherokee, with whom he spent the rest of his life.[5] Some of his descendants still occupy honored positions in the tribe.

[Page 148]Among the manuscript archives of South Carolina there was said to be, some 50 years ago, a treaty or agreement made with the government of that colony by the Cherokee in 1684, and signed with the hieroglyphics of eight chiefs of the lower towns, viz, Corani, the Raven (Ka'lanû); Sinnawa, the Hawk (Tlă'nuwă); Nellawgitehi, Gorhaleke, and Owasta, all of Toxawa; and Canacaught, the great Conjuror, Gohoma, and Caunasaita, of Keowa. If still in existence, this is probably the oldest Cherokee treaty on record.[1]

What seems to be the next mention of the Cherokee in the South Carolina records occurs in 1691, when we find an inquiry ordered in regard to a report that some of the colonists "have, without any proclamation of war, fallen upon and murdered" several of that tribe.[2]

In 1693 some Cherokee chiefs went to Charleston with presents for the governor and offers of friendship, to ask the protection of South Carolina

---

[3] Mooney, op. cit., pp. 34-35.

[4] Document of 1699, quoted in South Carolina Hist. Soc. Colls., I, p. 209; Charleston, 1857.

[5] Haywood, Nat. and Aborig. Hist. Tennessee, p. 233, 1823.

[1] Noted in Cherokee Advocate, Tahlequah, Indian Territory, January 30, 1845.

[2] Document of 1691, South Carolina Hist. Soc. Colls., I, p. 126.

against their enemies, the Esaw (Catawba), Savanna (Shawano), and Congaree, all of that colony, who had made war upon them and sold a number of their tribesmen into slavery. They were told that their kinsmen could not now be recovered, but that the English desired friendship with their tribe, and that the Government would see that there would be no future ground for such complaint.[3] The promise was apparently not kept, for in 1705 we find a bitter accusation brought against Governor Moore, of South Carolina, that he had granted commissions to a number of persons "to set upon, assault, kill, destroy, and take captive as many Indians as they possible [sic] could," the prisoners being sold into slavery for his and their private profit. By this course, it was asserted, he had "already almost utterly ruined the trade for skins and furs, whereby we held our chief correspondence with England, and turned it into a trade of Indians or slave making, whereby the Indians to the south and west of us are already involved in blood and confusion." The arraignment concludes with a warning that such conditions would in all probability draw down upon the colony an Indian war with all its dreadful consequences.[4] In view of what happened a few years later this reads like a prophecy.

About the year 1700 the first guns were introduced among the Cherokee, the event being fixed traditionally as having occurred in the girlhood of an old woman of the tribe who died about 1775.[5] In 1708 we find them described as a numerous people, living in the mountains northwest from the Charleston settlements and having sixty towns, but of small importance in the Indian trade, being "but ordinary hunters and less warriors."[6]

In the war with the Tuscarora in 1711-1713, which resulted in the expulsion of that tribe from North Carolina, more than a thousand southern Indians reenforced the South Carolina volunteers, among them being over two hundred Cherokee, hereditary enemies of the Tuscarora. Although these Indian allies did their work well in the actual encounters, their assistance was of doubtful advantage, as they helped themselves freely to whatever they wanted along the way, so that the settlers had reason to fear them

---

3 Hewat, South Carolina and Georgia, I, p. 127, 1778.

4 Documents of 1705, in North Carolina Colonial Records, II, p. 904; Raleigh, 1886.

5 Haywood, Nat. and Aborig. Tenn., p. 237, 1823; with the usual idea that Indians live to extreme old age, Haywood makes her 110 years old at her death, putting back the introduction of firearms to 1677.

6 Letter of 1708, in Rivers, South Carolina, p. 238, 1856.

almost as much as the hostile [Page 149] Tuscarora. After torturing a large number of their prisoners in the usual savage fashion, they returned with the remainder, whom they afterward sold as slaves to South Carolina.[1]

Having wiped out old scores with the Tuscarora, the late allies of the English proceeded to discuss their own grievances, which, as we have seen, were sufficiently galling. The result was a combination against the whites, embracing all the tribes from Cape Fear to the Chattahoochee, including the Cherokee, who thus for the first time raised their hand against the English. The war opened with a terrible massacre by the Yamassee in April, 1715, followed by assaults along the whole frontier, until for a time it was seriously feared that the colony of South Carolina would be wiped out of existence. In a contest between savagery and civilization, however, the final result is inevitable. The settlers at last rallied their whole force under Governor Craven and administered such a crushing blow to the Yamassee that the remnant abandoned their country and took refuge with the Spaniards in Florida or among the Lower Creeks. The English then made short work with the smaller tribes along the coast, while those in the interior were soon glad to sue for peace.[2]

A number of Cherokee chiefs having come down to Charleston in company with a trader to express their desire for peace, a force of several hundred white troops and a number of negroes under Colonel Maurice Moore went up the Savannah in the winter of 1715-16 and made headquarters among the Lower Cherokee, where they were met by the chiefs of the Lower and some of the western towns, who reaffirmed their desire for a lasting peace with the English, but refused to fight against the Yamassee, although willing to proceed against some other tribes. They laid the blame for most of the trouble upon the traders, who, "had been very abuseful to them of late." A detachment under Colonel George Chicken, sent to the Upper Cherokee, penetrated to "Quoneashee" (Tlanusi'yĭ, on Hiwassee, about the present Murphy) where they found the chiefs more defiant, resolved to continue the war against the Creeks, with whom the English were then trying to make peace, and demanding large supplies of guns and ammunition, saying that if they made a peace with the other tribes

---

[1] Royce, Cherokee Nation, Fifth Ann. Rep. Bureau of Ethnology, p. 140, 1888; Hewat, op. cit., p. 216 et passim.

[2] Hewat, South Carolina and Georgia, I, p. 216 et passim, 1778.

they would have no means of getting slaves with which to buy ammunition for themselves. At this time they claimed 2, 370 warriors, of whom half were believed to have guns. As the strength of the whole nation was much greater, this estimate may have been for the Upper and Middle Cherokee only. After "abundance of persuading" by the officers, they finally "told us they would trust us once again," and an arrangement was made to furnish them two hundred guns with a supply of ammunition, together with fifty white soldiers, to assist them against the tribes with which the English were still at war. In March, 1716, this force was increased by one hundred men. The detachment under Colonel Chicken returned by way of the towns on the upper part of the Little Tennessee, thus penetrating the heart of the Cherokee country.[3]

Steps were now taken to secure peace by inaugurating a satisfactory trade system, for which purpose a large quantity of suitable goods [Page 150] was purchased at the public expense of South Carolina, and a correspondingly large party was equipped for the initial trip.[1] In 1721, in order still more to systematize Indian affairs, Governor Nicholson of South Carolina invited the chiefs of the Cherokee to a conference, at which thirty-seven towns were represented. A treaty was made by which trading methods were regulated, a boundary line between their territory and the English settlements was agreed upon, and an agent was appointed to superintend their affairs. At the governor's suggestion, one chief, called Wrosetasatow(?) was formally commissioned as supreme head of the nation, with authority to punish all offenses, including murder, and to represent all Cherokee claims to the colonial government. Thus were the Cherokee reduced from their former condition of a free people, ranging where their pleasure led, to that of dependent vassals with bounds fixed by a colonial governor. The negotiations were accompanied by a cession of land, the first in the history of the tribe. In little more than a century thereafter they had signed away their whole original territory.[2]

---

[3] See Journal of Colonel George Chicken, 1715-16, with notes, in Charleston Yearbook, pp. 313-354, 1894.

[1] Journal of South Carolina Assembly, in North Carolina Colonial Records, II, pp. 225-227, 1886.

[2] Hewat, South Carolina and Georgia, I, pp. 297-298, 1778; Royce, Cherokee Nation in Fifth Ann. Rep. Bureau of Ethnology, p. 144 and map, 1888.

The document of 1716 already quoted puts the strength of the Cherokee at that time at 2, 370 warriors, but in this estimate the Lower Cherokee seem not to have been included. In 1715, according to a trade census compiled by Governor Johnson of South Carolina, the tribe had thirty towns, with 4, 000 warriors and a total population of 11, 210.[3] Another census in 1721 gives them fifty-three towns with 3, 510 warriors and a total of 10, 379,[4] while the report of the board of trade for the same year gives them 3, 800 warriors,[5] equivalent, by the same proportion, to nearly 12, 000 total. Adair, a good authority on such matters, estimates, about the year 1735, when the country was better known, that they had "sixty-four towns and villages, populous and full of children," with more than 6, 000 fighting men,[6] equivalent on the same basis of computation to between 16, 000 and 17, 000 souls. From what we know of them in later times, it is probable that this last estimate is very nearly correct.

By this time the colonial government had become alarmed at the advance of the French, who had made their first permanent establishment in the Gulf States at Biloxi Bay, Mississippi, in 1699, and in 1714 had built Fort Toulouse, known to the English as "the fort at the Alabamas," on Coosa River, a few miles above the present Montgomery, Alabama. From this central vantage point they had rapidly extended their influence among all the neighboring tribes until in 1721 it was estimated that 3, 400 warriors who had formerly traded with Carolina had been "entirely debauched to the French interest," while 2, 000 more were wavering, and only the Cherokee could still be considered friendly to the English.[7] From this time until the final withdrawal of the French in 1763 the explanation of our Indian wars is to be found in the struggle between the two nations for territorial and commercial supremacy, the Indian being simply the cat's-paw of one or the other. For reasons of their own, the Chickasaw, whose territory lay within the recognized limits of Louisiana, soon became [Page 151] the uncompromising enemies of the French, and as their position enabled them in a measure to control the approach from the Mississippi, the Carolina

---

3 Royce, op. cit., p. 142.

4 Document of 1724, in Fernow, Berthold, Ohio Valley in Colonial Days, pp. 273-275; Albany, 1890.

5 Report of Board of Trade, 1721, in North Carolina Colonial Records, II, p. 422, 1886.

6 Adair, James, American Indians, p. 227; London, 1775.

7 Board of Trade report, 1721, North Carolina Colonial Records, II, p. 422, 1886.

government saw to it that they were kept well supplied with guns and ammunition. British traders were in all their towns, and on one occasion a French force, advancing against a Chickasaw palisaded village, found it garrisoned by Englishmen flying the British flag.[1] The Cherokee, although nominally allies of the English, were strongly disposed to favor the French, and it required every effort of the Carolina government to hold them to their allegiance.

In 1730, to further fix the Cherokee in the English interest, Sir Alexander Cuming was dispatched on a secret mission to that tribe, which was again smarting under grievances and almost ready to join with the Creeks in an alliance with the French. Proceeding to the ancient town of Nequassee (Nĭkwăsĭ, at the present Franklin, North Carolina), he so impressed the chiefs by his bold bearing that they conceded without question all his demands, submitting themselves and their people for the second time to the English dominion and designating Moytoy, of Tellico, to act as their "emperor" and to represent the nation in all transactions with the whites. Seven chiefs were selected to visit England, where, in the palace at Whitehall, they solemnly renewed the treaty, acknowledging the sovereignty of England and binding themselves to have no trade or alliance with any other nation, not to allow any other white people to settle among them, and to deliver up any fugitive slaves who might seek refuge with them. To confirm their words they delivered a "crown," five eagle tails, and four scalps, which they had brought with them. In return they received the usual glittering promises of love and perpetual friendship, together with a substantial quantity of guns, ammunition, and red paint. The treaty being concluded in September, they took ship for Carolina, where they arrived, as we are told by the governor, "in good health and mightily well satisfied with His Majesty's bounty to them."[2]

In the next year some action was taken to use the Cherokee and Catawba to subdue the refractory remnant of the Tuscarora in North Carolina, but when it was found that this was liable to bring down the wrath of

---

1 Pickett, A. J., History of Alabama, pp. 234, 280, 288; reprint, Sheffield, 1896.

2 Hewat, South Carolina and Georgia, II, pp. 3-11, 1779; treaty documents of 1730, North Carolina Colonial Records, III, pp. 128-133, 1886; Jenkinson, Collection of Treaties, II, pp. 315-318; Drake, S. G., Early History of Georgia; Cuming's Embassy; Boston, 1872; letter of Governor Johnson, December 27, 1730, noted in South Carolina Hist. Soc. Colls., I, p. 246, 1857.

the Iroquois upon the Carolina settlements, more peaceable methods were used instead.³

In 1738 or 1739 the smallpox, brought to Carolina by slave ships, broke out among the Cherokee with such terrible effect that, according to Adair, nearly half the tribe was swept away within a year. The awful mortality was due largely to the fact that as it was a new and strange disease to the Indians they had no proper remedies against it, and therefore resorted to the universal Indian panacea for "strong" sickness of almost any kind, viz, cold plunge baths in the running stream, the worst treatment that could possibly be devised. As the pestilence spread unchecked from town to town, despair fell upon the nation. The priests, believing the visitation a penalty for violation of the ancient ordinances, threw away their sacred paraphernalia as things which had lost their protecting power. Hundreds of the warriors [Page 152] committed suicide on beholding their frightful disfigurement. "Some shot themselves, others cut their throats, some stabbed themselves with knives and others with sharp-pointed canes; many threw themselves with sullen madness into the fire and there slowly expired, as if they had been utterly divested of the native power of feeling pain."¹ Another authority estimates their loss at a thousand warriors, partly from smallpox and partly from rum brought in by the traders.²

About the year 1740 a trading path for horsemen was marked out by the Cherokee from the new settlement of Augusta, in Georgia, to their towns on the headwaters of Savannah River and thence on to the west. This road, which went up the south side of the river, soon became much frequented.² Previous to this time most of the trading goods had been transported on the backs of Indians. In the same year a party of Cherokee under the war chief Kâ'lanû, "The Raven," took part in Oglethorpe's expedition against the Spaniards of Saint Augustine.³

In 1736 Christian Priber, said to be a Jesuit acting in the French interest, had come among the Cherokee, and, by the facility with which he learned the language and adapted himself to the native dress and mode of life, had

---

3 Documents of 1731 and 1732, North Carolina Colonial Records, III, pp. 153, 202, 345, 369, 393, 1886.

1 Adair, American Indians, pp. 232-234, 1775.

2 Meadows (?), State of the Province of Georgia, p. 7, 1742, in Force Tracts, I, 1836.

2 Meadows (?), State of the Province of Georgia, p. 7, 1742, in Force Tracts, I, 1836.

3 Jones, C. C., History of Georgia, I, pp. 327, 328; Boston, 1883.

quickly acquired a leading influence among them. He drew up for their adoption a scheme of government modeled after the European plan, with the capital at Great Tellico, in Tennessee, the principal medicine man as emperor, and himself as the emperor's secretary. Under this title he corresponded with the South Carolina government until it began to be feared that he would ultimately win over the whole tribe to the French side. A commissioner was sent to arrest him, but the Cherokee refused to give him up, and the deputy was obliged to return under safe-conduct of an escort furnished by Priber. Five years after the inauguration of his work, however, he was seized by some English traders while on his way to Fort Toulouse, and brought as a prisoner to Frederica, in Georgia, where he soon afterward died while under confinement. Although his enemies had represented him as a monster, inciting the Indians to the grossest immoralities, he proved to be a gentleman of polished address, extensive learning, and rare courage, as was shown later on the occasion of an explosion in the barracks magazine. Besides Greek, Latin, French, German, Spanish, and fluent English, he spoke also the Cherokee, and among his papers which were seized was found a manuscript dictionary of the language, which he had prepared for publication—the first, and even yet, perhaps, the most important study of the language ever made. "Says Adair:

As he was learned and possessed of a very sagacious penetrating judgment, and had every qualification that was requisite for his bold and difficult enterprise, it was not to be doubted that, as he wrote a Cheerake dictionary, designed to be published at Paris, he likewise set down a great deal that would have been very acceptable to the curious and serviceable to the representatives of South Carolina and Georgia, which may be readily found in Frederica if the manuscripts have had the good fortune to escape the despoiling hands of military power.

He claimed to be a Jesuit, acting under orders of his superior, to introduce habits of steady industry, civilized arts, and a regular form of government among the southern tribes, with a view to the ultimate [Page 153] founding of an independent Indian state. From all that can be gathered of him, even though it comes from his enemies, there can be little doubt that he was a worthy member of that illustrious order whose name has been a synonym for scholarship, devotion, and courage from the days of Jogues and Marquette down to De Smet and Mengarini.¹

Up to this time no civilizing or mission work had been undertaken by either of the Carolina governments among any of the tribes within their borders. As one writer of the period quaintly puts it, "The gospel spirit is not yet so gloriously arisen as to seek them more than theirs," while another in stronger terms affirms, "To the shame of the Christian name, no pains have ever been taken to convert them to Christianity; on the contrary, their morals are perverted and corrupted by the sad example they daily have of its depraved professors residing in their towns."² Readers of Lawson and other narratives of the period will feel the force of the rebuke.

Throughout the eighteenth century the Cherokee were engaged in chronic warfare with their Indian neighbors. As these quarrels concerned the whites but little, however momentous they may have been to the principals, we have but few details. The war with the Tuscarora continued until the outbreak of the latter tribe against Carolina in 1711 gave opportunity to the Cherokee to cooperate in striking the blow which drove the Tuscarora from their ancient homes to seek refuge in the North. The Cherokee then turned their attention to the Shawano on the Cumberland, and with the aid of the Chickasaw finally expelled them from that region about the year 1715. Inroads upon the Catawba were probably kept up until the latter had become so far reduced by war and disease as to be mere dependent pensioners upon the whites. The former friendship with the Chickasaw was at last broken through the overbearing conduct of the Cherokee, and a war followed of which we find incidental notice in 1757,³ and which terminated in a decisive victory for the Chickasaw about 1768. The bitter war with the Iroquois of the far North continued, in spite of all the efforts of the Colonial governments, until a formal treaty of peace was brought about by the efforts of Sir William Johnson (12) in the same year.

The hereditary war with the Creeks for possession of upper Georgia continued, with brief intervals of peace, or even alliance, until the United States finally interfered as mediator between the rival claimants. In 1718

---

1 Adair, American Indians, pp. 240-243, 1775; Stevens, W. B., History of Georgia, I, pp. 104-107; Phila., 1847.

2 Anonymous writer in Carroll, Hist. Colls. of South Carolina, II, pp. 97-98, 517, 1836.

3 Buckle, Journal, 1757, in Rivers, South Carolina, p. 57, 1856.

we find notice of a large Cherokee war party moving against the Creek town of Coweta, on the lower Chattahoochee, but dispersing on learning of the presence there of some French and Spanish officers, as well as some English traders, all bent on arranging an alliance with the Creeks. The Creeks themselves had declared their willingness to be at peace with the English, while still determined to keep the bloody hatchet uplifted against the Cherokee.[4] The most important incident of the struggle between the two tribes was probably the battle of Tali'wa about the year 1755.[5]

By this time the weaker coast tribes had become practically extinct, and the more powerful tribes of the interior were beginning to take [Page 154] the alarm, as they saw the restless borderers pushing every year farther into the Indian country. As early as 1748 Dr. Thomas Walker, with a company of hunters and woodsmen from Virginia, crossed the mountains to the southwest, discovering and naming the celebrated Cumberland Gap and passing on to the headwaters of Cumberland River. Two years later he made a second exploration and penetrated to Kentucky River, but on account of the Indian troubles no permanent settlement was then attempted.[1] This invasion of their territory awakened a natural resentment of the native owners, and we find proof also in the Virginia records that the irresponsible borderers seldom let pass an opportunity to kill and plunder any stray Indian found in their neighborhood.

In 1755 the Cherokee were officially reported to number 2, 590 warriors, as against probably twice that number previous to the great smallpox epidemic sixteen years before. Their neighbors and ancient enemies, the Catawba, had dwindled to 240 men.[2]

Although war was not formally declared by England until 1756, hostilities in the seven years' struggle between France and England, commonly known in America as the "French and Indian War," began in April, 1754, when the French seized a small post which the English had begun at the present site of Pittsburg, and which was afterward finished by the French

---

4 Barcia, A. G., Ensayo Chronologico para la Historia General de la Florida, pp. 335, 336, Madrid, 1723.

5 For more in regard to these intertribal wars see the historical traditions.

1 Walker, Thomas, Journal of an Exploration, etc., pp. 8, 35-37; Boston, 1888; Monette (Valley of the Miss. I, p. 317; New York, 1848) erroneously makes the second date 1758.

2 Letter of Governor Dobbs, 1755, in North Carolina Colonial Records, v. pp. 320, 321, 1887.

under the name of Fort Du Quesne. Strenuous efforts were made by the English to secure the Cherokee to their interest against the French and their Indian allies, and treaties were negotiated by which they promised assistance.[3] As these treaties, however, carried the usual cessions of territory, and stipulated for the building of several forts in the heart of the Cherokee country, it is to be feared that the Indians were not duly impressed by the disinterested character of the proceeding. Their preference for the French was but thinly veiled, and only immediate policy prevented them from throwing their whole force into the scale on that side. The reasons for this preference are given by Timberlake, the young Virginian officer who visited the tribe on an embassy of conciliation a few years later:
I found the nation much attached to the French, who have the prudence, by familiar politeness—which costs but little and often does a great deal—and conforming themselves to their ways and temper, to conciliate the inclinations of almost all the Indians they are acquainted with, while the pride of our officers often disgusts them. Nay, they did not scruple to own to me that it was the trade alone that induced them to make peace with us, and not any preference to the French, whom they loved a great deal better. . . . The English are now so nigh, and encroached daily so far upon them, that they not only felt the bad effects of it in their hunting grounds, which were spoiled, but had all the reason in the world to apprehend being swallowed up by so potent neighbors or driven from the country inhabited by their fathers, in which they were born and brought up, in fine, their native soil, for which all men have a particular tenderness and affection.

He adds that only dire necessity had induced them to make peace with the English in 1761.[4]

In accordance with the treaty stipulations, Fort Prince George was built in 1756 adjoining the important Cherokee town of Keowee, on the headwaters of the Savannah, and Fort Loudon near the junction [Page 155] of Tellico River with the Little Tennessee, in the center of the Cherokee towns beyond the mountains.[1] By special arrangement with the influential chief,

---

3 Ramsey, Tennessee, pp. 50-52, 1853; Royce, Cherokee Nation, in Fifth Ann. Rep. Bur. of Ethnology, p. 145, 1888.

4 Timberlake, Henry, Memoirs, pp. 73, 74; London, 1765.

1 Ramsey, Tennessee, p. 51, 1853; Royce, Cherokee Nation, in Fifth Ann. Rept. Bur. of Ethnology, p. 145, 1888.

Ata-kullakulla (Ătă'-gûl"kălû'),² Fort Dobbs was also built in the same year about 20 miles west of the present Salisbury, North Carolina.³

The Cherokee had agreed to furnish four hundred warriors to cooperate against the French in the north, but before Fort Loudon had been completed it was very evident that they had repented of their promise, as their great council at Echota ordered the work stopped and the garrison on the way to turn back, plainly telling the officer in charge that they did not want so many white people among them. Ata-kullakulla, hitherto supposed to be one of the stanchest friends of the English, was now one of the most determined in the opposition. It was in evidence also that they were in constant communication with the French. By much tact and argument their objections were at last overcome for a time, and they very unwillingly set about raising the promised force of warriors. Major Andrew Lewis, who superintended the building of the fort, became convinced that the Cherokee were really friendly to the French, and that all their professions of friendship and assistance were "only to put a gloss on their knavery." The fort was finally completed, and, on his suggestion, was garrisoned with a strong force of two hundred men under Captain Demeré.⁴ There was strong ground for believing that some depredations committed about this time on the heads of Catawba and Broad Rivers, in North Carolina, were the joint work of Cherokee and northern Indians.⁵ Notwithstanding all this, a considerable body of Cherokee joined the British forces on the Virginia frontier.⁶

Fort Du Quesne was taken by the American provincials under Washington, November 25, 1758. Quebec was taken September 13, 1759, and by the final treaty of peace in 1763 the war ended with the transfer of Canada and the Ohio Valley to the Crown of England. Louisiana had already been ceded by France to Spain.

Although France was thus eliminated from the Indian problem, the Indians themselves were not ready to accept the settlement. In the North the confederated tribes under Pontiac continued to war on their own account

---

2 For notice see Ătă'-gûl"kălû', in the glossary.

3 Ramsey, op. cit., p. 50.

4 Letters of Major Andrew Lewis and Governor Dinwiddie, 1756, in North Carolina Colonial Records V, pp. 585, 612-614, 635, 637, 1887; Ramsey, op. cit., pp. 51, 52.

5 Letter of Governor Dobbs, 1756, in North Carolina Colonial Records, V, p. 604, 1887.

6 Dinwiddie letter, 1757, ibid., p. 765.

until 1765. In the South the very Cherokee who had acted as allies of the British against Fort Du Quesne, and had voluntarily offered to guard the frontier south of the Potomac, returned to rouse their tribe to resistance.

The immediate exciting cause of the trouble was an unfortunate expedition undertaken against the hostile Shawano in February, 1756, by Major Andrew Lewis (the same who had built Fort Loudon) with some two hundred Virginia troops assisted by about one hundred Cherokee. After six weeks of fruitless tramping through the woods, with the ground covered with snow and the streams so swollen by rains that they lost their provisions and ammunition in crossing, they were obliged to return to the settlements in a starving condition, having [Page 156] killed their horses on the way. The Indian contingent had from the first been disgusted at the contempt and neglect experienced from those whom they had come to assist. The Tuscarora and others had already gone home, and the Cherokee now started to return on foot to their own country. Finding some horses running loose on the range, they appropriated them, on the theory that as they had lost their own animals, to say nothing of having risked their lives, in the service of the colonists, it was only a fair exchange. The frontiersmen took another view of the question, however, attacked the returning Cherokee, and killed a number of them, variously stated at from twelve to forty, including several of their prominent men. According to Adair they also scalped and mutilated the bodies in the savage fashion to which they had become accustomed in the border wars and brought the scalps into the settlements, where they were represented as those of French Indians and sold at the regular price then established by law. The young warriors at once prepared to take revenge, but were restrained by the chiefs until satisfaction could be demanded in the ordinary way, according to the treaties arranged with the colonial governments. Application was made in turn to Virginia, North Carolina, and South Carolina, but without success. While the women were still wailing night and morning for their slain kindred, and the Creeks were taunting the warriors for their cowardice in thus quietly submitting to the injury, some lawless officers of Fort Prince George committed an unpardonable outrage at the neighboring Indian town while most of the men were away hunting.[1] The warriors could no longer be

---

[1] Adair, American Indians, 245-246, 1775; North Carolina Colonial Records, V, p. xiviii, 1887; Hewat, quoted in Ramsey, Tennessee, p. 54, 1853.

restrained. Soon there was news of attacks upon the back settlements of Carolina, while on the other side of the mountains two soldiers of the Fort Loudon garrison were killed. War seemed at hand.

At this juncture, in November, 1758, a party of influential chiefs, having first ordered back a war party just about to set out from the western towns against the Carolina settlements, came down to Charleston and succeeded in arranging the difficulty upon a friendly basis. The assembly had officially declared peace with the Cherokee, when, in May of 1759, Governor Lyttleton unexpectedly came forward with a demand for the surrender for execution of every Indian who had killed a white man in the recent skirmishes, among these being the chiefs of Citico and Tellico. At the same time the commander at Fort Loudon, forgetful of the fact that he had but a small garrison in the midst of several thousands of restless savages, made a demand for twenty-four other chiefs whom he suspected of unfriendly action. To compel their surrender orders were given to stop all trading supplies intended for the upper Cherokee.

This roused the whole nation, and a delegation representing every town came down to Charleston, protesting the desire of the Indians for peace and friendship, but declaring their inability to surrender their own chiefs. The governor replied by declaring war in November, 1759, at once calling out troops and sanding messengers to secure the aid of all the surrounding tribes against the Cherokee. In the meantime a second delegation of thirty-two of the most prominent men, [Page 157] led by the young war chief Oconostota (Ăgăn-stâta),[1] arrived to make a further effort for peace, but the governor, refusing to listen to them, seized the whole party and confined them as prisoners at Fort Prince George, in a room large enough for only six soldiers, while at the same time he set fourteen hundred troops in motion to invade the Cherokee country. On further representation by Atakullakulla (Ătă'-gûl'-kălû'), the civil chief of the nation and well known as a friend of the English, the governor released Oconostota and two others after compelling some half dozen of the delegation to sign a paper by which they pretended to agree for their tribe to kill or seize any Frenchman entering their country, and consented to the imprisonment of the party until all the warriors demanded had been surrendered for execution or otherwise. At this stage of affairs the smallpox broke out in the Cherokee

---

1 For notices see the glossary.

towns, rendering a further stay in their neighborhood unsafe, and thinking the whole matter now settled on his own basis, Lyttleton returned to Charleston.

The event soon proved how little he knew of Indian temper. Oconostota at once laid siege to Fort Prince George, completely cutting off communication at a time when, as it was now winter, no help could well be expected from below. In February, 1760, after having kept the fort thus closely invested for some weeks, he sent word one day by an Indian woman that he wished to speak to the commander, Lieutenant Coytmore. As the lieutenant stepped out from the stockade to see what was wanted, Oconostota, standing on the opposite side of the river, swung a bridle above his head as a signal to his warriors concealed in the bushes, and the officer was at once shot down. The soldiers immediately broke into the room where the hostages were confined, every one being a chief of prominence in the tribe, and butchered them to the last man.

It was now war to the end. Led by Oconostota, the Cherokee descended upon the frontier settlements of Carolina, while the warriors across the mountains laid close siege to Fort Loudon. In June, 1760, a strong force of over 1, 600 men, under Colonel Montgomery, started to reduce the Cherokee towns and relieve the beleaguered garrison. Crossing the Indian frontier, Montgomery quickly drove the enemy from about Fort Prince George and then, rapidly advancing, surprised Little Keowee, killing every man of the defenders, and destroyed in succession every one of the Lower Cherokee towns, burning them to the ground, cutting down the cornfields and orchards, killing and taking more than a hundred of their men, and driving the whole population into the mountains before him. His own loss was very slight. He then sent messengers to the Middle and Upper towns, summoning them to surrender on penalty of the like fate, but, receiving no reply, he led his men across the divide to the waters of the Little Tennessee and continued down that stream without opposition until he came in the vicinity of Echoee (Itse'yĭ), a few miles above the sacred town of Nĭkwăsĭ', the present Franklin, North Carolina. Here the Cherokee had collected their full force to resist his progress, and the result was a desperate engagement on June 27, 1760, by which Montgomery was compelled to retire to Fort Prince George, after losing nearly one hundred men in killed and wounded. The Indian loss is unknown.

[Page 158]His retreat sealed the fate of Fort Loudon. The garrison, though hard pressed and reduced to the necessity of eating horses and dogs, had been enabled to hold out through the kindness of the Indian women, many of whom, having found sweethearts among the soldiers, brought them supplies of food daily. When threatened by the chiefs the women boldly replied that the soldiers were their husbands and it was their duty to help them, and that if any harm came to themselves for their devotion their English relatives would avenge them.[1] The end was only delayed, however, and on August 8, 1760, the garrison of about two hundred men, under Captain Demeré, surrendered to Oconostota on promise that they should be allowed to retire unmolested with their arms and sufficient ammunition for the march, on condition of delivering up all the remaining warlike stores.

The troops marched out and proceeded far enough to camp for the night, while the Indians swarmed into the fort to see what plunder they might find. "By accident a discovery was made of ten bags of powder and a large quantity of ball that had been secretly buried in the fort to prevent their falling into the enemy's hands" (Hewat). It is said also that cannon, small arms, and ammunition had been thrown into the river with the same intention (Haywood). Enraged at this breach of the capitulation the Cherokee attacked the soldiers next morning at daylight, killing Demeré and twenty-nine others at the first fire. The rest were taken and held as prisoners until ransomed some time after. The second officer, Captain Stuart, for whom the Indians had a high regard, was claimed by Ata-kullakulla, who soon after took him into the woods, ostensibly on a hunting excursion, and conducted him for nine days through the wilderness until he delivered him safely into the hands of friends in Virginia. The chief's kindness was well rewarded, and it was largely through his influence that peace was finally brought about.

It was now too late, and the settlements were too much exhausted, for another expedition, so the fall and winter were employed by the English in preparations for an active campaign the next year in force to crush out all resistance. In June, 1761, Colonel Grant with an army of 2, 600 men, including a number of Chickasaw and almost every remaining warrior of the Catawba,[2] set out from Fort Prince George. Refusing a request from

---

1 Timberlake, Memoirs, p. 65, 1765.
2 Catawba reference from Milligan, 1763, in Carroll, South Carolina Historical Collections, II, p. 519, 1836.

Ata-kullakulla for a friendly accommodation, he crossed Rabun Gap and advanced rapidly down the Little Tennessee along the same trail taken by the expedition of the previous year. On June 10, when within two miles of Montgomery's battlefield, he encountered the Cherokee, whom he defeated, although with considerable loss to himself, after a stubborn engagement lasting several hours. Having repulsed the Indians, he proceeded on his way, sending out detachments to the outlying settlements, until in the course of a month he had destroyed every one of the Middle towns, 15 in all, with all their granaries and cornfields, driven the inhabitants into the mountains, and "pushed the frontier seventy miles farther to the west."

The Cherokee were now reduced to the greatest extremity. With some of their best towns in ashes, their fields and orchards wasted for two successive years, their ammunition nearly exhausted, many of [Page 159] their bravest warriors dead, their people fugitives in the mountains, hiding in caves and living like beasts upon roots or killing their horses for food, with the terrible scourge of smallpox adding to the miseries of starvation, and withal torn by factional differences which had existed from the very beginning of the war—it was impossible for even brave men to resist longer. In September Ata-kullakulla, who had all along done everything in his power to stay the disaffection, came down to Charleston, a treaty of peace was made, and the war was ended. From an estimated population of at least 5, 000 warriors some years before, the Cherokee had now been reduced to about 2, 300 men.[1]

In the meantime a force of Virginians under Colonel Stephen had advanced as far as the Great Island of the Holston—now Kingsport, Tennessee—where they were met by a large delegation of Cherokee, who sued for peace, which was concluded with them by Colonel Stephen on November 19, 1761, independently of what was being done in South Carolina. On the urgent request of the chief that an officer might visit their people for a short time to cement the new friendship, Lieutenant Henry Timberlake, a young Virginian who had already distinguished himself in active service,

---

1 Figures from Adair, American Indians, p. 227, 1775. When not otherwise noted, this sketch of the Cherokee war of 1760-61 is compiled chiefly from the contemporary dispatches in the Gentleman's Magazine, supplemented from Hewat's Historical Account of South Carolina and Georgia, 1778; with additional details from Adair, American Indians; Ramsey, Tennessee; Royce, Cherokee Nation; North Carolina Colonial Records, v., documents and introduction; etc.

volunteered to return with them to their towns, where he spent several months. He afterward conducted a delegation of chiefs to England, where, as they had come without authority from the Government, they met such an unpleasant reception that they returned disgusted.[2]

On the conclusion of peace between England and France in 1763, by which the whole western territory was ceded to England, a great council was held at Augusta, which was attended by the chiefs and principal men of all the southern Indians, at which Captain John Stuart, superintendent for the southern tribes, together with the colonial governors of Virginia, North Carolina, South Carolina, and Georgia, explained fully to the Indians the new condition of affairs, and a treaty of mutual peace and friendship was concluded on November 10 of that year.[3]

Under several leaders, as Walker, Wallen, Smith, and Boon, the tide of emigration now surged across the mountains in spite of every effort to restrain it,[4] and the period between the end of the Cherokee war and the opening of the Revolution is principally notable for a number of treaty cessions by the Indians, each in fruitless endeavor to fix a permanent barrier between themselves and the advancing wave of white settlement. Chief among these was the famous Henderson purchase in 1775, which included the whole tract between the Kentucky and Cumberland Rivers, embracing the greater part of the present State of Kentucky. By these treaties the Cherokee were shorn of practically all their ancient territorial claims north of the present Tennessee line and east of the Blue Ridge and the Savannah, including much of their best hunting range; their home settlements were, however, left still in their possession.[5]

[Page 160] As one consequence of the late Cherokee war, a royal proclamation had been issued in 1763, with a view of checking future encroachments by the whites, which prohibited any private land purchases from the Indians, or any granting of warrants for lands west of the sources of the streams flowing into the Atlantic.[1] In 1768, on the appeal of the Indians themselves, the British superintendent for the southern tribes, Captain

---

2 Timberlake, Memoirs, p. 9 et passim, 1765.
3 Stevens, Georgia, II, pp. 26-29, 1859.
4 Ramsey, Tennessee, pp. 65-70, 1853.
5 Royce, Cherokee Nation, in Fifth Ann. Rep. Bur. of Ethnology, pp. 146-149, 1888.
1 Royce, Cherokee Nation, op. cit., p. 149; Ramsey, Tennessee, p. 71, 1853

John Stuart, had negotiated a treaty at Hard Labor, in South Carolina, by which Kanawha and New Rivers, along their whole course downward from the North Carolina line, were fixed as the boundary between the Cherokee and the whites in that direction. In two years, however, so many borderers had crossed into the Indian country, where they were evidently determined to remain, that it was found necessary to substitute another treaty, by which the line was made to run due south from the mouth of the Kanawha to the Holston, thus cutting off from the Cherokee almost the whole of their hunting grounds in Virginia and West Virginia. Two years later, in 1772, the Virginians demanded a further cession, by which everything east of Kentucky River was surrendered; and finally, on March 17, 1775, the great Henderson purchase was consummated, including the whole tract between the Kentucky and Cumberland Rivers. By this last cession the Cherokee were at last cut off from Ohio River and all their rich Kentucky hunting grounds.[2]

While these transactions were called treaties, they were really forced upon the native proprietors, who resisted each in turn and finally signed only under protest and on most solemn assurances that no further demands would be made. Even before the purchases were made, intruders in large numbers had settled upon each of the tracts in question, and they refused to withdraw across the boundaries now established, but remained on one pretext or another to await a new adjustment. This was particularly the case on Watauga and upper Holston Rivers in northeastern Tennessee, where the settlers, finding themselves still within the Indian boundary and being resolved to remain, effected a temporary lease from the Cherokee in 1772. As was expected and intended, the lease became a permanent occupancy, the nucleus settlement of the future State of Tennessee.[3]

Just before the outbreak of the Revolution, the botanist, William Bartram, made an extended tour of the Cherokee country, and has left us a pleasant account of the hospitable character and friendly disposition of the Indians at that time. He gives a list of forty-three towns then inhabited by the tribe.[4]

---

2 Ramsey, op. cit., pp. 93-122; Royce, op. cit., pp. 146-149.

3 Ramsey, op. cit., pp. 109-122; Royce, op. cit., p. 146 et passim.

4 Bartram, Travels, pp. 366-372, 1792.

The opening of the great Revolutionary struggle in 1776 found the Indian tribes almost to a man ranged on the British side against the Americans. There was good reason for this. Since the fall of the French power the British Government had stood to them as the sole representative of authority, and the guardian and protector of their rights against constant encroachments by the American borderers. Licensed British traders were resident in every tribe and many had intermarried and raised families among them, while the border man looked upon the Indian only as a cumberer of the earth. The British superintendents, Sir William Johnson in the north and Captain [Page 161] John Stuart in the south, they knew as generous friends, while hardly a warrior of them all was without some old cause of resentment against their backwoods neighbors. They felt that the only barrier between themselves and national extinction was in the strength of the British Government, and when the final severance came they threw their whole power into the British scale. They were encouraged in this resolution by presents of clothing and other goods, with promises of plunder from the settlements and hopes of recovering a portion of their lost territories. The British Government having determined, as early as June, 1775, to call in the Indians against the Americans, supplies of hatchets, guns, and ammunition were issued to the warriors of all the tribes from the lakes to the gulf, and bounties were offered for American scalps brought in to the commanding officer at Detroit or Oswego.[1] Even the Six Nations, who had agreed in solemn treaty to remain neutral, were won over by these persuasions. In August, 1775, an Indian "talk" was intercepted in which the Cherokee assured Cameron, the resident agent, that their warriors, enlisted in the service of the King, were ready at a signal to fall upon the back settlements of Carolina and Georgia.[2] Circular letters were sent out to all those persons in the back country supposed to be of royalist sympathies, directing them to repair to Cameron's headquarters in the Cherokee country to join the Indians in the invasion of the settlements.[3]

---

1 Ramsey, Tennessee, pp. 143-150, 1853; Monette, Valley of the Mississippi, I, pp. 400, 401, 431, 432, and II, pp. 33, 34, 1846; Roosevelt, Winning of the West, I, pp. 276-281, and II, pp. 1-6, 1889.

2 Ramsey, op. cit., p. 143.

3 Quoted from Stedman, in Ramsey, op. cit., p. 162.

In June, 1776, a British fleet under command of Sir Peter Parker, with a large naval and military force, attacked Charleston, South Carolina, both by land and sea, and simultaneously a body of Cherokee, led by Tories in Indian disguise, came down from the mountains and ravaged the exposed frontier of South Carolina, killing and burning as they went. After a gallant defense by the garrison at Charleston the British were repulsed, whereupon their Indian and Tory allies withdrew.[4]

About the same time the warning came from Nancy Ward, a noted friendly Indian woman of great authority in the Cherokee Nation, that seven hundred Cherokee warriors were advancing in two divisions against the Watauga and Holston settlements, with the design of destroying everything as far up as New River. The Holston men from both sides of the Virginia line hastily collected under Captain Thompson and marched against the Indians, whom they met and defeated with signal loss after a hard-fought battle near the Long Island in the Holston (Kingsport, Tennessee), on August 20. The next day the second division of the Cherokee attacked the fort at Watauga, garrisoned by only forty men under Captain James Robertson, but was repulsed without loss to the defenders, the Indians withdrawing on news of the result at the Long Island. A Mrs. Bean and a boy named Moore were captured on this occasion and carried to one of the Cherokee towns in the neighborhood of Tellico, where the boy was burned, but the woman, after she had been condemned to death and everything was in readiness for the tragedy, was rescued by the interposition of Nancy Ward. Two other Cherokee detachments [Page 162] moved against the upper settlements at the same time. One of these, finding all the inhabitants securely shut up in forts, returned without doing much damage. The other ravaged the country on Clinch River almost to its head, and killed a man and wounded others at Black's station, now Abingdon, Virginia.[1]

At the same time that one part of the Cherokee were raiding the Tennessee settlements others came down upon the frontiers of Carolina and Georgia. On the upper Catawba they killed many people, but the whites took refuge in the stockade stations, where they defended themselves until General Rutherford came to their relief. In Georgia an attempt had been made by a small party of Americans to seize Cameron, who lived

---

4 Ramsey, op. cit., p. 162.
1 Ramsey, Tennessee, pp. 150-159, 1853.

in one of the Cherokee towns with his Indian wife, but, as was to have been expected, the Indians interfered, killing several of the party and capturing others, who were afterward tortured to death. The Cherokee of the Upper and Middle towns, with some Creeks and Tories of the vicinity, led by Cameron himself, at once began ravaging the South Carolina border, burning houses, driving off cattle, and killing men, women, and children without distinction, until the whole country was in a wild panic, the people abandoning their farms to seek safety in the garrisoned forts. On one occasion an attack by two hundred of the enemy, half of them being Tories, stripped and painted like Indians, was repulsed by the timely arrival of a body of Americans, who succeeded in capturing thirteen of the Tories. The invasion extended into Georgia, where also property was destroyed and the inhabitants were driven from their homes.[2]

Realizing their common danger, the border States determined to strike such a concerted blow at the Cherokee as should render them passive while the struggle with England continued. In accord with this plan of cooperation the frontier forces were quickly mobilized and in the summer of 1776 four expeditions were equipped from Virginia, North Carolina, South Carolina, and Georgia, to enter the Cherokee territory simultaneously from as many different directions.

In August of that year the army of North Carolina, 2, 400 strong, under General Griffith Rutherford, crossed the Blue Ridge at Swannanoa Gap, and following the main trail almost along the present line of the railroad, struck the first Indian town, Stikâ'yĭ, or Stecoee, on the Tuckasegee, near the present Whittier. The inhabitants having fled, the soldiers burned the town, together with an unfinished townhouse ready for the roof, cut down the standing corn, killed one or two straggling Indians and then proceeded on their mission of destruction. Every town upon Oconaluftee, Tuckasegee, and the upper part of Little Tennessee, and on Hiwassee to below the junction of Valley River—thirty-six towns in all—was destroyed in turn, the corn cut down or trampled under the hoofs of the stock driven into the fields for that purpose, and the stock itself killed or carried off. Before such an overwhelming force, supplemented as it was by three others simultaneously advancing from other directions, the Cherokee made but poor resistance, and fled with their women and children into the fastnesses of the

---

2 Roosevelt, Winning of the West, I, pp. 293-297, 1889.

Great Smoky Mountains, leaving their desolated fields and smoking towns behind them. As was usual in [Page 163] Indian wars, the actual number killed or taken was small, but the destruction of property was beyond calculation. At Sugartown (Kûlsetsi'yĭ, east of the present Franklin) one detachment, sent to destroy it, was surprised, and escaped only through the aid of another force sent to its rescue. Rutherford, himself, while proceeding to the destruction of the Hiwassee towns, encountered the Indians drawn up to oppose his progress in the Waya Gap of the Nantahala Mountains, and one of the hardest fights of the campaign resulted, the soldiers losing over forty killed and wounded, although the Cherokee were finally repulsed. One of the Indians killed on this occasion was afterwards discovered to be a woman, painted and armed like a warrior.[1]

On September 26 the South Carolina army, 1, 860 strong, under Colonel Andrew Williamson, and including a number of Catawba Indians, effected a junction with Rutherford's forces on Hiwassee River, near the present Murphy, North Carolina. It had been expected that Williamson would join the northern army at Cowee, on the Little Tennessee, when they would proceed together against the western towns, but he had been delayed, and the work of destruction in that direction was already completed, so that after a short rest each army returned home along the route by which it had come.

The South Carolina men had centered by different detachments in the lower Cherokee towns about the head of Savannah River, burning one town after another, cutting down the peach trees and ripened corn, and having an occasional brush with the Cherokee, who hung constantly upon their flanks. At the town of Seneca, near which they encountered Cameron with his Indians and Tories, they had destroyed six thousand bushels of corn, besides other food stores, after burning all the houses, the Indians having retreated after a stout resistance. The most serious encounter had taken place at Tomassee, where several whites and sixteen Cherokee were killed, the latter being all scalped afterwards. Having completed the ruin of the Lower towns, Williamson had crossed over Rabun Gap and descended

---

1 See No. 110, "Incidents of Personal Herosim." For Rutherford's expedition, see Moore, Rutherford's Expedition, in North Carolina University Magazine, February, 1888; Swain, Sketch of the Indian War in 1776, ibid., May, 1852, reprinted in Historical Magazine, November, 1867; Ramsey, Tennessee, p. 164, 1853; Roosevelt, Winning the West, I, pp. 294-302, 1889, etc.

into the valley of the Little Tennessee to cooperate with Rutherford in the destruction of the Middle and Valley towns. As the army advanced every house in every settlement met was burned—ninety houses in one settlement alone— and detachments were sent into the fields to destroy the corn, of which the smallest town was estimated to have two hundred acres, besides potatoes, beans, and orchards of peach trees. The stores of dressed deerskins and other valuables were carried off. Everything was swept clean, and the Indians who were not killed or taken were driven, homeless refugees, into the dark recesses of Nantahala or painfully made their way across to the Overhill towns in Tennessee, which were already menaced by another invasion from the north.[2]

In July, while Williamson was engaged on the upper Savannah, a force of two hundred Georgians, under Colonel Samuel Jack, had marched in the same direction and succeeded in burning two towns on [Page 164] the heads of Chattahoochee and Tugaloo Rivers, destroying the corn and driving off the cattle, without the loss of a man, the Cherokee having apparently fallen back to concentrate for resistance in the mountains.[1]

The Virginia army, about two thousand strong, under Colonel William Christian, rendezvoused in August at the Long Island of the Holston, the regular gathering place on the Tennessee side of the mountains. Among them were several hundred men from North Carolina, with all who could be spared from the garrisons on the Tennessee side. Paying but little attention to small bodies of Indians, who tried to divert attention or to delay progress by flank attacks, they advanced steadily, but cautiously, along the great Indian warpath toward the crossing of the French Broad, where a strong force of Cherokee was reported to be in waiting to dispute their passage. Just before reaching the river the Indians sent a Tory trader with a flag of truce to discuss terms. Knowing that his own strength was overwhelming, Christian allowed the envoy to go through the whole camp and then sent him back with the message that there could be no terms until the Cherokee towns had been destroyed. Arriving at the ford, he kindled fires

---

2 For Williamson's expedition see Ross Journal, with Rockwell's notes, in Historical Magazine, October, 1876; Swain, Sketch of the Indian War in 1776, in North Carolina University Magazine for May, 1852, reprinted in Historical Magazine, November, 1867; Jones, Georgia, II, p. 246 et passim, 1883; Ramsey, Tennessee, 163-164, 1853; Roosevelt, Winning of the West, I, pp. 296-303, 1889.

1 Jones, op. cit., p. 246; Ramsey, op. cit., p. 163; Roosevelt, op. cit., p. 295.

and made all preparations as if intending to camp there for several days. As soon as night fell, however, he secretly drew off half his force and crossed the river lower down, to come upon the Indians in their rear. This was a work of great difficulty, as the water was so deep that it came up almost to the shoulders of the men, while the current was so rapid that they were obliged to support each other four abreast to prevent being swept off their feet. However, they kept their guns and powder dry. On reaching the other side they were surprised to find no enemy. Disheartened at the strength of the invasion, the Indians had fled without even a show of resistance. It is probable that nearly all their men and resources had been drawn off to oppose the Carolina forces on their eastern border, and the few who remained felt themselves unequal to the contest.

Advancing without opposition, Christian reached the towns on Little Tennessee early in November, and, finding them deserted, proceeded to destroy them, one after another, with their outlying fields. The few lingering warriors discovered were all killed. In the meantime messages had been sent out to the farther towns, in response to which several of their head men came into Christian's camp to treat for peace. On their agreement to surrender all the prisoners and captured stock in their hands and to cede to the whites all the disputed territory occupied by the Tennessee settlements, as soon as representatives of the whole tribe could be assembled in the spring, Christian consented to suspend hostilities and retire without doing further injury. An exception was made against Tuskegee and another town, which had been concerned in the burning of the boy taken from Watauga, already noted, and these two were reduced to ashes. The sacred "peace town," Echota, had not been molested. Most of the troops were disbanded on their return to the Long Island, but a part remained and built Fort Patrick Henry, where they went into winter quarters.[2]

[Page 165]From incidental notices in narratives written by some of the participants we obtain interesting side lights on the merciless character of this old border warfare. In addition to the ordinary destruction of war—the burning of towns, the wasting of fruitful fields, and the killing of the defenders—we find that every Indian warrior killed was scalped, when opportunity permitted; women, as well as men, were shot down and afterward

---

[2] For the Virginia-Tennessee expedition see Roosevelt, Winning of the West, I, pp. 303-305, 1889; Ramsey, Tennessee, pp. 165-170, 1853.

"helped to their end"; and prisoners taken were put up at auction as slaves when not killed on the spot. Near Tomassee a small party of Indians was surrounded and entirely cut off. "Sixteen were found dead in the valley when the battle ended. These our men scalped." In a personal encounter—a stout Indian engaged a sturdy young white man, who was a good bruiser and expert at gouging. After breaking their guns on each other they laid hold of one another, when the cracker had his thumbs instantly in the fellow's eyes, who roared and cried "*canaly*"—enough, in English. "Damn you," says the white man, "you can never have enough while you are alive." He then threw him down, set his foot upon his head, and scalped him alive; then took up one of the broken guns and knocked out his brains. It would have been fun if he had let the latter action alone and sent him home without his nightcap, to tell his countrymen how he had been treated.

Later on some of the same detachment (Williamson's), seeing a woman ahead, fired on her and brought her down with two serious wounds, but yet able to speak. After getting what information she could give them, through a half-breed interpreter, "the informer being unable to travel, some of our men favored her so far that they killed her there, to put her out of pain." A few days later "a party of Colonel Thomas's regiment, being on a hunt of plunder, or some such thing, found an Indian squaw and took her prisoner; she being lame, was unable to go with her friends. She was so sullen that she would, as an old saying is, neither lead nor drive, and by their account she died in their hands; but I suppose they helped her to her end." At this place—on the Hiwassee—they found a large town, having "upwards of ninety houses, and large quantities of corn," and "we encamped among the corn, where we had a great plenty of corn, peas, beans, potatoes, and hogs," and on the next day "we were ordered to assemble in companies to spread through the town to destroy, cut down, and burn all the vegetables belonging to our heathen enemies, which was no small undertaking, they being so plentifully supplied." Continuing to another town, "we engaged in our former labor, that is, cutting and destroying all things that might be of advantage to our enemies. Finding here curious buildings, great apple trees, and white-man-like improvements, these we destroyed."[1]

While crossing over the mountains Rutherford's men approached a house belonging to a trader, when one of his negro slaves ran out and "was

---

1 Ross Journal, in Historical Magazine, October, 1867.

shot by the Reverend James Hall, the chaplain, as he ran, mistaking him for an Indian."[2] Soon after they captured two women and a boy. It was proposed to auction them off at once to the highest bidder, and when one of the officers protested that the matter should be left to the disposition of Congress, "the greater part swore bloodily that if they were not sold for slaves upon the spot they would kill and scalp them immediately." The prisoners were accordingly sold for about twelve hundred dollars.[3]

[Page 166] At the Wolf Hills settlement, now Abingdon, Virginia, a party sent out from the fort returned with the scalps of eleven warriors. Having recovered the books which their minister had left behind in his cabin, they held a service of prayer for their success, after which the fresh scalps were hung upon a pole above the gate of the fort. The barbarous custom of scalping to which the border men had become habituated in the earlier wars was practiced upon every occasion when opportunity presented, at least upon the bodies of warriors, and the South Carolina Legislature offered a bounty of seventy-five pounds for every warrior's scalp, a higher reward, however, being offered for prisoners.[1] In spite of all the bitterness which the war aroused there seems to be no record of any scalping of Tories or other whites by the Americans.

The effect upon the Cherokee of this irruption of more than six thousand armed enemies into their territory was well nigh paralyzing. More than fifty of their towns had been burned, their orchards cut down, their fields wasted, their cattle and horses killed or driven off, their stores of buckskin and other personal property plundered. Hundreds of their people had been killed or had died of starvation and exposure, others were prisoners in the hands of the Americans, and some had been sold into slavery. Those who had escaped were fugitives in the mountains, living upon acorns, chestnuts, and wild game, or were refugees with the British.[2] From the Virginia line to the Chattahoochee the chain of destruction was complete. For the present, at least, any further resistance was hopeless, and they were compelled to sue for peace.

---

2 Swain, Sketch of the Indian War of 1776, in Historical Magazine, November, 1867.
3 Moore's narrative, in North Carolina University Magazine, February, 1888.
1 Roosevelt, Winning of the West, I, pp. 285, 290, 303, 1889.
2 About five hundred sought refuge with Stuart, the British Indian superintendent in Florida, where they were fed for some time at the expense of the British Government (Jones, Georgia, II, p. 246, 1883).

By a treaty concluded at De Witts Corners in South Carolina on May 20, 1777, the first ever made with the new States, the Lower Cherokee surrendered to the conqueror all of their remaining territory in South Carolina, excepting a narrow strip along the western boundary. Just two months later, on July 20, by treaty at the Long Island, as had been arranged by Christian in the preceding fall, the Middle and Upper Cherokee ceded everything east of the Blue Ridge, together with all the disputed territory on the Watauga, Nolichucky, upper Holston, and New Rivers. By this second treaty also Captain James Robertson was appointed agent for the Cherokee, to reside at Echota, to watch their movements, recover any captured property, and prevent their correspondence with persons unfriendly to the American cause. As the Federal Government was not yet in perfect operation, these treaties were negotiated by commissioners from the four States adjoining the Cherokee country, the territory thus acquired being parceled out to South Carolina, North Carolina, and Tennessee.[3]

While the Cherokee Nation had thus been compelled to a treaty of peace, a very considerable portion of the tribe was irreconcilably hostile to the Americans and refused to be a party to the late cessions, especially on the Tennessee side. Although Ata-kullakulla sent word that he was ready with five hundred young warriors to fight for the Americans against the English or Indian enemy whenever called upon, [Page 167] Dragging-canoe (Tsiyu-gûnsi'nĭ), who had led the opposition against the Watauga settlements, declared that he would hold fast to Cameron's talk and continue to make war upon those who had taken his hunting grounds. Under his leadership some hundreds of the most warlike and implacable warriors of the tribe, with their families, drew out from the Upper and Middle towns and moved far down upon Tennessee River, where they established new settlements on Chickamauga Creek, in the neighborhood of the present Chattanooga. The locality appears to have been already a rendezvous for a sort of Indian banditti, who sometimes plundered boats disabled in the rapids at this point while descending the river. Under the name "Chickamaugas" they soon became noted for their uncompromising and never-ceasing hostility. In 1782, in consequence of the destruction of their towns

---

3 Royce, Cherokee Nation, in Fifth Ann. Rep. Bureau of Ethnology, p. 150 and map, 1888; Ramsey, Tennessee, pp. 172-174, 1853; Stevens, Georgia, II, p. 144, 1859; Roosevelt, Winning of the West, I, p. 306, 1889.

by Sevier and Campbell, they abandoned this location and moved farther down the river, where they built what were afterwards known as the "five lower towns," viz, Running Water, Nickajack, Long Island, Crow town, and Lookout Mountain town. These were all on the extreme western Cherokee frontier, near where Tennessee River crosses the State line, the first three being within the present limits of Tennessee, while Lookout Mountain town and Crow town were, respectively, in the adjacent corners of Georgia and Alabama. Their population was recruited from Creeks, Shawano, and white Tories until they were estimated at a thousand warriors. Here they remained, a constant thorn in the side of Tennessee, until their towns were destroyed in 1794.[1]

The expatriated Lower Cherokee also removed to the farthest western border of their tribal territory, where they might hope to be secure from encroachment for a time at least, and built new towns for themselves on the upper waters of the Coosa. Twenty years afterward Hawkins found the population of Willstown, in extreme western Georgia, entirely made up of refugees from the Savannah, and the children so familiar from their parents with stories of Williamson's invasion that they ran screaming from the face of a white man.[2]

In April, 1777, the Legislature of North Carolina, of which Tennessee was still a part, authorized bounties of land in the new territory to all able-bodied men who should volunteer against the remaining hostile Cherokee. Under this act companies of rangers were kept along the exposed border to cut off raiding parties of Indians and to protect the steady advance of the pioneers, with the result that the Tennessee settlements enjoyed a brief respite and were even able to send some assistance to their brethren in Kentucky, who were sorely pressed by the Shawano and other northern tribes.[3]

The war between England and the colonies still continued, however, and the British Government was unremitting in its effort to secure the active assistance of the Indians. With the Creeks raiding the Georgia and South

---

[1] Ramsey, op. cit., pp. 171-177, 185-186, 610 et passim; Royce, op. cit., p. 150; Campbell letter, 1782, and other documents in Virginia State papers, III, pp. 271, 571, 599, 1883, and IV, pp. 118, 286, 1884; Blount letter, January 14, 1793, American State Papers: Indian Affairs, I, p. 431, 1832. Campbell says they abandoned their first location on account of the invasion from Tennessee. Governor Blount says they left on account of witches.
[2] Hawkins, manuscript journal, 1796, with Georgia Historical Society.
[3] Ramsey, Tennessee, pp. 174-178, 1853.

Carolina frontier, and with a British agent, Colonel Brown, and a number of Tory refugees regularly domiciled at Chickamauga,[4] it was impossible for the Cherokee long to remain [Page 168] quiet. In the spring of 1779 the warning came from Robertson, stationed at Echota, that three hundred warriors from Chickamauga had started against the back settlements of North Carolina. Without a day's delay the States of North Carolina (including Tennessee) and Virginia united to send a strong force of volunteers against them under command of Colonels Shelby and Montgomery. Descending the Holston in April in a fleet of canoes built for the occasion, they took the Chickamauga towns so completely by surprise that the few warriors remaining fled to the mountains without attempting to give battle. Several were killed, Chickamauga and the outlying villages were burned, twenty thousand bushels of corn were destroyed, and large numbers of horses and cattle were captured, together with a great quantity of goods sent by the British Governor Hamilton at Detroit for distribution to the Indians. The success of this expedition frustrated the execution of a project by Hamilton for uniting all the northern and southern Indians, to be assisted by British regulars, in a concerted attack along the whole American frontier. On learning, through runners, of the blow that had befallen them, the Chickamauga warriors gave up all idea of invading the settlements and returned to their wasted villages.[1] They, as well as the Creeks, however, kept in constant communication with the British commander in Savannah. In this year also a delegation of Cherokee visited the Ohio towns to offer condolences on the death of the noted Delaware chief, White-eyes.[2]

In the early spring of 1780 a large company of emigrants under Colonel John Donelson descended the Holston and the Tennessee to the Ohio, whence they ascended the Cumberland, effected a junction with another party under Captain James Robertson, which had just arrived by a toilsome overland route, and made the first settlement on the present site of Nashville. In passing the Chickamauga towns they had run the gauntlet of the hostile Cherokee, who pursued them for a considerable distance

---

4 Campbell letter, 1782, Virginia State Papers, III, p. 271, 1883.

1 Ramsey, op. cit., pp. 186-188; Roosevelt, Winning of the West, II, pp. 236-238, 1889. Ramsey's statements, chiefly on Haywood's authority, of the strength of the expedition, the number of warriors killed, etc., are so evidently overdrawn that they are here omitted.

2 Heckewelder, Indian Nations, p. 327, reprint of 1876.

beyond the whirlpool known as the Suck, where the river breaks through the mountain. The family of a man named Stuart being infected with the smallpox, his boat dropped behind, and all on board, twenty-eight in number, were killed or taken by the Indians, their cries being distinctly heard by their friends ahead who were unable to help them. Another boat having run upon the rocks, the three women in it, one of whom had become a mother the night before, threw the cargo into the river, and then, jumping into the water, succeeded in pushing the boat into the current while the husband of one of them kept the Indians at bay with his rifle. The infant was killed in the confusion. Three cowards attempted to escape, without thought of their companions. One was drowned in the river; the other two were captured and carried to Chickamauga, where one was burned and the other was ransomed by a trader. The rest went on their way to found the capital of a new commonwealth.[3] As if in retributive justice, the smallpox broke out in the Chickamauga Band in consequence of the capture of Stuart's family, causing the death of a great number.[4]

[Page 169]The British having reconquered Georgia and South Carolina and destroyed all resistance in the south, early in 1780 Cornwallis, with his subordinates, Ferguson and the merciless Tarleton, prepared to invade North Carolina and sweep the country northward to Virginia. The Creeks under McGillivray, and a number of the Cherokee under various local chiefs, together with the Tories, at once joined his standard.

While the Tennessee backwoodsmen were gathered at a barbecue to contest for a shooting prize, a paroled prisoner brought a demand from Ferguson for their submission; with the threat, if they refused, that he would cross the mountains, hang their leaders, kill every man found in arms, and burn every settlement. Up to this time the mountain men had confined their effort to holding in check the Indian enemy, but now, with the fate of the Revolution at stake, they felt that the time for wider action had come. They resolved not to await the attack, but to anticipate it. Without order or authority from Congress, without tents, commissary, or supplies, the Indian fighters of Virginia, North Carolina, and Tennessee quickly assembled at the Sycamore shoals of the Watauga to the number

---

3 Donelson's Journal, etc., in Ramsey, Tennessee, pp. 197-203, 1853; Roosevelt, Winning of the West, II, pp. 324-340, 1889.

4 Ibid., II, p. 337.

of about one thousand men under Campbell, of Virginia, Sevier and Shelby, of Tennessee, and McDowell, of North Carolina. Crossing the mountains, they met Ferguson at Kings Mountain in South Carolina on October 7, 1780, and gained the decisive victory that turned the tide of the Revolution in the South.[1]

It is in place here to quote a description of these men in buckskin, white by blood and tradition, but half Indian in habit and instinct, who, in half a century of continuous conflict, drove back Creeks, Cherokee, and Shawano, and with one hand on the plow and the other on the rifle redeemed a wilderness and carried civilization and free government to the banks of the Mississippi.

They were led by leaders they trusted, they were wonted to Indian warfare, they were skilled as horsemen and marksmen, they knew how to face every kind of danger, hardship, and privation. Their fringed and tasseled hunting shirts were girded by bead-worked belts, and the trappings of their horses were stained red and yellow. On their heads they wore caps of coon skin or mink skin, with the tails hanging down, or else felt hats, in each of which was thrust a bucktail or a sprig of evergreen. Every man carried a small-bore rifle, a tomahawk, and a scalping knife. A very few of the officers had swords, and there was not a bayonet nor a tent in the army.[2]

To strike the blow at Kings Mountain the border men had been forced to leave their own homes unprotected. Even before they could cross the mountains on their return the news came that the Cherokee were again out in force for the destruction of the upper settlements, and their numerous small bands were killing, burning, and plundering in the usual Indian fashion. Without loss of time the Holston settlements of Virginia and Tennessee at once raised seven hundred mounted riflemen to march against the enemy, the command being assigned to Colonel Arthur Campbell, of Virginia, and Colonel John Sevier, of Tennessee.

Sevier started first with nearly three hundred men, going south along the great Indian war trail and driving small parties of the Cherokee before him, until he crossed the French Broad and came upon seventy of them on Boyds Creek, not far from the present Sevierville, on December 16, 1780.

---

[1] Roosevelt, Winning of the West, II, pp. 241-294, 1889; Ramsey, Tennessee, pp. 208-249, 1853

[2] Roosevelt, op. cit., p. 256.

Ordering his men to spread out [Page 170] into a half circle, he sent ahead some scouts, who, by an attack and feigned retreat, managed to draw the Indians into the trap thus prepared, with the result that they left thirteen dead and all their plunder, while not one of the whites was even wounded.[1]

A few days later Sevier was joined by Campbell with the remainder of the force. Advancing to the Little Tennessee with but slight resistance, they crossed three miles below Echota while the Indians were watching for them at the ford above. Then dividing into two bodies, they proceeded to destroy the towns along the river. The chiefs sent peace talks through Nancy Ward, the Cherokee woman who had so befriended the whites in 1776, but to these overtures Campbell returned an evasive answer until he could first destroy the towns on lower Hiwassee, whose warriors had been particularly hostile. Continuing southward, the troops destroyed these towns, Hiwassee and Chestuee, with all their stores of provisions, finishing the work on the last day of the year. The Indians had fled before them, keeping spies out to watch their movements. One of these, while giving signals from a ridge by beating a drum, was shot by the whites. The soldiers lost only one man, who was buried in an Indian cabin which was then burned down to conceal the trace of the interment. The return march was begun on New Year's day. Ten principal towns, including Echota, the capital, had been destroyed, besides several smaller villages, containing in the aggregate over one thousand houses and not less than fifty thousand bushels of corn and large stores of other provision. Everything not needed on the return march was committed to the flames or otherwise wasted. Of all the towns west of the mountains only Talassee, and one or two about Chickamauga or on the headwaters of the Coosa, escaped. The whites had lost only one man killed and two wounded. Before the return a proclamation was sent to the Cherokee chiefs, warning them to make peace on penalty of a worse visitation.[2]

---

[1] Roosevelt, Winning of the West, II, pp. 298-300, 1889; Ramsey, Tennessee, pp. 261-264, 1853. There is great discrepancy in the various accounts of this fight, from the attempts of interested historians to magnify the size of the victory. One writer gives the Indians 1, 000 warriors. Here, as elsewhere, Roosevelt is a more reliable guide, his statements being usually from official documents.

[2] Roosevelt, op. cit., pp. 300-304; Ramsey, op. cit., pp. 265-268; Campbell, report, January 15, 1781, in Virginia State Papers, I, p. 436. Haywood and others after him make the expedition go as far as Chickamauga and Coosa River, but Campbell's report expressly denies this.

Some Cherokee who met them at Echota, on the return march, to talk of peace, brought in and surrendered several white prisoners.[3] One reason for the slight resistance made by the Indians was probably the fact that at the very time of the invasion many of their warriors were away, raiding on the Upper Holston and in the neighborhood of Cumberland Gap.[4]

Although the Upper or Overhill Cherokee were thus humbled, those of the middle towns, on the headwaters of Little Tennessee, still continued to send out parties against the back settlements. Sevier determined to make a sudden stroke upon them, and early in March of the same year, 1781, with 150 picked horsemen, he started to cross the Great Smoky Mountains over trails never before attempted by white men, and so rough in places that it was hardly possible to lead horses. Falling unexpectedly upon Tuckasegee, near the present Webster, North Carolina, he took the town completely by surprise, killing several warriors and capturing a number of women and children. Two other principal towns and three smaller settlements were [Page 171] taken in the same way, with a quantity of provision and about 200 horses, the Indians being entirely off their guard and unprepared to make any effective resistance. Having spread destruction through the middle towns, with the loss to himself of only one man killed and another wounded, he was off again as suddenly as he had come, moving so rapidly that he was well on his homeward way before the Cherokee could gather for pursuit.[1] At the same time a smaller Tennessee expedition went out to disperse the Indians who had been making headquarters in the mountains about Cumberland Gap and harassing travelers along the road to Kentucky.[2] Numerous indications of Indians were found, but none were met, although the country was scoured for a considerable distance.[3] In summer the Cherokee made another incursion, this time upon the new settlements on the French Broad, near the present Newport, Tennessee. With a hundred horsemen Sevier fell suddenly upon their camp on Indian

---

3 Ramsey, op. cit., p. 266.

4 Roosevelt, op. cit., p. 302.

1 Campbell, letter, March 28, 1781, in Virginia State Papers, I, p. 602, 1875; Martin, letter, March 31, 1781; ibid., p. 613; Ramsey, Tennessee, p. 268, 1853; Roosevelt, Winning of the West, II, pp. 305-307, 1889.

2 Campbell, letter, March 28, 1781, in Virginia State Papers, I, p. 602, 1875.

3 Ramsey, op. cit., p. 269.

Creek, killed a dozen warriors, and scattered the rest.[4] By these successive blows the Cherokee were so worn out and dispirited that they were forced to sue for peace, and in midsummer of 1781 a treaty of peace—doubtful though it might be—was negotiated at the Long Island of the Holston.[5] The respite came just in time to allow the Tennesseeans to send a detachment against Cornwallis.

Although there was truce in Tennessee, there was none in the South. In November of this year the Cherokee made a sudden inroad upon the Georgia settlements, destroying everything in their way. In retaliation a force under General Pickens marched into their country, destroying their towns as far as Valley River. Finding further progress blocked by heavy snows and learning through a prisoner that the Indians, who had retired before him, were collecting to oppose him in the mountains, he withdrew, as he says, "through absolute necessity," having accomplished very little of the result expected. Shortly afterwards the Cherokee, together with some Creeks, again invaded Georgia, but were met on Oconee River and driven back by a detachment of American troops.[6]

The Overhill Cherokee, on lower Little Tennessee, seem to have been trying in good faith to hold to the peace established at the Long island. Early in 1781 the Government land office had been closed to further entries, not to be opened again until peace had been declared with England, but the borderers paid little attention to the law in such matters, and the rage for speculation in Tennessee lands grew stronger daily.[7] In the fall of 1782 the chief, Old Tassel of Echota, on behalf of all the friendly chiefs and towns, sent a pathetic talk to the governors of Virginia and North Carolina, complaining that in spite of all their efforts to remain quiet the settlers were constantly encroaching upon them, and had built houses within a day's walk of the Cherokee towns. They asked that all those whites who had settled beyond the boundary last established should be removed.[8] As was to have been expected, this was never done.

---

4 Ibid.; Roosevelt, op. cit., p. 307.

5 Ibid.; Ramsey, op. cit., pp. 267, 268. The latter authority seems to make it 1782, which is evidently a mistake.

6 Stevens, Georgia, II, pp. 282-285, 1859; Jones, Georgia, II, p. 503, 1883.

7 Roosevelt, Winning of the West, II, p. 311, 1889.

8 Old Tassel's talk, in Ramsey, Tennessee, p. 271, 1853, and in Roosevelt, op. cit., p. 315

[Page 172]The Chickamauga Band, however, and those farther to the south, were still bent on war, being actively encouraged in that disposition by the British agents and refugee loyalists living among them. They continued to raid both north and south, and in September, 1782, Sevier, with 200 mounted men, again made a descent upon their towns, destroying several of their settlements about Chickamauga Creek, and penetrating as far as the important town of Ustana'li, on the headwaters of Coosa River, near the present Calhoun, Georgia. This also he destroyed. Every warrior found was killed, together with a white man found in one of the towns, whose papers showed that he had been active in inciting the Indians to war. On the return the expedition halted at Echota, where new assurances were received from the friendly element.[1] In the meantime a Georgia expedition of over 400 men, under General Pickens, had been ravaging the Cherokee towns in the same quarter, with such effect that the Cherokee were forced to purchase peace by a further surrender of territory on the head of Broad River in Georgia.[2] This cession was concluded at a treaty of peace held with the Georgia commissioners at Augusta in the next year, and was confirmed later by the Creeks, who claimed an interest in the same lands, but was never accepted by either as the voluntary act of their tribe as a whole.[3]

By the preliminary treaty of Paris, November 30, 1782, the long Revolutionary struggle for independence was brought to a close, and the Cherokee, as well as the other tribes, seeing the hopelessness of continuing the contest alone, began to sue for peace. By seven years of constant warfare they had been reduced to the lowest depth of misery, almost indeed to the verge of extinction. Over and over again their towns had been laid in ashes and their fields wasted. Their best warriors had been killed and their women and children had sickened and starved in the mountains. Their great war chief, Oconostota, who had led them to victory in 1780, was now a broken old man, and in this year, at Echota, formally resigned his office in favor of his son, The Terrapin. To complete their brimming cup of misery the smallpox again broke out among them in 1783.[4] Deprived of the assistance of their former white allies they were left to their own cruel fate,

---

1 Ramsey, op. cit., p. 272; Roosevelt, op. cit., p. 317 et passim.
2 Stevens, op. cit., pp. 411-415.
3 Royce, Cherokee Nation, in Fifth Ann. Rep. Bureau of Ethnology, p. 151, 1888.
4 See documents in Virginia State Papers, III, pp. 234, 398, 527, 1883.

the last feeble resistance of the mountain warriors to the advancing tide of settlement came to an end with the burning of Cowee town,[5] and the way was left open to an arrangement. In the same year the North Carolina Legislature appointed an agent for the Cherokee and made regulations for the government of traders among them.[6]

RELATIONS WITH THE UNITED STATES—FROM THE FIRST TREATY TO

THE REMOVAL—1785-1838.

Passing over several unsatisfactory and generally abortive negotiations conducted by the various State governments in 1783-84, including the treaty of Augusta already noted,[7] we come to the turning point in the history of the Cherokee, their first treaty with the new [Page 173] Government of the United States for peace and boundary delimitation, concluded at Hopewell in South Carolina on November 28, 1785. Nearly one thousand Cherokee attended, the commissioners for the United States being Colonel Benjamin Hawkins, of North Carolina; General Andrew Pickens, of South Carolina; Cherokee Agent Joseph Martin, of Tennessee, and Colonel Lachlan McIntosh, of Georgia. The instrument was signed by thirty-seven chiefs and principal men, representing nearly as many different towns. The negotiations occupied ten days, being complicated by a protest on the part of North Carolina and Georgia against the action of the Government commissioners in confirming to the Indians some lands which had already been appropriated as bounty lands for State troops without the consent of the Cherokee. On the other hand, the Cherokee complained that 3, 000 white settlers were at that moment in occupancy of unceded land between the Holston and the French Broad. In spite of their protest these intruders were allowed to remain, although the territory was not acquired by treaty until some years later. As finally arranged the treaty left the Middle and Upper towns, and those in the vicinity of Coosa River, undisturbed, while the whole country east of the Blue Ridge, with the Watauga and

---

5 Ramsey, Tennessee, p. 280, 1853.
6 Ibid., p. 276.
7 See Royce, Cherokee Nation, op. cit., pp. 151, 152; Ramsey, op. cit., p. 299 et passim.

Cumberland settlements, was given over to the whites. The general boundary followed the dividing ridge between Cumberland River and the more southern waters of the Tennessee eastward to the junction of the two forks of Holston, near the present Kingsport, Tennessee, thence southward to the Blue Ridge and southwestward to a point not far from the present Atlanta, Georgia, thence westward to the Coosa River and northwestward to a creek running into Tennessee River at the western line of Alabama, thence northward with the Tennessee River to the beginning. The lands south and west of these lines were recognized as belonging to the Creeks and Chickasaw. Hostilities were to cease and the Cherokee were taken under the protection of the United States. The proceedings ended with the distribution of a few presents.

THE EASTERN TRIBES.

Besides the Iroquois and Shawano, the Cherokee remember also the Delawares, Tuscarora, Catawba, and Cheraw as tribes to the east or north with which they formerly had relations.

The Cherokee call the Delawares Anakwan"kĭ, in the singular Akwan"kĭ, a derivative formed according to usual Cherokee phonetic modification from Wapanaq'kĭ, "Easterners," the generic name by which the Delawares and their nearest kindred call themselves.

In the most ancient tradition of the Delawares the Cherokee are called Talega, Tallige, Tallige-wi, etc.[1] In later Delaware tradition they are called Kĭtu'hwa, and again we find the two tribes at war, for which their neighbors are held responsible. According to the Delaware account, the Iroquois, in one of their forays to the south, killed a Cherokee in the woods and purposely left a Delaware war club near the body to make it appear that the work had been done by men of that tribe. The Cherokee found the body and the club, and naturally [Page 174] supposing that the murder had been committed by the Delawares, they suddenly attacked the latter, the result being a long and bloody war between the two tribes.[1] At this time, i. e., about the end of the seventeenth century, it appears that a part at least

---

[1] Brinton, Lenape and Their Legends, p. 130 et passim, 1885; Schoolcraft, Notes on Iroquois, pp. 147, 305 et passim, 1847; Heckewelder, Indian Nations, pp. 47-50, ed. 1876.
[1] Heckewelder, op. cit., p. 54.

of the Cherokee lived on the waters of the Upper Ohio, where the Delawares made continual inroads upon them, finally driving them from the region and seizing it for themselves about the year 1708.[2] A century ago the Delawares used to tell how their warriors would sometimes mingle in disguise with the Cherokee at their night dances until the opportunity came to strike a sudden blow and be off before their enemies recovered from the surprise.

Later there seems to have been peace until war was again brought on by the action of the Shawano, who had taken refuge with the Delawares, after having been driven from their old home on Cumberland River by the Cherokee. Feeling secure in their new alliance, the Shawano renewed their raids upon the Cherokee, who retaliated by pursuing them into the Delaware country, where they killed several Delawares by mistake. This inflamed the latter people, already excited by the sight of Cherokee scalps and prisoners brought back through their country by the Iroquois, and another war was the result, which lasted until the Cherokee, tired of fighting so many enemies, voluntarily made overtures for peace in 1768, saluting the Delawares as Grandfather, an honorary title accorded them by all the Algonquian tribes. The Delawares then reprimanded the Shawano, as the cause of the trouble, and advised them to keep quiet, which, as they were now left to fight their battles alone, they were glad enough to do. At the same time the Cherokee made peace with the Iroquois, and the long war with the northern tribes came to an end. The friendly feeling thus established was emphasized in 1779, when the Cherokee sent a message of condolence upon the death of the Delaware chief White-eyes.[3]

The Tuscarora, formerly the ruling tribe of eastern North Carolina, are still remembered under the name Ani'-Skăla'lĭ, and are thus mentioned in the Feather dance of the Cherokee, in which some of the actors are supposed to be visiting strangers from other tribes.

As the majority of the Tuscarora fled from Carolina to the Iroquois country about 1713, in consequence of their disastrous war with the whites, their memory has nearly faded from the recollection of the southern Indians. From the scanty light which history throws upon their mutual relations, the two tribes seem to have been almost constantly at war with each

---

2 Loskiel, History of the [Moravian] Mission, pp. 124-127; London, 1794.
3 Heckewelder, Indian Nations, pp. 88-89, 1876.

other. When at one time the Cherokee, having already made peace with some other of their neighbors, were urged by the whites to make peace also with the Tuscarora, they refused, on the ground that, as they could not live without war, it was better to let matters stand as they were than to make peace with the Tuscarora and be obliged immediately to look about for new enemies with whom to fight. For some years before the outbreak of the Tuscarora war in 1711 the Cherokee had ceased their inroads upon this tribe, and it was therefore supposed that they were more busily engaged with some other people west of the mountains, these being probably the Shawano, whom they drove out of Tennessee about this time.[4] In the war of [Page 175] 1711-1713 the Cherokee assisted the whites against the Tuscarora. In 1731 the Cherokee again threatened to make war upon the remnant of that tribe still residing in North Carolina and the colonial government was compelled to interfere.[1]

The Cheraw or Sara, ranging at different periods from upper South Carolina to the southern frontier of Virginia, are also remembered under the name of Ani'-Suwa'lĭ, or Ani'-Suwa'la, which agrees with the Spanish form Xuala of De Soto's chronicle, and Suala, or Sualy, of Lederer. The Cherokee remember them as having lived east of the Blue Ridge, the trail to their country leading across the gap at the head of Swannanoa River, east from Asheville. The name of the stream and gap is a corruption of the Cherokee Suwa'lĭ-Nûññâ'hĭ, "Suwa'li trail." Being a very warlike tribe, they were finally so reduced by conflicts with the colonial governments and the Iroquois that they were obliged to incorporate with the Catawba, among whom they still maintained their distinct language as late as 1743.[2]

The Catawba are known to the Cherokee as Ani'ta'gwa, singular Ata'gwa, or Ta'gwa, the Cherokee attempt at the name by which they are most commonly known. They were the immediate neighbors of the Cherokee on the east and southeast, having their principal settlements on the river of their name, just within the limits of South Carolina, and holding the leading place among all the tribes east of the Cherokee country with the exception of the Tuscarora. On the first settlement of South Carolina there were

---

4 See Haywood, Nat. and Aborig. Hist. of Tennessee, pp. 220, 224, 237, 1823.
1 North Carolina Colonial Records, III, pp. 153, 202, 345, 369, 393, 1886.
2 Mooney, Siouan Tribes of the East (bulletin of the Bureau of Ethnology), pp. 56, 61, 1894.

estimated to be about 7, 000 persons in the tribe, but their decline was rapid, and by war and disease their number had been reduced in 1775 to barely 500, including the incorporated remnants of the Cheraw and several smaller tribes. There are now, perhaps, 100 still remaining on a small reservation near the site of their ancient towns. Some local names in the old Cherokee territory seem to indicate the former presence of Catawba, although there is no tradition of any Catawba settlement within those limits. Among such names may be mentioned Toccoa Creek, in northeastern Georgia, and Toccoa River, in north-central Georgia, both names being derived from the Cherokee Tagwâ'hĭ, "Catawba place." An old Cherokee personal name is Ta'gwădihĭ', "Catawba killer."

The two tribes were hereditary enemies, and the feeling between them is nearly as bitter to-day as it was a hundred years ago. Perhaps the only case on record of their acting together was in the war of 1711-13, when they cooperated with the colonists against the Tuscarora. The Cherokee, according to the late Colonel Thomas, claim to have formerly occupied all the country about the head of the Catawba River, to below the present Morganton, until the game became scarce, when they retired to the west of the Blue Ridge, and afterward "loaned" the eastern territory to the Catawba. This agrees pretty well with a Càtawba tradition recorded in Schoolcraft, according to which the Catawba—who are incorrectly represented as comparatively recent immigrants from the north—on arriving at Catawba River found their progress disputed by the Cherokee, who claimed original ownership of the country. A battle was fought, with incredible loss on both sides, but with no decisive result, although the [Page 176] advantage was with the Catawba, on account of their having guns, while their opponents had only Indian weapons. Preparations were under way to renew the fight when the Cherokee offered to recognize the river as the boundary, allowing the Catawba to settle anywhere to the east. The overture was accepted and an agreement was finally made by which the Catawba were to occupy the country east of that river and the Cherokee the country west of Broad River, with the region between the two streams to remain as neutral territory. Stone piles were heaped up on the battle field to commemorate the treaty, and the Broad River was henceforth called Eswau Huppeday (Line River), by the Catawba, the country eastward to Catawba River being left unoccupied.[1] The fact that one party had guns would bring this event within the early historic period.

The Catawba assisted the whites against the Cherokee in the war of 1760 and in the later Revolutionary struggle. About 100 warriors, nearly the whole fighting strength of the tribe, took part in the first-mentioned war, several being killed, and a smaller number accompanied Williamson's force in 1776.[2] At the battle fought under Williamson near the present site of Franklin, North Carolina, the Cherokee, according to the tradition related by Wafford, mistook the Catawba allies of the troops for some of their own warriors, and were fighting for some time under this impression before they noticed that the Catawba wore deer tails in their hair so that the whites might not make the same mistake. In this engagement, which was one of the bloodiest Indian encounters of the Revolution, the Cherokee claim that they had actually defeated the troops and their Catawba allies, when their own ammunition gave out and they were consequently forced to retire. The Cherokee leader was a noted war chief named Tsanĭ (John).

About 1840 nearly the whole Catawba tribe moved up from South Carolina and joined the eastern band of Cherokee, but in consequence of tribal jealousies they remained but a short time, and afterward returned to their former home, as is related elsewhere.

Other tribal names (of doubtful authority) are Ani'-Sa'ni and Ani'-Sawahâ'nĭ, belonging to people said to have lived toward the north; both names are perhaps intended for the Shawano or Shawnee, properly Ani'-Sawănu'gĭ. The Ani'-Gilĭ' are said to have been neighbors of the Anin'tsĭ or Natchez; the name may possibly be a Cherokee form for Congaree.

Tuscarora.—The Tuscarora, a southern tribe of the Iroquoian stock, formerly occupied an extensive territory upon Neuse River and its branches, in eastern North Carolina, and, like their northern cousins, seem to have assumed and exercised a certain degree of authority over all the smaller tribes about them. As early as 1670 Lederer described the Tuscarora "emperor" as the haughtiest Indian he had ever met. About the year 1700 Lawson estimated them at 1, 200 warriors (6, 000 souls?) in 15 towns. In 1711 they rose against the whites, one of their first acts of hostility being

---

[1] Catawba MS. from South Carolina official archives. Schoolcratt, Indian Tribes, III, pp. 293-4, 1853.

[2] Ibid., p. 294, 1853.

the killing of Lawson himself, who was engaged in surveying lands which they claimed as their own. In a struggle extending over about two years they were [Page 177] so terribly decimated that the greater portion fled from Carolina and took refuge with their kinsmen and friends, the Iroquois of New York, who were henceforth known as the Six Nations. The so-called "friendly" party, under Chief Blount, was settled upon a small reservation north of Roanoke River in what is now Bertie County, North Carolina. Here they gradually decreased by disease and emigration to the North, until the few who were left sold their last remaining lands in 1804. The history of the tribe after the removal to the North is a part of the history of the Iroquois or Six Nations. They number now about 750, of whom about 380 are on the Tuscarora Reservation in New York, the others upon the Grand River Reservation in Ontario.

Xuala, Suwali, Sara, or Cheraw.—For the identification and earliest notices of the Sara see historical note 8, "De Soto's Route." Their later history is one of almost constant hostility to the whites until their final incorporation with the Catawba, with whom they were probably cognate, about the year 1720. In 1743 they still preserved their distinct language, and appear to be last mentioned in 1768, when they numbered about 50 souls living among the Catawba. See Mooney, Siouan Tribes of the East, Bulletin of the Bureau of Ethnology, 1894.

Catawba.—The origin and meaning of this name, which dates back at least two centuries, are unknown. It may possibly come from the Choctaw through the Mobilian trade jargon. They call themselves Nieye, which means simply "people" or "Indians." The Iroquois call them and other cognate tribes in their vicinity Toderigh-rono, whence Tutelo. In the seventeenth century they were often known as Esaw or Ushery, apparently from *iswă'*, river, in their own language. The Cherokee name Ata'gwa, plural Ani'ta'gwa, is a corruption of the popular form. Their linguistic affinity with the Siouan stock was established by Gatschet in 1881. See Mooney, Siouan Tribes of the East.

The southern and western tribes: The Creek confederacy.—Next in importance to the Cherokee, among the southern tribes, were the Indians of the Creek confederacy, occupying the greater portion of Georgia and Alabama, immediately south of the Cherokee. They are said to have been called Creeks by the early traders on account of the abundance of small streams in their country. Before the whites began to press upon them their tribes held nearly all the territory from the Atlantic westward to about the watershed between the Tombigby and the Pearl and Pascagoula Rivers, being cut off from the Gulf coast by the Choctaw tribes, and from the Savannah, except near the mouth, by the Uchee, Shawano, and Cherokee. About the year 1800 the confederacy comprised 75 towns, the people of 47 of which were the Upper Creeks, centering about the upper waters of the Alabama, while those of the remaining 28 were the Lower Ceeks, upon the lower Chattahoochee and its branches (Hawkins). Among them were represented a number of tribes formerly distinct and speaking distinct languages. The ruling tribe and language was the Muscogee (plural, Muscogûlgee), which frequently gave its name to the confederacy. Other languages were the Alabama, Koasati, Hichitee, Taskigi, Uchee, Natchee, and Sawanugi or Shawano. The Muscogee, Alabama, Koasati, Hichitee, and Taskigi (?) belonged to the Muskhogean stock, the Alabama and Koasati, [Page 178] however, being nearer linguistically to the Choctaw than to the Muscogee. The Hichitee represent the conquered or otherwise incorporated Muskhogean tribes of the Georgia coast region. The Apalachi on Appalachee Bay in Florida, who were conquered by the English about 1705 and afterward incorporated with the Creeks, were dialectically closely akin to the Hichitee; the Seminole also were largely an offshoot from this tribe. Of the Taskigi all that is known has been told elsewhere.

The Uchee, Natchee, and Sawanugi were incorporated tribes, differing radically in language from each other and from the Muskhogean tribes. The territory of the Uchee included both banks of the middle Savannah, below the Cherokee, and extended into middle Georgia. They had a strong race pride, claiming to be older in the country than the Muscogee, and are probably identical with the people of Cofitachiqui, mentioned in the early Spanish narratives. According to Hawkins, their incorporation with the Creeks was brought about in consequence of intermarriages about the year 1729. The Natchee or Natchez were an important tribe residing in lower Mississippi, in the vicinity of the present town of that name, until driven out by the French about the year 1730, when most of them took refuge with the Creeks, while others joined the Chickasaw and Cherokee. The Sawanugi were Shawano who kept their town on Savannah River, near the present Augusta, after the main body of their tribe had removed to the North about 1692. They probably joined the Creeks about the same time as their friends, the Uchee. The Uchee still constitute a compact body of about 600 souls in the Creek Nation, keeping up their distinct language and tribal character. The Natchee are reduced to one or two old men, while the Sawanugi have probably lost their identity long ago.

According to Morgan, the Muscogee proper, and perhaps also their incorporated tribes, have 22 clans. Of these the Wind appears to be the leading one, possessing privileges accorded to no other clan, including the hereditary guardianship of the ancient metal tablets which constitute the palladium of the tribe. By the treaty of Washington in 1832, the Creeks sold all of their remaining lands in their old country and agreed to remove west of the Mississippi to what is now the Creek Nation in the Indian Territory. The removal extended over a period of several years and was not finally accomplished until 1845. In 1898 the citizen population of the Creek Nation numbered 14, 771, of whom 10, 014 were of Indian blood and the remainder were negroes, their former slaves. It appears that the Indian population included about 700 from other tribes, chiefly Cherokee. There are also about 300 Alabama, "Cushatta" (Koasati), and Muscogee in Texas. See also Hawkins, Sketch of the Creek Country; Gatschet, Creek Migration Legend; Adair, History of the American Indians; Bartram, Travels; The Five Civilized Tribes, Bulletin of the Eleventh Census; Wyman, in Alabama Historical Society Collections.

Chickasaw.—This tribe, of Muskhogean stock, formerly occupied northern Mississippi and adjacent portions of Alabama and Tennessee, and at an early period had incorporated also several smaller tribes on Yazoo River in central Mississippi, chief among which were the cognate Chokchuma. The name occurs first in the De Soto narrative. The Chickasaw language was simply a dialect of Choctaw, although the two tribes were hereditary enemies and differed widely in character, [Page 179] the former being active and warlike, while the latter were notoriously sluggish. Throughout the colonial period the Chickasaw were the constant enemies of the French and friends of the English, but they remained neutral in the Revolution. By the treaty of Pontotoc in 1832 they sold their lands east of the Mississippi and agreed to remove to Indian Territory, where they are now organized as the Chickasaw Nation. According to Morgan they have 12 clans grouped into two phratries. In 1890 the citizen population of the nation (under Chickasaw laws) consisted of 3, 941 full-blood and mixed-blood Chickasaw, 681 adopted whites, 131 adopted negroes, and 946 adopted Indians from other tribes, chiefly Choctaws. Under the present law, by which citizenship claims are decided by a Government commission, "Chickasaw by blood" are reported in 1898 to number 4, 230, while "white and negro" citizens are reported at 4, 818. See also Gatschet, Creek Migration Legend; The Five Civilized Tribes, Bulletin of Eleventh Census.

[Page 180] EXHIBIT H.

HISTORY OF THE TUSCARORAS.

[From Handbook of American Indians:]

TUSCARORA (*Skarū'rĕn*', "hemp gatherers," the *Apocynum cannabinum*, or Indian hemp, being a plant of many uses among the Carolina Tuscarora; the native form of this appellative is impersonal, there being no expressed pronominal affix to indicate person, number, or gender). Formerly an important confederation of tribes, speaking languages cognate with those of the Iroquoian linguistic group, and dwelling, when first encountered, on the Roanoke, Neuse, Taw (Torhunta or Narhontes), and Pamlico rs., N. C. The evidence drawn from the testimony of writers contemporary with them, confirmed in part by tradition, makes it appear that while occupying this primitive habitat the Tuscarora league was composed of at least three tribal constituent members, each bearing an independent and exclusive appellation. The names of these component members still survive in the traditions of the Tuscarora now dwelling in w. New York and s. Ontario, Canada. The first of these tribal names in *Kă'tĕ'nuā'kā*', i. e., "People of the Submerged Pine-tree;" the second *Akawĕñteākā*' (meaning doubtful); and the third, *Skarū'rĕn*', "Hemp Gatherers." Cusick (Hist. Six Nations, 34, 1828) wrote these tribal appellations "Kautanohakau," "Kauwetseka," and "Tuscarora," respectively, and (p. 31) refers also to the "Esaurora, or Tuscarora," from which it may be inferred that Esaurora is a synonym of Skarū'reĕ'. According to the same authority (p. 36), the Tuscarora, on traditionary evidence, possessed in early times the "country lying between the sea shores and the mountains, which divide the Atlantic

States," in which they had 24 large towns and could muster 6,000 warriors, probably meaning persons. Lawson, a better authority, wrote that in 1708 the Tuscarora had 15 towns and about 1,200 warriors—perhaps a minimum estimate of the true number of their fighting-men; and Johnson (Legends, etc., of the Iroquois, 1881) says that the Tuscarora in North Carolina had 6 towns and 1,200 warriors, which was probably approximately true of the Tuscarora proper. Col. Barnwell, the commander of the South Carolina forces in the war of 1711-12, said that the Tuscarora or "the enemy can't be less than 1,200 or 1,400 [warriors], which may be easily judged by their large settlements;" but Gov. Spotswood of Virginia placed their fighting strength at 2,000 men in 1711. According to Barnwell the Tuscarora had 3 towns on Pamlico r., of which one was Ucouhnerunt, but that most of their towns were on Neuse r., and its many affluents. Some indication of the extent of the territory claimed by the Tuscarora may be obtained from the terms of the truce declared between the Tuscarora and Col. Barnwell in 1712. It was agreed therein that the Tuscarora were "to plant only on Neuse River, the creek the fort is on, quitting all claims to other lands.... To quit all pretensions to planting, fishing, hunting or ranging to all lands lying between Neuse River and Cape [Page 181] Feare, that entirely to be left to the So. Carolina Indians, and to be treated as enemies if found in those ranges without breach of peace, and the enemy's line shall be between Neuse and Pamblico ... fishing on both sides Bear River." This would indicate that Cape Fear r. was the southern boundary of the Tuscarora territory.

History.—The data for the history of the Tuscarora are meager and fragmentary, hence while they were at first an important people of North Carolina, little is evidently known regarding them, and that little usually applies to only a part of the people. The first authentic information concerning the Tuscarora is that recorded by Lawson, the Surveyor General of North Carolina, who knew them well, having lived in close contact with them for many years. His History of Carolina, having been written about 1709 and published in 1718, contains nothing in regard to the Tuscarora during the most eventful period of their history, namely, that covering the years 1711 to 1713. During this time they fought two wars with the colonists of North Carolina, who were effectively aided by those of South Carolina and Virginia, reenforced by their tributary Indian allies. The first war began with the capture of Lawson and the Baron De Graffenried by about 60 Tuscarora and the condemnation to death of the former in September, 1711. Immediately following, a portion of the Tuscarora under Hencock, the Coree,

Pamlico, Matamuskeet, Bear Rivers, and Machapungo, conspired to cut off the whites, each one of the tribes agreeing to operate in its own district whence they were being driven by the steady encroachment of the colonists. This compact resulted in the massacre of about 130 of the colonists on September 22, 1711, on Trent and Pamlico Rrs., by the tribes mentioned. Col. Barnwell was sent by South Carolina to aid the hard-pressed colonists of North Carolina, and succeeded in driving the Tuscarora into one of their palisaded towns about 20 m. above Newbern, N. C., where he defeated them and later induced them to accept terms of peace; but Barnwell violated this treaty by seizing some of the Indians and sending them away into slavery. This was the beginning of the second war between the Tuscarora and their allies and the people of North Carolina. Again an appeal was made to South Carolina for aid, which responded by sending Col. James Moore with a small militia force and about 900 tributary Indians.

Of the Tuscarora, Lawson said that they possessed many amiable qualities; that, in fact, they were "really better to us than we have been to them, as they always freely give us of their victuals at their quarters, while we let them walk by our doors hungry, and do not often relieve them. We look upon them with disdain and scorn, and think them little better than beasts in human form; while with all our religion and education, we possess more moral deformities and vices than these people do." This attitude of the whites toward the Indians naturally led to the troubles later, which ended in much bloodshed and cruelty on both sides. Although the Tuscarora were regarded as mild, kind, peaceable, ingenious, and industrious, they were speedily brutalized by the vices of the colonists with whom they came in contact; their women were debauched by the whites, and both men and women were kidnapped to be sold into slavery. The colonists of North Carolina, like their Puritan brethren of New England, did not recognize in the Indian any right to the soil, hence the lands of the Tuscarora and of their Indian neighbors and allies were [Page 182] appropriated without thought of purchase. It is not strange, therefore, that such conduct on the part of the whites should eventually have awakened distrust and jealousy in the minds of the erstwhile amiable Tuscarora, which, fomented by these and other grievances, finally ripened into a hatred which led to resistance and reprisal.

Perhaps the most lucid and condensed statement of the wrongs suffered by the Tuscarora before vainly attempting to right them is contained in a petition made to the Provincial Government of Pennsylvania in 1710. More than a year before the massacre of 1711 the Tuscarora had officially formulated a number of proposals embodying their grievances and their desire to have these adjusted or removed by the conclusion of peace, and to this end they sent, through the Conestoga (Susquehanna), an embassy with these pacific overtures to the people and government of Pennsylvania. The governor and provincial council dispatched two commissioners to meet this embassy at Conestoga on June 8, 1710, where, in addition to the Tuscarora emissaries, they found Civility and four other Conestoga chiefs, and Opessa, the head chief of the Shawnee. In the presence of these officials the Tuscarora ambassadors delivered their proposals, attested by eight wampum belts, at the same time informing the Pennsylvania commissioners that these were sent as an overture for the purpose of asking for a cessation of hostilities until the following spring, when their chiefs and headmen would come in person "to sue for the peace they so much desired." By the first belt, the elder women and the mothers besought the friendship of the Christian people, the Indians and the government of Pennsylvania, so they might fetch wood and water without risk or danger. By the second, the children born and those about to be born, implored for room to sport and play without the fear of death or slavery. By the third, the young men asked for the privilege to leave their towns without the fear of death or slavery to hunt for meat for their mothers, their children, and the aged ones. By the fourth, the old men, the elders of the people, asked for the consummation of a lasting peace, so that the forest (the paths to other tribes) be as safe for them as their palisaded towns. By the fifth, the entire tribe asked for a firm peace. By the sixth, the chiefs asked for the establishment of a lasting peace with the government, people, and Indians of Pennsylvania, whereby they would be relived from "those fearful apprehensions they have these several years felt." By the seventh, the Tuscarora begged for a "cessation from murdering and taking them," so that thereafter they would not fear "a mouse, or anything that ruffles the leaves." By the eighth, the tribe, being strangers to the people and government of Pennsylvania, asked for an official path or means of communication between them.

Stripped of metaphor and the language of diplomacy, the purport of this message is plain; it was the statement of a tribe at bay, that in view of the large numbers of their people who were being kidnaped to be sold into slavery or who were being killed while seeking to defend their offspring and their friends and kindred they desired to remove to a more just and friendly government than that whence they came. At this time there was no war between them and the white people; there had as yet been no massacre by the Tuscarora, no threat of hostility on the part of the Indians, yet to maintain peace and to avoid the impending shedding of blood they [Page 183] were even then willing to forsake their homes. The commissioners of Pennsylvania, however, informed the delegates, among other things, that "to confirm the sincerity of their past carriage toward the English, and to raise in us a good opinion of them, it would be very necessary to procure a certificate from the government they leave, to this, of their good behaviour, and then they might be assured of a favourable reception" (Min. Prov. Coun. Pa., II, 511, 1852). The Conestoga ("Seneques") chiefs present at this conference stated that by the advice of their council it had been determined to send these belts, brought by the Tuscarora, to the Five Nations. It was the reception of the belts with their pitiful messages by these Five Nations that moved the latter to take steps to shield and protect the Tuscarora, which gave so much apprehension to the northern colonies.

The rapid encroachment of the whites on the lands of the Tuscarora and their Indian neighbors for a period of 60 years after the first settlements, although there was an air of peace and harmony between the two races, were wrongs which dwarfed in comparison with the continued practice of kidnaping their young to be sold into slavery. This was the true cause of the so-called Tuscarora War in 1711-1713. This phase of the question is overlooked or quite disregarded by most historians; but years before the massacre of 1711, Tuscarora Indians were brought into Pennsylvania and sold as slaves, a transaction that excited grave apprehension in the minds of the resident Indian tribes. To allay as much as possible this growing terror among them, the provincial council of Pennsylvania enacted in 1705 that, "Whereas the importation of Indian slaves from Carolina, or other places, hath been observed to give the Indians of this province some umbrage for suspicion and dissatisfaction," such importation be prohibited after March 25, 1706. This enactment was based solely on expediency and self-interest, since it was evident that the Indians to the southward were in a general commotion. During the Tuscarora War an act was passed, June 7, 1712, forbidding the importation of Indians, but providing for their sale as slaves to the highest bidder in case any should be imported for that purpose. It is known that the prisoners of Col. Barnwell and Col. Moore were all sold as slaves, even the northern colonies being canvassed for a market for them; indeed, the Boston News Letter of 1713 contained an advertisement offering these very Indians for purchase.

According to De Graffenried, Surveyor Gen. Lawson in 1709-10 settled his people, the Swiss and Palatines, on the south bank of Trent River, on a tongue of land called Chattawka, formed by the Trent and the Neuse in North Carolina, in a hot and unhealthful situation. De Graffenried bitterly complained that the surveyor general was dishonest for having charged him a "heavy price" for it, and for the consequences of his not knowing that Lawson had no title to the land and that the place was still inhabited by the Indians, although the surveyor general had attested that the land was free of encumbrance and unoccupied. This encroachment on the Indian lands was one of the fundamental causes of the so-called Tuscarora War. It is well known that the Coree, together with their close allies, the hostile Tuscarora, in 1711 took vengeance on the Swiss and Palatines settled on Trent River, killing about 70 of them, wounding many others, [Page 184] and destroying much of their property. De Graffenried says that one of the several causes of the war was the "rough treatment of some turbulent Carolinians, who cheated those Indians in trading, and would not allow them to hunt near their plantations, and under that pretense took away from them their game, arms, and ammunition," and that the despised Indians being "insulted in many ways by a few rough Carolinians, more barbarous and inhuman than the savages themselves, could not stand such treatment any longer and began to think of their safety and of vengeance. What they did they did very secretly."

In a letter of Maj. Christopher Gale to his brother, November 2, 1711, he describes a condition, fairly representative of the times, as to the relations between the whites and the Indians around them. During an attack on one of the many small garrisons maintained for the protection of the settlements, "a number of Indian prisoners of a certain nation, which we did not know, whether they were friends or enemies, rose in the garrison, but were soon cut to pieces, as those on the outside repelled. In the garrison were killed 9 men, and soon after 39 women and children sent off for slaves." This shows that for the purposes of slavery little distinction, if any, was made between one tribe and another.

De Graffenried, while a captive among the hostile Tuscarora, negotiated, subsequent to the execution of the unfortunate Lawson, a private treaty with them by offering to every one of the chiefs of the 10 villages of the hostiles a cloth jerkin, 2 bottles of powder, 500 grains of small shot, 2 bottles of rum, and something more to the head chief for his own ransom. Among other things he agreed to remain neutral during the continuance of the war, and that he, the "said governor of the German colony, promises to remain within his limits and to take no more lands from them without due warning to the king [head chief] and his nation." Thus De Graffenried admitted taking Indian lands without consulting the Indians, although he says elsewhere, "It must be observed that it was neither I nor my colony who were the cause of that terrible slaughter or Indian war," apparently overlooking the fact that the greatest massacre was among his own Swiss and Palatines, indicating that the Indians thus resented the wrongs committed by him and his people.

In order to secure the aid of the Catawba ("Flatheads") against the hostile Tuscarora, the Carolina authorities promised them that in the event of success in the war the Indians were to obtain goods "cheaper than formerly." But after faithfully aiding the Carolinians in 1711-1713 in dispersing the hostile Tuscarora, the Catawba were deceived as to the promised reduction in the price of goods sold to them, and from this misunderstanding arose the troubles leading later to the Catawba War in 1714-15 (N. Y. Doc. Col. Hist., v, 444, 1855).

The chiefs of the Five Nations, in conference with Gov. Hunter at Albany, September 25, 1714, acquainted him with the fact that the "Tuscarora Indians are come to shelter themselves among the Five Nations; they were of us and went from us long ago, and now are returned and promise to live peaceably among us. And since there is peace now everywhere we have received them. Do give a belt of wampum. We desire you to look upon the Tuscaroras that are come to live among us as our children, who shall obey our commands [Page 185] and live peaceably and orderly" (N. Y. Doc. Col. Hist., v, 387, 1855). This proposal, for it was practically such, was not yet accepted by the New York government in 1715 (ibid., 413).

On June 23, 1712, Gov. Hunter, of New York, wrote to the Lords of Trade that "the war betwixt the people of North Carolina and the Tuscarora Indians is like to embroil us all," and expressed the fear that under French instigation the Five Nations would fulfill their threat to joint the Tuscarora (ibid., 343). Again, on September 10, 1713, Hunter wrote to Secretary Popple that "the Five Nations are hardly to be diswaded from sheltering the Tuscaruro Indians, which would embroil us all," and expressed regret that he had no funds with which to buy presents to be employed in dissuading them from forming an alliance with the Tuscarora.

On September 10, 1713, an Onondaga chief, in conference with commissioners from Gov. Hunter at Onondaga, said: "Brother Corlaer says the

Queen's subjects towards the south are now at war with the tus-Carorase Indians. These Indians went out heretofore from us, and have settled themselves there; now they have got into war and are dispersed. * * * They have abandoned their castles and are scattered hither and thither; let that suffice; and we request our Brother Corlaer to act as mediator between the English of Carrelyna and the Tuskaroras that they may no longer be hunted down, and we assure that we will oblige them not to do the English any more harm, for they are no longer a nation with a name, being once dispersed" (N. Y. Doc. Col. Hist., v, 376, 1855).

In 1717 Gov. Hunter, of New York, informed the Five Nations that there were Virginia traders who still bartered with the Tuscarora, thus showing that, contrary to the common opinion, there were still a part of these Indians in Carolina and southern Virginia.

In a letter dated at Narhantes Fort, February 4, 1712, Col. Barnwell gives a list of the various tribes of Southern Indians who composed his motley army. In his own spelling these were: The Yamasses, Hog Logees, Apalatchees, Corsaboy, Watterees, Sagarees, Catawbas, Suterees, Waxams, Congarees, Sattees, Pedees, Weneaws, Cape Feare, Hoopengs, Wareperes, Saraws, and Saxapahaws. Fort Narhantes, according to Barnwell, was the largest and most warlike town of the Tuscarora. It was situated about 27 miles below a former settlement of the Saxapahaw or "Shacioe Indians," which these Indians had been forced to abandon along with others at the beginning of February, 1712, by the Narhantes Tuscarora, who had fallen upon them and had killed 16 persons, owing to the refusal of the Saxapahaw to join the Tuscarora against the English. The Saxapahaw had just reached the Wattomas when Barnwell arrived there. After reaching Neuse River, Barnwell numbered his men before crossing, and found that he had 498 Indians and 33 white men. He complained that there was a great desertion of the Indians; that only 67 remained of Capt. Bull's 200. On taking Fort Narhantes, "head Town of ye Tuscaruros," on January 30, 1712, he and his men were greatly surprised and puzzled to find within two log houses much stronger than the outer fort. After gaining an entrance, he says, while "we were putting the men to the sword, our Indians got all the slaves and the plunder, only one girl we gott." This was the strongest fort in that part of the country. His loss was 7 white men killed and at least 32 wounded; the Indian loss was 6 killed and 28 [Page 186] wounded; the Tuscarora loss was 52 men killed and at least 10 women, and 30 prisoners. Barnwell was much chagrined at his great loss, "with no greater execution of ye enemy." De Graffenried, in speaking of this encounter, says he "marched against a great Indian village, called Core, about 30 miles distant from Newbern, drove out the King and his forces, and carried the day with such fury that, after they had killed a great many, in order to stimulate themselves still more, they cooked the flesh of an Indian 'in good condition' and ate it." So it appears that Narhantes was a Coree village, whose King was called Cor Tom. Barnwell then advanced on Catechna, or King Hencock's town, in which had taken refuge a medley of Indians from the Weetock, Bay, Neuse, Cor, Pamlico, and a portion of the Tuscarora tribe. After two assaults, which the Indians successfully repulsed, Barnwell, in order to save from massacre the white prisoners within the fort, induced the Indians to enter into a truce with him on condition that the white prisoners be liberated; and he returned to Newbern with his small army for refreshment. Barnwell had hoped for great honors and gifts from North Carolina, but being disappointed in this hope, and wishing to return home with his forces with some profit, he lured, under pretense of peace, a large number of the Indians to the neighborhood of Cor village and then broke the truce by capturing them and carrying them away to be sold into slavery. This naturally incensed the Tuscarora and other Carolina Indians, and caused them to lose all confidence in the word of a white man. This change of affairs resulted in repeated raids by the Indians along Neuse and Pamlico Rivers, and "the last troubles were worse than the first."

Solicitations by the North Carolina authorities were made to the government of South Carolina for new aid, which was granted, under Col. Moore, with a body of 33 white men and more than 900 Indian allies, who were probably reenforced by North Carolina recruits. His objective point was the palisaded town of Catechna, or Hencock's village. In a letter dated March 27, 1713, to President Pollock, of North Carolina, just after he had taken the palisaded town of "Neoheroka," in Greene County, N. C., which lay on his route to Catechna, he reported that the attack was begun on the 20th and that on the morning of the 23d "wee had gott ye fort to ye ground." He states that the prisoners taken were 392, that the scalps taken in the fort numbered 192, that there were 200 killed and burned in the fort, and 166 persons killed and taken "out of ye fort on ye Scout," a total of 950. His own loss was 22 white men killed and 36 wounded; the loss of his Indians was 35 killed and 58 wounded. This severe loss so awed the Tuscarora that they abandoned Fort "Cohunche," situated at Hencock's town, and migrated northward toward the territory of the Five Nations.

Prior to the arrival of Col. Moore, President Pollock had entered into an arrangement with Tom Blunt, the leading chief of the "Northern Tuscarora," to seize Chief Hencock, who was the reputed head of the hostile Tuscarora, and to bring him alive to the President for the purpose of adjusting their mutal difficulties and to negotiate peace. Blunt's Tuscarora were to destroy the hostiles who had taken part in the massacre and to deliver hostages for their own good behavior—this arrangement was to continue only until the new year. After the defeat of the Tuscarora by Moore, another treaty was made [Page 187] with Tom Blunt and his Tuscarora, thus leaving as hostile only the small tribes of the Coree, Matamuskeet, and Catechna. All of Moore's Indians except about 180 returned to South Carolina to sell their captives into slavery. With the remaining forces Moore soon reduced and drove away the few remaining hostiles.

The date of the adoption of the Tuscarora into the Council Board of the League of the Iroquois, through the Oneida, their political sponsors, is indefinite, judging from the differing dates, ranging from 1712 to 1715, given by various well-informed writers. In their forced migration northward the Tuscarora did not all decamp at once. The hostiles and their most apprehensive sympathizers were most probably the first to leave their ancient homes in North Carolina. On the total defeat and dispersion of the hostile Tuscarora and their allies in 1713, the scattered fragments of tribes fled and sought asylum with other tribes, among whom their identity was not always maintained. Although the Five Nations gave asylum to the fugitive Tuscarora, there is also abundant evidence that, for political reasons perhaps, the Tuscarora were not for many years after their flight from North Carolina formally admitted into the Council Board of the League of the Five Nations as a constitutive member. The fact is that the Tuscarora were 90 years in removing from their North Carolina home to more friendly dwelling-places in the north, and there is no evidence that they were formally incorporated into the confederation of the Five Nations, as a coequal member, before September, 1722. On September 6, 1722, Gov. Burnet held a conference with the Five Nations at Albany, at which Gov. Spotswood, of Virginia, was present. For the purpose of preventing forays between the Five Nations and their allies on the one hand, and the Southern Indians on the other, Spotswood induced the Five Nations to consent to the running of a dividing line along the Potomac and the high ridge of the Allegany Mountains. This agreement was made in the name of the Five Nations and the Tuscarora, indicating that the latter had become a factor in the councils of the League of the Iroquois. In closing the conference, it is stated that the Indians "gave six shouts—five for the Five Nations and one for the castle of Tuscaroras, lately seated between the Oneidas and Onondagas." The record continues that at the conclusion of this conference, on September 13, the Five Nations sought a special interview with the governor of Pennsylvania, and that on September 14 the governor received "the 10 chiefs of the Five Nations, being two from each, together with two others, said to be of the Tuscororoes." This appears to be the first official mention of the Tuscarora as taking part in the management of the public affairs of the league. The Tuscacora mentioned here, however, did not include those who dwelt on the Juniata and on the Susquehanna at Oquaga and its environs, nor those still in North Carolina.

In a petition of John Armstrong for land lying in Tuscarora Valley, on Juniata River, Pa., about 6 miles from the mouth of Tuscarora Creek, the Indians living there at that time are called Lakens; this land was taken up by Armstrong on February 3, 1755. On the same day George Armstrong obtained a warrant for land situated on the south side of Tuscarora Creek, "opposite to the settlement of the Indians, called Lackens." It would thus appear that at this date this band of Tuscarora were known, at least locally, as Lakens or Lackens.

[Page 188]Elias Johnson, in his legends, says that it was the Seneca who first adopted the Tuscarora as a constituent member of the league. This, however, is at variance with the common but authentic traditions of all the tribes and with the official statement of Col. (afterward Sir) William Johnson to the Oneida, made at Mount Johnson, September 8, 1753. He said, "Brethren of Oneida. * * * My best advice is to have your castles as near together as you conveniently can with the Tuscaroras, who belong to you as children, and the Scanihaderadighroones, lately come into your alliance or families, which makes it necessary for me to fix a new string to the cradle which was hung up by your forefathers when they received the Tuscaroras, * * * to feed and protect."

After the close of the war of 1711-1713 in North Carolina, the neutral Tuscarora, with remnants of allied tribes still remaining in that country, were placed under the rule of Chief Tom Blunt, or Blount, by treaty with the provincial government of North Carolina. From an act of the General Assembly of North Carolina, in 1778, it is learned that Withmell Tuffdick was then the ruling chief; but the last ruling chief of the North Carolina Tuscarora was Samuel Smith, who died in 1802.

In 1767, the renown of the Moravian mission station at Friedenshuetten (q. v.) in Pennsylvania was so great that many Indians from various tribes, including the Tuscarora, probably from Oquaga, Ingaren, and vicinity, were constantly stopping there. Many passed through it merely to see a place so famous for its hospitality. In May, 1766, seventy-five Tuscarora, according to Loskiel, on their way from North Carolina, halted here and remained for some weeks. They are described as lazy and "refuse to hear religion." During their stay the Tuscarora were so alarmed at the sight of the first snow that they left their huts down by the river and took refuge with the missionaries. A number of Tuscarora arrived at the mission to remain there; these had planted their crops during 1766 at the mouth of Tuscarora Creek, Wyoming County, Pa.

On December 16, 1766, Sir William Johnson received at Mount Johnson, N. Y., 160 Tuscarora who had just arrived from North Carolina. They complained to him that on their way thither they had been robbed at Paxtang, in Pennsylvania, of their horses and other property to the value of about $300.

Later the Tuscarora on the Susquehanna, dwelling at Oquaga and in its vicinity, had lands assigned them by the Oneida, their political sponsors. These lands were bounded on the east by Unadilla River, on the west by the Chenango, and on the south by the Susquehanna. In the northern part of this allotment were situated the towns of Ganasaraga, on the site of Sullivan, Madison County, N. Y., and Kannehsuntahkeh. A number of the Tuscarora lived with the Oneida in their chief village. On these lands a large portion of the Tuscarora remained until the events of the Revolution displaced them. By the terms of the treaty of Fort Herkimer in 1785 with the State of New York, to which the Tuscarora were nominal parties, the Oneida, the original proprietors of the lands then occupied by the Tuscarora, conveyed to New York the lands of the Tuscarora and retained the proceeds of the sale; thus the Tuscarora were again without a home. Thereafter they became dispersed. Later they had a village called Junastriyo (Tcunästri' io') in the Genessee Valley, [Page 189] below Avon, N. Y.; another, called Jutaneaga (Tcutäněñ" kiä'), at the fork of Chittenango Creek; and another called Kanhato (Kǎ'n'ha"nǔ').

According to Johnson (legends, etc.), a part of the fugitive Tuscarora settled at a point about 2 miles west of Tamaqua, Schuylkill County, Pa., where they planted apple trees and lived for a number of years. It is probable that it was these Tuscarora who later removed to Oquaga, in the vicinity of which they had three other towns in 1778. Another band of fugitives settled in Tuscarora Valley (as it was called later from them), on Juniata River, Pa. They remained here at least as late as 1762. In a minute of a conference held at Lancaster, Pa., August 11, 1762, between Lieut. Gov. Hamilton of Pennsylvania and delegates from the Ohio Delawares, the Tuscarora of Oquaga and Lower Tuscarora, the Shawnee, the Kickapoo, the Wea, and the Miami, it is stated that six Tuscarora were present, of whom three were chiefs, who brought from their people a letter in which they asked the governor to furnish them with a pass, saying, "We should be glad to be informed of the state and behavior of our brethren in Tuscarora Valley, and to have some directions about the way, as we propose to make them a visit, and also should be glad of a pass or recommendation in writing, that we may be friendly received on our way to and at the valley."

Major portions of the Oneida and the Tuscarora, in accordance with standing agreements with the United Colonies, remained faithful to the American cause during the Revolution. When the Indian allies of the British, even some of their brethren of the Six Nations, learned that a majority of the Tuscarora had cast their lot with the Colonies, they invaded the Tuscarora country, burned their lodges, and destroyed their crops and other property. Thus again by the fortunes of war the Tuscarora were scattered and homeless. A large party of these settled at a place called Oyonwayea, or Johnson's Landing, in Niagara County, N. Y., about 4 miles east of the outlet of Niagara River, at the mouth of Four Mile Creek, in order not to be directly among the many Indians friendly to the British cause camped around Fort Niagara. At the close of the war, two families, probably clans, of Tuscarora from Oyonwayea, made their way to the northeast limits of their present reservation, where they found many walnuts and butternuts, and a fine stream. Here they decided to winter. Being missed from Oyonwayea, scouts were sent out, who found them in their newly chosen settlement, a situation so favorable that, after the gratuitous cession of their former home among the Oneida, Oyonwayea was abandoned and all the families removed to the new site. Although the Tuscarora had only a tacit permission from the Seneca to reside at this place, the last settlement became the foundation of the present Tuscarora reservation in New York. At the treaty held at Genessee, September 15, 1797, between Robert Morris and the Seneca Tribe, the Tuscarora chiefs complained for the first time since their admission to the councils of the league, that the Five Nations had from time to time allotted lands to their people, but that each time these lands had been included in a subsequent cession to the whites, and that the

Tuscarora had received nothing in return for their right of occupancy or for their improvements. The justice and merits of their complaint having been acknowledged by the Five Nations, Morris reserved to the Tuscarora, [Page 190] by grant, 2 square miles, covering their settlement on the ridge mentioned above, and the Seneca thereupon granted them an adjoining square mile. About 1800-1802 a deputation was sent to North Carolina to learn whether they could obtain funds in payment for the lands they formerly occupied there, with the result that, by aid of the North Carolina Legislature, they were able to lease the Carolina lands, which yielded a fund of $13, 722. This sum enabled the Secretary of War in 1804, under authority of Congress, to purchase 4, 329 acres for the Tuscarora from the Holland Land Co., adjoining the 3 square miles already occupied by them. Such is the origin of the land holdings of the New York Tuscarora.

It was while the Tuscarora deputation was in North Carolina that the remnant of the tribe still residing there was brought to the north and joined their brethren in New York State.

The Tuscarora in sympathy with those of the Six Nations that adhered to the cause of Great Britain in the Revolution were granted lands in severalty on Grand River Reservation, Ontario.

The evangelizing work of Christian missionaries began among the Tuscarora in western New York as early as 1805 under the patronage of the New York Missionary Society. At first there were only six persons among the Tuscarora willing to abjure their ancient faith and customs, at least in name and appearance, and join in the missionary work; the remainder were generally strongly averse to the work of the missionaries. So violent were the struggles between the two unequal parties that in the spring of 1820 the "pagans" succeeded in inducing about 70 persons to emigrate to Canada, where they settled among the pagans of the Six Nations on the Grand River Reservation, Ontario. The church membership at this time was 16 persons. Little progress was apparent in the education of the Tuscarora, although the New York Society had maintained a school among them.

Ethnology.—The Tuscarora in New York are governed by a council of irresponsible chiefs, for the Indians have forgotten and so neglect the means to be employed in enforcing the will of the clan in case a chief fails in his plain duty; the criminal law of New York at this point nullifies the early sovereignty of the clan over its members. In common with the other tribes of the Iroquoian linguistic stock, the Tuscarora traced the descent of blood through the line of the mother, and made the civil and official military chieftainships hereditary in the *ohwatcira* of certain clans (see *Clans*) over which the women chiefs and the elder women presided. The simplest political unit was the *ohwatcira*, of which one or more constituted a clan, which was the simplest organized political unit. The Tuscarora were constituted of at least eight clans, which primitively were organized into phratries. There are no data, other than those furnished by tradition and analogy, as to the organization of the Tuscarora confederation. The clans were exogamic as to their own members, as were also the phratries in primitive times. The Tuscarora of New York being completely isolated from any of their own people who still profess their ancient dogmas and beliefs and who still practice their ancient rites and ceremonies, have preserved only a hazy recollection of their early customs, ceremonies, and rites; even less do they comprehend the meaning of the ceremonies still practiced by the so-called pagan members of cognate tribes. They are all professed [Page 191] Christians, and so turn away from the old forms of thought and practice of their ancestors.

The exact number of clans still existing among the Tuscarora is not definitely known, for the native authorities themselves do not agree on the number and the names of those still recognized—some informants give seven, while others with equal credibility give eight. There is likewise some diversity in regard to the correct names of certain clans. One list has Bear, Wolf, Turtle, Beaver, Deer, Eel, and Snipe; another has Bear, Eel, Large Turtle, Small Turtle, Beaver, Deer, Wolf, and Snipe; still another list has Bear, Eel, Deer, Turtle, Gray Wolf, Yellow Wolf, Beaver, and Snipe; and yet another is like the last, except that the Turtle clan is replaced by the clans Small Turtle and Large Turtle. Like differences appear in the lists of clans of the other Iroquois tribes.

The names of the civil chiefs still in use among the present two divisions of the Tuscarora (that in Ontario and the other in western New York) are: (A) *Säkwari"çrä'* (Sacharissa), 'The spear trailer'; *Ni'hawĕñāñ'ä'*, 'His voice is small'; *Hotio'kwawă"kĕn'*, 'He holds or grasps the multitude,' or possibly, 'He holds or grasps his own loins'; these three belong to the Turtle clan. (B) *Näkāiĕñ'iĕn'* (signification not clear); *Utakwa'tej'a'*, 'The Bear clib'; *Ionĕñtchānĕñ"nākĕn'*, 'Its fore-paw pressed against its breast'; these three belong to the Bear clan. (C) *Nāio'kāwenă* (signification not known); *Neiotchă'k'doñ'*, 'It is bent'; these two belong to the Wolf clan. (D) *Karoñdawă"kĕn'*, 'One is holding the tree'; *Thanādăk'hwă'* (signification not clear); these two belong to the Snipe clan. (E) *Kari'hĕñ'tiä'*, 'It goes along teaching'; *Niʻhnoʻkāʼwä*, 'He annoints the hide'; *Näkäʻhĕñwăʻçʻhĕñ*, 'It is twenty canoes'; these three belong to the Beaver clan. Among the Canadian Tuscarora on Grand River Reservation, Ontario, the first and last names of the Turtle clan, the first title of the Wolf clan, and the first title of the Snipe clan appear to be the only ones now in use, although these four titles are questionably also in use among the New York Tuscarora.

There is no definite information available as to the former and more complete organization into clan phratries. Some of the translations of the chieftain titles above would seem to indicate that they were originally designations of some habit, attitude, or other characteristic feature of the clan tutelary or patron, questionably called "totem." The clan name, with one or two exceptions, is not the ordinary name of the clan guardian or patron, but is rather descriptive of some feature or attitude, or is the name of the usual habitat, of the tutelary; for example, the name of the Bear clan signifies literally, 'Broken-off tail'; that of the Plover or Killdee (Snipe) 'Clean-sand people'; that of the Beaver, 'People of the stream'; that of the Turtle clan, 'Climbing-the-mountain people,' named from the position of the turtle basking, etc. It is probable that plover killdee should be substituted in the foregoing lists of clans, for the name clearly refers to the killdee's habit of running along the clean sand at the water's edge.

De Graffenried gives (N. C. Col. Rec., I, 905 et seq.) an interesting account of the preparations made for the execution of Lawson and himself by the hostile Tuscarora. In the open space or public square mentioned there was a large fire, near which was the shaman or high priest, a grizzled sorcerer, who made two white rings on the ground, [Page 192] whether of flour or white sand was not stated. In front of the two victims was placed a wolf skin, and a short distance farther there stood an Indian in a terrifying posture, holding in one hand a knife and in the other a tomahawk; he was apparently the executioner. He did not move from the spot. On the farther side of the fire were assembled young men, women, and children, who danced with weird and frightful contortions and attitudes. In the center of the circle of dancers were seated two singers who intoned a dismal song, "rather fit to provoke tears and anger than joy." Within the circle of dancers the shaman stood unterrified, uttering his threatenings and adjurations and performing his exorcisms against the foes of his people and their *orenda* or "medicine," when there would come a pause in the dancing. Finally, with shouts and howls the dancers ran into the neighboring forests. In a short time they returned with their faces painted black, white, and red, in bands, and with their hair loose and flying, oiled and sprinkled with fine down or cotton from the cattail flag and with small white feathers, and some returned arrayed in all kinds of furs. After their return, the dance was renewed. Back of the two victims stood a double line of armed warriors who kept their posts until everything was over; back of this guard was the council of war, whose members were seated on the ground in a circle, gravely deliberating on the fate of the two noted prisoners. Finally, they acted on the advice of "King" Tom Blunt, the headchief of their neighbors, "the villages of the Tuscaroros," properly so called, that King Hencock should liberate De Graffenried, and could deal with Lawson as he and his council pleased. The manner of Lawson's death, as learned from Indian information, is found in a letter of Maj. Christopher Gale to his brother, Nov. 2, 1711, wherein it is said that the Indians stuck the unfortunate prisoner "full of fine small splinters of torchwood, like hogs' bristles, and so set them gradually on fire." De Graffenried was not permitted to know how Lawson was executed.

To this account of the Tuscarora method of preparing for the execution of captives may be added their triumphal ceremonies which De Graffenrid says they performed after their defeat of a relief party of Swiss and Palatines. He reports that they built bonfires at night, and especially a large one in the place of executions, where they raised "three wolf's hides, figuring as many protectors or gods," to which offerings, consisting of their jewels, were made by the women. In the middle of the cricle, the chief shaman performed all manner of contortions, conjurations, and imprecations against the enemies of his country, while the populace danced in a circle around the wolf hides.

The council of "King" Hencock, which consisted of 40 elders, was called by the Tuscarora, according to De Graffenried, the "Assembly of the Great," a translation of the Tuscarora terms for the council of chiefs, the general word for chief signifying 'one is great,' either in size or position. At the council before which Lawson and De Graffenried were tried the "forty elders" were seated around a great fire kindled in a large open space devoted to important festivals and public executions. On this occasion these chiefs and the accused were seated on rush mats, which were customarily provided for the comfort of guests as a mark of deference and honor. Although the two captives were acquitted by the first council, they were again [Page 193] tried before a second council, after Lawson incautiously had had a bitter quarrel with Cor Tom, the chief of Cor town, who was not at the first council. The two captives were not given mats upon which to sit, and Lawson was condemned to death and De Graffenried was acquitted.

Lawson asserts that the most powerful tribe "scorns to treat or trade with any others, of fewer numbers and less power in any other tongue but their own, which serves for the lingua of the country; with which we travel and deal." As an example of this, the Tuscarora are cited. Being the most numerous tribe in North Carolina, their language was necessarily understood by some persons in every town of all the neighboring tribes.

The Tuscarora carried on a pernicious trade in rum with the Indians dwelling to their westward. In 1708 rum had been but recently introduced among the latter, chiefly by the Tuscarora, who transported it in rundlets several hundred miles, amongst other Indians. They sold it at "so many mouthfuls for a buckskin, they never using any other measure," the buyer always choosing a man having the largest mouth possible to accompany him to the market, and the mouthful was scrupulously emptied into a bowl brought for the purpose. The Tuscarora also traded with the Shakori and Occaneechi, selling them wooden bowls and ladles for rawhides.

Their lodges, usually round in form, were constructed of poles, covered with the bark of cypress, red or white cedar, or sometimes pine. At one place Lawson met more than 500 Tuscarora in one body in a hunting camp. They had constructed their lodges with bark, "not with round tops, as they commonly use, but ridge fashion, after the manner of most Indians." Among them he found much corn, while meat and venison were scarce, because of the great number of people, for although they were expert hunters, they were too populous for one range.

According to Lawson, the native Tuscarora of North Carolina had rather flat bodies, due probably to the fact that in early infancy the children were swathed to cradle-boards. He adds: "They are not of so robust and strong bodies as to lift great burdens, and endure labor and slavish work, as Europeans are; yet some that are slaves prove very good and laborious." They were dextrous and steady, and collected in the use of their hands and feet; their bearing was sedate and majestic; their eyes were commonly full and manly, being black or dark hazel in color, and the white of the eye was usually marbled with red lines; their skin was tawny, and somewhat darkened by the habit of anointing it with bear's oil and a pigment resembling burnt cork. When they wished to be very fine they mixed with the oil a certain red powder made from a scarlet root growing in the hilly country. This root was held in great esteem among them, selling it one to another at a very high price, on account of the distance from which it came and the danger to which they were exposed in obtaining it. The Tuscarora and other Indians attempted to cultivate this plant, but it would not grow in their land. As a substitute they sometimes used puccoon root, which also has a crimson color, but this dyed the hair an ugly hue. The heads even of the aged were scarcely ever bald; their teeth were tinged yellow from smoking tobacco, to which habit both men and women were much addicted; [Page 194] they, however, did not snuff or chew tobacco. They plucked the hair from their faces and bodies. There were but few deformed or crippled persons among them.

The Tuscarora had many dances suitable to various occasions; these as a rule were accompanied with public feasts prepared under the direction of the women chiefs. Every dance had its peculiar song, but probably was not changed for every occasion on which the dance was performed, although Lawson states that "all these songs are made new for every feast; nor is one and the same song sung at two several festivals. Some one of the nation, which has the best gift of expressing their designs, is appointed by their king and war captains to make these songs." To these festivals the people came from all the towns within 50 or 60 m., "where they buy and sell several commodities."

The Tuscarora, in like measure with the northern Iroquois, were passionately given to gaming, frequently stripping one another of every piece of property available. Sometimes they went even so far as to bet themselves away to the winner, readily becoming his slave until he or his relatives could pay the redemption price; nevertheless they bore their losses with great equanimity, no matter how ruinous they were. Among their games was that of a bundle of 51 split reeds about 7 in. in length and neatly made. The game consisted in throwing a part of the bundle before an opponent, who must on sight guess the number thrown. It is said that experts were able to tell the number correctly ten times in ten throws. A set of these reeds was valued at a dressed doeskin. The Tuscarora also had the well-known bowl and plum-seed game, which is such an important adjunct to the thanksgiving festivals of the northern Iroquois. They also had a number of other games, but some of their neighbors had games which they did not have.

There were feasts among the Tuscarora when several villages united to celebrate some event or when two or more tribes assembled to negotiate peace. There were feasts and dances of thanksgiving, and invocations to the gods that watched over their harvests, when their crops were garnered and when the first fruits of the year were gathered.

Population.—No trustworthy estimates of the Tuscarora population at any given date, exclusive of those of Lawson and Barnwell, previous to 1830, are available for the entire Tuscarora people. The earliest and perhaps most authoritative estimate of the total Tuscarora population at a given time was that of Lawson in 1708. His estimate of 15 towns and 1, 200 fighting men would indicate a population of about 4, 800 at that date; Col. Barnwell's figures are somewhat larger than Lawson's, though they appear to be conservative; his estimate was 1, 200 to 1, 400 warriors, or a maximum population of about 5, 600 persons. The estimate of Chauvignerie in 1736 was 250 warriors, or about 1, 000 persons. His estimate was restricted to the Tuscarora living near Oneida, N. Y., hence did not include those living in North Carolina or on the Susquehanna and Juniata rs. Other estimates of this group give them 1, 000 (1765), 2, 000 (1778), 1, 000 (1783) 400 (1796), in the United States; 414 (1885) in New York and an equal number in Canada, or a total of 828; 364 (1909) in New York, and 416 (1910) in Canada, a total of 780.

[Page 195]*Settlements.*—The following Tuscarora towns have been mentioned in writings pertaining to this people: Annaooka, Chunaneets, Coerntha, Cohunche, Conauhkare, Contahnah, Cotechney, Coram, Corutra, Eno, Ganasaraga, Ganatisgowa, Harooka, Harutawaqui, Ingaren, Junastriyo, Jutaneaga, Kanhato, Kaunehsuntahkeh, Kenta, Kentanuska, Naurheghne, Nonawharitse, Nursoorooka, Nyuchirhaan, Ohagi, Oonossora, Oneida (in part), Oquaga, Shawhiangto, Tasqui, Tiochcrungwe, Tonarooka, Torhunte, Tosneoc, Tuscarora, Unanauhan, Ucouhnerunt. Some of these towns were in North Carolina, others on Juniata r. in Pennsylvania, others on the Susquehanna in Pennsylvania, others on the Susquehanna in New York, while others were s. of Oneida Lake in New York, and one in Genessee Valley. The exact situation of the majority of these towns is not definitely known. In some instances the Tuscarora shared a town with other tribes, as was the case at Anajot (Oneida, or Ganowarohare) and Onohoquaga.

Treaties.—The Tuscarora have taken part in the following treaties between the United States and the Six Nations: Ft. Stanwix, N. Y., Oct. 22, 1784; Ft. Harmar, Ohio, Jan. 9, 1789; Canandaigua (Konondaigua), N. Y., Nov. 11, 1794; Oneida, N. Y., Dec. 2, 1794; Buffalo Creek, N. Y., Jan. 15, 1838.

For further information consult Elias Johnson (native Tuscarora), Legends, Traditions and Laws of the Iroquois, or Six Nations, and History of the Tuscorora Indians, 1881; Documents Relating to the Colonial History of

New York, I-XI, 1855-61; Documentary History of New York, I-IV, 1849-51; Pennsylvania Archives, I-XII, 1852-56 Minutes of the Provincial Council of Pennsylvania (Colonial Records), I-XVI, 1852-53; South Carolina Historical and Genealogical Magazine, I-X, especially IX and X; Virginia Magazine, I-XV, 1893-1908; Lawson, History of Carolina, 1714, repr. 1860; Publications of the Buffalo Hist. Soc., especially Vol. VI. (J. N. B. H.)

[Page 196] EXHIBIT I.

HISTORY OF THE OLD CHERAWS.

[From Gregg's History of the old Cheraws.]

CHAPTER I.

Indian tribes in Carolina—Extent of their territory—Other tribes—Pedees—Kadapaws—Localities of each—Their origin—Advent of the Catawbas—Their tradition—Subsequent relation to tribes on the Pedee—Lederer's narrative—Localities identified—Sara, where—First mention in public records of tribes on the Pedee—Visit of the Cheraws to Charlestown—Governor's visit to the Congerees—Interview with Pedees—Governor Glenn writes to Governor Clinton—Evans's Journal—Cheraws visit Charlestown—Smallpox prevails—Removal of Cheraws and union with Catawbas—Catawba History—Languages of tribes on the Pedee—Meaning of "Cheraw"—"Pedee"—Indian remains on the Pedee—Indian habits and customs—Lawson's narrative—Last of Cheraws and Catawbas.

There is a sad chapter in the history of the New World: it is that relating to the aborigines of America—a people, as all accounts agree, distinguished for many noble traits, but invariably degenerating in character and habit as they have come in contact with the "pale-faces," and taken up their mournful line of march toward the setting sun.

When first known to the colonists, South Carolina is said to have contained not less than 28 tribes of Indians, with settlements extending from the ocean to the mountains. Of these tribes but a few names survive to mark the localities they once inhabited; and these, with such scattered remains as the waste of time and the leveling work of the white man have spared, are the only memorials left to tell of their early occupancy of the soil. Of the tribes which dwelt upon the Pedee and its tributaries, the Saras, or Saraws, as they were first called—afterwards Charrows, Charraws, and Cheraws—occupied the region still identified by the name; their territory extending thence to the coast, and along the coast from the Cape Fear to the Pedee. This extensive region has been assigned to the Cheraws by one of the most eminent ethnologists of America, as among the sites of the Indian tribes when first known to the Europeans, about the year 1600, along the coast of the Atlantic.[1]

If such was the extent of their territory at that early period, it would indicate a population which must have been greatly diminished, when, upon the approach of the Catawbas, a half century later, the supremacy of the Cheraws over the smaller tribes around them, and even over their own distinct nationality, would seem to have been lost, or at least unacknowledged. Within these early territorial limits of the Cheraws, and along the middle and lower parts of the valley of the river, must be assigned the Pedees; and about the mouth of the river, the Winyaws. The Kadapaws were found on Lynches Creek, after the name of which tribe that stream was called [Page 197]

[Page 198]

[Page 199] in the Indian tongue. Of these, the Cheraws—however they may have been diminished in number by disease and war, or perchance by some dismemberment of their nation, and the removal of many, of which no record or tradition remains—continued to be the dominant race on the Pedee; the others having ever been reckoned among the smaller and inferior tribes. Of their origin nothing is known beyond the conjectures of ethnologists. They have been assigned, but upon what grounds does not appear, to the extensive family of Algonkins. These occupied that portion of North America on the east extending from 35° to 60° north latitude, and reaching along the northern line of extension almost to the Pacific on the west. Beyond this, as the track of aboriginal descent and migration begins to be traced back, even conjecture is lost in a sea of uncertainty.

---

1 See map annexed, by the late Albert Gallatin, Vol. I, of Transactions of American Ethnological Society,

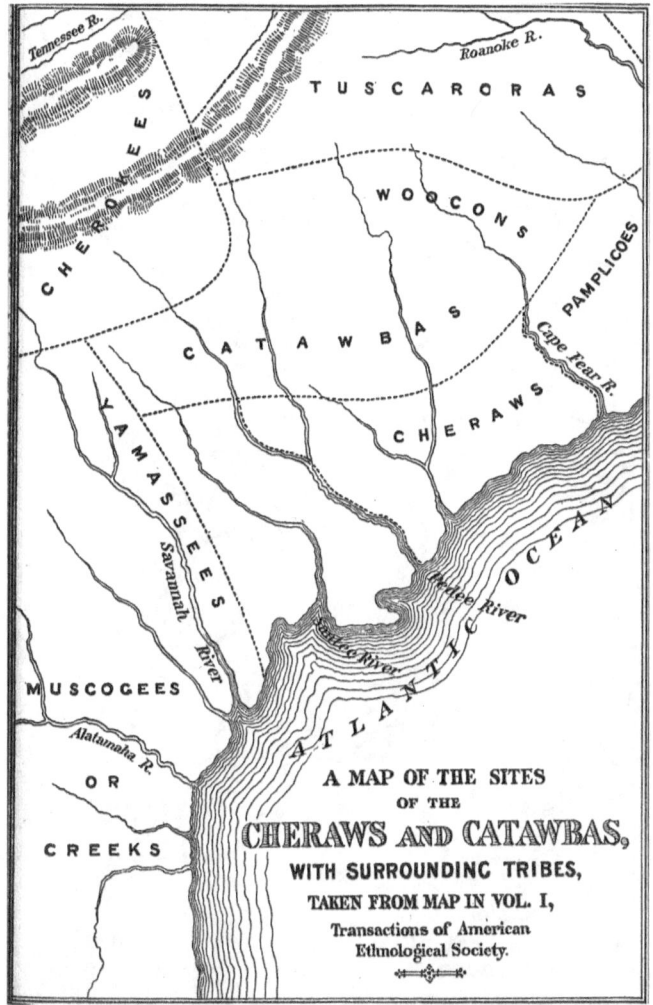

Map of the sites of the Cheraws and Catawbas. From Gregg's History of the Old Cheraws.

The tribes on the Pedee continued in their feeble and disconnected state (the Cheraws maintaining the supremacy) until the arrival of the Catawbas from the north, with the history of whom their own was ever after to be inseparably blended.

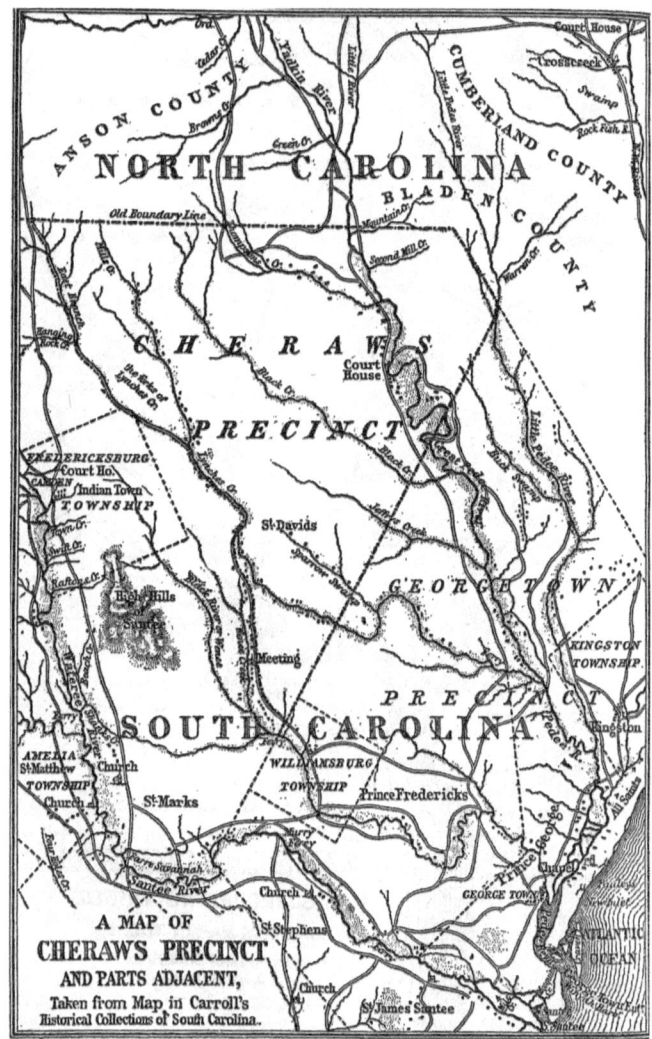

Map of Cheraws precinct. From Gregg's History of the old Cheraws.

According to their tradition,[1] as it has been handed down to very recent times, the Catawbas, at a period prior or not long subsequent to the

---

[1] For this interesting traditional account, as given by the Catawbas, the author is indebted to W. H. Thomas, Esq., of Qualla Town, N. C., who has been intimately connected with them, as their head man, or chief, since their removal to the western part of that State.

discovery and settlement of North America by the whites, occupied a region far to the northward, from whence, in course of time, they removed to the south. Being a numerous and warlike race, they vanquished the tribes with whom they came successively in conflict on the way, until they met the Cherokees on the banks of the river, afterwards called by their own name, Catawba.

Here, as the tradition relates, a sanguinary battle ensued between them, which lasted from morning until night, darkness alone serving to put an end to the conflict. The loss on both sides was heavy, though neither party gained the victory. They slept on the field of blood among their dead and wounded. With the approach of morning, propositions of peace were made by the Catawbas and accepted by the Cherokees. According to the terms of the agreement, the former were to occupy the country east of the river, and the latter the territory on the west. Here they solemnly agreed to live together as brothers; and, after burying their dead, and erecting piles of stones as monuments alike to their common loss and of the peace and friendship established between them, returned to their encampments, ever afterwards sacredly observing the terms of the compact. This tradition of the Catawbas is confirmed throughout by the fuller details which ethnological research has added to their history. They appear to have been a Canadian tribe, and to have left their ancient home about the year 1650, pursued by the Connewangas, a superior and more warlike tribe, with whom they had come in conflict. Forced thus to remove, they turned their faces to the southward, and fought their way, when necessary to do so, until they approached the headwaters of the Kentucky River. Here a separation took place, the larger number becoming absorbed in the great families of the Chickasaws and Choctaws.

The remainder of the tribe stopped in what was afterwards known as Bottetourt County, Va., but without making any permanent settlement.

[Page 200]They removed thence in the year 1660, continuing their journey to the south, and, as Adair wrote,
settled on the east side of a broad, purling river, that heads in the great blue ridge of mountains, and empties itself into Santee River, in Amelia township, then running eastward of Charlestown, disgorges itself into the Atlantic.

On the banks of this river, the Eswa Tavora (as it was called in the Indian tongue), they met the Cherokees, whose extensive territory ran thence to the westward, and there followed the sanguinary conflict, of which some account has been given.

In this battle 1, 000 of the bravest warriors were lost on each side, greatly reducing the force of the Catawbas, and doubtless making a permanent impression on their spirit as a warlike race, for which they had been so celebrated in the earlier periods of their history.

How the approach of the Catawbas was regarded by the Cheraws, and whether any conflict ensued between them, tradition does not inform us. The approach of a strong and formidable tribe was generally regarded by the Indians as a hostile demonstration and claim to dominion. Already, doubtless, the decline of the Cheraws had commenced and made such progress as to unfit them for contesting the claim to supremacy. It was to be the story of a continuous decline, and of a race scattered or absorbed into another superior to themselves, the beginning of the last and most mournful chapter in their history. A portion of the Cheraws, however, must have remained distinct and independent for more than a century later, as will be found in tracing their subsequent course. They were henceforth to be wanderers, the remains of their once extensive dominion, with those of the smaller tribes around them, having passed away to the Catawbas. The territory of the latter was placed in 34° north latitude, being bounded on the north and northeast by North Carolina; on the east and south by South Carolina; and about west and southwest by the Cherokee nation.[1]

The smaller tribes on the waters of the Pedee, appear after this period to have had but a nominal existence. They had doubtless degenerated through the operation of those wasting and destructive agencies at work in the history of the aboriginal races; and, in addition, had undergone the process, common among the Indians, of becoming absorbed in their conquerors or in the larger tribes around them.

In this instance they were merged chiefly in the Catawbas. About the year 1743, the language of the Catawbas is said to have consisted of 20 different dialects, of which the "Katahba" was the standard, or court dialect, the "Cherah" being another. Scarcely anything beyond a bare allusion to them by name is found relating to the tribes on the Pedee in the earliest accounts of the Indians of Carolina. With the exception of the Cheraws, they were reckoned among the smaller and inferior tribes, most of whom had

---

[1] Adair, p. 224.

then greatly degenerated and were rapidly approaching extinction. Brief allusions are found at an early period to the several tribes in the acts of the assembly, passed for the regulation and support of the Indian trade. The larger tribes on the northern and western boundaries of the Province engaged the attention of the Government almost exclusively. [Page 201] The Catawbas formed a sort of barrier against their incursions, and of them there is frequent mention.

Of the Cheraws the first distinct relation in any contemporaneous record, is found in the explorations of John Lederer, "in three several marches from Virginia to the west of Carolina and other parts of the Continent; begun in March, 1669, and ended in September, 1670."[1]

Such at least is the case if we are to understand by "Sara," as he writes it, the locality of the "Saraws," as they were sometimes called, or Cheraw Indians. Thus, in one of his journeys, Lederer says:

I departed from Watery the one-and-twentieth of June, and keeping a west course for near thirty miles, I came to Sara. Here I found the ways more level and easy. I did likewise, to my no small admiration, find hard cakes of white salt among them; but whether they were made of sea-water or taken out of saltpits I know not, but am apt to believe the latter, because the sea is so remote from them. From Sara I kept a southwest course until the five-and-twentieth of June, and then I reached Wisacky. This three days' march was more troublesome to me than all my travels besides, for the direct way which I took from Sara to Wisacky is over a continued marsh overgrown with weeds, from whose roots spring knotty stumps, as hard and sharp as flint.

I was forced to lead my horse most part of the way, and wonder that he was not either plunged in the bogs or lamed by those rugged knots. This nation is subject to a neighbor king residing upon the bank of a great lake called Ushery, environed of all sides with mountains and Wisacky marsh.[2]

There is great difficulty throughout Lederer's narrative, as Dr. Hawks more than once remarks, in determining the routes by which he passed and the localities described. If by "Watery," the Wateree of the present day is to be understood, he could not by going west 30 miles to "Wisacky," and

---

1 For a full account of this early American traveler, the reader is referred to Dr. Hawks' History of North Carolina, Vol. II, pp. 43-63, with maps annexed.
2 Hawks's History of North Carolina, Vol. II, p. 49.

thence three days' march by a southwest course to "Ushery," have reached the Santee; for by "Ushery" the Santee was meant, if the authority quoted by Dr. Hawks is correct: Col. Byrd, he adds, says that the Indians living on the Santee River were called "Usheries." If, on the other hand, amid the confusion of names which could not have been very well defined at that early period, we may understand by "Watery" the Pedee of the present day, a journey of 30 miles to the west would have brought Lederer to Lynche's Creek, the "Wisacky," and three days' march from thence southwestwardly along the swamp of Wateree, would have enabled him to reach the Santee, environed by the "High Hills" which have since become so famous, called by this early explorer, "Mountains," and with an almost impenetrable swamp of vast extent, to which his description of a "marsh overgrown with reeds," would very well answer.

In support of this view, we find in Oldmixon's History of Carolina, published in 1708, reason for supposing that the Pedee was then called by that name (Watery). Describing the six counties into which Carolina, North and South, was then divided, he begins with Albemarle, on the borders of Virginia. Then follows an account of Clarendon County, in which, he says:
is the famous promontory, called also Cape Fear, at the mouth of Clarendon River, called also Cape Fear River. The next river is named Waterey River, or Winyan, about twenty-five leagues distant from Ashley River: it is capable of receiving large [Page 202] ships, but inferior to Port Royal, nor is yet inhabited. There is another small river called Wingon River, and a little settlement honoured with the name of Charles-town, but so thinly inhabited that 'tis not worth taking notice of. We come now to South Carolina, which is parted from North by Zantee River. The adjacent county is called Craven County.[1]

It is evident that the "Waterey" here spoken of, was the Waccamaw, or the lower Pedee, and not the Wateree of the present day.

The Pedee being a much longer stream than the Waccamaw, it is not impossible that though the latter was known by the name of Waterey, or Winyan near its mouth, the former being supposed to form its extension higher up, was also in like manner designated. Dr. Hawks remarks:
Watery, Sara, Wisacky, and Ushery, would all appear to have been in South Carolina, the last directly west of Charles-town. If he made his journey

---

[1] Oldmixon's History, in Carroll's Collections, Vol. II, p. 446.

then, entering the State somewhere in Robeson County, he must have crossed in a south-western line, and passing through Robeson County into South Carolina, must have traversed that State also in its entire width. The time occupied would not have been sufficient for it. Lederer's Itinerary presents difficulties which we confess we cannot satisfactorily solve.[2]

If, as is here conjectured, Lederer passed through Robeson County into South Carolina, the supposition we have made will appear the more probable. And it brings to light the fact never before suggested or imagined, perhaps, that the Pedee in the earlier days of aboriginal history was known as "Sara." If it was so, the time and reason of the change to Pedee can be left to conjecture only.

It might have taken place after the advent of the Catawbas and been brought about by them in order that such a standing memorial of the "Sara" dominion might be forever obliterated; or, what is yet more probable, the "Sara" territory, once embracing the region higher up but afterwards confined to the coast, the Pedees, if succeeding to it, would naturally have called the river after their own name.

The earliest mention in the provincial records of any of the tribes inhabiting the Valley of the Pedee, is found in the proceedings of the Council or Upper House of Assembly, December 15th, 1732.[3] It is in these words:

Mr. Sanders and Mr. Waties came from the Lower House with the following message. We herewith send your excellency a letter of great moment to this Government, relating to the murder of a Pedee Indian by one Kemp. We desire your excellency to take the proper measures to prevent the ill consequences of it by causing the offender to be apprehended and brought to justice, or otherwise as your excellency shall see fit.

Upon reading the message from the Lower House of Assembly, and likewise the letter therein mentioned, complaining that one Kemp, or Camp, an overseer at Black River, or Georgetown, has barbarously murdered one of the Pedee Indians,

Ordered, That James Neale, Esq., provost marshal, do immediately attach the said Kemp, or Camp, and bring him before his excellency the governor, in Charlestown, to be dealt with according to law, and that all constables

---

[2] Hawks's History of North Carolina, Vol. II, p. 52.
[3] Council Journal, No. 5, p. 258, secretary of state's office, Columbia.

and other officers and subjects of His Majesty be aiding and assisting to the said provost marshal in the execution of this order.

[Page 203]This proceeding of the House was based upon the following facts:

Appeared before this board, Thomas Burton and Wm. Kemp, and upon the affidavit of Thomas Burton, and the information of Wm. Kemp concerning the fact of an Indian fellow being killed, name Corn-White Johnny, his excellency issued the following order: "On the 17th January, 1733, in council, upon hearing this day the information of William Kemp, relating to the death of Corn-White Johnny, and the affidavit of Thomas Burton, it is ordered that King Harry, Captain Billy, George and Dancing Johnny, and some of the relations of the deceased, be and appear before me the second Wednesday in February next ensuing, to give an account of what they know of the death of the said Indian, and that Wm. Kemp do attend at the same time; likewise that Mr. John Thompson, jun., is desired to acquaint the said Indians of this order.

This record is of interest now as evincing the jealous care exercised by the Provincial Government for the protection of those scattered and defenseless remnants of the Indian tribes whose domain was fast passing away from them and who continued faithful to the whites to the close of their history.

Of the result of the proceedings referred to no further account appears.

We have next a brief but interesting notice[1] of a visit made to Charlestown by a few of the leading men of the Cheraws and Catawbas in July, 1739.

On Saturday last,

said the Gazette of that day,

arrived in this town eleven of the chief men among the Catawbas and Cheraw Indians, who came to pay a visit to his honour the lieutenant governor and inform him that some time since a party of their people went out to war, and not meeting with their enemies had cut off a white family

---

1 South Carolina Gazette, June 30—July 7, 1739. For access to this invaluable historical collection—a complete file of the old Gazettes, commencing about 1730—the author is indebted to the courtesy of A. H. Mazyck, Esq., of the Charleston Library. Only a few of the earlier numbers of the Gazette are missing. At a later period a small portion was burned.

on the borders of Virginia; that upon complaint made to them of the said barbarous murder they examined into the facts and had put five of the ringleaders to death; and that they were determined to prosecute in the same rigorous manner any of their people who for the future should be found guilty of the like cruel practices. They met with a kind reception from his honour the lieutenant governor, and having received the usual presents from the country they set out this day on their return home, well pleased and content.

The signal punishment visited by these tribes upon the murderers of the whites indicated their fidelity to the Provincial Government, which continued to be as true as it was lasting.

Of the Pedees mention is made a few years later.
In council March 2, 1743, his excellency the governor signed the following order to Mr. Commissary Dart, viz, to provide for the Pedee Indians now in town the following particulars, viz:

Presents.—To the three head men, each of them, a gun and knife; to the others, each of them, a knife. For the three women, each of them, a looking-glass, twenty bullets, half a pound vermilion to be divided among them.

Also, an order on Col. Brewton for ten pounds of gunpowder for use of said Indians.[2]

The Pedees are mentioned again with the Catawbas in the following year. "In council, 25th July, 1744, the governor admitted four Pedee Indians to an interview in the council chamber, who informed his excellency that seven Catawbas had been barbarously murdered by the Notchee Indians, who live among them," which horrible deed having been confirmed by Mr. Matthew Beard, who lives at Goose Creek, who had certain intelligence of the same, saying that the said Catawbas being drunk near Fuller Cowpen, near the four holes, seven [Page 204] of them while asleep were murdered by the Notchees; which affair being taken into consideration, his excellency, by the advice of His Majesty's council, ordered the following letter to be dispatched away relating to that subject:

SO. CA., July 28, 1744.

---

2 Council Journal, No. 11, p. 133.

SIR: I have received information of an unlucky accident which happened about a week ago, at or near the store belonging to the late Major Fuller, somewhere about the Four Holes, where some Notchee Indians have fallen upon and killed five or six of the Catawbas, being instigated thereto by a person who keeps that store. The Catawbas, as I understand, have already set out to take their revenge, which has obliged the Notchees and Pedees to come further down among the settlements for shelter. I must therefore desire the favor of you to interpose in this matter, and to prevent, as far as you are able, any bloodshed, till this matter is fully enquired into. Then the guilty may be punished, and if you find it necessary, to interpose with the militia in your parts to keep the peace. This I write at the desire of His Majesty's council. I hear they are at Mr. Beard's plantation, in the neighborhood.

I am, with truth, yours,

JAMES GLEN.[1]

To Hon. WM. MIDDLETON, Esq.

About two years after this, the governor, as was usual when any difficulty occurred with the Indians, or to preserve their friendship and maintain a due influence over them, made a visit into the interior, at a certain place on the Congarees, appointed by him for an interview with the Catawbas, of which the following account was preserved:[2]

The governor arrived at Congarees 27 April, 140 miles distance hence, where, on the bank of the Santee, the king and a few of the head men met him. Yenabe Yalangway, the king—the old leader, Captain Taylor, Nafkebee, and some others awaited on his excellency. The next day the governor addressed them. A place being erected for the governor to sit under, and the union flag hoisted, our men were drawn out in two lines, through which the Indians marched, when they were received with drums beating and colours flying, and saluted with some small pieces of cannon; after they had all taken the governor by the hand, and the king with some of his headmen, had placed himself near his excellency, a person was sworn truly to interpret all that should pass betwixt the governor and the Indians; and

---

1 Council Journal, No. 11, pp. 413, 414.
2 Gazette, June 2, 1746.

then his excellency addressed them in words, the purport of which was to dissuade them from agreeing to a proposition which had been made to them by some of the other Indian nations to join in a French war against the people of Carolina. After which, presents were distributed, consisting chiefly of powder, guns, pistols, paint, &c. The governor had that morning received an express from Mr. Brown (who trades amongst the Catawbas) acquainting him that some of the Pedees and Cheraws (two small tribes who have long been incorporated with the Catawbas), intended to leave them, which might prove of dangerous consequence at a time when they were so closely attacked by their enemies, the Northern Indians. Mr. Brown therefore entreated that, if possible, such a separation might be prevented.

The governor ordered the rammers of all the pistols which he had delivered to the Indians to be laid upon the table, desiring that such as were Pedees and Charraws might advance, and they, being in a body near him, he spoke to them in these words: "It gives me great concern, my friends, to hear that you entertain the least thought of leaving the Catawbas, with whom you have been so long and so closely united. This union makes you strong, and enables you to defend yourselves and annoy your enemies; but should you ever separate, you would thereby weaken yourselves, and be exposed to every danger. Consider that if you were single and divided, you may be broke as easily as I break this stick" (at the same time breaking one of the rammers); "but if you continue united together, and stand by one another, it will be as impossible to hurt or break you, as it is impossible for me to break these," (his excellency then taking up a handful of rammers).

After this, they all promised to continue together in their camp. The governor then directed himself to the king of the Catawbas, telling him that he would expect his answer. To which the king replied at some length, assuring the governor of their friendship and fidelity.

[Page 205] The pledge of fidelity renewed on this occasion was faithfully observed by these Indians throughout all their subsequent history. Though often tempted by artful representations and large promises to take up arms against the people of Carolina, they could never be persuaded to do so. Throughout the Indian wars, and the contest with the mother country, they continued steadfast in their devotion to their early friends and allies, well meriting the aid and protection extended to them by the State in the latter stages of their decline and weakness.

That the Pedees owned slaves will appear from the following notice, published in the Gazette of the day, August 30-September 6, 1748:

Taken up by Michael Welch, overseer to the subscriber, on an island called Uchee Island, a Negro fellow, who gives the following account of himself, viz, that he belonged formerly to Mr. Fuller, and was by him sold to Billy, king of the Pedee Indians; that the Catawba Indians took him from King Billy, and carried him to their nation; and that in endeavoring to make his escape from the Catawbas, he was lost in the woods, and had been so a considerable time before he was taken. He is a middle-sized fellow, and a little pot-bellied; says his name is Fortune, but is suspected to have another name which he does not care to own. Any person having any right or property in the said fellow may apply to the subscriber, now in Charlestown.

ISAAC MARKSDALE.

The Pedees and other smaller tribes, who now led a wandering life, were in constant danger of being enticed off by the more powerful and hostile nations of Indians, to join them in their predatory excursions.

The following letters indicate the anxiety felt on the subject by the Catawbas, as well as by the Provincial Government at this period. The first[1] was addressed by the king of the Catawbas to his excellency, James Glen, Esq.:

There are a great many Pedee Indians living in the settlements that we want to come and settle amongst us. We desire for you to send for them, and advise them to this, and give them this string of wampum in token that we want them to settle here, and will always live like brothers with them. The Northern Indians want them all to settle with us; for, as they are now at peace, they may be hunting in the woods or straggling about, killed by some of them, except they join us, and make but one nation, which will be a great addition of strength to us.

THE (his x mark) KING.

---

1 Indian Book, Vol. III, pp. 163, 164, in secretary of state's office, Columbia, S. C.

CATAWBAS, *21st November, 1752.*

During the previous year, viz, May 24, 1751, Gov. Glen had written to Gov. Clinton, of New York, respecting the Congress of Indians to be holden at Albany, for the purpose of uniting the different friendly tribes, and preserving their friendship as a bulwark against the more hostile. Of that letter, the following extract will suffice:

Our first care ought to be to make all Indians that are friends with the English friends also among themselves; and for that reason I hope you and the other governors and commissioners will heartily join your interest in removing all the obstacles to a peace, in reconciling all the differences, and cementing together in a closer union the northern and southern Indians, under the name of Norw*d*. Indians. I include not only the six nations, the Delewares, the Susquehanna Indians, but all the different tribes who may be in friendship with them, particularly those on the Ohio River; as under the name of Southward Indians, I comprehend the Cherokees, the Catawbas, the Creeks (called sometimes Muscogee), the Chickasaws, and such part of the Choctaws as are in our interest, and all tribes in friendship with these nations, or that live amongst our settlements, such as Charraws, Uchees, Pedees, Notches, Cape Fears, or other Indians; and I hope that all prisoners on each side will be mutually delivered back.[2]

On the 14th of October, 1755, John Evans made a visit to the Catawbas, by order of his excellency, Gov. Glen. From his journal [Page 206] the following extracts are taken, and will be found chiefly interesting here, as containing some information respecting the Pedees:

October 17th.—Met a Catawba man and woman, and informed by them, that in the summer, the Cherrackees and Notchees had killed some Pedees and Waccamaws in the white people's settlements.

18th.—I got into the Catawbas. King Hazler was gone a hunting the day before; the next morning they sent for him, and he came in that night.

Before he got into the nation, I made it my care to inquire of the Pedees if they could not tell what people killed the Pedees at Goose Creek, where the boys were that was taken prisoners: answered, "They could not tell who they were, but understood it was the Notchees and Cherokees that did the mischief."

---

2 Indian Book, Vol. II, p. 96.

21st.—The king and head man met, and desired to know what I was come for. I told them that there was two Pedee women killed and scalped, and two boys carried away from out of the settlements, and that it was done by some of their nation; and one Notchee, which was called the Notchee Doctor, and his excellency, the governor, had sent me to demand the boys; and I then and there demanded these boys. I further acquainted them that his excellency, the governor, desired that they would not come into the settlements without they were sent for. The white people might mistake them, and do them a mischief, believing them to be enemy Indians. I further said, that it was his excellency, the governor's pleasure, that the Catawba people should not attempt to carry away any of the Indians that are now living in the settlements up to their nation on any pretence whatever without his permission first. Their answer was, that old men should always speak truth; and the most of them were grey-headed; and they, for their parts, did not hurt the Pedees, and did not know or believe the mischief was done by any belonging to that nation; and further said, that when the Northward Indians were in their nation, they bound the same three women and two men; and the Catawbas released the three women, but the Northward Indians carried the men away.

22nd.—I set out from the Catawba nation homeward, and at night came to a camp of Pedees. I acquainted them with my errand to the nation, and desired them to let me know, if they could, who it was that killed and scalped the Pedee women, and carried the boys away. Lewis Jones, their chief, answered, that soon after the Pedees were killed, he went down from the nation to the settlements to inquire what harm was done by Goose Creek. He met a Pedee Indian, named Prince, who lived in the settlements; and Prince told him, that a day or two before the mischief was done, there was five Cherokees and one Notchee seen to go by Monck's Corner, and Lewis John said, he did believe they scalped the women, and carried the boys away.[1]

The Cheraws, following the example of the Catawbas, were true to the English, as they continued to be to the colonists throughout the Revolution and afterwards.

---

1 Indian Book, Vol. V, pp. 94, 95.

They cheerfully endured the hardships of distant journeys when called upon for aid. In the *South Carolina Gazette* of June 2, 1759, this account was given:

On Tuesday last, 45 Charraws, part of a nation of Indians incorporated with the Catawbas, arrived in town, headed by King Johnny, who brought to the governor the scalp of a French Indian, which he had taken near Loyal-Henning. He and several others that are with him here, were with Gen. Forbes during the whole expedition against Fort Du Quesne. There chief business seems to be, to see his excellency and receive presents.

In the latter part of this year the great scourge of the red man appeared amongst them and carried off many Indans in this part of the Province. In the Gazette of December 8-15, 1759, was this sad account of its ravages:

It is pretty certain that the smallpox has lately raged with great violence among the Catawba Indians, and that it has carried off near one-half of that nation, by throwing themselves into the river as soon as they found themselves ill. This distemper has since appeared among the inhabitants at the Charraws and Waterees, where many families are down, so that unless especial care is taken, it must soon spread through [Page 207] the whole country, the consequences of which are much to be dreaded. The smallpox went almost through the Province in the year 1738, when it made prodigious havoc, and has ever since been kept out of it by the salutary laws enacted for that purpose.

So destructive and rapidly exterminative had been this disease among the Indians from its first introduction that its appearance brought on a spirit of frenzy and desperation. Ignorant and grossly superstitious, they regarded it as a visible embodiment of the Spirit of Evil—the sentence of wrath from heaven let loose upon them, from which there was no escape. In this state of mind the disease found abundant food for keeping itself alive and completing the work of destruction. The white families at the "Charraws" and "Waterees," who appear to have suffered severely at this period, were doubtless unprepared for such a visitant, and having not the means of prevention or cure at command, yielded for a time, like their savage neighbors, to the fell destroyer. At a later period, about the time of the Revolution, some of the Catawba warriors having visited Charlestown, there contracted the disease again, and returning, communicated it to their nation, which, according to contemporaneous accounts, came well nigh being exterminated. It was after this, having been sorely thinned by disease, that they were advised by their friends to invite the Cheraws to move up and unite with them as one tribe. The Cheraws here spoken of by the writers of the day must have been a part of the tribe which had maintained its independence probably in the region lower down the Pedee or on the coast, where they led a proud but feeble existence. That some of them should have refused to submit to what must have seemed to be the yoke of a foreign invader is not surprising. But their doom was sealed. No longer able to maintain their isolated sway, or to resist the destructive agencies at work among them, a weak and declining remnant, like the Catawbas themselves, they gladly accepted the invitation to unite their future with that of their brethren who had gone before them.

And now was seen their last journey as the representatives of a nation of ancient renown.

Mournful as it was short, the march was soon ended; and henceforth these broken fragments were to constitute but one nation, under the name of Catawbas. For awhile, as at the first, the Cheraws retained their own language, though ordinarily using the Catawba.

They lived in harmony together, their early feuds forgotten, and the jealousies of other days obliterated by those common wants and saddened recollections which were henceforth to mark their declining history. Within the memory of persons now living a few of the Cheraws have visited the upper Pedee, to take a last look at the localities which their own traditions had identified as the homes of their fathers. About the year 1700 the Catawbas numbered 1, 500 warriors. Only a half century later this proud band had dwindled away to 400. Their principal settlement about this latter period was on the Wateree, where their country was described as being "an old waste field, seven miles in extent, with several others of smaller dimensions; which shows," it was added, "that they were formerly a numerous people, to cultivate so much land, with their dull stone axes, before they had an opportunity of trading with the English, or allowed others to incorporate with them."[1]

[Page 208]In 1787 they were the only organized tribe, under a distinct name of its own, in South Carolina.

Their town, "Catawba," contained then about 450 inhabitants, of which not more than 150 were fighting men. In 1798 they are said to have been in the habit of holding an anniversary meeting of a sadly interesting character.

---

1 Adair.

It was intended to commemorate their former greatness by recounting the numbers and deeds of their ancestors, of which tradition had kept them informed.[1] Well might the Catawbas have been proud of their history. And well may South Carolina cherish the memory of a people who maintained their friendship and their active devotion inviolate throughout the long and trying period of conflicts waged successively with savage foes, and those of the same language and blood who came to reduce their American brethren to a state of worse than colonial vassalage!

Of the liberal provision made for the Catawbas in later times by the Legislature of South Carolina it is unnecessary to speak.

A portion of them had removed at an earlier period to Buncombe County, N. C., west of the Blue Ridge, and thither the miserable remnant, with few exceptions, followed a few years since. Reduced in numbers by disease and intermarriage, by the contracted territory to which they had been confined while yet unfitted, by the slow process through which the Indian must always pass, for agricultural pursuits; and withal, by those habits of idleness and dissipation which the custom of leasing their lands to the whites, and the consequent want of employment had subjected them; drunken and wandering from place to place, their condition became as abject as it had once been elevated among the red men of Carolina. "In this rapidly declining tribe," says an eminent authority of recent times, "we behold the remnant of the defeated, long-lost, and celebrated tribe of the Eries." It is hoped that their history, in the materials of which the public records of the State abound, will one day, as it deserves, be fully written.

Of the languages of the Indian tribes once inhabiting the valley of the Pedee scarce a vestige is left, except the names of the rivers and a few localities. The same remark may be made of all the tribes which were found at the first approaches of the white man on the coast of Carolina, from Cape Hatteras to the Savannah.[2]

Of the meaning of "Cheraw," reasoning from the affinities of the Indian tongues, a probable conjecture may be hazarded. In Cherah, or Chera, as it seems at certain periods of Indian history to have been called, is found a close affinity with Chera-kee. In the language of the Chera-kees, Cherah, or Chera, means fire. If, then, as seems highly probable, Cherah is identical

---

[1] Barton's New View, p. 51.
[2] Transactions of American Ethnological Society, Vol. II, p. 115

with Serah, or Saraw, or Sara—as Lederer called it—now Cheraw, it may be conjectured to have meant the fire town. The site of the present town of Cheraw, which has retained the name, with slight changes, from an early period, may have been the scene of an extensive conflagration when occupied by the Indians; or, being situated on a high bluff, and visible as a point of observation and alarm for miles across, it may have been a signal station, as such prominent localities often were, to gain the knowledge of an enemy's approach, or other danger, and hence may have been called Cherah; in Cherokee, the fire town: or, as may seem [Page 209] yet more probable, in another view; if, about the period of their first distinct existence as a tribe, being possibly an offshoot from the Cherakees, at the era of some internal struggle and partial dismemberment of that once powerful and widely extended nation, the Cherahs, or Cheraws, were noted as fire eaters, as some of the Indian tribes have been, the original of the name may be found in this circumstances—Cheraw meaning fire eaters. After all, however, it is one of those points, the original of language in the aboriginal races, which, without the light of contemporaneous history, must ever remain involved in more or less of darkness and uncertainty.

Of the meaning of "Pedee" nothing is known. It has even been made a question whether the name is of Indian origin; and the opinion has been advanced that it is not, on the ground that it appears to have been unknown prior to the English colonial settlements. Hence it is conjectured that it was of subsequent origin, having had its beginning, perhaps, in the initials of a white man's name, as of Patrick Daly, for example—P. D.—first carved upon a tree, then Indianized, and so changed into Pedee, as we now have it. This theory, however, is wholly untenable.

That the name is not mentioned by the earliest writers is readily accounted for by the fact that the Pedees, if ever a people of any note, had then become an insignificant tribe; whereas only the more powerful nations of Indians engaged attention at first, or were so much as known by name. The earliest mention of Pedee is found in the account of the Eleven Townships, one of which was to be laid out on that river. This was about the year 1731-32.[1] But then it was spoken of as having already been in familiar use. It was spelt, too, not as if it had come from two capital letters, the initials of a proper name.

---

1 Carroll's Historical Collections, Vol. II, p. 124.

Both the analogy and euphony of the Indian tongue indicate, beyond all doubt, that Pedee had the same original as Santee, Congaree, Wateree, Uchee, and Sewee, all of unquestionable Indian birth, and the names of neighboring and cognate tribes. That the name Pedee does not appear in the earliest published accounts of Carolina may be attributed to the fact that for a considerable time after the first settlement of the province, scarcely anything was known of that part of the State, because out of the line of the main route of travel, far in the interior, and at a later period only coming into notice.

Of the Indian remains on the Pedee which are still to be seen, though but little trace is left, there is nothing distinguishable from those in other parts of the State, of which full accounts have been given. In some instances these remains are so numerous as to indicate the existence of once populous settlements. These settlements, as usually the case with the aborigines, were made upon the banks of rivers and other large streams, on account of the fertility of the soil, for fishing purposes, and other facilities thereby afforded.

In most instances on the Pedee where these remains are yet to be seen are found large collections of fragments of potware of varied shapes, sizes, and devices. It is difficult even to conjecture why such quantities of these were deposited at points not far removed from each other. They could scarcely have been the result of large [Page 210] accumulations in those places where the potware was made, for they are generally found to be well-finished specimens of their kind, and evidently parts of vessels which were once in use. Nor does it appear to be a well-founded opinion, sometimes advanced, that upon the sudden breaking up of the Indian settlements, for whatever cause, these vessels of ornament or use were heaped together in one confused mass, and with such other chattels as could not be removed abandoned forever. Their appearance indicates that they were broken by violence; and what is more remarkable, of all the specimens taken up at random in any single locality, scarcely any two are found to be exactly alike in outward device and finish.

The ornamental lines and figures on the exterior are in many cases well executed, and for the untutored savage exhibit a high degree of art. The questions, how they were broken, why collected in such strangely mingled masses, and why other remains, as the pipe, the arrowhead, the stone ax, etc., are not generally found among them, will remain unanswered; and like so much else we would fain know respecting these early occupants of the soil, continue perhaps among the secret things of their history.

A large vase or jar,[1] of 3 gallons' capacity, was washed up a few years since by the waters of a freshet on the east bank of the Pedee, in Marlborough district, near Spark's Ferry. It is in a state of almost entire preservation, but not so highly finished as are many of the broken specimens which have been recovered. Like those to which Lawson alludes in his account of the Congerees, this jar has a hole in the bottom, not smoothly cut, but roughly and irregularly made, as if punched through by some blunt instrument after the vessel was finished. Lawson supposes that they were sometimes used for burial purposes and that the holes were made in the bottom to let off the morbid juices of the body going to decay. Some of the specimens of potware found are highly finished, and upon the whole appear to warrant the conclusion arrived at by the first and most thoughtful travelers among our Indian tribes, and since clearly demonstrated by the results of later explorations, that those whom the Europeans found on their first discovery and settlement of the country were not the ancient dwellers in this part of the New World.

The earthen pots,

says Lawson—

are often found under ground and at the foot of the banks, where the water has washed them away. They are for the most part broken in pieces; but we find them of a different sort, in comparison of those the Indians use at this day, who have had no others ever since the English discovered America. The bowels of the earth can not have altered them, since they are thicker, of another shape and composition, and nearly approach to the urns of the ancient Romans.[2]

We are told that they made earthen pots of very different sizes, so as to contain from 2 to 10 gallons; large pitchers to carry water, bowls, dishes, platters, basins, and a prodigious number of other vessels of such antiquated forms that it would be almost impossible to describe them.

Some of the specimens, in a fragmentary form, and others in a state of preservation, which were found on the Pedee, are of different shapes and

---

1 This vessel was presented to the Cheraw Lyceum by Col. J. D. Wilson, of Darlington.

2 Lawson, pp. 169, 170.

curiously finished. Of these one is very small, not holding [Page 211] more than a gill, and seems to have been used for paint or some other valuable liquid.

Another,[1] of which the lower portion only is left, has the exact shape, the outward finish, and as much the appearance of a pineapple as if it had been carefully fashioned after that as a model. The process of glazing was simple, and consisted in placing the vessels over a large fire of smoky pitch pine, which made them smooth and shining. "Their lands abounded in proper clay for that use, and even with porcelain, as has been proved by experiment." When first discovered on the coast, the Indians were found to cultivate a variety of grains and vegetables. The process of clearing their lands has been minutely described. Their stone axes, of which specimens have been found on the Pedee, resembled a wedge or smith's chisel and weighed from 1 to 2 or 3 pounds. They twisted two or three tough hickory slips about 2 feet long around the notched head of the ax and by means of this simple contrivance deadened the trees by cutting through the bark, after which they fell by decay or, having become thoroughly dry, were easily burned.

With these trees they kept up their annual holy fire. In the first clearing of their plantations they only barked the larger timber, cut down the saplings and underwood, and burned them in heaps. As the suckers put up, they chopped them off close by the stump, and so made fires to deaden the roots till in time they also decayed. The burning of the grass and underwood in the forests is said to have been an ancient custom of the Indians. This may account for the fact, which has been mentioned in connection with the first settlements by the whites in the interior, that in many places the woods were found open to such an extent that even small objects could be seen to a great distance. These burnings were practiced by the Indians, as we are told,

in order to allure the deer upon the new grass, as also to discover the impressions of their enemies' tracks in the new burnt ground, distinguishable to their women and children, in case the raven should be sick or out of the way (thus they call the lookout, whose business it is to recognize the avenues of their towns), who, as well as any other Indian (as they all apply themselves to hunting), are by practice so keen and precise that they can

---

1 This was also presented to the Cheraw Lyceum by Col. Wilson.

distinguish and follow a track, be it of a white man, negro, Indian, or be it of a bear, deer, or wolf, horse or cow, even on hard bottom, not admitting of impression so as on soft ground, although covered all over with leaves so that the ground itself is not visible, and even bare of any grass or bushes, which by their irregular bend may indicate a creature—human or animal—having trod upon or brushed by it.[2]

Having cleared their lands in the primitive manner before described, the Indians used, in planting and tilling, their own made instruments. Afterwards a common hoe was the only implement employed in the cultivation of the soil. They prepared their corn for use by beating it till the husks came off, then boiling it in large earthen pots. For pounding the corn, mortars were made by cautiously burning a large log to a proper level and length, then placing a fire on the top and wet clay around it, in order to give the interior a proper shape. When the fire was extinguished, or occasion required, they chopped the inside with their stone instruments, patiently continuing the process until they finished the vessel for the intended purpose.

[Page 212]In certain localities on the Pedee, which appear to have been the centers[1] of their once extensive settlements, many tumuli were once to be seen.

They were similar to some of those described by Bartram[2] in East Florida, near the river St. Juan, "where," he observes—
I found the surface of the ground very uneven by means of little mounts and ridges. I had taken up my lodging on the border of an ancient burying-ground; sepulchers or tumuli of the Yamassees, who were here slain by the Creeks in their last decisive battle. These graves occupied the whole grove, consisting of two or three acres of ground.

During a visit of the author in 1859 to the upper part of Marlborough district, near the North Carolina line, a mound was pointed out to him which is related by tradition to have been the scene of an Indian battle. On a subsequent occasion it was visited for the purpose of exploration. It appears to have been raised originally but a few feet above the surface of the adjoining level, and had been almost entirely washed down. Its dimensions

---

2 De Brahm's Philosophico-Historico-Hydrogeography of South Carolina, Georgia, and East Florida, 1751. Edited and republished by Plowden C. J. Weston, 1856, p. 189.

2 Bartram's Travels in the Carolinas, Georgia, East and West Florida, 1773-74.

were about ten by fifteen feet. Many years before, a partial excavation had been made, and in digging down on this occasion for a short distance small pieces of bone were found mixed with the earth throughout, so that no opinion could be formed as to the depth of the first layer of bodies. Four feet below the surface a point was reached where the soil had not been disturbed, and a little below this were found from four to six skeletons, lying regularly, in a horizontal position, with the feet to the east, having evidently been placed in two layers. The larger bones were in a comparative state of preservation, and one of the jawbones with the teeth entire, apparently of a person about middle age. With the bones were found a stone hatchet, a beautiful arrowhead, and a pipe, and strange to relate, the smell of tobacco about the pipe was perceptible for several hours after the exhumation. The tradition relating to the battle and the burial was well founded, and carried them nearly a century back.

As to tobacco, the Indians affirmed, as some of the earliest travelers among them inform us, that the use of it was known to them before the Europeans discovered the continent. The skill of the Indians in medicine, in certain diseases, was remarkable, the process of cure being simple and expeditious. The knowledge of some of the most valuable plants now in use was derived from them.[3]

Some of the customs of the Indians of Carolina indicated a degree of kindness and social affection, as well as an appreciation of duty, of which they are not generally supposed to have been possessed. When, for example, one of their own nation had suffered any loss by fire, or otherwise, he was ordered to make a feast, to which all the tribe was invited. After they had partaken of the feast, one of their speakers, generally a grave old man, delivered a harangue, informing them of the particulars of the loss sustained, and of their duty under such circumstances. After which, every man, according to his quality, threw down some present upon the ground, of beads, skins, furs, or other valuables, which often amounted to treble the loss incurred.

So, if one wished to build a canoe, or make a cabin, they rendered his assistance, saying, "There were several works which one man [Page 213] could not effect, and that therefore they must help him; otherwise their society would fall, and they would be deprived of those urgent necessities

---

3 Lawson, p. 172.

which life requires." If a woman lost her husband, and had a large family of children to maintain, she was always assisted. The young men of the tribe were made to plant, reap, and do anything she was not capable of doing herself. At the same time they would not suffer anyone to be idle, but compelled all to employ themselves in some work or other.[1]

As to religion, they believed generally that the world was round, and that there were two spirits, the one good and the other bad. The good spirit they reckoned to be the author and maker of everything. It was He, they said, who gave them the fruits of the earth, and taught them to hunt, fish, and be wise enough to overpower the beasts of the wilderness and all other creatures, that they might be assistant and beneficial to man. They did not believe that the Good Spirit punished any man in this life, or that to come, but that he delighted in doing good, and in making his creatures wise and happy. The bad spirit (who lived, as they thought, separate from the Good Spirit) they made the author of sickness, disappointment, loss, hunger, travail, and all the misfortunes that human life is incident to. Some of our aborigines were found to have traditions of the great Deluge, and of this event they gave a curious description. Of some of their practices, and one in particular, Lawson gives a singular account. He says—

Several customs are found in some families, which others keep not; as, for example, the families of the Mach-a-pangas use the Jewish custom of circumcision, and the rest do not; neither did I ever know any other amongst the Indians that practiced any such thing; and perhaps if you ask them what is the reason they do so, they will make you no manner of answer; which is as much as to say, I will not tell you.[2]

They seem to have been unwilling, for the most part, to give any account of their customs, particularly those of a religious character.

And so, the same writer remarks, that he knew them, for days together, to be amongst their idols and dead kings, though he could never get admittance to their sacred places to see what they were doing. The fact of their practicing idolatry at all has been positively denied by other travelers, who profess to have informed themselves of all that relates to their habits and customs. It is likely that the different tribes, remote from each other, and possibly of different origin, differed much in their customs and traditional

---

1 Lawson, pp. 178-179.
2 Lawson, pp. 210, 211.

observances, and hence the conflicting accounts which have been given. Of one custom, remarkable as it is suggestive, which Lawson affirms to have prevailed among the Indians of Carolina, and of which no other writer is believed to give any account, it may gratify the curiosity of the reader to be informed. It is very certain that it must have nipped the risings of aboriginal Young Americanism in the bud, leaving to a far superior race to exhibit, in the management of their youth, much more indecision and weakness. There is one most abominable custom—

Says Lawson—

which they call husquenauing their young men, which I have not made any mention of yet.

Most commonly once a year, or at farthest once in two years, these people take up so many of their young men as they think are able to undergo it and husquenaugh them, which is to make them obedient and respective to their superiors, and (as they [Page 214] say) is the same to them as it is to us to send our children to school to be taught good breeding and letters. This house of correction is a strong, large cabin, made on purpose for the reception of the young men and boys that have not passed this graduation already, and it is always at Christmas that they husquenaugh their youth, which is by bringing them into this house and keeping them dark all the time, where they more than half starve them. Besides, they give them pellitory bark and several intoxicating plants that make them go driving mad as ever were any people in the world. You may hear them make the most dismal cries and howlings that ever human creatures expressed, all which continues about five or six weeks; and the little meat they eat is the nastiest, loathsome stuff, and mixed with all manner of filth its possible to get. After the time is expired, they are brought out of the cabin, which never is in the town, but always a distance off, and guarded by a jailer or two, who watch by turns. And when they first come out they are poor as ever any creatures were; for you must know several die under this diabolical purgation. Moreover, they really either are or pretend to be drunk, and do not speak for several days; I think, 20 or 30, and look so ghastly and are so changed that its next to an impossibility to know them again, although you was never so well acquainted with them before. I would fain have gone into the madhouse and seen them in their time of purgatory, but the king would not suffer it, because he told me that they would do me or any other white man an injury that ventured in amongst them; so I desisted. They play this prank with girls as well as boys, and I believe it is a miserable life they endure, because I have known several of them run away at that time to avoid it. Now, the savages say, if it was not for this, they could not keep their youth in subjection: besides, that it hardens them after to the fatigues of war, hunting, and all manner of hardship which their way of living exposes them to. Besides, they add, that it carries off those infirm, weak bodies that would have been only a burden and disgrace to their nation, and saves the victuals and clothing for better people that would have been expended on such useless creatures.[1]

Lawson is the only one of the early Indian travelers in South Carolina, except Lederer, who passed through those parts of the State inhabited by the ancient dwellers on the Pedee. A large part of his book, however, is taken up with the natural history of North Carolina. He commenced a journey from Charleston, December 28, 1700, passed up the Santee and Wateree Rivers, and thence probably across to the Yadkin, and through North Carolina into Virginia. Among the Catawbas he must have met with the Cheraws and Pedees, if not in the parts higher up on our own river, though he does not mention them by name. In speaking, therefore, of the Carolina Indians generally, his remarks will apply to these, as well as others more particularly mentioned.

A few years after he was put to death in a most barbarous manner by the Indians in eastern North Carolina, to which State he had rendered most important service as surveyor general, as well as by his interesting account of the natural history of that region.

The author at one time cherished the hope of procuring some valuable traditional matter as to the Cheraws through William H. Thomas, Esq., of North Carolina, of whom mention has already been made. It was thought not unlikely that during his long and familiar intercourse with the Catawbas, Mr. Thomas might have gathered from their traditions something of the history of the Cheraws before the union of the tribes; but the hope was disappointed. The tradition of the Catawbas, already related, seem to be all they have preserved. Every other source of information now accessible has been exhausted. And with the account here given, meager and unsatisfactory as it is, we must be content, leaving these early occupants of the soil, proud and valiant and numerous as they once were, in that darkness

---

[1] Lawson, pp. 233-234.

and oblivion to which the red man, as he has receded westward before the advancing tide of civilization, has ever been consigned.

[Page 215] EXHIBIT J.

HISTORY OF THE CATAWBAS.

[From Hand Book of American Indians.]

CATAWBA (probably from Choctaw *katápa*, 'divided,' 'separated,' 'a division.'—Gatschet). The most important of the eastern Siouan tribes. It is said that Lynche Creek, S. C., east of the Catawba territory, was anciently known as Kadapau; and from the fact that Lawson applies this name to a small band met by him southeast of the main body, which he calls Esaw, it is possible that it was originally given to this people by some tribe living in east South Carolina, from whom the first colonists obtained it. The Cherokee, having no *b* in their language, changed the name to Atakwa, plural Anitakwa. The Shawnee and other tribes of the Ohio valley made the word Cuttawa. From the earliest period the Catawba have also been known as Esaw, or Issa (Catawba *iswă*, 'river'), from their residence on the principal stream of the region, Iswa being their only name for the Catawba and Watereers. They were frequently included by the Iroquois under the general term Totiri, or Toderichroone, another form of which is Tutelo, applied to all the southern Siouan tribes collectively. They were classed by Gallatin (1836) as a distinct stock, and were so regarded until Gatschet visited them in 1881 and obtained a large vocabulary showing numerous Siouan correspondences. Further investigations by Hale, Gatschet, Mooney, and Dorsey proved that several other tribes of the same region were also of Siouan stock, while the linguistic forms and traditional evidence all point to this eastern region as the original home of the Siouan tribes. The alleged tradition which brings the Catawba from the north, as refugees from the French and their Indian allies about the year 1660, does not agree in any of its main points with the known facts of history, and, if genuine at all, refers rather to some local incident than to a tribal movement. It is well known that the Catawba were in a chronic state of warfare with the northern tribes, whose raiding parties they sometimes followed, even across the Ohio.

The first notice of the Catawba seems to be that of Vandera in 1579, who calls them Issa in his narrative of Pardo's expedition. Nearly a century later, in 1670, they are mentioned as Ushery by Lederer, who claims to have visited them, but this is doubtful.

Lawson, who passed through their territory in 1701, speaks of them as a "powerful nation" and states that their villages were very thick. He calls the two divisions, which were living a short distance apart, by different names, one the Kadapau and the other the Esaw, unaware of the fact that the two were synonyms. From all accounts they were formerly the most populous and most important tribe in the Carolinas, excepting the Cherokee. Virginia traders were already among them at the time of Lawson's visit. Adair, 75 years later, says that one of the ancient cleared fields of the tribes extended 7 [Page 216] miles, besides which they had several smaller village sites. In 1728 they still had 6 villages, all on Catawba River, within a stretch of 20 miles, the most northern being named Nauvasa. Their principal village was formerly on the west side of the river, in what is now York County, S. C., opposite the mouth of Sugar Creek. The known history of the tribe till about 1760 is chiefly a record of petty warfare between themselves and the Iroquois and other northern tribes, throughout which the colonial government tried to induce the Indians to stop killing one another and go to killing the French. With the single exception of their alliance with the hostile Yamasi, in 1715, they were uniformly friendly toward the English, and afterwards kept peace with the United States, but were constantly at war with the Iroquois, Shawnee, Delawares, and other tribes of the Ohio Valley, as well as with the Cherokee. The Iroquois and the Lake tribes made long journeys into South Carolina, and the Catawba retaliated by sending small scalping parties into Ohio and Pennsylvania. Their losses from ceaseless attacks of their enemies reduced their numbers steadily, while disease and debauchery introduced by the whites, especially several epidemics of smallpox, accelerated their destruction, so that before the close of the 18th century the great nation was reduced to a pitiful remnant. They sent a large force to help the colonists in the Tuscarora war of 1711-1713, and also aided in expeditions against the French and their Indian allies at Fort Du Quesne and elsewhere during the French and Indian war. Later it was proposed to use them and the Cherokee against the Lake tribes under Pontiac in 1763. They assisted the Americans also during the Revolution in the defense of South Carolina against the British, as well as in Williamson's expedition against the Cherokee. In 1738 smallpox raged in South Carolina and worked great destruction, not only among the whites, but also among the Catawba and smaller tribes. In 1759 it appeared again, and this time destroyed nearly half the tribe. At a conference at Albany, attended by delegates from the Six Nations and the Catawba, under the auspices of the colonial governments, a treaty of peace was made between these two tribes. This peace was probably final as regards the Iroquois, but the western tribes continued their warfare against the Catawba, who were now so reduced that they could make little effectual resistance. In 1762 a small party of Shawnee killed the noted chief of the tribe, King Haiglar, near his own village. From this time the Catawba ceased to be of importance except in conjunction with the whites. In 1763 they had confirmed to them a reservation, assigned a few years before, of 15 miles square, on both sides of Catawba River, within the present York and Lancaster Counties, S. C. On the approach of the British troops in 1780 the Catawba withdrew temporarily into Virginia, but returned after the battle of Guilford Court House, and established themselves in 2 villages on the reservations known respectively as Newton, the principal village, and Turkey Head, on opposite sides of Catawba River. In 1826 nearly the whole of their reservation was leased to whites for a few thousand dollars, on which the few survivors chiefly depended. About 1841 they sold to the State all but a single square mile, on which they now reside. About the same time a number of the Catawba, dissatisfied with their condition among the whites, removed to the eastern Cherokee in western North Carolina, but finding their position among [Page 217] their old enemies equally unpleasant, all but one or two soon went back again. An old woman, the last survivor of this emigration, died among the Cherokee in 1889. A few other Cherokee are now intermarried with that tribe. At a later period some Catawba removed to the Choctaw Nation in Indian Territory and settled near Scullyville, but are said to be now extinct. About 1884 several became converts of Mormon missionaries in South Carolina and went with them to Salt Lake City, Utah.

The Catawba were sedentary agriculturists, and seem to have differed but little in general customs from their neighbors. Their men were respected, brave, and honest, but lacking in energy. They were good hunters, while their women were noted makers of pottery and baskets, arts which they still preserve. They seem to have practiced the custom of head flattening to a limited extent, as did several of the neighboring tribes. By reason of their dominant position they gradually absorbed the broken tribes of South Carolina, to the number, according to Adair, of perhaps 20.

In the early settlement of South Carolina, about 1682, they were estimated at 1, 500 warriors, or about 4, 600 souls; in 1728 at 400 warriors, or about 1, 400 persons. In 1738 they suffered from smallpox; and in 1743, after incorporating several small tribes, numbered less than 400 warriors. In 1759 they again suffered from smallpox, and in 1761 had some 300 warriors, or about 1, 000 people. The number was reduced in 1775 to 400 souls; in 1780 it was 490; and in 1784 only 250 were reported. The number given in 1822 is 450, and Mills gives the population in 1826 as only 110. In 1881 Gatschet found 85 on the reservation, which, including 35 employed on neighboring farms, made a total of 120. The present number is given as 60, but as this apparently refers only to those attached to the reservation, the total may be about 100.

See Lawson, History of Carolina, 1714 and 1860; Gatschet, Creek Migration Legend, I-II, 1884-88; Mooney (1) Siouan Tribes of the East, Bull. 22, B. A. E., 1894, (2) in 19th Rep. B. A. E., 1900; H. Lewis Scaife, History and Condition of the Catawba Indians, 1896. (J. M.)

[Page 218] EXHIBIT K.

HISTORY OF THE CHERAWS.

[From Handbook of American Indians.]

CHERAW.—An important tribe, very probably of Siouan stock, formerly ranging in central Carolina, east of the Blue Ridge, from about the present Danville, Va., southward to the neighborhood of Cheraw, S. C., which takes its name from them. In numbers they may have stood next to the Tuscarora among the North Carolina tribes, but are less prominent in history by reason of their almost complete destruction before the white settlements had reached their territory. They are mentioned first in the De Soto narrative for 1540, under the name Xuala, a corruption of Suali, the name by which they are traditionally known to the Cherokee, who remember them as having anciently lived beyond the Blue Ridge from Asheville. In the earlier Carolina and Virginia records they are commonly known as Saraw, and at a later period as Cheraw. We first hear of "Xuala province" in 1540, apparently in the mountain country southward from Asheville. In 1672, Lederer, from Indian information, located them in the same general region, or possibly somewhat farther northeast, "where the mountains bend to the west," and says that this portion of the main ridge was called "Sualy Mountain" from the tribe. This agrees with Cherokee tradition. Some years later, but previous to 1700, they settled on Dan River near the south line of Virginia, where the marks of their fields were found extending for several miles along the river by Byrd, in 1728, when running the dividing line between the two colonies. There seem to have been two villages, as on a map of 1760 we find this place designated as "Lower Saura Town," while about 30 miles above, on the south side of the Dan and between it and Town Fork, is another place marked "Upper Saura Town." They are also alluded to by J. F. D. Smyth (Tour in United States, 1784), who says the upper town was insignificant. About the year 1710, being harassed by the Iroquois, they abandoned their home on the Dan and moving southeast joined the Keyauwee. The colonists of North Carolina being dissatisfied at the proximity of these and other tribes, Gov. Eden declared war against the Cheraw, and applied to Virginia for assistance. This Gov. Spotswood refused, as he believed the people of Carolina were the aggressors; nevertheless the war was carried on against them and their allies by the Carolinas until the defeat and expulsion of the Yamasi in 1716. During this period complaint was made against the Cheraw, who were declared to be responsible for most of the mischief done north of Santee River, and of endeavoring to draw into their alliance the smaller coast tribes. It was asserted by the Carolinians that arms were supplied them from Virginia. At the close of the Yamasi war the Cheraw were dwelling on the upper Pedee near the line between the Carolinas, where their name is perpetuated in the town of Cheraw, S. C. Their number in 1715, according to Rivers, was 510, but this estimate probably included the [Page 219] Keyauwee. Being still subject to attack by the Iroquois, they finally—between 1726 and 1739—became incorporated with the Catawba, with whom at an earlier date they had been at enmity. They are mentioned as with the Catawba but speaking their own distinct dialect as late as 1743 (Adair). In 1759 a party of 45 "Charraws," some of whom were under their chief, "King Johnny," joined the English in the expedition against Fort Du Quesne. The last notice of them is in 1768, when their remnant, reduced by war and disease to 50 or 60, were still living with the Catawba. (J. M.)

[Page 220] EXHIBIT KK.

HISTORY OF THE CHEROKEES.

[From Handbook of American Indians.]

CHEROKEE.—A powerful detached tribe of the Iroquoian family, formerly holding the whole mountain region of the southern Alleghenies, in southwestern Virginia, western North Carolina and South Carolina, northern Georgia, eastern Tennessee, and northeastern Alabama, and claiming even to the Ohio River. The tribal name is a corruption of Tsálăgĭ or Tsárăgĭ, the name by which they commonly called themselves, and which may be derived from the Choctaw *chiluk-ki*, "cave people," in allusion to the numerous caves in their mountain country. They sometimes also call themselves *Ani'-Yûñ'wiyâ'*, "real people," or *Ani'-Kĭtu'hwagĭ*, "people of Kituhwa," one of their most important ancient settlements. Their northern kinsmen, the Iroquois, called them *Oyata'gecronoñ'*, "inhabitants of the cave country" (Hewitt), and the Delawares and connected tribes called them *Kittuwa*, from the settlement already noted. They seem to be identical with the Rickohockans, who invaded central Virginia in 1658, and with the ancient Talligewi, of Delaware tradition, who were represented to have been driven southward from the upper Ohio River region by the combined forces of the Iroquois and Delawares.

The language has three principal dialects: (1) *Elatĭ*, or Lower, spoken on the heads of Savannah River in South Carolina and Georgia; (2) Middle, spoken chiefly on the waters of Tuckasegee River in western North Carolina, and now the prevailing dialect on the East Cherokee reservation; (3) Âtăli, Mountain or Upper, spoken throughout most of upper Georgia, eastern Tennessee, and extreme western North Carolina. The lower dialect was the only one which had the r sound, and is now extinct. The upper dialect is that which has been exclusively used in the native literature of the tribe.

Traditional, linguistic, and archæologic evidence shows that the Cherokee originated in the North, but they were found in possession of the southern Allegheny region when first encountered by De Soto in 1540. Their relations with the Carolina colonies began 150 years later. In 1736 the Jesuit (?) Priber started the first mission among them, and attempted to organize their government on a civilized basis. In 1759, under the leadership of Âganstâ'ta (Oconostota), they began war with the English of Carolina. In the Revolution they took sides against the Americans, and continued the struggle almost without interval until 1794. During this period parties of the Cherokee pushed down Tennessee River and formed new settlements at Chickamauga and other points about the Tennessee-Alabama line. Shortly after 1800 missionary and educational work was established among them, and in 1820 they adopted a regular form of government modeled on that of the United States. In the meantime large numbers of the more conservative Cherokee, wearied by the encroachments of the whites, had crossed the Mississippi and made [Page 221] new homes in the wilderness in what is now Arkansas. A year or two later Sequoya (q. v.), a mixed blood, invented the alphabet, which at once raised them to the rank of a literary people.

At the height of their prosperity gold was discovered near the present Dahlonega, Ga., within the limits of the Cherokee Nation, and at once a powerful agitation was begun for the removal of the Indians. After years of hopeless struggle under the leadership of their great chief, John Ross, they were compelled to submit to the inevitable, and by the treaty of New Echota, December 29, 1835, the Cherokee sold their entire remaining territory and agreed to remove beyond the Mississippi to a country there to be set apart for them—the present (1905) Cherokee Nation in Indian Territory. The removal was accomplished in the winter of 1838-39, after considerable hardship and the loss of nearly one-fourth of their number, the unwilling Indians being driven out by military force and making the long journey on foot. On reaching their destination they reorganized their national government, with their capital at Tahlequah, admitting to equal privileges the earlier emigrants, known as "old settlers." A part of the Arkansas Cherokee had previously gone down into Texas, where they had obtained a grant of land in the eastern part of the State from the Mexican Government. The later Texan revolutionists refused to recognize their rights, and in spite of the efforts of Gen. Sam Houston, who defended the Indian claim, a conflict was precipitated, resulting, in 1839, in the killing of the Cherokee chief, Bowl (q. v.), with a large number of his men, by the Texan troops and the expulsion of the Cherokee from Texas.

When the main body of the tribe was removed to the West several hundred fugitives escaped to the mountains, where they lived as refugees for a time, until, in 1842, through the efforts of William H. Thomas, an influential trader, they received permission to remain on lands set apart for their use in western North Carolina. They constitute the present Eastern Band of Cherokee, residing chiefly on the Qualla Reservation, in Swain and Jackson Counties, with several outlying settlements.

The Cherokee in the Cherokee Nation were for years divided into two hostile factions, those who had favored and those who had opposed the treaty of removal. Hardly had these differences been adjusted when the Civil War burst upon them. Being slave owners and surrounded by southern influences, a large part of each of the Five Civilized Tribes of the Territory enlisted in the service of the Confederacy, while others adhered to the National Government. The territory of the Cherokee was overrun in turn by both armies, and the close of the war found them prostrated. By treaty in 1866 they were readmitted to the protection of the United States, but obliged to liberate their negro slaves and admit them to equal citizenship. In 1867 and 1870 the Delawares and Shawnee, respectively, numbering together about 1, 750, were admitted from Kansas and incorporated with the nation. In 1889 the Cherokee commission (see Commission) was created for the purpose of abolishing the tribal governments and opening the Territories to white settlement, with the result that after 15 years of negotiation an agreement was made by which the government of the Cherokee Nation came to a final end March 3, 1906; the Indian lands were divided, and the Cherokee Indians, native and adopted, became citizens of the United States.

[Page 222]The Cherokee have seven clans, viz: Ani'-wa'"ya (Wolf), Ani'-Kawĭ' (Deer), Ani'-Tsi'skwa (Bird), Ani'-wâ'dĭ (Paint), Ani'-Sahâ'ni, Ani'-Ga'tâgéwĭ, Ani'-Gilâ'hĭ. The names of the last three can not be translated with certainty. There is evidence that there were anciently 14, which by extinction or absorption have been reduced to their present number. The Wolf clan is the largest and most important. The "seven clans" are frequently mentioned in the ritual prayers and even in the printed laws of the tribe. They seem to have had a connection with the "seven mother towns" of the Cherokee, described by Cuming in 1730 as having each a chief, whose office was hereditary in the female line.

The Cherokee are probably about as numerous now as at any period in their history. With the exception of an estimate in 1730, which placed them at about 20, 000, most of those up to a recent period gave them 12, 000 or 14, 000, and in 1758 they were computed at only 7, 500. The majority of the earlier estimates are probably too low, as the Cherokee occupied so extensive a territory that only a part of them came in contact with the whites. In 1708 Gov. Johnson estimated them at 60 villages and "at least 500 men" (Rivers, S. C., 238, 1856). In 1715 they were officially reported to number 11, 210 (Upper, 2, 760; Middle, 6, 350; Lower, 2, 100), including 4, 000 warriors, and living in 60 villages (Upper, 19; Middle, 30; Lower, 11). In 1720 they were estimated to have been reduced to about 10, 000, and again in the same year reported at about 11, 500, including about 3, 800 warriors (Gov. Johnson's Rep. in Rivers, op. cit., 93, 94, 103, 1874). In 1729 they were estimated at 20, 000, with at least 6, 000 warriors and 64 towns and villages (Stevens, Hist. Ga., I, 48, 1847). They are said to have lost 1, 000 warriors in 1739 from smallpox and rum, and they suffered a steady decrease during their wars with the whites, extending from 1760 until after the close of the Revolution. Those in their original homes had again increased to 16, 542 at the time of their forced removal to the West in 1838, but lost nearly one-fourth on the journey, 311 perishing in a steamboat accident on the Mississippi. Those already in the West before the removal were estimated at about 6, 000. The Civil War in 1861-1865 again checked their progress, but they recovered from its effects in a remarkably short time, and in 1885 numbered about 19, 000, of whom about 17, 000 were in Indian Territory, together with about 6, 000 adopted whites, negroes, Delawares, and Shawnee, while the remaining 2, 000 were still in their ancient homes in the East. Of this eastern band, 1, 376 were on Qualla Reservation, in Swain and Jackson Counties, N. C.; about 300 are on Cheowah River, in Graham County, N. C., while the remainder, all of mixed blood, are scattered over eastern Tennessee, northern Georgia, and Alabama. The eastern band lost about 300 by smallpox at the close of the Civil War. In 1902 there were officially reported 28, 016 persons of Cherokee blood, including all degrees of admixture, in the Cherokee Nation in the Territory, but this includes several thousand individuals formerly repudiated by the tribal courts. There were also living in the nation about 3, 000 adopted negro freedmen, more than 2, 000 adopted whites, and about 1, 700 adopted Delaware, Shawnee, and other Indians. The tribe has a larger proportion of white admixture than any other of the Five Civilized Tribes. See Mooney, Myths of Cherokee Indians. (Hand Book of American Indians, Bulletin 30, Bureau American Ethnology.)

[Page 223] EXHIBIT L.

LEGISLATION RELATIVE TO INDIANS OF ROBESON COUNTY.

Exhibit L1.

[Amendments (to the constitution of North Carolina) proposed by a convention of delegates of the people of North Carolina, on the 11th of July, 1835, and ratified by the people on the second Monday of November, in the same year.]

SECTION 111.

CLAUSE 3. No free negro, free mulatto, or free person of mixed blood, descended from negro ancestors to the fourth generation, inclusive (though one ancestor of each generation may have been a white person), shall vote for members of the senate or house of commons.

Exhibit L2.

[Revised code of North Carolina, enacted by the general assembly at the session of 1854.]

CRIMES AND PUNISHMENTS—CHAPTER 34.

SEC. 80. If any clerk of the court of pleas and quarter-sessions shall knowingly issue any license for marriage between any free person of color and a white person; or if any clergyman, minister of the gospel, or justice of the peace shall knowingly marry any such free person of color to a white person, the person so offending shall be guilty of a misdemeanor.

MARRIAGE—CHAPTER 68.

SEC. 7. All marriages since the eighth day of January, eighteen hundred and thirty-nine, and all marriages in future between a white person and a free negro, or free person of color, to the third generation, shall be void.

Exhibit L3.

[Constitution of North Carolina, amendment of 1857—Proposed by the general assembly in 1854, December 11, 1856, and January 8, 1857, and ratified by the people the first Thursday in August, 1857.]

Every free white man of the age of twenty-one years, being a native or naturalized citizen of the United States, and who has been an inhabitant of the State for twelve months immediately preceding the day of any election, and shall have paid public taxes, shall be entitled to vote for a member of the senate for the district in which he resides.

[Page 224] *Exhibit L4.*

[The constitution of the State of North Carolina of 1868, as amended.]

ARTICLE VI.

SUFFRAGE AND ELIGIBILITY TO OFFICE.

SECTION 1. Every male person born in the United States, and every male person who has been naturalized, twenty-one years of age, and possessing the qualifications set out in this article, shall be entitled to vote at any election by the people in the State, except as herein otherwise provided.

SEC. 4. Every person presenting himself for registration shall be able to read and write any section of the Constitution in the English language; and before he shall be entitled to vote he shall have paid on or before the first day of May of the year in which he proposes to vote, his poll tax for the previous year, as prescribed by Article V, section 1, of the Constitution. But no male person who was, on January 1, 1867, or at any time prior thereto, entitled to vote under the laws of any State in the United States wherein he then resided, and no lineal descendant of any such person, shall be denied the right to register and vote at any election in this State by reason of his failure to possess the educational qualifications herein prescribed: *Provided,* He shall have registered in accordance with the terms of this section prior to December 1, 1908. The general assembly shall provide for the registration of all persons entitled to vote without the educational qualifications herein prescribed, and shall, on or before November 1, 1908, provide for the making of a permanent record of such registration, and all persons so registered shall forever thereafter have the right to vote in all elections by the people in this State, unless disqualified under section 2 of this article: *Provided,* Such person shall have paid his poll tax as above required.

Exhibit L5.

[Constitution of North Carolina, annotated by Connor and Cheshire.]

1. ALL MEN EQUAL.

1. Indians and free persons of color before 1868. The Cherokee, Croatan, and other Indians living in North Carolina are citizens of the State and amenable to the laws.

State *v.* Wolf, 145 N. C., 440; State *v.* Tachanatah, 64 N. C., 614.

Before the constitution of 1868 and the thirteenth amendment to the Constitution of the United States *free persons of color* were citizens of North Carolina; and this was so even after the right to vote was taken from such persons.

State *v.* Manuel, 20 N. C., 144 (20), where Gaston, J., says: "Upon the Revolution no other change took place in the laws of [Page 225] North Carolina than was consequent upon the transition from a colony, dependent on a European King, to a free and sovereign State. Slaves remained slaves. British subjects in North Carolina became North Carolina free men. Foreigners until made members of the State continued aliens. Slaves manumitted here became free men and, therefore, if born within North Carolina, are citizens of North Carolina—and all free persons born within the State are born citizens of the State." (This case was cited with approval by Mr. Justice Curtis in his dissenting opinion in the Dred Scott case, 60 U. S. (19 Howard) 573.—Editors.)

(State *v.* Manuel, *supra,* was subsequent to the convention of 1835, which deprived free negroes of their right to vote. For an interesting debate upon the origin, basis, and history of their right to vote, see "Debates in convention, 1835," pp. 72, 351.—Editors.)

2. *Civil and political rights.* The constitution (of North Carolina) was not intended to enforce social equality, but only civil and political equality.

State *v.* Hairston, 63 N. C., 452, holding (before the adoption of Art. XLV, sec. 8) that Rev. Code, ch. 68, sec. 7, declaring intermarriages between white persons *and persons of color* void, is not a discrimination in favor of one race against another, but applies equally to all races and is valid and still in force.

Exhibit L5½.

[Laws of North Carolina, 1885, chapter 51.]

AN ACT To provide for separate schools for Croatan Indians in Robeson County.

Whereas the Indians now living in Robeson County claim to be descendants of a friendly tribe who once resided in eastern North Carolina on the Roanoke River, known as the Croatan Indians; therefore,

The General Assembly of North Carolina do enact:

SECTION 1. That the said Indians and their descendants shall hereafter be designated and known as the Croatan Indians.

SEC. 2. That said Indians and their descendants shall have separate schools for their children, school committees of their own race and color, and shall be allowed to select teachers of their own choice, subject to the same rules and regulations as are applicable to all teachers in the general school law.

SEC. 3. It shall be the duty of the county board of education to see that this act is carried into effect, and shall for that purpose have the census of all the children of said Indians and their descendants between the ages of six and twenty-one taken, and proceed to establish such suitable school districts as shall be necessary for their convenience, and take all such other and further steps as may be necessary for the purpose of carrying this act into effect without delay.

SEC. 4. The treasurer and other proper authorities, whose duties it is to collect, keep, and apportion the school fund, shall procure [Page 226] from the county board of education the number of children in said county between the ages of six and twenty-one, belonging to said Indian race, and shall set apart and keep separate their pro rata share of said school funds, which shall be paid out upon the same rules in every respect as are provided in general school law: *Provided*, That where any children, descendants of Indians as aforesaid, shall reside in any district in which there are no schools, as provided in this chapter, the same shall have the right to attend any of the public schools in said county for their race, and shall be allowed to draw their share of public school fund upon the certificate of the school committee in the district in which they reside, stating that they have thus removed and are entitled to attend public schools.

SEC. 5. The general school law shall be applicable in all respects to this chapter, where the same is not repugnant to or inconsistent with this act. This act shall only apply to Robeson County. All laws and clauses of law in conflict with this act are hereby repealed.

SEC. 6. That this act shall be in force from and after its ratification.

(In the General Assembly read three times and ratified this the 10th day of February, A. D. 1885.)

Exhibit L6.

[Laws of North Carolina, chapter 400.]

AN ACT To establish a normal school in the county of Robeson.

The General Assembly of North Carolina do enact:

SECTION 1. That W. L. Moore, James Oxendine, James Dial, Preston Locklear, and others who may be associated with them, and their successors, are hereby constituted a body politic and corporate, for educational purposes, in the county of Robeson, under the name and style of the trustees of the Croatan Normal School, and by that name may have perpetual succession, may sue and be sued, plead and be impleaded, contract and be contracted with, to have and to hold school property, including buildings, lands, and all appurtenances thereto, situated in the county of Robeson, at any place in said county to be selected by the trustees herein named, provided such place shall be located between Bear Swamp and Lumber River in said county; to acquire by purchase, donation, or otherwise, real and personal property for the purpose of establishing and maintaining a school of high grade for teachers of the Croatan race in North Carolina.

SEC. 2. That the trustees at their organization shall elect one of their own number president of the board of trustees, whose duties shall be such as develoves upon such officers in similar cases, or such as shall hereafter be defined by said trustees.

SEC. 3. That said trustees shall have full power to rent, lease, mortgage or sell any real or personal property for the purpose of maintaining said school, discharging indebtedness, or reinvesting the proceeds for a like purpose: *Provided,* That the liabilities of said trustees shall affect only the property owned by said trustees for educational purposes and shall not affect the private credit of said trustees.

[Page 227]SEC. 4. That the trustees whose names are mentioned in the first section of this act shall have power to select three additional trustees from the Croatan race in such manner as they may determine.

SEC. 5. That said trustees shall have full power and authority to employ a teacher or teachers in said normal school under such regulations as the said trustees may determine.

SEC. 6. That said board of trustees shall have full power to fill all vacancies by death, removal, or otherwise in said board: *Provided,* a majority vote of all the trustees shall be necessary to a choice.

SEC. 7. That the sum of five hundred dollars is hereby appropriated to the support of said school annually for two years, and no longer, commencing with the first day of January, one thousand eight hundred and eighty-eight, said sum to be paid out of the general educational fund: *Provided,* That said sum thus appropriated shall be expended for the payment of services rendered for teaching and for no other purpose; said sum to be paid in semiannual payments upon warrants drawn by State superintendent of public instruction upon receipt by said superintendent of report of trustees of said school showing the number of teachers employed, the amount paid to teacher, the number of students in attendance during the term of six months next preceding the first day of July, one thousand eight hundred and eighty-eight, first day of January, one thousand eight hundred and eighty-nine, first day of July, one thousand eight hundred and eighty-nine, and first day of January, one thousand eight hundred and ninety.

SEC. 8. That all property, real and personal, acquired by purchase, donation, or otherwise, as long as it is used for educational purposes, shall be exempt from taxation, whether on the part of the State or county.

SEC. 9. That no person shall sell any spirituous liquors within two miles of the location of said school, and any person violating this section shall be guilty of a misdemeanor, and upon conviction shall be fined not less than ten dollars nor more than thirty dollars, or imprisoned not less than ten days nor more than thirty days, or both at the discretion of the court.

SEC. 10. *Provided,* That no person shall be admitted into said school as a student who has not attained the age of fifteen years; and that all those who shall enjoy the privileges of said school as students shall previously obligate (themselves) to teach the youth of the Croatan race for a stated period.

SEC. 11. That this act shall be in force from and after its ratification.

(In the General Assembly read three times, and ratified this 7th day of March, A. D. 1887.)

Exhibit L7.

[Laws of North Carolina, session of 1887, chapter 254.]

AN ACT To amend section one thousand eight hundred and ten of the code.

The General Assembly of North Carolina do enact:

SECTION 1. That section one thousand eight hundred and ten of the Code of North Carolina be amended by adding thereto the words: "That all marriages between an Indian and a negro or between an [Page 228] Indian and a person of negro descent to the third generation, inclusive, shall be utterly void: *Provided,* This act shall only apply to the Croatan Indians."

SEC. 2. This act shall be in force from and after its ratification.

(In the general assembly read three times, and ratified this 7th day of March, A. D. 1887.)

Exhibit L8.

[Laws of North Carolina, session of 1889, chapter 458.]

AN ACT To amend chapter fifty-seven, acts of one thousand eight hundred and eighty-five, in reference to the schools of Croatan Indians in Richmond County.

The General Assembly of North Carolina do enact:

SECTION 1. That the citizens of Richmond County who are Croatan Indians, or the descendants of such who are known as such, or who have a distinct race identity as such, shall be entitled to the same school privileges and benefits as are granted to other Croatan Indians in Robeson County under the provisions of said act of one thousand eight hundred and eighty-five, chapter fifty-one, and the act or acts subsequent to and amendatory of the act of one thousand eight hundred and eighty-five.

SEC. 2. That this act shall be in force from and after its ratification.

(Ratified the 11th day of March, A. D. 1889.)

Exhibit L9.

[Laws of North Carolina, session of 1889, chapter 60.]

AN ACT To amend the laws of 1885 and 1887 so as to provide additional educational facilities for the Croatan Indians, citizens of Robeson County, North Carolina.

The General Assembly of North Carolina do enact:

SECTION 1. That Chapter Fifty-one, section two, of the Laws of One thousand eight hundred and eighty-five be amended by adding after the word "law" in the last line of said section the words, "and there shall be excluded from such separate schools for the said Croatan Indians all children of the negro race to the fourth generation."

SEC. 2. That section seven, Chapter Four hundred, of the Laws of One thousand eight hundred and eighty-seven be amended as follows: Strike out in lines two and three the words, "for two years and no longer;" strike out in line fifteen all after the words "eighty-eight," and insert "and every six months thereafter."

SEC. 3. That section ten of said Chapter Four hundred, Laws of One thousand eight hundred and eighty-seven, be amended by striking out in line three the word "fifteen" and inserting the word "ten" in lieu thereof.

SEC. 4. This act shall be in force from and after its ratification.

(Ratified the 2d day of February, A. D. 1889.)

[Page 229] *Exhibit L10.*

[Public laws of North Carolina, session of 1897, chapter 536.]

AN ACT In relation to the Croatan Normal School in Robeson County.

The General Assembly of North Carolina do enact:

SECTION 1. That there shall be placed to the credit of the Croatan Normal School of Robeson County out of the general educational fund in the hands of the State treasurer, the sum of two hundred and eighty-one 25.100 dollars, being the unexpended appropriation for the year 1895; and the treasurer is hereby authorized to pay Prof. P. B. Hiden, upon the approval of his claim by the board of trustees and the commissioners of Robeson County, out of the above $281 & 25/100, the sum of forty ($40) dollars for services heretofore rendered in 1896.

SEC. 2. This act shall be in force from and after its ratification.

(Ratified the 9th day of March, A. D. 1897.)

Exhibit L11.

[Public laws of North Carolina, session of 1911, chapter 168.]

AN ACT To empower the trustees of the Indian School of Robeson County to transfer title to property of said school by deed to State board of education, and to provide for the appointment of trustees for said school.

The General Assembly of North Carolina do enact:

SECTION 1. That in accordance with the recent action of the trustees, in meeting assembled, of the Croatan State normal school, known as the Indian Normal School of Robeson County, situated near Pembroke, North Carolina, said school being incorporated under Chapter Four hundred, Public Laws of One thousand eight hundred and eighty-seven, which action of the trustees of said school has been duly certified to by the president, C. R. Sampson, and the secretary, A. A. Locklear, the said trustees are hereby empowered to convey by deed to the State board of education the title to all property of said school, and the State board of education is hereby authorized to accept same.

SEC. 2. That the State board of education shall appoint seven members of the Indian race, formally known as Croatans, to be constituted the board of trustees of said school, as follows: Two members for the term of two years, two for the term of four years, and three for the term of six years; and, at the expiration of these terms, their successors shall be appointed by the State board of education for a term of six years.

SEC. 3. That the board of trustees of said Indian normal school Robeson County shall have the power to employ and discharge teachers, to prevent negroes from attending said school, and to exercise the usual functions of control and management of said school, their action being subject to the approval of the State board of education.

SEC. 4. That all laws and clauses of laws in conflict with this act are hereby repealed.

SEC. 5. This act shall be in force from and after its ratification.

(Ratified this the 8th day of March, A. D. 1911.)

[Page 230] *Exhibit L12.*

[Public Laws of North Carolina, Session of 1911, Chapter 215.]

AN ACT To change the name of the Indians in Robeson County and to provide for said Indians separate apartments in the State hospital.

The General Assembly of North Carolina do enact:

SECTION 1. That Chapter Fifty-one of the Public Laws of North Carolina, session of eighteen hundred and eighty-five, be, and the same is hereby, amended by striking out the words "Croatan Indians" wherever the same occur in said chapter and inserting in lieu thereof the words "Indians of Robeson County."

SEC. 2. That in all laws enacted by the General Assembly of North Carolina relating to said Indians subsequent to the enactment of said Chapter Fifty-one of the Laws of Eighteen hundred and eighty-five, the words "Croatan Indians" be, and the same are hereby, stricken out and the words "Indians of Robeson County" inserted in lieu thereof.

SEC. 3. And that the said Indians residing in Robeson and adjoining counties which have heretofore been known as Croatan Indians, together with their descendants, shall hereafter be known and designated as "Indians of Robeson County," and by that name shall be entitled to all the rights and privileges conferred by any of the laws of North Carolina upon the Indians heretofore known as Croatan Indians.

SEC. 4. That the school situated near the town of Pembroke, in Robeson County, known as Croatan Indian Normal School, shall hereafter be known and designated as "The Indian Normal School of Robeson County," and in that name shall be entitled to all of the privileges and powers heretofore conferred by any law of the State of North Carolina or any laws hereafter enacted for the benefit of said school.

SEC. 5. That the board of directors for the State Hospital for the Insane at Raleigh are hereby authorized and directed to provide and set apart at said hospital, as soon after the passage of this act as practicable, suitable apartments and wards for the accommodation of any of said Indians of Robeson County who may be entitled under the laws relating to insane persons to be admitted to said hospital.

SEC. 6. That the sheriff, jailer, or other proper authorities of Robeson County shall provide in the common jail of Robeson County and in the Home for the Aged and Infirm of Robeson County separate cells, wards, or apartments for the said Indians of Robeson County, in all cases where it shall be necessary under the laws of this State to commit any of said Indians to said jail or County Home for the Aged and Infirm.

SEC. 7. That all laws and clauses of laws in conflict with this act are hereby repealed.

SEC. 8. That this act shall be in force from and after its ratification. (Ratified this 8th day of March, A. D. 1911.)

[Page 231] *Exhibit L13.*

[Public Laws of North Carolina, Session of 1913, Chapter 123.]

AN ACT To restore to the Indians residing in Robeson and adjoining counties their rightful and ancient name.

The General Assembly of North Carolina do enact:

SECTION 1. That Chapter Two hundred and fifteen of the Public Laws of North Carolina, session one thousand nine hundred and eleven, be, and the same is hereby, amended by striking out in the last line of said section one the words "Indians of Robeson County," and inserting in lieu thereof the words "Cherokee Indians of Robeson County."

SEC. 2. That section two of said Chapter Two hundred and fifteen of the Public Laws of North Carolina, session one thousand nine hundred and eleven, be, and the same is hereby, amended by striking out the words "Indians of Robeson County," in the fifth line of said section two, and inserting in lieu thereof the words "Cherokee Indians of Robeson County."

SEC. 3. That said Chapter Two hundred and fifteen of the Public Laws of North Carolina, session one thousand nine hundred and eleven, be further amended by striking out the words "Indians of Robeson County," in line four of said section three, and inserting in lieu thereof the words "Cherokee Indians of Robeson County."

SEC. 4. That the Indians residing in Robeson and adjoining counties who have heretofore been known as "Croatan Indians" or "Indians of Robeson County," together with their descendants, shall hereafter be known and designated as "Cherokee Indians of Robeson County," and by that name shall be entitled to all the rights and privileges heretofore or hereafter conferred by any law or laws of the State of North Carolina upon the Indians heretofore known as the "Croatan Indians" or "Indians of Robeson County," including all such rights and privileges as have been conferred upon said Indians by Chapter Two hundred and fifteen of the Public Laws of North Carolina, session one thousand nine hundred and eleven.

SEC. 5. Neither this act nor any other act relating to said "Cherokee Indians of Robeson County" shall be construed so as to impose on said Indians any powers, privileges, rights, or immunities or any limitations on their power to contract, heretofore enacted with reference to the Eastern Band of Cherokee Indians residing in Cherokee, Graham, Swain, Jackson, and other adjoining counties in North Carolina, or any other band or tribe of Cherokee Indians other than those now residing, or who have, since the Revolutionary War, resided in Robeson County, nor shall said "Cherokee Indians of Robeson County," as herein designated be subject to the limitations provided in section nine hundred and seventy-five and nine hundred and seventy-six of the revisal of one thousand nine hundred and five of North Carolina.

SEC. 6. That Chapter Two hundred and fifteen of the Public Laws of North Carolina, session one thousand nine hundred and eleven, be further amended by striking out the words "Indian Normal School of Robeson County," in the third and fourth lines of said section four of said Chapter Two hundred and fifteen, and inserting in lieu thereof the words "Cherokee Indian Normal School of Robeson County."

[Page 232]SEC. 7. That all laws and clauses of laws in conflict with the provisions of this act are hereby repealed.

SEC. 8. That this act shall be in force and effect from and after its ratification.

(In the general assembly read three times and ratified this the 11th day of March, 1913.)

Exhibit L14.

[Public Laws of North Carolina, Session of 1913, Chapter 199.]

AN ACT To provide for the maintenance and support of the Indian Normal School of Robeson County.

The General Assembly of North Carolina do enact:

SECTION 1. That in addition to the sum of two thousand two hundred and fifty dollars ($2, 250) appropriated by the General Assembly of North Carolina, session of nineteen hundred and thirteen, for the maintenance of the Indian Normal School of Robeson County, the further sum of five hundred dollars is hereby annually appropriated for the years one thousand nine hundred and thirteen and one thousand nine hundred and fourteen for the support and maintenance of said school.

SEC. 2. That the appropriation herein made shall be drawn out by the auditor upon his warrant, and thereupon shall be charged by the State treasurer to the account of said school.

SEC. 3. That this act shall be in force from and after its ratification.

(In general assembly read three times and ratified this the 12th day of March, 1913.)

[Page 233] EXHIBIT M.

CORRESPONDENCE RELATIVE TO THE INVESTIGATION OF THE CONDITION, TRIBAL RIGHTS, ETC., OF THE INDIANS OF ROBESON COUNTY, N. C.

JULY 23, 1914.

Mr. O. M. MCPHERSON, *Special Agent.*
My DEAR MR. MCPHERSON, Upon the receipt of these instructions, or as soon thereafter as practicable, you will proceed to North Carolina for the purpose of investigating the affairs of the Croatan Indians of Robeson and adjoining counties of that State, as provided for by Senate resolution 410.

This resolution reads:

Resolved, That the Secretary of the Interior be, and he hereby is, directed to cause an investigation to be made of the condition and tribal rights of the Indians of Robeson and adjoining counties of North Carolina, recently declared by the Legislature of North Carolina to be Cherokees, and formerly known as Croatans, and report to Congress what tribal rights, if any, they have with any band or tribe; whether they are entitled to or have received any lands, or whether there are any moneys due them, their present condition, their educational facilities, and such other facts as would enable Congress to determine whether the Government would be warranted in making suitable provision for their support and education.

Extreme care should be exercised by you in obtaining all pertinent facts relative to the condition and tribal rights of these Indians, in order that this office may be prepared to submit to the next Congress, through the department, full information responsive to said resolution.

Very truly, yours,

CATO SELLS,
Commissioner.

DEPARTMENT OF THE INTERIOR,

OFFICE OF INDIAN AFFAIRS,

Washington, July 24, 1914.

SIR: The United States Senate, on June 30, 1914, passed a resolution (S. Res. 410) directing the Secretary of the Interior to cause an investigation to be made of the condition and tribal rights, educational facilities, etc., of the Indians of Robeson and adjoining counties in North Carolina, commonly known as Croatans, and to make a report to Congress respecting their rights, etc.

I have been detailed to make the investigation called for by said Senate resolution.

I will thank you very much to send me, to Lumberton, N. C., at your earliest convenience, such facts and information from the files and records of your office, or from other sources, respecting the said Indians as are available.

[Page 234]I especially desire to learn the number of these Indians by counties, the number paying taxes in each county, the amount of personal taxes, amount of real-estate taxes, and other facts relating to their history or rights as may be shown by the records of your office or as are available from other sources. I will be pleased to receive any information concerning them which would enable the Secretary of the Interior better to comply with the terms of said Senate resolution. An early response will be appreciated.

I inclose a self-addressed envelope for reply, which will not require postage.

Very respectfully,

O. M. MCPHERSON,
Special Indian Agent.

DEPARTMENT OF THE STATE AUDITOR,

Raleigh, N. C., July 28, 1914.

DEAR SIR: Answering your letter of July 24, which you handed me this date, I give you the following information, taken from the records of this department:

	1912	1913
ROBESON COUNTY.		
Number Indian polls.....	960	1,010
Value property listed for taxation.....	$493,900	$506,094
SCOTLAND COUNTY.		
Number Indian polls.....	38	44
Value property listed for taxation.....	$6,500	$5,689
HOKE COUNTY.		
Number of Indian polls.....	13	28
Value property listed for taxation.....	$3,574	$4,463

The records on file in this department from Cumberland, Bladen, and Columbus Counties do not show any Indian polls.

Yours, truly,

W. P. WOOD, *State Auditor.*
By BAXTER DURHAM, *Tax Clerk.*

DEPARTMENT OF THE INTERIOR,

OFFICE OF INDIAN AFFAIRS,

Washington, July 24, 1914.

SIR: The United States Senate, on June 30, 1914, passed a resolution (S. Res. 410) directing the Secretary of the Interior to cause an investigation to be made of the condition and tribal rights, educational facilities, etc., of the Indians of Robeson and adjoining counties [Page 235] in North Carolina, commonly known as Croatans, and to make a report to Congress respecting their rights, etc.

I have been detailed to make the investigation called for by said Senate resolution.

I will thank you very much to send me, to Lumberton, N. C., at your earliest convenience, such facts and information from the files and records of your office, or from other sources, respecting the said Indians as are available.

I especially desire to be advised of the number of said Indians, their location as to counties, the number of school age, the number and character of established schools, the number attending school in each county, together with the provision that the State of North Carolina has made for the education of said Indians; in short, I desire to obtain full information respecting the educational facilities provided the Croatans. An early response will be appreciated.

I inclose to you for reply a self-addressed envelope which will require no postage.

Very respectfully,

O. M. MCPHERSON,
Special Indian Agent.

OFFICE OF SUPERINTENDENT OF PUBLIC INSTRUCTION,

STATE OF NORTH CAROLINA,

Raleigh, August 3, 1914.

DEAR SIR: Your letter of July 24 to the superintendent of public instruction of North Carolina was referred to me for reply. We have no statistics on the Croatan Indians other than the school population for Robeson County. Mr. Joyner's report for 1911-12 shows that there were 2, 183 Croatans of school age—6 to 21 years—in Robeson County; 1, 159 enrolled in the public schools, with an average daily attendance of 602. In addition to this we enrolled in the Indian Normal School at Pembroke 134 pupils, with an average attendance of 105.

In sections 4236 to 4242, inclusive, you will find the law establishing this normal school. The sections referred to are in volume 2 of the revisal of 1905 of North Carolina. You will find the amendment in the laws of 1907, 1911, 1913. Section 4086 of the revisal provides for separate schools for the descendants of the Croatan Indians now living in Robeson and Richmond Counties. Sections 4168-4171, inclusive, indicate the manner in which this law is to be carried out. You will see in the matter of education in the elementary schools these Indians are put on the same footing as the other races.

Very truly, yours,

E. E. SAMS,
Supervisor Teacher Training.

WASHINGTON, D. C., July 24, 1914.

SIR: The United States Senate on June 30, 1914, passed a resolution (S. Res. 410) directing the Secretary of the Interior to cause an investigation [Page 236] to be made of the condition and tribal rights of the Indians of Bobeson and adjoining counties in North Carolina, commonly known as

Croatans, and to make a report to Congress respecting their condition, rights, etc.

Said resolution is as follows:

Resolved, That the Secretary of the Interior be, and he hereby is, directed to cause an investigation to be made of the condition and tribal rights of the Indians of Robeson and adjoining counties of North Carolina, recently declared by the Legislature of North Carolina, to be Cherokees, and formerly known as Croatans, and report to Congress what tribal rights, if any, they have with any band or tribe; whether they are entitled to or have received any lands, or whether there are any moneys due them, their present condition, their educational facilities, and such other facts as would enable Congress to determine whether the Government would be warranted in making suitable provision for their support and education.

Special Agent O. M. McPherson has been detailed to make the investigation called for by said Senate resolution.

You are requested to communicate with the special agent at Lumberton, N. C., giving him all the information shown by the files of your agency, and such other information as you can obtain from other sources, concerning the subject matter of said resolution. Please make this matter special, and furnish Special Agent McPherson with the information at the earliest practicable date.

Very respectfully,

E. B. MERRITT,
Assistant Commissioner.

CHEROKEE, N. C., July 28, 1914.

MY DEAR MR. MCPHERSON: I am in receipt of a letter from the Indian office saying that you had been put in charge of certain investigations among the Croatan Indians of Bobeson and adjoining counties of North Carolina and directing me to furnish you with all the information available at this place to aid you in the work.

Since the Croatans and the Cherokees have never been connected either officially or socially the Cherokees refusing to recognize the Croatans there is very little in our files that will be of service to you in the work. During my time here I have seen only a very few letters with reference to the Croatans, and I believe that they were copies of letters from former Supt. Kyselka to the department telling the department that the Croatans were trying to get an act through the North Carolina Legislature making them Cherokees. If you so desire I will hunt up all of the correspondence with reference to the matter and will send you either the originals or the copies as you may desire.

I have always been interested in Croatan affairs, yet I think they have nothing in common with our Cherokees.

In connection with your work you had better come to Cherokee and get some of our cold water and fine air. It must be rather warm down there just now.

Assuring you of all of the aid I am possible to give in your new undertaking, I am,

Very respectfully,

JAMES E. HENDERSON,
Superintendent.

[Page 237]LUMBERTON, N. C., July 30, 1914.

MY DEAR MR. HENDERSON: I have received your letter of July 28, referring to a recent Indian office letter directing you to furnish me, in connection with the investigation I am making of the condition and tribal rights, etc., of the Indians of Robeson and adjoining counties of North Carolina, as authorized by Senate Resolution 410, all the information in your files relating to the proposed investigation. You refer to certain correspondence had by your predecessor, Supt. Kyselka, with the Indian office, concerning the Croatan Indians.

I will thank you very much to send me copies of all correspondence in your files relating in any way to the so-called Croatan Indians; I think it proper that the originals should remain on file in your office. Please send me also copies of all papers, printed matter, etc., at your command which would be of value to me in said investigation.

An early response will be appreciated.

Would, indeed, be glad to have some of your pure water and fine air, though the weather just now is very comfortable.

Very respectfully,

O. M. MCPHERSON,
Special Indian Agent.

CHEROKEE, N. C., August 5, 1914.

MY DEAR MR. MCPHERSON: Answering yours of July 30, I will say that we have been looking through the files in this office for papers that you might be able to use, but am sorry to say that to this time we have been unable to find anything. I remember to have seen a letter from Mr. Kyselka to the department with reference to the matter since I have been here. I will keep up the search and will forward to you anything I am able to find. Since the Cherokees have had nothing whatever to do with the Robeson County Indians, I fear that we will be able to find very little that will throw light on the subject.

I trust that you can make it convenient to come to Cherokee before you leave Lumberton. I have always had a desire to go to that locality and hope that I can pay you a visit before you leave there.

With the kindest regards, I am, very respectfully,

JAMES E. HENDERSON,
Superintendent.

DEPARTMENT OF THE INTERIOR,

OFFICE OF INDIAN AFFAIRS,

Washington, July 24, 1914.

SIR: The United States Senate, on June 30, 1914, passed a resolution (S. Res. 410) directing the Secretary of the Interior to cause an investigation to be made of the conditions and tribal rights, educational facilities, etc., of the Indians of Robeson and adjoining counties [Page 238] in North Carolina, commonly known as Croatans, and to make a report to Congress respecting their rights, etc.

I have been detailed to make the investigation called for by said Senate resolution.

I will thank you very much to send me, to Lumberton, N. C., at your earliest convenience, such facts and information from the files and records of Columbus County office as are available respecting the number of Croatan Indians, if any, in your county; the number of families; the number of children of school age; number attending school; school facilities provided by the State and county for said Indians; the kind and value of their property in the county and amount of taxes paid by them; also any other information respecting said Indians which would enable the Secretary of the Interior better to comply with the terms of said Senate resolution. An early response will be appreciated.

I inclose a self-addressed envelope for reply, which will not require postage.

Respectfully,

O. M. MCPHERSON,
Special Indian Agent.

CHADBOURN, N. C., July 28, 1914.

DEAR SIR: So far as I can learn our files show no record of any Indians residing in Columbus County. There are a few scattering ones who have come down from Robeson, but this number is so small that no provision has been made for them in our schools.

Mr. K. B. Council, of Wananish, N. C., knows more about those who call themselves Indians in our county than anyone else. He has made a special study of their history and could give you some valuable information concerning them. We have a few in our county who claim to be Indians but who have always been recognized as colored people. Some of these are petitioning us to recognize them as Indians, but because of the lack of knowledge of their ancestors we have not yet been able to grant their request.

I seriously doubt whether or not we have any pure-blooded Indians in the county except a few scattering from Robeson.

Yours, truly,

F. T. WOOTEN,
County Superintendent.

LUMBERTON, N. C., July 29, 1914.

DEAR SIR: The United States Senate on June 30, 1914, passed a resolution (S. Res. 410) directing the Secretary of the Interior to cause an investigation to be made of the condition and tribal rights, educational facilities, etc., of the Indians of Robeson and adjoining counties of North Carolina, and to make a report to Congress respecting their tribal rights, etc.

[Page 239]I have been detailed to make the investigation called for by said Senate resolution.

Mr. F. T. Wooten, superintendent of schools of Columbus County, has advised me that you are well informed concerning the history and condition of the Croatan Indians, and could probably give me some valuable information concerning them.

I will thank you very much to give me at your earliest convenience a very full statement relating to the history and condition of said Indians. An early reply will be appreciated.

Very respectfully,

O. M. MCPHERSON,
Special Indian Agent.

LUMBERTON, N. C., July 29, 1914.

MY DEAR MR. SELLS: Referring to my instructions of July 23, 1914, to proceed to North Carolina and to investigate the condition, etc., of the Indians of Robeson County, and adjoining counties in North Carolina, as directed by Senate resolution No. 410, dated June 30, 1914, I beg to invite your attention to that part of the resolution reading:

* * * and report to Congress what tribal rights, if any, they have with any band or tribe; whether they are entitled to or have received any lands, or whether there are any moneys due them * * *

These are matters which an investigation in the field can not readily develop, and I will thank you very much to advise me at your earliest convenience what the files, records, and papers of the Indian office show on these subjects.

An early reply will be very much appreciated.

Very respectfully,

O. M. MCPHERSON,
Special Indian Agent.

DEPARTMENT OF THE INTERIOR,

OFFICE OF INDIAN AFFAIRS,

Washington, August 4, 1914.

MY DEAR MR. MCPHERSON: The office is in receipt of your letter of July 29, 1914, regarding the tribal rights, etc., of Indians of Robeson and adjoining counties of North Carolina, otherwise known as Croatans.

The main file relative to these Indians is now in your possession, and, it is believed, contains all the information now available. It further appears that you consulted the records of the "old files" relative to the Croatans before your departure from this city.

For your further information, however, there is inclosed a copy of a report of June 6, 1914, to the Congress on Senate resolution 344.

Very truly yours,

C. F. HAUKE,
Second Assistant Commissioner.

[Page 240]DEPARTMENT OF THE INTERIOR,

Washington, June 6, 1814.

MY DEAR SENATOR: The department is in receipt of your letter of April 29, 1914, transmitting a copy of Senate resolution 344, Sixty-third Congress, second session, providing for an investigation of the present condition, educational facilities, etc., of alleged Cherokee Indians in "Robeson and adjoining counties of North Carolina."

The department has heretofore made reports to Congress on the conditions of these Indians, based upon an investigation made by a supervisor of Indian schools in 1912 in connection with school matters, and for the information of your committee there is inclosed a copy of his report of March 2, 1912. That report shows substantially as follows:

First. The Croatan Indians, as these people are called, number about 10, 000 people, of whom about 7, 000 reside in Robeson County. The ancestry of these Indians has been much in doubt in the past, but they are now recognized as having originated from the white colonists of the lost colony of the Roanoke and the Indians from remnants of several powerful southern tribes.

Second. These Indians show several positively different types, having no Indian language and no distinctive customs, and being unable to communicate with other Indians except through the medium of the English language.

Third. Until the year 1835 the Croatans were allowed to vote, own slaves, build churches and schoolhouses, and live as comfortably as their white neighbors. The right of suffrage was denied them in 1835, but the Croatans rebelled continuously until they were again recognized as citizens in 1885 and given their right as such.

Fourth. There are but few full bloods among the Croatans, although a large majority of them seem to be at least three-fourths Indian. They are classed as good citizens, are quite industrious, law abiding, and are said to be much interested in education.

Fifth. The Croatans own 28, 092 acres of good land, assessed at present $334, 212, which is considerably below its actual value. Their personal property schedules $205, 205, and they pay $1, 247 in poll taxes. They are considered good farmers and raise as much cotton to the acre as many of the white planters. Some of the Indians are poor, but several of them have very good homes, the owners being worth from $6, 000 to $10, 000 each.

Sixth. The State of North Carolina is doing for the Croatans just what the State of New York is doing for her Indians, giving them a fair common school education. There are 26 Indian district schools, with an enrollment of 1, 094 pupils, and in addition, the State has established a so-called normal school at Pembroke for these Croatan day schools.

The following is an excerpt from the Indian census of North Carolina as of June 1, 1890:

A body of people residing chiefly in Robeson County, North Carolina, known as the Croatan Indians, are generally white, showing the Indian mostly in actions and habits. They were enumerated by the regular census enumerator in part as whites. They are clannish and hold with considerable pride to the traditions that they are descendants of the Croatans of the Raleigh period of North Carolina and Virginia.

[Page 241]Mr. Hamilton McMillan, of Fayetteville, North Carolina, in 1888 published a pamphlet of 27 pages, the title page of which is as follows: "Sir Walter Raleigh's lost colony * * * with the traditions of an Indian tribe in North Carolina, Wilson, North Carolina." This pamphlet is to show that Raleigh's colony was carried off by the Indians, and that the Croatan Indians of North Carolina are their descendants. Mr. McMillan also, in answering an inquiry in reference to the Croatans, wrote the following to the Commissioner of Indian Affairs:

RED SPRINGS, N. C., *July 17, 1890.*

* * * The Croatan Tribe lives principally in Robeson County, North Carolina, though there is quite a number of them settled in counties adjoining in North and South Carolina. In Sumter County, South Carolina, there is a branch of the tribe, and also in east Tennessee. In Macon County, North Carolina, there is another branch, settled there long ago. Those living in east Tennessee are called "Melungeans," a name also retained by them here, which is a corruption of "Melange," a name given them by early settlers (French), which means mixed. * * * In regard to their exodus from Roanoke Island their traditions are confirmed by maps recently discovered in Europe by Prof. Alexander Brown, member of the Royal Historical Society of England. These maps are dated in 1608 and 1610, and give the reports of the Croatans to Raleigh's ships which visited our coast in those years. * * * The particulars of the exodus preserved by tradition here are strangely and strongly corroborated by these maps. There can be little doubt of the fact

that the Croatans in Robeson County and elsewhere are the descendants of the Croatans of Raleigh's day.

From information available at this time, it does not appear that the Croatans ever affiliated with or have been recognized by the Eastern Cherokee Indians. No money or land is due the Croatans from the Government. The department will be glad to make a further investigation of the affairs of these Indians, but a sufficient amount should be appropriated to defray the expense thereof. It is estimated this would require about $1, 000.

Cordially, yours,

A. A. JONES,
First Assistant Secretary.

LUMBERTON, N. C., July 29, 1914.

DEAR SIR: On June 30, 1914, the United States Senate passed a resolution (S. Res. 410) directing the Secretary of the Interior to cause an investigation to be made of the condition and tribal rights, educational facilities, etc., of the Indians of Robeson and adjoining counties of North Carolina, and to make a report to Congress respecting their tribal rights, etc.

I have been detailed to make the investigation called for by said Senate resolution. I have a copy of your booklet entitled "Sir Walter Raleigh's Lost Colony."

I would regard it as a favor, in the interests of the Indians, if you would furnish me with any information you have concerning said Indians not contained in your pamphlet.

Please send me, also, any information at your command concerning the location of the scattered members of the tribe, not residing in Robeson County, their present condition, their present school facilities, and what the State of North Carolina is doing for the education of the young members of the tribe.

An early reply will be appreciated.

Very respectfully,

O. M. MCPHERSON,
Special Indian Agent.

[Page 242]RED SPRINGS, N. C., August 2, 1914.

DEAR SIR: Circumstances beyond my control have prevented a reply to your recent favor relative to the Indians of Robeson County.

Tradition is the Indian's history. The Indians in Robeson are known as Croatans. Croatan is the Indian name for an island on the eastern coast of North Carolina, and the early English naturally called the Indians there Croatans from the locality where they were located, and so they are designated today. These Indians call themselves Cherokees. During past 30 years I have interviewed hundreds of them, and the inquiry as to their origin was, without an exception, in favor of their being Cherokees. They pointed to the great roads leading to the mountains in western North Carolina by which their ancestors traveled to the eastern coast. These great roads are the Lowrie Road, an ancient trail along the coast when the ocean extended far west of the present coast line, and the Morganton Road, once an Indian trail but in past century improved by United States Government and made straight. There was another great trail now known as the Yadkin Road, these roads converging near the present town of Fayetteville.

All the tribes in North Carolina, except the Tuscaroras, were originally Cherokee if we accept tradition. The Tuscaroras were at war with the Cherokee Nation, which was a mountain tribe using the eastern portion of our State as a hunting ground. Permanent settlements were made along these great trails, and the Indians traveled back and forth along these trails, and occasionally imigrants from eastern North Carolina now travel on the old Lowrie Road toward the Pedee and Catawba Rivers. The Indians on the coast were friendly to white men at first, and those now known as Croatans claim that they were always the friends of white men; that they received the white colony left on Roanoke Island in 1587, and amalgamated with them. They have about 40 family names among them that are found in the families left in Roanoke Island as preserved by Haklyt. See Hawks' History of North Carolina, vol. 1.

These Indians, numbering nearly 6,000, have no records. The oldest deed in Robeson County is one made by George II to Henry Berry and James Lowrie in 1732. This deed was lost through carelessness of a surveyor. I have seen and handled that deed, which called for 100 acres of land in upper Robeson, now Hoke, at present owned by Hon. D. P. McEachern, of Red Springs.

I was in search of different persons among these people many years ago, and they located some of them in Florida, western North Carolina, and New Mexico. Many of the Indians in Robeson County in 1713 joined "Bonnul" in fighting the Tuscaroras near Pamlico Sound. ("Bonnul" was Gen. Barnwell.) Handed down from father to son through many generations is the universal tradition that their ancestors were Cherokees.

Since their recognition as a separate race they have made wonderful progress. Their hatred of the Negro is stronger than that entertained by Caucasians.

A crowd of Indians from Macon County was present before a joint committee of the senate and house in 1913, in Raleigh, N. C., and lined up with them were Indians from Robeson. The resemblance [Page 243] was very striking, so much so that Senator G. B. McLeod, coming before the committee, mistook the western Cherokees as Robeson County Indians.

I am pleased to learn that you will spend some time in your invesgation. You will find much ignorance among them as to their origin, as they leave the traditions of the tribe to the old chroniclers of the tribe, and these chroniclers are passing away.

Several of these Indians have lived among the Cherokees in Indian Territory—notably Washington Lowrie, now living but a helpless invalid. Their ancestors fought for American independence and again served in War of 1812. See records in office of adjutant general at Raleigh, N. C.

The names *Lowrie* and *Lochlayah* and *Oxendine* are the only Indian dian names I can find among them, and these are Cherokee names.

Wishing you abundant success in your work and with my best wishes,

I am, respectfully, yours,

HAMILTON MCMILLAN.

P. S.—I am somewhat an invalid, and my penmanship may trouble you to decipher.

H. MCMILLAN.LUMBERTON, N. C., July 30, 1914.

DEAR SIR: I have been sent to Lumberton, N. C., by the Secretary of the Interior to make an investigation of the condition and tribal rights of the

Indians residing in Robeson and adjoining counties in North Carolina. I am advised by Hon. W. P. Wood, State auditor, that there are a few Indians in Hoke County.

I will thank you very much to send me, to Lumberton, N. C., at your earliest convenience, such facts and information as are shown by the records and files of Hoke County respecting the number of Indians in your county; the number of families; number of children of school age; number attending school; the school facilities provided by the State and county for the Indians; the kind and value of their property; amount of their property listed for taxation, and any other information respecting the Indians which you think would be of value to me in the investigation I am making. An early response will be appreciated.

Very respectfully,

O. M. MCPHERSON,
Special Indian Agent.

BOARD OF EDUCATION, HOKE COUNTY,

Raeford, N. C., August 4, 1914.

DEAR SIR: In reply to your letter, I will give you what information I can concerning the Indians in Hoke County. There has never been a census of the county taken since it was established, three years ago, and consequently the only information that I can give will have to come from the tax books.

[Page 244]I think that there are a few Indians and part Indians scattered about all over the county, but in the tax books they are listed separately in two townships, Allendale and Antioch. Their polls and property is as follows:

Polls, $32. Value live stock, $2, 782; farming utensils, etc., $529; household and kitchen furniture, etc., $250; bicycles, etc., $15; jewelry, $9; land, 6 acres, value $60. Total value personal property, $3, 584; total, real and personal property, $3, 644.

We have never been able to get a complete census of the school children, but I think that there are about 65 or 70. We established a school for them last year, but they taught only two months of school, at a salary of $25 per month. The enrollment was 33. We are planning to establish another school for them the coming year and to continue the one they had last year.

The Indians that we have, as you see from the amount of land that they own, are not permanent settlers, but tenants. This being the case, it is a pretty hard problem to know just how to deal with them. I would be very glad if you could suggest some way that we can deal with them in the way of education. They are good laborers and are continually spreading out into new territory. They are mixed in with the whites and colored people, and we have to maintain three separate schools covering the same territory, and this, as you know, is very expensive.

I would be glad to have you visit this county while you are in this section, and for you to see the exact status of the Indians here. If you can come up for a day or two, let me know in advance so that I can be here to meet you.

Very truly, yours,

J. A. MCGOOGAN,
County Superintendent.

LUMBERTON, N. C., August 4, 1914.

DEAR SIR: I am advised that Col. Fred. A. Olds, secretary North Carolina Historical Association, early in the summer of 1908 made a visit to the Croatan Indians of Robeson County, N. C., and wrote an extended account of his visit, which was published in the Charlotte Observer of June 21, 1908. If a copy of said issue is available for distribution I will thank you very much to send me a copy. I am making an investigation of the affairs of the Croatan Indians in obedience to Senate resolution 410.

Very respectfully,

O. M. MCPHERSON,
Special Indian Agent.

CHARLOTTE, N. C., August 10, 1914.

DEAR SIR: In reply to your letter of recent date, we regret to state that we are unable to furnish you with a copy of The Observer of June 21, 1908. The only copy we have of this is in our bound file. It covers about 12 columns, or nearly 2 pages in our paper. If at [Page 245] any time you are in this city we will be glad to lend you our files so that you can read this article, or we could have same typewritten for 5 cents per typewritten sheet.

Yours, very truly,

THE OBSERVER CO.,

PAUL H. BROWN,
Circulation Manager.

DEPARTMENT OF THE INTERIOR,

OFFICE COMMISSIONER INDIAN AFFAIRS,

Washington, August 4, 1914.

MY DEAR Mr. MCPHERSON: I understand there is to be a meeting of the Croatan Indians on the 11th of August and that this meeting is likely to develop more or less things of interest along the line of your inquiry. Consequently, I suggest that you take advantage of the coming together of this body of Indians, and thereby acquire all the additional dependable information possible.

It is my desire that you shall get at the exact facts regardless of resolutions or expressions of interest. It is the facts we want, and on them alone will we be able to draw satisfactory conclusion. Please make your investigation thorough to the end that there will be no occasion for its repetition, as we are now being called upon to do.

Sincerely yours,

CATO SELLS,
Commissioner.

LUMBERTON, N. C., August 6, 1914.

MY DEAR Mr. SELLS: I have the honor to acknowledge the receipt of your letter of August 4, 1914, concerning my investigation of the condition, tribal rights, etc., of the Indians of Robeson and adjoining counties in North Carolina.

I beg to say in reply that prior to the receipt of your letter I had made arrangements to attend the meeting of the so-called Croatan Indians at Pembroke, on August 11, and had so advised the leading Indians of the band.

On Monday, August 3, I visited the homes of a large number of Indians living southwest of Lumberton in what are known as the Sampson and Hunt settlements. I took notes of their condition and conferred freely with them concerning their history, tribal rights, needs, conditions, and as to what Congress could best do for them. Tuesday, August 4, I conferred with a large number of the Indians in Lumberton, along the same lines, who had come in by arrangement to meet me for such a conference. Yesterday I spent the entire day at Pembroke in a similar conference with the Indians of the Pembroke neighborhood, and conferred with a very large number. I had made arrangements to visit the homes of the Indians of the Pembroke district to-day, but had to postpone the trip on account of rainy weather. I shall go to-morrow if the weather permits, and shall spend Monday in [Page 246] a similar visit to a different part of the Indian settlement; and as I have said, I shall attend the Indian meeting at Pembroke on August 11.

I wish to assure you that I am making my investigation as thorough as possible, and shall put forth my best efforts to get at the "bottom facts."

With kindest regards, I am, very sincerely yours,

O. M. MCPHERSON,
Special Indian Agent.

INDIAN MASS MEETING, TUESDAY, AUGUST 11.

There will be a mass meeting of the Indians at the normal school building in the town of Pembroke on Tuesday, August 11, 1914, at 10 o'clock in the forenoon, for the purpose of considering all matters in which the Indians are interested both with reference to schools, the change of name, and any other business which may be necessary.

This meeting is called at the request of Senator Simmons and Congressman Godwin for the purpose of getting our people together upon important matters. The time and place of meeting have been agreed upon by representatives of every section. We urgently request the Indians not only of Robeson, but of all adjoining counties, to attend this meeting, as matters of the greatest importance will be transacted.

Senator Simmons, Congressman Godwin, and others have been invited to be present and address our people.

Let as many as possible bring dinner.

STEPHEN A. HAMMOND,
G. H. C., Order of Redmen.

J. A. HUNT,
G. F. M., Order of Rainbow.

DEPARTMENT OF THE INTERIOR,

Washington, August 14, 1914.

DEAR SIR: If you have not already done so, I will thank you very much to send me by return mail, the property statistics, from the records of your office, of the so-called Croatan Indians of Robeson County.

An early reply would be very much appreciated.

Very respectfully,

O. M. MCPHERSON,
Special Indian Agent.

Washington, D. C., September 15, 1914.

No reply has been received from the auditor of Robeson County to the above request for information.

O. M. MCPHERSON,
Special Indian Agent.

[Page 247]DEPARTMENT OF THE INTERIOR,

Washington, August 14, 1914.

DEAR SIR: If you have not already done so, I will thank you very much to send me by return mail the school statistics of the so-called Croatan Indians of Robeson County for the school years 1912 and 1913.

An early reply would be very much appreciated.

Very respectfully,

O. M. MCPHERSON,
Special Indian Agent.

BOARD OF EDUCATION, ROBESON COUNTY,

Lumberton, N. C., August 19, 1914.

DEAR SIR: Replying to your favor of few days ago, in regard to the Indian schools of Robeson County, I beg to submit the following statistics, as they appear of record in this department:

Scholastic year 1912-13.

Census (6 to 21).....	2, 643
Enrollment (6 to 21).....	1, 662
Average daily attendance (6 to 21).....	970

Twenty-seven different schools were taught by 32 different teachers (21 male and 11 female teachers). These schools were taught in 27 different buildings, which, together with sites on which they stood, were valued at $7, 900. The average length of term was 85.70 days for all Indian schools in the county. In the special-tax districts the term averaged 111.43; in those districts which did not have a special tax the term averaged 80.54 days. During the year 1912-13, $500 was expended for repairs on school buildings and $5, 475.25 for teachers' salaries.

Scholastic year 1913-14.

Census.....	2,948
Enrollment (6 to 21).....	1,854
Average attendance (6 to 21).....	1,164

Twenty-seven different schools were taught by 36 different teachers. We had the same number of school buildings as in the former year, but $1,160 was spent during the year for new buildings, repairs, etc., bringing the total valuation up to $9,060. The average length of term in all the Indian schools of the county was 102.66 days, in the special-tax schools 104, and in those districts which do not have special tax 100.30 days; $6,410.25 was paid for teachers' salaries. The Indians at present have nine special-tax districts and a number of others will probably be established this year.

It might be well to note that in the figures given above, the census includes all the children of school age in the county, while the figures giving the enrollment and average attendance include only those in the county public schools and do not include those who enrolled and attended at the State normal at Pembroke.

[Page 248]As it now stands these people have no educational opportunities beyond those offered by the local public schools and the State normal at Pembroke. When these have been completed there are no other institutions anywhere in this section of the country to which they can go for industrial or professional training.

Yours, very truly,

J. R. POOLE.

DEPARTMENT OF THE INTERIOR,

OFFICE OF INDIAN AFFAIRS,

Washington, August 19, 1914.

DEAR SIR: Referring to our conversation before I left Lumberton, I have to advise you that so far as I now know I shall submit my report in the matter of the investigation of the Indians of Robeson and adjoining counties in North Carolina, before I take my vacation. Any matter which you care to submit in connection with the investigation should be sent to the Commissioner of Indian Affairs as early as practicable.

Very respectfully,

O. M. MCPHERSON,
Special Indian Agent.

THE BANK OF LUMBERTON,

Lumberton, N. C., August 28, 1914.

DEAR SIR: I have your letter of the 19th, and just as soon as I can get a little time I will try and send you the further data in regard to the Indians of Robeson County. I will probably send this in in the next two weeks. If that will be satisfactory, please let me know.

Yours, truly,

A. W. MCLEAN.

DEPARTMENT OF THE INTERIOR,

OFFICE OF INDIAN AFFAIRS,

Washington, August 31, 1914.

DEAR SIR: Answering your letter of August 28, you are advised that any matter reaching me by September 7 or 8 will be in time for consideration in my report of investigations of the Indians of Robeson County.

Very respectfully,

O. M. MCPHERSON,
Special Indian Agent.

[Page 249]PEMBROKE, N. C., August 25, 1914.

Mr. MCPHERSON.

SIR: I am writing you a few lines to let you hear from me. I am well at present, truly hoping you the same. I will ask you a favor if it is not out of order for you to answer. If you please let me know about what date you will be able to make your report to the Indian Commissioner, as I would like to come up there about that time, and I hope that I am not out of order by asking you this favor.

Write at once to yours truly,

WM. LOWRY.

DEPARTMENT OF THE INTERIOR,

OFFICE OF INDIAN AFFAIRS,

Washington, August 28, 1914.

DEAR SIR: I have received your letter of August 25, inquiring when I will file my report in the matter of the investigation of the affairs of the Indians of Robeson County, N. C.

In reply you are advised that I expect to be able to file my report in said case about September 15. It must be understood that this is only an approximate date, as some unforeseen event might delay the filing of my report several days. Will be glad to see you at Washington whenever you can make it convenient to come.

Very respectfully,

O. M. MCPHERSON,
Special Indian Agent.

PEMBROKE, N. C., August 27, 1914.

DEAR SIR: Do you think it necessary for the committee to be in Washington at the time when you submit your report for your visit to Robeson County?

Mr. Wm. Lowrie, Abner Chavis, and myself are the committee. Kindly advise me at your earliest convenience.

Very respectfully,

W. R. LOCKLEAR.

DEPARTMENT OF THE INTERIOR,

OFFICE OF INDIAN AFFAIRS,

Washington, August 29, 1914.

DEAR SIR: I have received your letter of August 27, inquiring whether it will be necessary for the committee of Indians to be in Washington when I file my report in the matter of the investigation directed by Senate resolution No. 410.

In response, you are advised that in my opinion it will not be necessary for your committee to be here when I file my report; I [Page 250] can not see what the committee could accomplish by being here at that time.

In the ordinary course of business my report will be sent to the Secretary of the Interior, and by him will be transmitted to Congress, in case he is of the opinion that my report covers all the essential facts. Whatever your committee can accomplish will be through the proper committees in Congress.

Very respectfully,

O. M. MCPHERSON
Special Indian Agent.

ST. PAULS, N. C., September 1, 1914.

DEAR SIR: Please grant me this privilege of writing you. I am well and trust you are enjoying life with the greatest of pleasure. I do this to hear from you. Can you tell me anything that is good about our affairs? Would you like to have my picture with my hunting suit?

And if so, I will mail you one.

Yours truly,

A. CHAVIS.

DEPARTMENT OF THE INTERIOR,

OFFICE OF INDIAN AFFAIRS,

Washington, September 3, 1914.

DEAR Mr. CHAVIS: I have received you letter of September 1st, inquiring whether I have anything good to tell you about the affairs of the Robeson County Indians, and whether I would like to have one of your pictures taken in your hunting suit.

In reply you are advised that I have not yet filed my report in the investigation of the affairs of the Robeson County Indians; I hope to be able to file my report within a week.

I regret that I did not take a camera with me so that I could have procured a large number of pictures of the Indians. However, I would be glad to have your picture for my own use, but I could not use one picture to advantage in my report.

Very truly yours,

O. M. MCPHERSON,
Special Indian Agent.

WASHINGTON, D. C., August 29, 1914.

DEAR MR. MCPHERSON: Referring to our conversation in regard to the matter of the Croatan Indians of North Carolina, I beg to hand you herewith a copy of H. R. 19036 introduced January 29, 1910, by Mr. Godwin, entitled a bill to change the name of the Croatan Indians of the State of North Carolina to their original name, Cherokee.

I also inclose you an extract concerning the Croatan Indians from the first volume of the Hand Book of American Indians. If there [Page 251] is any further information I can furnish you concerning these people, kindly let me know.

Yours, very truly,

CHARLES J. KAPPLER.

P. S.—I also inclose a copy of the hearings had before the House Committee on Indian Affairs on S. bill 3258 "To acquire a site and erect buildings for a school for the Indians of Robeson County, N. C., and for other purposes," which passed the Senate. This bill was an effort to do something for these Indians.

[H. R. 19036, Sixty-first Congress, second session.]

IN THE HOUSE OF REPRESENTATIVES.

JANUARY 24, 1910.—Mr. Godwin introduced the following bill; which was referred to the Committee on Indian Affairs and ordered to be printed.

A BILL To change the name of the Croatan Indians of the State of North Carolina to their original name, Cherokee.

Whereas the Croatan Indians who now reside in the State of North Carolina are a branch of the Cherokee Tribe of Indians and are desirous of changing their name to the original name, Cherokee: Now, therefore,

Be it enacted by the Senate and House of Representatives of the United States of America in Congress assembled, That the name of the band of Croatan Indians in said State of North Carolina be, and the same is hereby, changed to Cherokee, by which name they shall be hereafter known and designated.

[Hand Book of American Indians, Bulletin 30, part 1, page 365.]

CROATAN. A village in 1585 on an island then called by the same name, which appears to have been that on which Cape Lookout is situated, on the coast of Carteret County, N. C. The inhabitants seem to have been independent of the chiefs of Secotan. It is thought that the lost colony of Lane, on Roanoke Island, joined them, and that traces of the mixture were discernible in the later Hatteras Indians. (J. M.)

Croatan.—Lane (1586) in Smith (1629), Virginia, 1, 92, repr. 1819. *Croatoan.*—Strachey (ca. 1612), Virginia, 43, 145, 1849. *Crooton.*—Lane, op. cit., 86.

CROATAN INDIANS. The legal designation in North Carolina for a people evidently of mixed Indian and white blood, found in various eastern sections of the State, but chiefly in Robeson County, and numbering approximately 5, 000. For many years they were classed with the free negroes, but steadily refused to accept such classification or to attend the negro schools or churches, claiming to be the descendants of the early native tribes and of white settlers who had intermarried with them. About 20 years ago their claim was officially recognized and they were given a separate legal existence under the title of "Croatan Indians," on the theory of descent from Raleigh's lost colony of Croatan (q. v.). Under this name they now [Page 252] have separate school provision, and are admitted to some privileges not accorded to the negroes. The theory of descent from the lost colony may be regarded as baseless, but the name itself serves as a convenient label for a people who combine in themselves the blood of the wasted native tribes, the early colonists or forest rovers, the runaway slaves or other negroes, and probably also of stray seamen of the Latin races from coasting vessels in the West Indian or Brazilian trade.

Across the line in South Carolina are found a people, evidently of similar origin, designated "Redbones." In portions of western North Carolina and eastern Tennessee are found the so-called "Melungeons" (probably from French melange, "mixed"), or "Portuguese," apparently an offshoot from the Croatan proper, and in Delaware are found the "Moors." All of these are local designations for peoples of mixed race with an Indian nucleous differing in no way from the present mixed-blood remnants known as Pamunkey, Chickahominy, and Nansemond Indians in Virginia, excepting in the more complete loss of their identity. In general, the physical features and complexion of the persons of this mixed stock incline more to the Indian than to the white or negro.

See Metis, Mixed Bloods. (J. M.)

www.ingramcontent.com/pod-product-compliance
Lightning Source LLC
Chambersburg PA
CBHW030333240426
43661CB00052B/1613